OUT OF THE CHANNEL

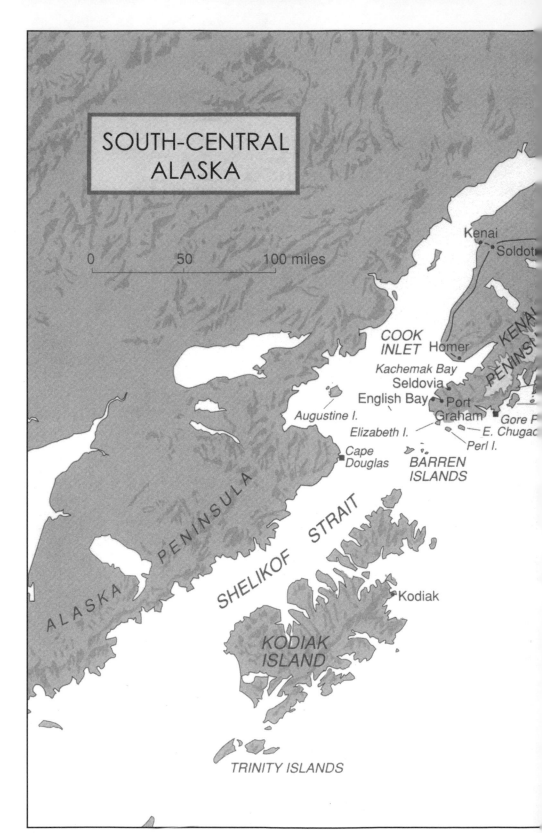

SOUTH-CENTRAL ALASKA

0   50   100 miles

Kenai
Soldot

COOK
INLET   Homer   KENAI
Kachemak Bay   PENINS
Seldovia
English Bay   Port
Graham   Gore P
Augustine I.   E. Chugac
Elizabeth I.   Perl I.
Cape   BARREN
Douglas   ISLANDS

ALASKA PENINSULA   SHELIKOF STRAIT

Kodiak

KODIAK
ISLAND

TRINITY ISLANDS

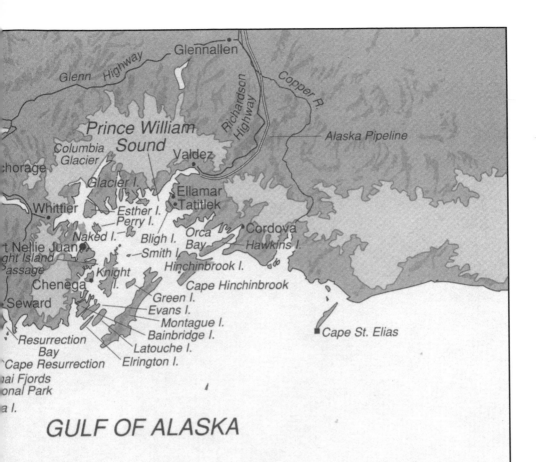

Glennallen

Glenn   Highway

Copper R.

Richardson Highway

Prince William
Sound

Alaska Pipeline

Columbia
Glacier

chorage

Valdez

Glacier I.

Ellamar
Tatitlek

Whittier

Esther I.
Perry I.

Cordova

Naked I.

Bligh I.

Orca
Bay

Hawkins I.

t Nellie Juan

Smith I.

ght Island

Knight

Hinchinbrook I.

assage

Chenega

I.

Cape Hinchinbrook

Seward

Green I.
Evans I.
Montague I.
Bainbridge I.
Latouche I.
Elrington I.

Cape St. Elias

Resurrection
Bay
Cape Resurrection

ai Fjords
onal Park

a I.

GULF OF ALASKA

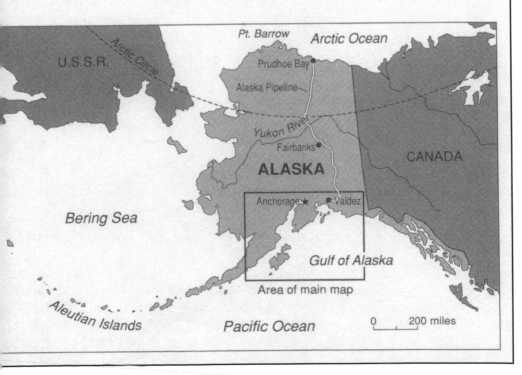

Pt. Barrow   Arctic Ocean

Arctic Circle

U.S.S.R.

Prudhoe Bay

Alaska Pipeline

Yukon River

Fairbanks

CANADA

ALASKA

Bering Sea

Anchorage ★   Valdez

Gulf of Alaska

Area of main map

Aleutian Islands

Pacific Ocean

0   200 miles

OUT OF THE CHANNEL

THE <u>EXXON VALDEZ</u> OIL SPILL IN PRINCE WILLIAM SOUND

JOHN KEEBLE

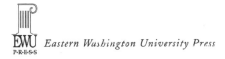

EWU
P·R·E·S·S
Eastern Washington University Press

Portions of this book appeared in different form in the *Village Voice*, (May 16, 1989), and in *Season of Dead Waters*, edited by Helen Frost (Breitenbush Books, 1990). Further writings and revised, reprinted material appeared after the publication of the HarperCollins edition in *Village Voice* (July 23, 1991); *Perspective* (fall, 1991); the *Amicus Journal*, (spring, 1993); *Outside* (March 1994); *Technological Disaster at Valdez; Readings On a Contemporary Social Problem*, edited by S. Picou, D. Gill, and M. Cohen, (Kendall-Hunt Publishing Co., 1996); and in *Listening to the Land: Conversations About Nature, Culture, and Eros*, edited by Derrick Jensen (Sierra Club Books, 1995).

Library of Congress Cataloging-in-Publication Data

Keeble, John 1944-

Out of the channel : the *Exxon Valdez* oil spill in

Prince William Sound / by John Keeble.

p. cm.

ISBN 091005553X (pbk.)

ISBN 0910055548 (hbk.)

Includes Bibliographical References

1. Oil spills — Environmental aspects — Alaska — Prince William Sound Region. 2. Oil spills — Economic aspects — Alaska — Prince William Sound Region. 3. Tankers — Accidents — Environmental aspects — Alaska — Prince William Sound Region. 4. *Exxon Valdez* (Ship) 5. Alyeska Pipeline Service Company. I. Title

TD427.P4K38 1999

363.738/2/097983—dc 21   98-054435

                                                                      CIP

To individuals of these, and more, to all of them, snagged in the channel . . .

Phalacrocorax pelagicus, Oceanodroma furcata, Charadrius semipalmatus, Brachyramphus marmoratus, Uria aalge, Cepphus columba, Lunda cirrhata, Haliaeetus leucocephalus, Ursus arctos, Odocoileus hemionus, Enhydra lustris, Phoca vitulina, Megaptera novaeangliae, Orcinus orca, Oncorhynchus gorbuscha, Hippoglossus stenolepsis, Katharina tunicata, Musculus niger, Saxidomus giganteus, Pycnopodia helianthoides, Solaster dawsoni, Zostera marina, Chlorophycophyta, Anonyx . . .

In Memoriam.

CONTENTS

II. MONEY

ACKNOWLEDGMENTS

With the exception of industry and government officials, and eventually of members of the scientific community who for one reason and another were not permitted to speak to the press, it was rare to find people in and out of Alaska who were not willing to share freely their insights and experiences with the Alaskan and other oil spills. Many, but not all, of those who spoke to me are mentioned in the pages that follow. I am grateful to each of them. Others took it upon themselves to inform me to a degree well beyond the immediate requirements. Among these were Charles Jurasz, Peter Jurasz, Lynn Schooler, Hild Sandstede, Mei Mei Evans, Richard Newman, Riki Ott, Kathy Conlan, Dan Reed, Bruce Stewart, Gordon Robilliard, Nancy Bird, Ken Adams, Gerald McCune, Marilyn Leland, and Rick Steiner. I am also indebted to the Exxon Corporation for information provided to me, to Arco Oil for support in the form of a tour of North Slope facilities, to the office of my congressman, Thomas J. Foley, for documents and advice speedily given, and especially to the editors of the *Village Voice*, who displayed their trust by first sending me to Valdez.

As I traveled, there were those who not only gave me the advantage of their knowledge but also offered their friendship, and the comfort of a meal, a place to take a shower, or to sleep. Among these were Larry Smith of Homer, and his mother, Luella Smith, Vivien and John Mickelson of Seldovia, Susan and Ron Chappell of Anchorage, Belle and Pete Mickelson, Heather and

Max McCarty, Kelly Weaverling and Susan Ogle, and Brenda Guest, all of Cordova. John Oliver of Moss Landing Marine Institute and David Grimes of Cordova each added immeasurably to my understanding and made what would prove to be indispensable arrangements to put me in direct contact with the waters of Prince William Sound. I am grateful to my fellow writers, Tess Gallagher and Barry Lopez, for advice given at critical moments, and to my editor, Ted Solotaroff, for his enduring patience and care.

Despite her own busy schedule, my wife, Claire, helped to keep my ever mounting stacks of documents organized and put in library time for me, and along with my three sons and then soon-to-be daughter-in-law, Susan Romano, otherwise supported this unexpected obsession. More than that, my family provided a backdrop of constancy and hope against which the events in Alaska came to be cast. The sense of my great good luck in having my life stitched together with their lives was a thing I carried with me always in my travels and my witnessing of the struggles of others to restore themselves in the disaster's aftermath. Many of them had been shaken to their roots and discovered that the very groundwork of the ties by which they had previously connected themselves to the world had been sundered.

October, 1990

NOTE ON THE SECOND EDITION

When the opportunity arose for the reissue of this book, the first temptation was to revise it completely in the light of the greater understanding I felt I had come to after the passage of several years. Since I have continued to this day to closely follow oil spill related events in Alaska and to return to Prince William Sound on a regular basis and, thus, to extend my research, I have certainly felt that my level of education had improved, not only in the broad sense, but also for certain particulars that had eluded my full comprehension at the time the book was first completed. Finally, however, and on the advice of friendly readers, it seemed wise to preserve as it was that element of the book which is the account of a citizen-witness before whose transfixed and yet inquiring eyes the disturbing events that immediately followed the oil spill unfolded.

Thus, for this edition, my approach to the original text has been, first, to gladly correct those errors of fact, detail, and omission as they were pointed out to me, and second, to enter into the text more current material where it may be done unobtrusively. The appearance since I completed work on the original edition in the fall of 1990 of several other books and hundreds of articles and reports on the subject has aided in this effort. Such material often appears in footnote form. What updating of the text has been done will usually be evident by its nature, e.g. the yields of fisheries after 1990, the effectiveness of bioremediation as a cleanup method as it was revealed after

1991, and the increasingly precise scientific projections of habitat degradation and animal mortality from the spill. Certain events and developments,
however, required a fresh treatment. These would include the terms and sometimes bewildering results of the 1991 settlement between the Exxon Corporation, the U.S. Justice Department, and the state of Alaska (at $1.025 bil-
lion, the largest environmental settlement in the history of the United States),
the successful (and very thinly reported) 1993 fishermen's blockade of the
tanker channel in Prince William Sound, the various ensuing suits over the
oil spill, the changes in shipping procedures and regulations in Prince William Sound, and the devastation of clear-cutting by Native corporations on
and near the waters of the sound, which actually brackets the oil spill in time
and into which settlement monies entered as a surprising factor. To this end,
I have completely revised and expanded the conclusion in this edition.

Even in the new conclusion the book remains a blend of memoir, sometimes strong in its opinion, and of carefully researched fact. I do not pretend
to complete objectivity concerning the meaning of the *Exxon Valdez* oil spill.
My first interest in it, or in the two spills — oil, and then money — was in
the effects upon natural habitat, wildlife, and upon the rudiments of being
for the people of Prince William Sound. My second interests were in science
and the politics of resource extraction in the West. I have assumed, however,
a consensual agreement with my readers on the nature of fact as we know it,
and have taken great pains to be accurate and to not misrepresent anything
or anyone. Early on in my investigations, back in 1989, I perceived that what
I was witnessing in Prince William Sound was "a parable for future eventualities we must face." I still see it so, but because of our country's astonishing
assumption during the last few years of its role as the single leading corporate nation of the world, or as the principal trading house for corporate
superproprietors, and the public's willing acceptance of this, I now feel much
less optimistic about the time frame within which such eventualities might
be recognized. The effort behind the reissue of this book is done in the hope
that renewing the telling of the parable may encourage interest in its call for
health and spiritual balance.

I could not have revisited this book without the aid of an array of steadfast people, many of whom regretfully pass unnamed. During the seven years
between the publication of the original HarperCollins edition and this one, I
received invaluable help from Arco Oil, the Exxon Valdez Oil Spill Trustees
Council, and the public relations officers and librarians of the Oil Spill Information Center in Anchorage, particularly from L.J. Evans, as well as from
other people, including Richard Fineberg, Marie Smith Jones, Dune Lankard,

Craig Lee, Craig Matkin, Susan Ogle, Riki Ott, Captain Jeffrey Portillo of the *Arco Spirit*, Pamela Smith, Eva Saulitas, and Rick Steiner. Special thanks go to the Eastern Washington University Foundation for a Faculty Research Grant; to Denise Shannon of my literary agency; to my research assistant at Eastern Washington University, Matt Spaur; my research assistants at the University of Alabama, Robert Boliek and especially Brendan Cooney who put in long, painstaking hours in a computer war with the new text; to James J. McAuley, Christopher Howell, and Scott Poole of Eastern Washington University Press; and for her great insight and editorial expertise, to Julie Mayeda. Finally, I am grateful to Natalie Fobes for making her remarkable photographs a part of this record, and to David Grimes, for being my friend and wise confidant throughout.

December, 1998

1 OIL

1   INTRUDERS

. . . the structure of every organic being is related, in the most essential yet often hidden manner, to that of all the other organic beings, with which it comes into competition for food or residence, or from which it has to escape, or on which it preys.

— Charles Darwin, *The Origin of Species*, 1859

On June 15, 1989, 82 days after the grounding of the *Exxon Valdez*, I walked along a Prince William Sound beach of coarse sand and pebbles with Peter Slattery of Moss Landing Marine Institute and Gordon Robilliard, vice president of Entrix, a private environmental consulting company based in San Diego. Both men are marine biologists. A semipalmated plover appeared in our path. It was a sandpiperlike bird, small, leggy, and colored to keep itself secret — tan on top and white beneath, with a black breast band. It limped in front of us, one outstretched wing dragging on the ground. The three of us stopped. The plover stumbled toward a narrow creek that drained into the sea, then disappeared over the edge of the bank.

When we changed our course to the left, it appeared again, chirping wildly. It flew toward us, landed, and limped off. Peter moved farther along and the plover straggled in his path. Gordon and I swung to the right. A second plover appeared with precisely the same infirmity as the first. It chirped at us. The plover near Peter chirped back. The sound they exchanged was like a very thin, hysterical cry. It was a decoy activity, we realized. The second plover stopped right in front of Gordon's boot and spread out one wing, placing itself in a position of extreme vulnerability. I glanced over at Gordon, a large man, bearded, heavyset, possessed of a sharp wit and at times an aggressive sense of irony. It was he who had introduced me to the phrase "the Bambi effect" as a description of the emotional and ideological turbulence awakened by the wholesale death of sea otters following the grounding of the *Exxon Valdez*. He gazed down at the plover and smiled faintly. In an instant of alarm, I thought he might step out and crush the bird.

I was wrong. He didn't move a muscle, and no doubt would never have considered harming the plover. On the contrary, the alarm was within myself, a tangle of feeling and instinct and sense that pleasured in the beauty of the bird, the pale brown and white, its delicacy of color and structure, the small, dark yellow bill with the black tip, and that at the same time was awakened to the curiosity of the bird's action, its apparent pliancy in the face of death. I found an ancient demon in myself, the killer who arose to salute the power in Gordon's position, but also another perhaps equally ancient thing, the taboo, the corrective sense to take a breath and simply watch and trust. Gordon stepped back. The bird darted off to our right and settled among the small stones. To the left, Peter stood still. There, the first bird limped along, dragging its wing. It disappeared back into the creek bed. It wished to lead Peter that way. The space of 30 square yards or so that we occupied in the company of the birds had grown radiant and taut like a drumhead. To our right, Gordon and I saw them then, the two plover chicks, no larger than my big toe and the same color exactly as the pebbles. Peter came to look. The second parent darted from one chick to the other and away. It feigned nesting activity among the pebbles, as if to distract us. Plovers make their shallow nests, or "scrapes," among the pebbles and right out in the open.

It sat still for a moment, but then as if wrenched into desperation by our presence, it came back to its chicks, first to one, the other, and then away again.

The three of us moved off, down along the creek bed, across its mouth, and up a gravel bar that overlooked a broad estuary. The estuary, fed by two rivers, is called Useless Cove, probably because it is not deep enough to accommodate boats. We stopped when we saw a large brown bear in it, loping through the shallows. Its motion seemed effortless, and yet in a moment it had crossed to the tall grass on the far side directly opposite us, and then into the trees. Its retreat scared up a flock of Canada geese. They churned out of the water, flew seaward and then circled back toward the mountains. We glimpsed water up there on the lower slopes, several broad catch basins and meandering outlets flashing in the sun. The geese vanished, dropping below a tree line to settle in an unseen pond.

Chastened, we retraced our steps to where the creek met the sea. A quarter mile to our left the orange Zodiac inflatable that had motored us here from our ship was beached, and not far from it I could see the figure of Kathy Conlan, a crustacean specialist from the Canadian National Museum of Natural Sciences. She was crouched and bent forward so that her face almost touched the ground. Her fingers were in the sea wrack, which she happily raided for just the sort of tiny littoral life plovers liked to eat, small crabs, amphipods, snails . . . We were on the mainland, on a long, gently sloping beach between Long Point and Flent Point just west of the mouth of Columbia Bay. Back past Kathy and the Zodiac, past Flent Point, around the corner, and not visible to us but deep in the recesses of Columbia Bay, was the Columbia Glacier. Across the water before us was Glacier Island. Bits of ice had drifted to the shore where we stood, and large, blue-colored chunks of it floated out in the water. In the maritime trade the large chunks are called "growlers" after the sound they make when they rub against the hull of a ship. Similar chunks and even larger ones, called "bergy bits," floated free past Glacier Island toward Valdez Arm. The bergy bits were the size of a train car or small house, big enough to wreak havoc with an oil tanker.

The water lapped against the shore. The booming sound of the glacier calving could be heard in the distance. It was like sporadic thunder, but a more self-contained sound without the ripping quality of thunder. The sound came from huge masses of ice shearing loose from the face of the ice floe and falling into the water. The glacier was retreating. It sloughed off huge quantities of ice, especially during the spring, summer, and fall. At the height of its activity, it could release 14 million tons of ice a day. Past the northern edge of Glacier Island, we could see the mouth of the long fjord called Valdez Arm, which was the tanker channel, and faintly the dark blue hump of Bligh Island, so named in 1794 by Captain George Vancouver, who at that time was still seeking the mythical Northwest Passage that would connect the Atlantic with the Pacific. As a young man, Vancouver had served with William Bligh under James Cook. In 1778, searching for the same passage, Cook had entered the waters of what he would call Sandwich Sound, after his patron, and what his mapmakers would re-name Prince William Sound.

Eighty-two days earlier, Gordon, Peter, and I might have been able to see the *Exxon Valdez* aground on Bligh Reef. There was no oil on this beach, nor in the water, not a trace of it, the first such place we'd seen in days. Northeastward along the arm some 40 miles from where we stood was Port Valdez and the city of Valdez itself.

CHAPTER

2 THE SCREENS ON THE STAGE

The result of that brave setting out of the Pilgrims has been an atavism that thwarts and destroys. The agonized spirit, that has followed like an idiot with undeveloped brain, governs with its great muscles, babbling in a text of the dead years. Here souls perish miserably, or, escaping, are bent into grotesque designs of violence and despair. It is an added strength thrown to a continent already too powerful for men. One had not expected that this seed of England would come to impersonate, and to marry, the very primitive itself; to creep into the very intestines of the settlers and turn them against themselves, to befoul the New World.

It has become "the most lawless country in the civilized world," a panorama of murders, perversions, a terrific ungoverned strength, excusable only because of the horrid beauty of its great machines. Today it is a generation of gross know-nothingism, of blackened churches where hymns groan like chants from stupefied jungles, a generation universally eager to barter permanent values (the hope of an aristocracy) in return for opportunist material advantages, a generation hating those whom it obeys.

What prevented the normal growth? Was it England, the northern strain, the soil they landed on? It was, of course, the whole weight of the wild continent that made their condition of mind advantageous, forcing it to reproduce its own likeness, and no more.

— William Carlos Williams, *In the American Grain*, 1925

The name is pronounced *Valdeez*. The place was first called Puerto Valdes, so named in 1790 by the Spanish explorer Salvador Fidalgo, in honor of Admiral Antonio Valdes, the commander of the Spanish Navy. The purpose of Fidalgo's voyage was to reassert the dominion of the fading Spanish empire over regions into which Russia was expanding. As it happened, Spain would hold nothing in Alaska, but Fidalgo's foray deep into the tricky waters of the sound was remarkable for the fact that it was done with a sailing vessel. The remnants of his appearance here are a few names — Valdez, Cordova, and Port Gravina. Port Fidalgo, a fjord just south and east of Bligh Island, was later named in honor of the Spanish explorer by Captain George Vancouver.

Valdez was not "settled" until 1898, and then mainly by Americans from the upper Midwest who had their own way of saying the word. It is suggested that since 1898 was the year of the Spanish American War, the current pronunciation was born of anti-Spanish sentiment. Valdez is situated in south-central Alaska at 61 degrees north, or at approximately the same latitude as Leningrad and the Shetland Islands. It is 375 miles south of the Arctic Circle. The average temperature is 38 degrees and the annual precipitation is near to 60 inches, much of that in the form of snow. The reason for the town's existence is the elongated, protected, and ice-free oval of water called Port Valdez. The town is built at sea level, although the mass of nearby mountains gives it the impression of elevation. Down at the docks, the open space across the bay provides a view of the Chugach Mountains, the jagged peaks backed endlessly by jagged peaks, the sheer rock faces, snow, the long fingers of ice and plunging, glaciated crevasses. At the back of town, the mountains come near. Within five miles several peaks rise to 5,000 feet. They give the sense of tremendous weight bearing straight down. Up there is the "wild," the cold, the heady contrast of dark stone and radiant ice.

On Good Friday in 1964, Valdez was destroyed by the tsunami, or scismic wave, that followed the 9.2 Alaskan earthquake and swept up Valdez Arm to the Port of Valdez. Thirty-three people died, most of whom were taken by surprise on the pier. The port installations and 325 homes were destroyed. What remained of the old town was razed and a new one was rebuilt on another site, on what is referred to as "stable" ground — a somewhat higher habitat that the planners considered more secure from disruptive natural forces. The slate had been wiped clean. The new site was filled, graded, tamped down, and on it were placed buildings of the type known as "modular." The residential section is laid out on a grid. There and throughout the downtown, metal siding and sameness are preeminent, and the idiosyncrasies granted by the passage of time are held to a minimum. There has been talk of introducing a Swiss architectural theme for the sake of the tourist trade. But for now there remains a stripped-away look to the place, even in the summer . . . streets, poured concrete curbs, square houses, and bright patches of dirt, not even much in the way of weed and bramble poking up through the crevices.

Architecturally, the town seems to grant that it is merely transitional to yet another condition. Though comfortable enough within, insulated, well-equipped, and modern, the buildings are shelters only, or high-tech tents. Up the highway as it passes by the airport are more houses, more individuated and more responsive to the terrain, but here in town the buildings seem to acknowledge nothing quite so much as the flimsiness of their hold, the ephemerality of their purpose, and the much greater power of what lies beyond their walls.

Throughout recent history change has come to this town in rushes of irresistible, transformational force, both natural and commercial: following the Canadian Klondike strike of 1897, the Alaskan gold strikes for which the Port of Valdez served as an entryway; the discovery of copper in the Copper River Delta in 1900; the completion of the Richardson Road to Fairbanks in 1919; the earthquake of 1964; the completion of the 800-mile Alaska pipeline from the North Slope to the Valdez terminal in 1977; the 11-million-gallon oil spill from the *Exxon Valdez* in 1989.[1]

---

[1] Eleven million gallons (rounded out from 10.8) is the figure almost universally accepted and reported during the months and years following the oil spill. Questions have arisen, however, concerning the accuracy of that figure. See Chapter 5 for a discussion of this question.

By road, Valdez is 300 miles from Anchorage, close to 300 from Fairbanks, and nearly 3,000 from Seattle. Anchorage has become the economic center of Alaska, thanks to the military presence following World War II and the ensuing development of commercial air transport. It's a "mother city" with a vengeance. Its importance as a trading and financial center far exceed what its population of 250,000 would suggest. Due to ice floes and heavy sediment loads, the Anchorage harbor is intrinsically inferior to the natural harbors of both Valdez in the sound and Seward over on the Kenai Peninsula, but through improvements it has come to serve as Alaska's primary docking point for ships carrying goods and equipment. By sea on a route the oil tankers sometimes travel between Cook Inlet and Valdez, the distance to Anchorage is in the neighborhood of 500 miles.

The road from Valdez to Anchorage winds first northward along the drainages through the Chugach Range on the Richardson Highway, and then back southwesterly on the Glenn Highway. During the pipeline boom of the mid-1970s and the construction of the terminal in Valdez, the town abruptly swelled from about 1,000 to 8,000 residents. The stocks on the shelves of its stores grew sparse, and it was not uncommon for people to drive the hundred miles to Glennallen or even on to Anchorage to shop. Here and in the other small towns along the water, the people have continued out of need and desire to turn toward what is made available through one pipeline or another. There are fish canneries, but otherwise little is made here, not clothing, cans, or paper, almost nothing manufactured, and no food grown except in gardens cultivated by experts in the hazards of cold, short summers, and ponderous shade.

There is hunting, and there is the sea. Some in Valdez and, no doubt, a higher proportion of the people in what would prove to be the region affected by the oil spill — Prince William Sound, the Kenai Peninsula, and Kodiak Island — rely to some degree upon the sustenance nature provides. Some, such as the Native people of the villages, rely heavily upon hunting, gathering, and fishing. Many of the newcomers — white people, by and large — hunt and fish for some of their food, but they have nothing like the intricate and delicately balanced system of subsistence or the concomitant spiritual way of seeing that the Native people have formed over time. Most white people no longer possess anything approaching the required knowledge of the natural world to sustain such a system. There are exceptions.

Following years of political conflict within Alaska and in the U.S. Congress over the question of Native land rights, and then triggered by commercially viable oil strikes on the Alaskan North Slope, the Alaska Native Claims

Settlement Act (ANCSA) was passed in 1971. It is one of the most complex single pieces of legislation ever written. So filled is it with historical and economic ironies that at times the positions taken by Native and white people in relation to its consequences turn common expectation on its head. The act was designed by the late Senator Henry "Scoop" Jackson of Washington State to remove the legal obstacles to pipeline construction, and it is regarded by some as an Orwellian scheme on a grand scale for social engineering and assimilation. It purports to have extinguished aboriginal title to all Alaskan lands, and places ownership of what were previously ancestral lands in the hands of for-profit "Native corporations" with the shares held by tribal members and set to mature in 1991, at which time shareholders could sell off their assets. This is decidedly not the reservation system common to what Alaskans refer to as the "lower forty-eight." In Alaska, the boards of Native Regional and Village Corporations as established by ANCSA, facing sometimes monumental legal bills resulting from the years of litigation, and lacking other means of generating immediate revenue, were put in the position of seeking resource development by outsiders on their lands, which in many cases consists precisely of what they were resisting in the first place. Failing such development, they faced the prospect of bankruptcy and thus of losing control of their lands in that fashion.

Placed under such duress, and following the example of other corporations, the governing boards of Native corporations have on occasion facilitated the capitalization of their lands. In response, certain contingents from the white culture (environmentalists, in particular) have attempted to apply the brakes to Native development while other white and Asian resource developers remain poised to use Native ownership and economic opportunism as a Trojan horse by which to advance their interests. Finally, it should be understood that the long tradition of enmity between the peoples, which goes back to British and American overfishing, overhunting, and mining in the nineteenth and early twentieth centuries, and further back to forced labor and the wholesale movement of Native communities into what might be properly called penal colonies during the Russian fur trade of the early nineteenth century, had already honed the blades of the present edgy entanglement.

For the moment, however, treating the situation in the terms of the dichotomy with which outsiders are familiar, it can be said that for those Native people who follow what is called (in a peculiar dissonance of sociological jargon) the "subsistence lifestyle,"[2] the exchange is immediate and wealth in

---

[2] Subsistence is also a legal and political question in Alaska. A federal law passed in 1980 established the subsistence use of fish and game as the highest-priority application of the

the form of stores set against winter is measured in the here and now: salmon, herring, clam, mussel, urchin, sea cucumber, chiton, crab, roe, sea lion, seal, deer, bear, porcupine, duck, mink, berry, wood ... This way of life is followed fairly strictly in some villages and by some Native people in the predominantly white towns, and for all Natives it provides a sometimes comforting and sometimes discomforting backdrop to contemporary economic realities. For the white people, on the other hand, the measure of wealth has nearly always been elsewhere: in the eighteenth and nineteenth centuries, the furs taken to China to trade for silk and tea, and the goods of the Orient returned to Europe, later, the gold traded on the basis of a rate of exchange set in New York, and now the timber shipped to Japan, and the ore, and the North Slope petroleum shipped to the West Coast of the lower forty-eight and refined and sold there as a federally mandated hedge against shortfalls in the international market.[3]

The people here, and especially the people of Valdez, whose economic lives since the seventies have been driven by the Trans-Alaska Pipeline System (TAPS), have lived simultaneously in touch with two worlds: the old world of the wilderness that presses close upon them, or the persistent "idea," at least, of that old world, and the new world out there where the terms of exchange are placed in the hands of the powerful and seem to be in a state of ceaseless revolution. The people depend upon all the petroleum-powered pipelines, the air traffic to Anchorage, and the traffic by sea or land to Valdez to

resource, and defines subsistence as "the customary and traditional uses by rural Alaska residents of wild, renewable resources for direct personal or family consumption as food, shelter, fuel, clothing, tools or transportation, for the making and selling of handicraft articles out of "nonedible" byproducts of fish and wildlife resources taken for personal or family consumption, and for the customary trade, barter or sharing for personal or family consumption." State priority laws were passed in 1978 and 1986. The 1986 law reestablishes that only rural residents can be considered subsistence users. The question reemerged in 1990 in the form of a proposed rural subsistence priority amendment to the Alaska State Constitution, following a State Supreme Court decision to the effect that existing laws discriminated against urban hunters and fishermen. The legislature deadlocked on the issue through two special sessions called by Governor Steve Cowper. The issue pitted tourism interests and outfitters (professional hunters) against Native subsistence interests. Left unresolved, subsistence management will return to the jurisdiction of the federal Fish and Wildlife Service. This raises the question of states' rights relative to federal management, which is a frequently recurring issue in Alaska that nearly always turns upon the disposition of resources. In a typically Alaskan twist, oil lobbyists, no doubt heeding the extent to which Alaskan lands are owned by Native Corporations, supported the proposed amendment.

[3] Through the Trans-Alaska Pipeline System Authorization Act of 1973, Congress approved the construction of the pipeline with the stipulation that North Slope crude oil

bring them their food, their computers and VCRs, books, microwaves, clothing, food, the toys for their children, the machinery with which to run their shops, the equipment with which to outfit their boats, the boats themselves, the modular components with which to construct their buildings. Shipping is a serious business here, and shipping crude oil out of Valdez is especially serious. The play between the hardiness of life on an outpost and the reliance upon distant and powerful centers of commerce is presented in Valdez with particular clarity and force.

Alaska is a resource colony, or economic territory. From it are drawn ore, timber, fish, and petroleum. At the same time, Alaska has been a state since 1959. The contrarieties of big externally financed and federally mandated industry on the one hand, and on the other, self-governance by a group of people strongly given to doing things their own way, whose small numbers (under 600,000) give them unusually ready access to state government and who, further, are divided among themselves between embracing what they have and capitalizing on the tailings of the industries of extraction, repeat the histories of all the western states. However, because the demand for raw materials has increased so dramatically in the twentieth century and the means for extracting them have grown so much more advanced, the replay tape is running at high speed. It's the last such tape the United States gets to roll within its own boundaries.

As the images on the tape flicker by, the mythos of a nation divides evermore tellingly against itself. The mythos, as we have long learned to think about it, is split between what, on the one hand, was once the sense of the boundlessness of the wilderness, first in the east, then the south, and then to the west and north, the liberating hope and the promise of endlessly stocked gardens, the promise of engagement with a wild world, the terror and rapturous romance and even the sense of right alignment that people experience when they allow their lives to join with natural forces, and on the other hand, the impulse to procure that place for its material holdings, to compel it into service, and to subject it to the instruments of extraction, or in William Carlos Williams's terms, the "horrid beauty" of our "great machines." The split-mindedness, though shaped by differing national identities, goes way back into the early European explorations of North America. James Cook, sailing for the British and seeking the illusory trade route of the River of the West, was also what Williams would call a great "voluptuary," a master seaman and

production be reserved for domestic use. This act was reinforced in its substance by several subsequent acts and amendments. In 1996, however, legislation passed Congress and was signed into law by President Bill Clinton that allowed for the export of North Slope oil, thus changing substantively the dynamics of Alaskan oil production.

proficient natural observer, a man of physical vigor, one who came to love where he was and what he found as he sailed the world, and yet who finally paid for the weirdness of his opportunism at Hawaii in 1779. He became a complicitor by allowing his crews to extract bounty for themselves, the "white gods" of the ships, until at last the Natives at Kealakekua Bay stabbed Cook from behind with a dagger. In their rage, they passed the dagger among themselves so as to share in the destruction of the fallen captain.

The Russians, principally during the eighteenth and nineteenth centuries, pursued the sea otter and fur seal trade by establishing posts along the coastal regions of Alaska. Their interest, like that of other invaders, was shaped by their belief in their right to dispossess "inferior" and "barbaric" races, to establish a true faith, and mainly to corner the economic benefits of dominion. Some, however, who stayed behind — such as Ivan Veniaminov, who became Russian Orthodoxy's "apostle of Alaska," and who took the trouble to study Native language and to immerse himself in Native culture while establishing the "true faith," allowed the schism of thought to begin to break up into its more beneficent voluptuary pieces.

The Americans, Meriwether Lewis and William Clark, were voluptuaries in their own differing ways. The one, Lewis, was an intellectual, and the other, Clark, a master practitioner, and they shared enough of each other's nature to make a union suited to the task of the journeying from Saint Louis to the Pacific, which they reached in 1805. They accomplished this in a manner respectful of the place and the Indians who inhabited it, but they, too, were guided by the same overriding purpose. Their charge, given by President Thomas Jefferson, was to find the stream which "may offer the most direct and practicable water communication across [the] continent, for the purposes of commerce." At a time when the Spanish, British, Russian, and American mercantile armatures were skirmishing over possession of the North American Pacific Coast, Lewis and Clark sought the same illusory river Cook had sought. Failing to find it, they otherwise took hold of the land route to the west for the benefit of American commerce. The loss of the illusion would be soon mended by stitching in the paths to the Pacific — trails, rails, highways, air routes, and pipelines.

Two hundred twenty years after the Russians began establishing posts along Alaska's Pacific coast, 211 years after Cook set anchor at Snug Corner Cove just inside what would be called Port Fidalgo, 199 years after Fidalgo plied the tricky waters of the sound, 184 years after Lewis and Clark reached the coast of Oregon, 165 years after Ivan Veniaminov arrived in the Aleutians, 122 years after the sale of Alaska to the United States, then (following nearly a century of proprietary exploration and political wrangling), 30 years after statehood was granted to Alaska, and 12 short years after the first oil flowed through the pipeline from the North Slope to Valdez, Captain Joseph Hazelwood entered Prince William Sound the master of a great machine — Exxon Shipping's newest and most advanced tanker, the *Exxon Valdez*.[4] Ten years before, at the age of 32, he had become the youngest captain in Exxon's fleet, and he quickly gained a reputation in the industry for his seamanship, his feel for the vessels, and for his uncanny ability to extricate them from dangerous situations. He was a man of intelligence and skill, who wanted mainly to be at sea, who despised the paperwork, the ever-mounting tailings of commercial bureaucracy that had become increasingly his obligation.

Whether or not it had anything to do with the grounding of his ship, Hazelwood had a weakness for alcohol, which would turn out to be the dagger passed through the news media so that the nation could share in his destruction. Hazelwood, too, bore the burden of the enduring contradiction — in his case, the promise of engagement with what he loved, the sea, and the blunting of that promise by the oil delivery system he served. As it happens, the balance at this time continues to be tipped toward those who, as Williams (writing in New Jersey between the two world wars) put it, would compel the wilderness to fit their own image and nothing more. This, as well as the clear need to sweep away that contradiction, and all the corollary economic and ethical questions attached to locating the line between necessary and excessive use of resources, make the central issue of the oil spill of Good Friday, March 24, 1989. The story of the spill is a parable for the future eventualities we must face.

The groups of people working one resource or another take on a character and a political stance. The fishermen,[5] of which Valdez has a significant number, may well be the quintessential Alaskans of the moment. They deal with live, replenishable things that swim at times willy-nilly in the water. They need to be attuned to the natural world. Their work is dangerous and requires intelligence and physical skill. Their catch is sold mainly to Japan. They are often deeply invested, but the more successful among them bring in six-figure incomes. Because of weak regulation and heavy, company-financed

[4] The fact that Hazelwood was given the command of this ship spoke of his company's regard for his abilities.

[5] There are many fisherwomen in Alaska. In 1989, I was urged by several of them that they preferred to be called fishermen. Since that time the gender-nonspecific term, fishers, has come into currency. While acknowledging this, I am staying with the preference as it was indicated to me at the time.

fishing during the territorial days of the first half of the twentieth century, the runs of salmon, which are the staple fish of the industry in south-central Alaska, had become dangerously depleted by the fifties and sixties. In response a cooperative effort was launched by the state, the fish processors, and the fishermen themselves. There is now a significant salmon hatchery system, a marriage of science, technology, free enterprise, and nature, placed under the common proprietorship of the state and the fishermen. Although not without a downside, since there is evidence that the wild stocks of salmon suffer in the presence of large numbers of hatchery fish, the system has so far accomplished two positive things. It helped to restore the salmon runs (by the eighties, returns of salmon from the hatcheries in Prince William Sound alone numbered in the tens of millions), and it strengthened the economic niche for a class of entrepreneurial fishermen, who are in some respects an economic throwback, harking to the Hamiltonian ideal of the independent producer.

The fishermen came into 1989 as aware as any other group of the need for the custodianship of resources, or of their resources, at least. The fishermen, too, are in touch with the two worlds, the old world of fish, the new world of aerial spotting and Japanese markets. They are articulate, aggressive, fiercely self-reliant, well-educated, and politically, if not the most powerful, as vigorous as any group in Alaska. They came out of 1989 even more aware of the frailty of resources, and more aggressive, and, finally, divided against themselves. Aside from the residents of the subsistence villages, the oil spill affected no group of people as tellingly as it affected the fishermen. They found themselves cast into a classic confrontation between their form of small, agrarian-based capitalism and big capitalism, to which power of the first rank belongs.

The petroleum industry is the Hudson Bay Fur Trading Company of contemporary Alaska, or "superproprietor." Because of its power — the power to employ, to enrich the state treasury, to transform whatever it touches, to create its own science, to eclipse small and middle-sized businesses, the power of a constituency that consists of all gasoline-purchasing Americans, and the power of its ties to "national security" — avenues were left open to sloppiness, inattentiveness, profiteering, influence peddling, graft, and to the collaboration in word and deed among the producers, state and federal agencies, the Coast Guard, and both the Alaskan public and the public of the United States at large. All of this made the oil spill from the *Exxon Valdez* inescapable.

These, then, are some of the screens against which the oil spill was cast: (1) the general use of Alaska as a resource colony, which presumes the alien-ability of the natural world; (2) the politics, economics, and spirituality of the Native population, appreciable numbers of whom still regard the natural world as inalienable; and (3) the needs and methods of the fishing industry. In addition, there are: (4) the ineffectiveness of federal regulatory agencies, especially the Environmental Protection Agency (EPA) and the United States Fish and Wildlife Service (USFWS); the ineffectiveness of Alaska's state regulatory agencies, especially the Department of Environmental Conservation (DEC) and the Alaska Department of Fish and Game (ADFG), and the compromise of information, especially of scientific information; and finally (5), the extent to which capital and the industries of extraction, especially the oil industry, drive public policy, and also the extent to which the American public through its own wastefulness allows itself to be held captive by oil. Culpability for what would be the largest oil tanker spill in the history of the United States, and arguably, the most destructive spill in the history of the world, is shared.[6]

A larger backdrop is the petroleum companies themselves. Beginning with the formation in the late nineteenth century of the Rockefeller Standard Oil trust (the ancestor of Exxon) and extending through World War I, the 1928 Redline Agreement which apportioned the resources of the Ottoman Empire among European and American interests, through World War II, the 1956 Suez War, the formation of the Organization of Petroleum Exporting Countries (OPEC) — which sought to restructure the world eco-

[6] Larger tanker spills, such as the 1967 *Torrey Canyon* spill (35 million gallons) off the Isles of Scilly at the mouth of the English Channel, and the more recent 1989 *Kharg 5* spill (37 million gallons) off the Moroccan coast, may cause less biological damage if the shorelines are less affected. Marine life at and near the shorelines is far denser than it is in open seas. Also, lighter oils, which evaporate more quickly, are less damaging. Even the 1978 *Amoco Cadiz* spill (close to 60 million gallons), which profoundly affected the shorelines of the French coast, seems to have caused less destruction than did the "reported" 11 million gallons from the *Exxon Valdez*. By way of example, estimates put bird mortality from the *Torrey Canyon* spill at 30,000, from the *Amoco Cadiz* at 20,000, and from the *Exxon Valdez* at numbers ranging from 260,000 to 600,000. There have been tanker spills since the 1989 *Exxon Valdez* spill, including the 42-million-gallon spill from the *Haven* off the coast of Italy in 1991, the 23.8-million-gallon spill from the *Aegean Sea* off the coast of Spain in 1992, the 78-million-gallon spill from the *Maersk Navigator* off the northern tip of Indonesia and the 26-million-gallon spill from the *Braer* off the Shetland Islands, both in 1993, and the 75,000 tonnes spill from the *Sea Empress* off the coast of Wales. Damaging as the likes of these tanker spills are, none of them seems to have exceeded the mortality rates of wildlife following the *Valdez* spill. There are, of course, other forms of extremely damaging spills such as the 1979 Ixtoc blowout of nearly 140 million gallons in the Gulf of Mexico, the concatenation of spills and ruptures during the 1991 Persian Gulf War, and the 1994 84-million-gallon spill from pipeline rupture in Siberia.

nomic order — and the 1973 embargo, the petroleum internationals came to be involved as an agent in most of the critical world economic and political events of the twentieth century. These have included battles, shooting and otherwise, over the oil resources of the various Middle Eastern countries, as well as, say, Angola, Venezuela, Nigeria, and Mexico. Petroleum is the primary energy source of industrialized societies, and it remains the principal fuel by which the machines of war are run. It is fundamental to strategic concerns, and because of the United States's early expertise in petroleum technology, it is directly tied to U.S. domination during the twentieth century. The petroleum internationals regularly act in concert to set production rates and prices, and the connection between their interests and the interests of their titular parent countries is extremely murky. In the case of the United States, foreign policy at times follows on the heels of oil interests. Sometimes, as with offshore and onshore oil exploration by Texaco, Mobil, and Exxon in South Africa, for example, the U.S. government has found itself backed into a political corner. The oil companies and the U.S. government would see the discovery of oil fields almost anywhere, including South Africa, as a means of relieving the dependency on Middle Eastern oil. At the same time, a substantial portion of the U.S. population was demanding an embargo against apartheid. This is but one typical and relatively well-defined example of the type of moral dilemma the international activity of the petroleum companies has consistently produced — mainly in the Middle East. Although the traditional major oil companies are products of the industrialized West, the complexity and extent of their international activities raises the question of whether or not they owe allegiance to any one country. From the perspective of an oil company like Exxon, the Alaskan oil spill had to be a minor, though surprisingly aggravating event in a history that includes leveraging heads of state and weathering African and Middle Eastern wars.

There are several very substantial edifices in Valdez: the elaborate and well-fitted community center just above the docks, the $11 million high school in town, and the Valdez grain terminal beyond the edge of town. They're all tied to oil revenues, which comprise about 85 percent of the state treasury. The grain terminal was built in the early 1980s to facilitate export of products in accordance with the state of Alaska's agricultural plan. The plan for agricultural self-sufficiency failed, it is argued, because of a classic, state-supported boondoggle in which the farming practices of the northern Great Plains were foisted upon the Alaskan interior. Alaska had oil money to burn. Now, the towering silo stands empty.

The strongest testimony by far to the presence of serious money in Valdez is the terminal operated by the Alyeska Pipeline Service Company, which along with the pipeline itself is owned by a consortium of oil companies, otherwise known as the Seven Sisters.[7] Built into a mountainside just across the bay from Valdez, the terminal has a Third Reich appearance. The egg-colored concrete holding tanks look like huge pillbox bunkers. There are 18 tanks in all, and each holds about a half-million barrels of crude oil.[8] Adding in smaller storage facilities, there is a total capacity at the terminal of 9.2 million barrels. There is an average flow through the pipeline from the North Slope drilling sites into the tanks at the terminal of 1.8 million barrels per day. This comes to over 650 million barrels a year. Even the numbers attached to Alaskan resources, both in the quantities of material and in dollars, tend to become so staggering that they veer toward incomprehensibility. A day's shutdown of the pipeline costs the oil industry millions of dollars. Between 1969 and 1987, the state took in an average of $1.5 billion a year in taxes, and the federal government close to $2 billion. During the same period, the oil industry made on average $2.4 billion in profit from Alaskan production and transportation. These facts, together with the fact that the bargain struck in Congress sends a portion of Alaskan oil revenues into a permanent fund whose principal is expected to reach $10 billion by 1991, and from which every Alaskan — man, woman, and child — receives an annual dividend check from the fund of between $800 and $1,000, explain the pressure to keep the oil flowing. When the question of dividends comes up, some Alaskans will quickly explain that their checks are put toward their children's education, or donated to an environmental cause, but the permanent fund has nevertheless turned into a persuasive device for the oil interests. By it, Alaskans are kept constantly aware that the money tap is trickling in their kitchen, too.

Built at a cost of over $8 billion, the pipeline and terminal were at the time the largest private construction project in the history of the United States. The Prudhoe Bay Oil Field is now one of several North Slope fields that feeds into TAPS. It was the first field to be put into production, the twelfth largest field in the world, and the largest to be discovered in North America. It accounts for one-fourth of the total domestic U.S. production,

[7] BP Exploration, Incorporated (a British-based international), 50.01 percent; ARCO Pipeline Company, 21.35 percent; Exxon Pipeline Company, 20.34 percent; Mobil Alaska Pipeline Company, 4.08 percent; Amerada Hess Pipeline Corporation, 1.5 percent; Phillips Alaska Pipeline Company, 1.36 percent; and Union Alaska Pipeline Company, 1.36 percent. These percentages will change with the late 1990's spate of oil company mergers.
[8] One barrel equals 42 gallons.

and through 1996, for one-eighth of U.S. consumption. From the startup in 1977 through 1990, more than 6 billion barrels had been shipped from Prudhoe Bay, and over 700 wells have been drilled in the field. At this time, about 9.4 billion barrels of oil are expected to be recovered from the 23.5 billion barrels that remain in place. The tapped reserves are declining, however, and there is strong pressure from the industry to explore for new fields and to develop known fields, particularly fields to the west of Prudhoe Bay or to the east on or near the Arctic National Wildlife Refuge (ANWR), which might be tied into the existing pipeline system.[9]

The purpose of the terminal is simple. It's the big bladder at the end of the pipeline. Its storage tanks are reservoirs that hold crude oil for the tankers that come to carry the oil away to the lower West Coast. The obligation for managing the terminal and the pipeline fell to the Alyeska Pipeline Service Company. Alyeska had been formed precisely in order to centralize, first, the construction of the pipeline and terminal, and later, the operating and cleanup capabilities. Certain requirements were attached to terminal construction and its operations as conditions to the approval Congress granted to build the pipeline in 1971. These included incinerators to burn off sludge and toxic vapors, monitoring systems to determine the amount of oil and other toxins in ballast dumped into the harbor, and a state-of-the art oil spill contingency plan. As the years passed, however, Alyeska junked many safeguards and never built others.

It never built 14 of the storage tanks that had been called for. It never built the incinerator to destroy toxic sludge produced by the terminal's operations. Contrary to its promises, it used less expensive carbon steel rather than stainless steel on the miles of pipe in the vapor recovery system intended to draw off the poisonous crude oil gases that collect in the tops of the storage tanks. At the end of the vapor recovery system were incinerators intended to destroy the hydrocarbons in the vapors by burning them at high temperatures (1,400 degrees Fahrenheit). The pipe in the vapor recovery system sprang dozens of leaks and the incinerators regularly operated below the required temperatures, with the result that ever more vapors were released into the atmosphere and the incinerators fell ever more deeply into disrepair. Between 1980 and 1985, the vapor recovery system was shut down an average of one in every five days.

Besides that, the state of Alaska estimated that as many as 1,000 tons of hydrocarbons a week entered the air through vents on the decks of the tank-

---

[9] Advances in recovery technology, price increases, or both would raise the amount of recoverable oil, as will newly discovered and opened offshore and onshore fields.

ers, but Alyeska — taking a position that presaged its role in the cleanup of the *Exxon Valdez* spill — argued that emissions from tankers were not its responsibility. In this regard, it is important to remember that this is not just a matter of general environmental principle, but that there are workers on the premises and a town just across the way. Responsibility for tanker emissions apparently fell through a large crack, and it becomes apparent in this as in other failures either of omission or commission that what was originally an attempt to centralize and streamline accountability on the part of the oil companies within Alyeska had resulted in the deflection of scrutiny.

Alyeska had promised that there would be a fleet of double-hulled tankers coming into the Port of Valdez, but virtually all the ships that have called here, including the *Exxon Valdez*, were single-hulled. It was also expected that the terminal would enlarge its capacity as the volume of crude oil "through-put" increased. By 1989, the volume had increased fourfold since the startup of the plant, but the terminal itself was the same size as when it was constructed in 1977.

As oil prices began to fall in the early eighties, due to the oil glut, the owners of Alyeska ordered deep cost-cutting measures. James Woodle, who had been the Coast Guard Commander for the Port of Valdez and then an Alyeska Marine Superintendent, saw his budget cut by a third just when he assumed his new duties. Woodle resigned his post not long before the spill, but said, "Based on my experience with Alyeska, the only surprise is that disaster didn't strike sooner. There was an overall attitude of petty cheapness. I was shocked at the shabbiness of the operation."

The matter of water quality in the Port of Valdez has been a point of contention for years, particularly as it pertained to the treatment of ballast water. The tankers must carry ballast as they travel to the Alyeska terminal; without it, they would be unstable. On the ships, ballast water is stored in the same tanks that will be filled with oil, and when pumped out the ballast carries an oil residue. It is Alyeska's obligation to clean the ballast water in its ballast treatment plant before discharging it into the Port of Valdez, but Alyeska never installed the planned system for continuous monitoring of the water released into the harbor, and it dismantled heaters designed to separate oil from the water because the heaters were difficult to maintain. Alyeska initially had a permit to dump water containing highly toxic hydrocarbons in quantities of as high as nine parts per million, which is a dangerous level. Upon expiration of the permit in 1983, state and federal regulators required that new permits reduce the limits by as much as 85 percent, but Alyeska continued to dump out high levels of hydrocarbons while tying up the EPA in administrative wrangles.

In 1985, regulators charged Alyeska with releasing sludge from the holding tanks through the ballast water system and discharging it into the water together with the ballast water. While internal Alyeska records showed that in 1980 Alyeska was seeking ways to dispose of 4,200 cubic yards of sludge, George Nelson, the Alyeska president, stated that the terminal had only produced 480 cubic yards of sludge in nine years of operation. Alyeska then at first refused to comply with an EPA subpoena for an investigation of water quality, and following an EPA suit, Nelson, according to EPA attorneys, avoided appointments with the EPA, although his deposition was eventually taken. Alyeska continued to fight state and federal regulators' demands to cut discharge of toxic hydrocarbons.

Alyeska employees gave accounts not simply of sloppy operations but also of deliberate falsification of test results. Steve Eward, a technician from 1977 to 1980, reported that he was frequently ordered to disconnect the meter that measured how much treated ballast water was being flushed into the harbor. James Woodle said that Alyeska avoided meeting EPA standards for treated ballast water by sending samples to Seattle for testing so that by the time it was tested some of the pollutants would have decayed. Erline Blake, a technician in Alyeska's testing laboratory from 1977 to 1983, said that it was "standard operating procedure" to doctor test results.[10]

Finally, the advanced system, or contingency plan, for dealing with oil spills went through a similar evolution — from a bright promise to virtually nothing at all. Testifying on behalf of Alyeska and the oil companies for the approval of the pipeline in 1971, a senior petroleum specialist for British Petroleum, L. R. Beynon, stated at Department of Interior hearings that Alyeska's contingency plan would "detail methods for dealing promptly and effectively with any oil spill which may occur, so that its effects on the environment will be minimal. We have adequate knowledge for dealing with oil spills and improvements in techniques and equipment are continuing to become available through worldwide research. The best equipment, materials and expertise, which will be made available as part of the oil spill contingency plan, will make operations in Port of Valdez and Prince William Sound the safest in the world." Eighteen years later, following the *Exxon Valdez* spill, the chief of the EPA, William Reilly, would say, "One of the things that impressed me in Alaska was how inadequate is the technology that we have

---

[10] New concerns include the introduction via ballast water of exotic species of marine organisms potentially harmful to the Prince William Sound ecosystem.

to deal with these spills, how relatively primitive it all is, skimmers that collect five hundred gallons an hour in the face of ten million [gallons spilled], dispersants that have a lot of toxicity. . . ."

Often, the drills conducted in order to maintain readiness for oil spills dissolved into comedy. During a drill in the early 1980s, a boat carrying the top Alyeska manager and a group of oil industry executives ran aground. In 1982, Alyeska dismantled the crew that had been devoted to oil spill response and either reassigned or laid off the workers. The response equipment began to fall into disrepair. In 1984, a drill generally beset with confusion had to be canceled when a containment boom sank. In a report to his superiors, a state inspector, Tom McCarty, wrote that Alyeska's spill response capability had "regressed to a dangerous level." In 1985, an Alyeska official declined to practice deploying a hose during a sloppily run drill because "it would be too much trouble to roll it up again."

A former oil spill coordinator for Alyeska, Jerry Nebel, said, "We knew exactly what was coming, where we were supposed to be, and we still messed it up. Drills were a farce, comic opera." In March of 1988, Alyeska conducted an inventory of cleanup equipment but could find only half of the emergency lights. The other half, it was later discovered, were being readied for use in Valdez's winter carnival. Half the required length of six-inch hose was missing, and so was some 3,700 feet of boom,[11] nearly 15 percent of the required amount, and eight of ten blinking barricades listed in the contingency plan were nowhere to be found. Duane Thompson, who worked from 1985 to 1989 for Alyeska and for Earthmovers, a company that had a maintenance contract with Alyeska, told me that the cleanup personnel took only a verbal test to prepare for spills, and that because personnel were constantly being shifted into other duties, there were at any one time very few people on duty who even knew how to run the equipment. The oil spill drills, Thompson said, "were a joke." State drills would be announced as long as three months ahead of time. "And then," Thompson said, "they'd drop oranges in the water because an orange has about the same buoyancy as a tar ball. We'd get out there on the day of the drill, sit around, and eat oranges."

---

[11] Boom, a staple of oil spill cleanup equipment, is a floating fence. It comes in various grades and sizes and may be linked together in sections to make a chain hundreds of yards long. It may include oil-absorbent material. From a distance, it looks like a long hose laid out on the water. Although it is most effective for containing small spills in calm waters, it may also be heavily constructed and come with skirts attached to its bottom and splash shields attached to its top for use in rough waters. Its usefulness decreases dramatically with large spills and in open, heavy waters, or when subjected to strong tidal currents.

Another factor in the Alyeska situation was the role played by the agency charged with the primary regulatory duties, Alaska's Department of Environmental Conservation. DEC acquired its function as a result of a land exchange between the federal and state governments prior to the construction of the terminal, which exempted the U.S. Department of Interior from its regulatory capacity. In the days and months following the *Exxon Valdez* spill, DEC became deeply involved as the principle arm of the state government, and DEC Commissioner Dennis Kelso became widely admired for his willingness to stand up to the oil industry. But for years the state agency had been seriously underfunded and had devolved into the second smallest agency in state government. The lack of funding and the tendency of middle- and upper-level DEC officials to overlook Alyeska transgressions bespoke the ability of oil interests to influence state government. Before the spill, Kelso had not read the oil spill contingency plan, and the largest of a handful of fines levied against Alyeska was $10,000 for a 1986 air-pollution conviction. Bills to increase the DEC budget and its monitoring capabilities consistently died in the legislature. The original staff of three full-time inspectors assigned to Alyeska had been reduced to one part-time inspector.

The ultimate penalty to Alyeska's repeated violations, or what Bob LaResche, Alaska's oil spill coordinator after the spill, would call "the Nuke," was simply to shut down the pipeline. Of course, this was never considered by either the state or federal government. There was far too much money at stake, and the infrastructure that had been formed between oil interests and state government was too dense and too heavy to move. A shutdown, which technically speaking the state had the power to apply, would have been tantamount to declaring war on itself, and on the nation. LaResche would say, ". . . if we didn't like Alyeska's contingency plan, we could shut down the pipeline, and that would last five or six hours until the National Guard arrived."

For ten years, the DEC representative in Valdez had been Dan Lawn. A big, bearded man, rather given to bluster, Lawn was regarded by some of his own colleagues as a troublemaker, and he was disliked by Alyeska officials. At one point in 1986 Alyeska officials threw him off Alyeska premises while he was videotaping operations. After the *Exxon Valdez* spill, other Alaskans would come to regard Lawn as a kind of outlaw hero within the government bureaucracy.

In 1982, Lawn had reported to his supervisor that the Alyeska contingency plan was "superficial at best." Lawn went on to say that "all our experience with Alyeska oil spill recovery rates indicates that the recovery rates listed [by Alyeska] are eighty percent too high." In 1984, Lawn reported that there had "taken place a general disemboweling of the Alyeska Valdez terminal operational plan. . . . Most knowledgeable and competently trained individuals have either quit, been terminated, or transferred up the line." Regarding his role as a DEC monitor, Lawn wrote, the department was too "underbudgeted and understaffed to adequately inspect the terminal and keep in touch with Alyeska's day-to-day operations. . . . Unfortunately, this has been a signal to Alyeska that the state is no longer interested in the Trans-Alaska Pipeline project. Alyeska has consistently broken promises made to the state of Alaska and the federal government prior to our granting permission to build the terminal. We can no longer ignore the routine monitoring of Alyeska, unless we do not care whether a major catastrophic event occurs." The extent to which the oil industry and state government were enmeshed with one another is attested to by the tendency of officials to treat Lawn as if he were a "whistleblower," even though his assignment was designed to be adversarial. His job was to report violations. He was an inspector for the state government, and yet he found himself left outside the very channel that employed him.

Each month, 80 ships — or between two and three of them a day — were loaded at the terminal before setting out across Prince William Sound toward the Gulf of Alaska, and thence to ports on the lower West Coast. Alyeska and oil industry officials pointed to the fact that prior to the *Exxon Valdez* spill, over 8,000 ships had passed in and out of the Port of Valdez "without incident." In fact, there had been numerous near misses, including one as early as 1979 when the supertanker *Prince William Sound* lost power and steering in high winds. The tanker was within half an hour of foundering on the rocks when a wind shift moved it back into deeper waters and it regained power. There were also common occurrences of small spills within the Port of Valdez.

The condition of the Valdez fleet generally has been subject to question, and this makes another panel in the fifth screen — the ways in which the petroleum industry has driven public policy — against which the grounding of the *Exxon Valdez* must be cast. During the 1970s tankers were replaced as a matter of course, but during the 1980s — again, because of declining petroleum prices — the oil companies cut back sharply on purchases of new tankers. United States law requires that American-built tankers be used to transport Alaskan crude, but no American shipyard had built a supertanker for years. On average, the age of the ships in the Alaskan fleet is 15 years greater than that of the U.S. fleet otherwise. The Gulf of Alaska is also the roughest water any U.S. tanker would have to travel. Because of their size and the weight they carry, which is meticulously distributed over the multiple tanks, the ships are designed to flex. They are made from heavy gauge plate steel joined by high-tensile welds. Even in relatively mild waters, one can stand on the deck of a tanker, or look down from the bridge, and watch as the deck "racks" rhythmically in overlapping sets of diagonal ripples. At first, this makes for an unnerving sight, and yet because of the scale of the ship and its load, it is also necessary. Over the long term, however, one result of the twisting and heaving is metal fatigue and the resultant cracking, and the greatest fear is that a severely cracked tanker would simply break apart at sea, or ground and then break apart, as did the *Amoco Cadiz*.

An analysis by the U.S. Coast Guard, the Marine Structural Casualty Study, compiled between 1984 and 1986 and released in 1988, found that the rate of structural failures among tankers traveling Alaskan waters was unusually high. Although tankers of the Alaskan fleet represented only about one-eighth of the large ships in the survey, they suffered more than half the cracks and other structural failures. Commander Tom Purtell of the Coast Guard's Marine Investigation Division observed that 44 structural fractures were found in 30 tankers and 8 freighters included in the study, which surveyed a total of 445 ships of more than 10,000 tons. All of the ships with multiple fractures were Alaska-fleet tankers. "It seemed relevant to us," Purtell said, "that thirteen percent of the population suffered fifty-two percent of the casualties."

In January 1989, the tanker *Thompson Pass* leaked 72,000 gallons of oil into Port Valdez. This was the largest spill up to that time in Prince William Sound. The *Thompson Pass*, a British Petroleum tanker, had been observed to be leaking in San Francisco, but company officials there decided to send it on to Alaska for one more load before repairing it. In the Port of Valdez, the boom that had been placed around the tanker was left unwatched and before long the oil leaking from the ship rode the water, overwhelmed the boom, and spilled over its top. It took the Alyeska cleanup crew 15 days to recover the oil. Two weeks after the *Thompson Pass* spill, another tanker, the *Cove Leader*, spilled an additional 2,500 gallons into Port Valdez.

The fishermen based in Prince William Sound are represented by Cordova District Fishermen United (CDFU). When I talked in April 1989 with Ken Adams, a member of the CDFU board of directors, he was careful to make clear to me that CDFU was not a union but something akin to a lobby that was willing to take legal action on behalf of its membership. Based in Cordova, a fishing community some 70 miles east of Valdez, CDFU's 600 members represent well over half of the fishing permit holders in what is termed the Area E fishery — Prince William Sound. CDFU had opposed the construction of the pipeline from the start and then had fought to have the pipeline extended down through Canada to the lower forty-eight. At the very time pipeline construction was about to begin, the fishermen were initiating the salmon hatchery system in Prince William Sound. CDFU filed suit against the Secretary of the Interior's approval of pipeline and terminal construction. In 1973 the suit, by then consolidated with suits from environmental and Native groups, received a favorable ruling in a federal district court. The decision was subsequently upheld by the Supreme Court, but proponents of the existing plan turned to Congress and late in 1973 legislation was introduced to circumvent the court rulings and to foreclose all court challenges to construction based upon environmental grounds. In the Senate, a tie vote on the legislation was broken by Vice President Spiro Agnew.

In 1985, and in conjunction with Charles (Chuck) Hamel, an oil broker, CDFU filed a notice of intent to sue again over mismanagement of the ballast water treatment plant at the terminal and the discharge of toxic pollutants into the Port of Valdez. This notice was followed by the joint compliance order issued by EPA and DEC, requesting Alyeska to build a system to monitor, remove, and dispose of sludge. The response to this compliance order was spotty. Throughout the time since the construction of the pipeline and terminal, CDFU, believing that the hatchery system and the fisheries generally were under threat, has had an extremely rocky relationship with Alyeska. In 1987, CDFU entered into the heated debate over whether or not to open the Arctic National Wilderness Refuge (ANWR) to oil exploration. CDFU hoped that this controversy would awaken national attention to the pollution problems in the Port of Valdez and to the oil industry's generally poor record of self-evaluation and performance.

When word of the *Thompson Pass* spill reached John Devens, the mayor of Valdez, he set about forming a committee to investigate safety problems at Alyeska. What he learned about Alyeska and water and air pollution alarmed him — rather surprisingly at that late date. A town meeting was called for Thursday evening, March 23. Alyeska declined the invitation to send a representative, and Devens invited Fredericka (Riki) Ott instead to travel to Valdez from her home in Cordova to give a presentation on the Alyeska terminal and marine transport of oil. Ott was a member of the CDFU board of directors. An energetic woman with a reputation for speaking her mind, she holds a master's degree in oil pollution and a Ph.D. in sediment toxicology as well as an Area E salmon drift gillnet permit. As it happened, bad weather grounded the flights from Cordova to Valdez, but the Valdez people arranged to hear Ott's presentation by teleconference. These were the two worlds of Alaska again — the old world of the outpost in which natural forces had the power to shut things down, set against the new world of communications. The people were willing to accommodate themselves to both.

Ott rode her bicycle into Cordova and at 7:00 P.M. gave her talk, speaking for two hours into a teleconference microphone. She spoke of oil revenues and Alaskan politics, of unauthorized design changes in the Alyeska terminal, of its overloaded pollution control systems, of its failure to live up to its promises, of the fact that the entire terminal was monitored by only one part-time DEC employee (Dan Lawn), of the condition of the tanker fleet. Like many of the fishermen, she believed that it was not a question of whether or not a major oil spill would happen, but of when it would. She spoke of the petroleum consortium's increasing incapability to clean up and contain a major spill. She said, "Given the high frequency of tankers into Port Valdez, the increasing age and size of that tanker fleet, and the inability to quickly contain and clean up an oil spill in the open water of Alaska, fishermen feel that we are playing a game of Russian roulette.

"When, not if," she went on, "The Big One does occur and much or all of the income from a fishing season is lost, compensation for processors, support industries and local communities will be difficult if not impossible to obtain."

Afterwards, Ott was pleased with the questions her talk had provoked. Little did she know that at the time she spoke, her prophecy on behalf of fishermen was in the process of being fulfilled. She went home, stoked her fire, and turned in. In less than 12 hours she awoke to hear acting CDFU president Jack Lamb banging on her door and found herself cast into the vanguard of the grassroots response to the spill she'd dreaded.

3 THE CHANNEL

The Gulf of Alaska extends southeasterly toward the Alexander Archipelago and southwesterly toward Kodiak Island. It is the threshold to the Pacific from south-central Alaska. As the crow flies, the edge of the gulf is about 60 miles from Valdez. By ship — because narrows, shallows, and islands must be negotiated — it is farther.

Roughly 30 by 75 miles and cast between the gulf and Valdez rather in the shape of a trapezoid is Prince William Sound, which the *Exxon Valdez* was scheduled to traverse. Port Valdez lies at the upper, northeastern corner of the trapezoid, dug into the mainland and pitched off eastward from the Valdez Arm. Once a tanker leaves the terminal, negotiates Valdez Narrows and Valdez Arm, and passes between Bligh Island and Glacier Island, the target becomes Hinchinbrook entrance, which lies between Hinchinbrook and Montague Islands.

The contours of the sound are most strongly characterized by the radical irregularity of its shorelines. No rendering will accurately capture the detail of the shoreline. Because the geological formations are recent, relatively speaking, much of the shoreline in the sound is indented with countless tiny coves and inlets into which small craft might be drawn, and the shorelines themselves and the reefs are rocky. The beaches are far from flat. They're frequently bounded by sheer, heavily striated rock faces. They are often composed of cobbled stone. Sometimes they're coarsely sanded, as was the beach off Flent Point that Peter Slattery, Gordon Robilliard, Kathy Conlan, and I walked. The irregularity of the formations further increases the surface exposed to the water, to the tides which run at a rate up to three knots and ebb and flow between a low of minus 3 feet to a high of 16 feet. A thumbnail accounting of shoreline surface area is 1,800 miles of mainland shoreline and 1,200 miles of shoreline along rocks and islands.

On and in these irregular surfaces, in all the cracks and crevices of the tidepools and estuaries, the near shore, the intertidal zone, live a host of tiny creatures: amphipods, copepods, sea worms, clams, crabs, mussels, periwinkles, starfish, shrimp, urchins . . . Here, too, is the plant life, the algae, kelp, fucus, and eel grass which the creatures may colonize and upon which they feed. From deeper waters come fish and ten species of marine mammals — seals, sea lions, whales, porpoises, and between 10,000 and 12,000 sea otters. From shore come over 30 species of land mammals, including bear, mountain goat, fox, wolf, lynx, deer, beaver, mink, river otter, marten, porcupine, wolverine, and human beings. There are the seabirds, more than 200 species of them, some of which are permanent residents and others of which are migratory. Great concentrations of migratory birds arrive between March and June, sometimes in flocks of hundreds of thousands. The total numbers of birds that pass through the sound are in the millions. There are 3,000 bald eagles. Each of these creatures, the amphipod, the crab, the mussel, the seal, the otter, the killer whale, the Sitka blacktailed deer, the semipalmated plover, murrelet, pelagic cormorant, tern, scoter, goose, and eagle, has its own life, its details of feeding and resting, of flight and predation, of courtship, of egg laying, and of nurturing young in the hollows and inlets, out in the open or hidden in the cracks and crevices. Rich and dense with life, the shoreline is the margin, the cutting edge of the action between earth and sea.

There are natural hazards to traffic in the sound. There is good weather and more bad — sudden squalls, fog, and high winds. One day in six is clear.[12]

[12] The outer coast of Prince William Sound is considered the rainiest place in the world at

The weather kept Riki Ott from flying to Valdez on March 23. It affects boats differently according to their size. During a storm, a fishing boat might pull into a protected cove and set anchor. On the night of March twenty-third, reports of ice floating from Columbia Glacier into the tanker channel put the *Exxon Valdez* an hour behind schedule.

The glaciers and other freshwater outlets into the sound affect the level of salinity, the water temperature, and so marine life in all its detail. The water surface of the sound measures approximately 2,500 square miles, and its dimensions otherwise include the subaquatic world. The mountains on the land merely happen to be higher than the mountains beneath the water. The sound varies in depth from next to zero at, say, Bligh Reef, to 2,850 feet off Lone Island, and there are surprises, even for experienced boat people. There are more channels under there, canyons, sand bars, and tidal flats that change shape, underwater eddies and powerful crosscurrents that interact with other forces — the wind, the tide, the predominant current.

All this, the large habitat, is the arena for the March 24 grounding, and through it, at a depth of about 80 fathoms, runs the channel designated for tanker traffic. But for a stretch at the Valdez Arm and running through Valdez Narrows, there are two lanes, incoming and outgoing. Beginning with the Port of Valdez, the outward path runs southwesterly through the narrows, out the arm and alongside Freemantle Point. Here the pilot must be wary of the growlers and bergy bits that float free from Columbia Glacier, which is the largest of 20 tidewater glaciers in the sound. In 1973 the balance of the glacier was disturbed by an abrupt emptying of a glacially dammed lake. The glacier's rapid retreat in recent years is an event not anticipated in the planning of the pipeline and terminal. Over the next 20 to 50 years, the glacier is expected to lose over two cubic miles of ice annually, and a new fjord will be created.[13] The chunks of ice are sometimes huge, white and pale blue and streaked with black mud. Birds gather on them. Seals rest on them. The drifts move out from Columbia Bay and around Glacier Island and sometimes fill the shipping channels, causing the ships to change their route, as would the *Exxon Valdez*, and immediately before it the *Arco Juneau*.

---

sea level. Port Chalmers on Montague Island has recorded more than 300 inches of precipitation in a year.

[13] "Jokulhumps," the periodic floods that drain ice-dammed lakes, are common around glaciers. Columbia Glacier is retreating rapidly now because it was the last in the sound to finally recede off its terminal moraine, or its stabilizing mound of rocks and debris pushed forward by the glacier's last advance. Once the glacier terminus melts off the moraine into the deeper water behind, the glacier's retreat becomes dramatic and miles of new fjord can be created in just a few decades.

The channel passes Bligh Reef, which is marked with a lighted buoy, and then from a point that lies midway between Glacier and Bligh islands, it swings first southerly and then southeasterly in the direction of Hinchinbrook Entrance. The openness of the water in this section provides a greater margin of safety. In good light, the Naked Island complex becomes visible off the starboard side. In the distance, Knight Island rises to view. Even in the summer the peaks of Knight Island are snowcapped. Narrow and spindly-looking, they rake the sky. The peaks seem a vertical recapitulation of the complication of the island's ragged shoreline. The lower slopes are dark blue, nearly black. Big enough to be mistaken for the mainland, Knight Island seems to float on the water. Straight ahead lies the opening between Hinchinbrook and Montague Islands. Between Knight Island and the channel are smaller islands — Smith Island, Little Smith, Seal. The color of the water is a pale blue tinged with green and the milk color of glacial silt. Terns and gulls float in the water, riding the swells. Cranes might fly overhead. A pod of killer whales might pass by. If there's a tanker in the channel, fishing boats will give it wide berth, darting clear of its ponderous trajectory. The green in the water gives the appearance of depth to the blue and the milkiness gives it an opacity. This makes an extraordinary mineral-like color that I would see again and again and for which I had no name. Aquamarine does not suffice. Even in good weather, the seas darken and take on a hard chop as the ship approaches Hinchinbrook Entrance. In bad weather, it can be a treacherous place.

THE
IMAGINARY
JOURNEY OF
CAPTAIN

4 JOSEPH
HAZELWOOD

These days, after much of the media hype and lunacy has abated, [I am] left simply with a gut feeling of frustration. Had to learn the hard way the lexicon of the 80's and discover exactly what "spin" means. The truth hasn't been allowed to come to the fore either for any number of legal reasons or it wasn't lurid enough for print or airing.

Oh well, I'll get my day(s) in court soon enough and the cause [of the oil spill] will seem pretty mundane and simple after all.

— Joseph Hazelwood in a letter to a friend, quoted in *Time*, July 24, 1989

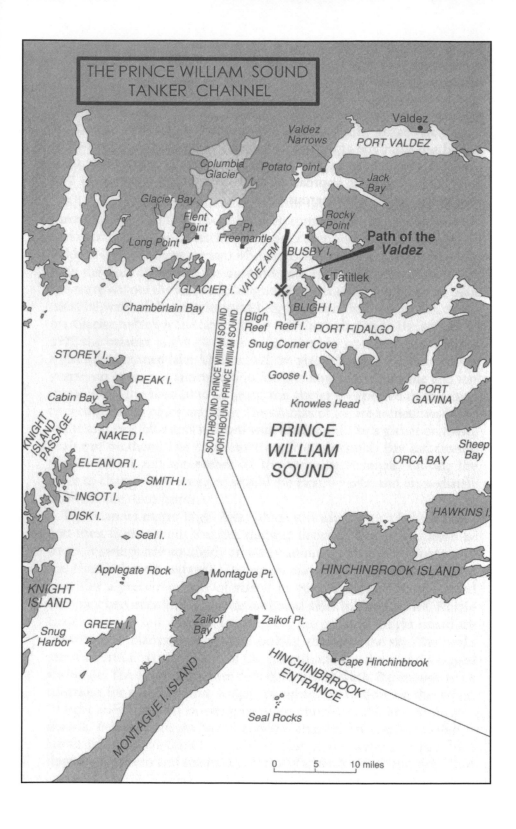

THE PRINCE WILLIAM SOUND
TANKER CHANNEL

Valdez

PORT VALDEZ

Valdez
Narrows

Columbia
Glacier

Potato Point

Jack
Bay

Glacier Bay

Flent
Point

Rocky
Point

Path of the
Valdez

Long Point

Pt.
Freemantle

BUSBY I.

Tatitlek

GLACIER I.

VALDEZ ARM

Chamberlain Bay

Bligh
Reef

BLIGH I.

Reef I.

PORT FIDALGO

Snug Corner Cove

STOREY I.

SOUTHBOUND PRINCE WILLIAM SOUND
NORTHBOUND PRINCE WILIIAM SOUND

Goose I.

PEAK I.

Cabin Bay

Knowles Head

PORT
GAVINA

KNIGHT ISLAND PASSAGE

NAKED I.

PRINCE
WILLIAM
SOUND

ORCA BAY

Sheep
Bay

ELEANOR I.

SMITH I.

INGOT I.

HAWKINS I.

DISK I.

Seal I.

Applegate Rock

Montague Pt.

HINCHINBROOK ISLAND

KNIGHT
ISLAND

Snug
Harbor

GREEN I.

Zaikof
Bay

Zaikof Pt.

HINCHINBROOK
ENTRANCE

Cape Hinchinbrook

MONTAGUE I. ISLAND

Seal Rocks

0   5   10 miles

And taking Jakonaan's head, all three went off towards Galilee.
As it was very heavy, they each carried it in turn.

— Gustave Flaubert, "Herodias," 1877

On Wednesday, March 22, following a passage through rough seas
in the Gulf of Alaska, the *Exxon Valdez* arrived in Port Valdez and docked at
the Alyeska Terminal at 10:48 P.M.

Chief Mate James Kunkel and Captain Hazelwood were on the bridge
of the ship. The crew spent the night on board. The ship measured 166 feet
at the beam and 987 feet from bow to stern — longer than three football
fields and a couple hundred feet shorter than the Empire State Building is
tall. The 1,286,738 barrels of crude oil she would take on was a little under
her capacity of 1,484,829 barrels, or 211,000 deadweight tons.

Early the next morning, the crew began the laborious process of discharging ballast water and filling the 12 cargo tanks with crude, which included handling the chicksans (loading arms) from the terminal to the ship
and at all times meticulously monitoring the flow of water out of the ballast
tanks and of oil into the various cargo tanks so as to maintain the proper
stress levels in the ship. By 7:24 P.M. on Thursday, March 23 — minutes
before Riki Ott began her telecommunication to Valdez — the loading was
completed, and the final checks were being made. The crew members who
worked the deck during the day — including Able Bodied Seamen (A.B.)
Maureen Jones and Robert Kagan, Third Mate Gregory Cousins, Second
Mate Lloyd LeCain, and Chief Mate Kunkel — were all tired.

Kunkel, who was in charge of all deck operations including docking and
loading procedures. Having stayed up from the time of arrival until 8:00 A.M.
the following morning, Kunkel then took a nap, arose at noon, worked the
deck again until 4:00 P.M., and went on his normal 4:00 to 8:00 watch.[14] If
the congressionally mandated requirement that officers have six hours' off-
duty time within the 12-hour period prior to departure had been adhered to,
the *Exxon Valdez* would never have cast off that night. The required rest

[14] Bridge watches — that is, command of the ship's navigation and its piloting — were
divided equally among the three mates. Each took a shift of 4 hours every 12 hours. In
addition to taking his turn on watch, the chief mate had command of deck operations. The
captain, who also functions as a chief executive, had command of all operations. In a four-
mate system the chief mate and captain would not stand regularly scheduled watches, but
would stand in as required. In the three-mate system, such as that in place on the *Exxon
Valdez* and most other tankers at the time, the chief mate is performing double duty.

period, however, was rarely observed. In testimony before the National Transportation Safety Board, Exxon Ship Group Coordinator Captain William Deppe would say, "We don't have any program to give six hours of rest to any deck officer before we get under way."

It has proved difficult to determine just what was binding and what was not in the maze of federal, state, Coast Guard, and company regulations that govern the crewing and operations of tankers in Prince William Sound. As a matter of practice, general crew fatigue was common on tankers following loading and unloading. In a cost-cutting measure that had little regard for safety, Exxon had used the increasing automation of ships as a justification for reducing the size of its crews. At the same time, the company pressed for as speedy a product delivery as possible. The result was that it was impossible for crews to both do the work and adhere to manning regulations. Remarkably, prior to the spill, Exxon Shipping had an additional objective of reducing crew levels even further by 1990 — from 20 to 16. This is a company that was part of an energy conglomerate (Exxon Corporation) that reported net revenues to its stockholders of $5.3 billion in 1988 and of $3.5 billion, after oil spill expenditures, in 1989.

Joseph Hazelwood spent part of Thursday in the town of Valdez. Between 11:00 A.M. and noon, he made several phone calls from the office of an oil agency, the Alaska Maritime Agency. From there he went to the Pizza Palace and had lunch with his chief engineer, Jerzy Glowacki, his radio electronics officer, Joel Roberson, and the man who would pilot the *Exxon Valdez* out of the harbor and Valdez Arm, William Murphy. According to Glowacki, Hazelwood drank iced tea during lunch. From the Pizza Palace, Hazelwood, Roberson, and Glowacki went to the Pipeline Club, a bar popular with tanker crews, and there, by the accounts of witnesses, Hazelwood drank either two or three vodkas "straight up." In his interview with Coast Guard investigators, Hazelwood said that he'd had two beers.

From the Pipeline Club, Hazelwood, Glowacki, and Roberson returned to downtown Valdez. Hazelwood entered a shop to order Easter flowers for his wife and daughter, then rejoined Glowacki and Roberson in the Pizza Palace, where Glowacki ordered pizza to take to the ship's engineers. There, Hazelwood drank something, but witnesses have not confirmed what it was.[15] The three took a cab to the pipeline terminal, passed through the gate, where

[15] In the civil trial, completed in 1994, and in which Hazelwood and Exxon, Inc., had been called as co-defendants, there was also conflicting testimony over how many times Hazelwood was seen in the Pipeline Club, how many drinks he had, whether they were double Vodka shots or singles. At the Pizza Palace, according to a witness, he ordered another vodka. Hazelwood testified that he believed he left the last drink untouched.

a policy on alcohol — in the form of its possession, being under its influence, or having imbibed it within four hours of ship duty, the last of which Hazelwood had done — was to have been enforced. They climbed the gangway to the *Exxon Valdez*. It was raining and the gangway was steep, but neither Roberson nor Glowacki noticed any hesitation in Hazelwood's step.

Following the loading of the ship, Third Mate Cousins had run the standard systems check on the navigational and electronic gear. At 7:48 P.M. the test was successfully completed. At 8:20, Pilot Murphy arrived on the bridge. Pilots are employed by Alyeska, and at that time one was required on each tanker as it passed in and out between the terminal and Rocky Point at the mouth of Valdez Arm. After Murphy's arrival, Cousins was relieved by Chief Mate Kunkel at the bridge so that Cousins could go down to his docking station to direct the handling of the lines. It was then, at about 8:30, that Captain Hazelwood appeared, and that Murphy smelled alcohol on his breath. Murphy's observation would make the newspapers soon afterwards and be taken as evidence of Hazelwood's drunkenness, although Murphy had otherwise detected no evidence of impairment in the captain.

Hazelwood went below with a shipping agent for Alaska Maritime Agencies, Patricia Caples, in order to complete paperwork pertaining to the cargo. Later, at Hazelwood's trial, Caples would first testify that she detected a "slight sway" in his step, that his eyes were watery, and that he "seemed jolly." When cross-examined, she acknowledged that the watery eyes might have been due to the fact that he'd just come in from the cold damp weather outside, that the sway she'd observed had been extremely slight, and that his jolliness might have been her impression as it was cast in relation to the last time she'd seen him — the night before, following his arrival after a passage through rough seas.

In about ten minutes, Caples departed for shore and Hazelwood returned to the bridge. From this point, throughout the journey, and continuing past the events that followed the grounding, no one on the ship observed any deficiency in Hazelwood's demeanor or in his ability to give clear, concise orders. While damaging reports of Hazelwood's drinking had been widely circulated, there is no incontrovertible evidence that Hazelwood was drunk at the time of the spill. His crew members, interviewed by the FBI between April 5 and 12, 1989, would unanimously assert that he showed no sign of intoxication before or after the grounding. Not one of them testified to smelling alchohol on his breath that night, nor did any know of previous instances of intoxication on board ship. His officers, in particular, would affirm that he was a fine captain and "excellent ship handler." The Coast Guard would find the measures he took to secure the ship after the gounding to be exemplary.

The blood alcohol test administered to him ten hours following the grounding would give a reading of 0.061 percent, or a little more than half the 0.1 percent drunk-driving limit in the state of Alaska and 50 percent higher than the 0.04 percent limit set by the Coast Guard for seamen operating a ship. A toxicologist who testified at his trial conjectured through a controversial process called retrograde extrapolation (calculating backwards) that his blood alcohol level at the time of the grounding might have been 0.22 percent, which likely would have left him staggering drunk. It would seem equally possible that Hazelwood took a belt sometime in the period between the grounding and the blood test. Hazelwood himself had claimed to have consumed two Moussy beers during that period, but two of them would never have produced the 0.061 percent blood test reading. A search of Hazelwood's quarters conducted by Coast Guard investigator Mark Delozier produced no evidence of alcohol, although Delozier admitted that he had not examined all the cupboards. In a claim reported by the news media early on, but which grew increasingly dubious during courtroom testimony, Delozier's search of the quarters was followed by the appearance of his Coast Guard colleague, the health services technician Scott M. Connor, who'd been called out to take the blood samples. Connor claimed to have seen a bottle of Jack Daniels left out on a shelf in the captain's quarters, in plain view for anyone to see. No one else did see it, and Connor admitted under cross-examination in court that he might have the image of the bottle "superimposed with another event from my life."

Because of the lack of Coast Guard provisions for the possibility that blood samples might have to be taken from a tanker crew, the samples themselves followed their own quixotic journey. The only available health technician — Connor — had merely happened to be in Valdez on other business when he was called to the ship to take samples. When he returned to shore, he temporarily placed the samples against his motel room window in hopes of keeping them cool, then stored them in the walk-in refrigerator in the galley of the Valdez Coast Guard station. The next day he carried them to Anchorage, put them in his own refrigerator, and finally turned them over to an Anchorage Coast Guard commander. By all early reports, the samples had arrived safely at Chem West Analytical Laboratories in Sacramento, California, but later — in July 1990, well after Hazelwood's trial in Anchorage — it was learned that the samples had been misidentified by either Connor or the lab.[16]

---

[16] During the 1994 civil trial, the mislabeling of the samples became crucial to Hazelwood's defense team's argument that the trail of the samples was impossible to follow.

The Anchorage jury rejected the prosecution's arguments regarding Hazelwood's drunkenness, but testimony at that trial otherwise established that Hazelwood had violated Coast Guard and Exxon rules concerning alcohol consumption prior to boarding his ship. Although this is speculation, it seems possible that by making him tired or distracted, whatever drinking he did in town may well have been a part of the web of factors that indirectly influenced the coming catastrophe.

At the time, Hazelwood was 42 years old. In retrospect, two qualities in his record would rise to prominence: first, his problems with alcohol and, second, his rare intelligence and skill as a mariner. He began drinking at weekend parties while a student at the New York Maritime College, an elite and rigorous state-run school in the Bronx. Later, he earned a reputation as a hard drinker among some of his fellow seamen, who said that he also had a sense of when to stop so that his performance would not be seriously impaired. In 1984, while off duty, he was arrested for drunk driving in Huntington, New York. At the urging of a friend and Exxon supervisor, Captain Mark Pierce, Hazelwood entered a rehabilitation program. Through a coincidence, the Exxon brass became aware of his problems, and company records showed that according to Hazelwood's physician, he was "depressed . . . demoralized," and had been "drinking excessively [and] episodically," which resulted in "familial and vocational dysfunction." In May 1985, an Exxon administrative manager, Ben C. Graves, addressed a memo to the company law department which reported that in the past Hazelwood had by his own admission returned "to vessels in port in an intoxicated state on several occasions, and that shipmates of Hazelwood's reported that he had violated company alcohol policy on at least several occasions."

Hazelwood was given a 90-day leave following his first drunk driving arrest and then returned to duty. By 1988 he had resumed heavy drinking, and according to reports his marriage of 20 years was on the verge of divorce. He was arrested once again for drunk driving. Despite Exxon's strict policy on alcohol, and despite Exxon Chairman L. G. Rawl's postgrounding letter to a Senate investigating committee, which claimed that from the time of Hazelwood's rehabilitation he had become "the most closely scrutinized individual in the company,"[17] Hazelwood's second arrest and his renewed drink-

---

[17] For reasons of liability, it seems to have been important to Exxon to separate Hazelwood's personal failing from company failings. State of Alaska documents, including its "Findings and Recommendations" to the National Transportation Safety Board, suggest that it has been interested in establishing, first, Hazelwood's drunkenness, and second, in tying that to Exxon's responsibilities. In the 1994 civil trial, Hazelwood and Exxon were tried as codefendants. Here, too, Exxon strove to separate itself from Hazelwood.

ing apparently did not awaken company notice. Even the occasional report to Exxon officials of seeing Hazelwood drinking in public, as happened in San Francisco two weeks before the grounding, did not lead to firm action. The truth is that he was hardly monitored. The reason Exxon eventually offered for its leniency was that the company did not want to set a precedent that would discourage employees with drinking problems from coming forward voluntarily for help.

From the time of his boyhood on Long Island, New York, Hazelwood was drawn to the sea. Even as a teenage member of the Sea Scouts he distinguished himself for calm and courage by climbing the 50-foot mast of a schooner to haul in a mainsail that had been blown out by a violent storm. Upon graduating from New York Maritime College, he was one of a select group of his classmates hired by Esso, as Exxon was then called. His first commanding officer, Steve Brelsford, said that Hazelwood "had that sixth sense about seafaring that enables you to smell a storm on the horizon or watch the barometer and figure how to outmaneuver it." In 1985, Hazelwood's command, the *Exxon Chester*, ran into a freak storm off the Carolinas. High winds knocked out the ship's radar and electronics gear, and with 30-foot waves and 50-knot winds overcoming the vessel, some of the crew prepared to abandon ship. Hazelwood calmed them, rigged a makeshift antenna, and guided the *Chester* out of the storm, only to be chastised by company officials for bringing the ship back to home port for repair instead of taking it on to its destination. In 1987 and 1988, under his command, the *Exxon Valdez* received a prestigious company award for "safety and performance."

At 9:12 P.M. on the twenty-third, the *Exxon Valdez* cleared the dock and set out under the escort of the tug *Stalworth*. Pilot Murphy had command and in his company on the bridge were Hazelwood and Kunkel. A.B. Harry Claar was posted as a lookout on the bow, and the helmsman was A.B. Paul Radtke. The helmsman's duties at this point consisted of following the pilot's directions for steering the ship. In other words, he turned the wheel to the proper setting, which was registered before him on a rudder indicator. The wheel itself was nothing like the romantic image of a ship's wheel, the long wooden spokes tipped with brass, but a foot-and-a-half disk that communicated its position to the ship's rudder by a hydraulic system. Between 15 and 30 seconds would pass before the ship noticeably responded to a course change. The bridge itself was not the least bit rustic, but more like a highly secured stateroom, well-appointed, spacious, carpeted, loaded with technical gear — control consoles, radar screens, radio equipment, a Loran (long range navigation device by which position is determined by radio signals), a depth finder, and rudder indicators, five in all, including one in the adjacent chart room.

At about 9:35, Hazelwood went back down to his quarters to take care of more paperwork. He would not return until an hour and a half later, just before Murphy was to disembark at the pilots' station at Rocky Point. In Hazelwood's absence, the contingent left at the bridge — Murphy, Kunkel, and Claar — fell outside guidelines requiring that there be two officers on the bridge in such waters. These and other guidelines, such as the requirement that watch commanders have an endorsement for Prince William Sound (which Cousins, who would soon take the command, did not have), were murkily established and seemingly not always followed. Murphy, an old friend of Hazelwood's, would testify that it wasn't "unusual for masters to leave the bridge periodically . . . [though] it wasn't typical, probably, to be gone that long."[18]

At 9:50, Cousins returned to the bridge from the deck to relieve Kunkel. Kunkel went to his quarters to sleep and would not awaken until a few minutes after midnight, when he heard a noise like a car running its side against a stone wall. Customarily he would have expected to come back on watch at 4:00 the next morning, but Hazelwood, knowing his chief mate's state of fatigue, had agreed to stand watch in his stead. It's important to note this, because in addition to the paperwork he was to complete, it raises the possibility that one reason for Hazelwood's spending so much time in his quarters following embarkation was that he, too, wanted to rest. Second Mate Lloyd LeCain, who was scheduled to come on watch at midnight, had also put in long hours, and Cousins himself, who had agreed to stand watch a little past midnight in order to allow LeCain more time in bed, had had no more than three and a half hours' rest in the 12 hours prior to resuming his work. This was the fashion in which the crew cobbled together its duty so as to accommodate the period of high demand while it took on its cargo.

At 10:20, the ship passed Entrance Island near the mouth of the Port of Valdez and began her turn into Valdez Narrows. There was fog at first. Here, traffic was restricted to one-way passage only, and as the fog lifted the land grew visible on either side of the ship as a darkness deeper than the sky. The sea was calm. The wind was light. The tide was rising, but the currents were weak. There had been reports of ice ahead in Valdez Arm. The ship moved

---

[18] Several years later, in 1994, I traveled between Long Beach and Valdez on the *Arco Spirit*, a tanker of a similar class as the *Valdez*. The captain of that ship, Jeffrey Portillo, emphatically stated what I learned to be the view of many captains: "He should never have left the bridge."

gently through the night, its huge diesel power plant felt on the bridge as a tremor like the rumble of a distant train. At 10:45, the marker light at Entrance Point came abeam. Eight minutes later the channel broadened and the ship passed the light at Potato Point on her starboard side.

As the ship came out of the narrows, visibility stretched to eight miles, well enough to take sightings on the lights mounted ahead at Point Freemantle, Rocky Point, and Busby Island. The ship entered Valdez Arm, where two lanes were established for inbound and outbound traffic. Hazelwood now returned to the bridge, and the ship's engine was reduced from half ahead to slow ahead to allow for the disembarkation of Pilot Murphy at Rocky Point — a place, some would argue afterwards, that had been selected as the staging area for pilots more for reasons of convenience than for navigational safety. Here, the tankers were still running at a relatively low speed, and in foul weather the waters would be less choppy than at Hinchinbrook Island, which had been the original staging area. Also, the distance itself back to Valdez was shorter — a cost-saving factor.[19]

Hazelwood directed Cousins and the lookout, Radtke, to assist in disembarking the pilot. At 11:24, Murphy was off, climbing down the side of the tanker to the pilot's boat that cruised alongside. Cousins was gone for a little over ten minutes. The state of Alaska would charge that the fact that there was only one officer on the bridge and no lookout again violated the Exxon Manual, which required a lookout and two officers on the bridge during Condition C — a measure of navigational hazard that indicated closely bounded waters or limited visibility. There would be dispute, however, over whether or not the ship was in fact in Condition C.

Hazelwood called the Coast Guard-administered Vessel Traffic Service (VTS) to report Murphy's departure, and then again several minutes later to request permission to change from the outbound to inbound lane. He was preparing for a maneuver to take the ship around the ice from Columbia Glacier. Gordon Taylor, who was then on duty at the VTS, testified that it was common for tankers to change lanes, and that as the ice flow increased it was not uncommon for them to deviate from the shipping channel entirely. He and his relief at the VTS Watch, Bruce Blandford, indicated that the focus of their radar was on the narrows, and that it often did not reach to Bligh Reef — a fact that many of the officers navigating tankers through

---

[19] Months later, speaking before the Commonwealth Club, Admiral James Watkins, Secretary of the Department of Energy, would say, "It's preposterous that we took the pilot off at the harbor entrance. It's easier to do there, but that's not enough." Currently, following changed regulations, the pilot gets on and off approaching and departing ships at Bligh Reef.

Prince William Sound had not been informed of. The radar system had been downgraded as a cost-saving measure during the early 1980s, even though the Coast Guard operations manual still stipulated that Valdez Arm, which extended to Bligh Reef, be "continually monitored."

When Blandford came on duty just before midnight, Taylor told him that the radar image of the *Exxon Valdez* was "getting hard to hold onto." Blandford made no effort to see or contact the ship, and described this practice as "routine." He went downstairs to make himself a sandwich. The VTS was administered by the Coast Guard. The condition of the radar system and the general sloppiness with which the VTS monitored the *Exxon Valdez* and apparently all tankers that passed into and out of Valdez, together with the little known fact that blood tests administered to Taylor and Blandford afterwards showed, respectively, traces of marijuana, and alcohol use (but in Blandford's case not incontrovertibly linked to consumption prior to or during his watch), would eventually result in the investigation of the grounding being taken over from the Coast Guard by the National Transportation Safety Board (NTSB). Possible Coast Guard culpability would become a factor in later settlement negotiations between the U.S. government, Alaska, and Exxon.

The ice in the shipping channel was heavy. The *Exxon Valdez* had been informed of this prior to departure, and now, though the weather had misted up, the ice was visible by sight and quite clearly on the radar screen, a little over two miles before them. It stretched in a cone shape clear across the lanes from Point Freemantle to within nine-tenths of a mile of Bligh Reef. This presented Hazelwood with two alternatives: either slow the ship down and go through the ice or go around where the ice was thinnest. By 11:24, the ship was back up close to 11 knots, the speed at which it maneuvered most effectively. A function of design and load, this is contrary to the common belief that the slower the ship goes, the better it handles.

Hazelwood informed Cousins that they would "divert around the ice" and then ordered a course change to 200 degrees and shortly afterward to 180 degrees south, which would take them to a point just off Busby Island. Hazelwood ordered helmsman Claar to put the ship on autopilot, or the "iron mike," without informing Cousins. Since the ship would not respond to steering maneuvers while on autopilot, this command was, for a time, widely regarded as a contributing factor to the grounding, and evidence of Hazelwood's disarranged state of mind, although it was probably a brief stop-gap measure on Hazelwood's part while arrangements were being made on the bridge. Moments later, when Robert Kagan came to relieve Claar at the helm, Claar said, "I'm steering one-eight-zero and I'm on the iron mike."

Cousins, who was standing next to Claar testified that he — Cousins — took the ship off autopilot. Disengaging the autopilot consisted of pushing a lighted button on the console. If the ship had not been disengaged from autopilot, this should have been evident by a light mounted on the steering stand that indicated when the autopilot was engaged. Nevertheless, that the autopilot was not disengaged and that this was not discerned when an attempt was made to turn the ship, or that the autopilot was mistakenly re-engaged, remain possible causes of what was about to happen.

Hazelwood told Cousins that he wanted to "bring it down to abeam of Busby, and then cut back to the lanes." Cousins went to the chart room and plotted the course. According to Cousins, Hazelwood had gone through the course change with him three times. In his testimony at Hazelwood's trial, which was slightly at variance with his previous testimony before the NTSB, Cousins said that he fully understood his orders, and that there was no doubt in his mind that the maneuver could be made. Cousins said, "He asked if I felt comfortable with what we were going to do and I said, yes. He said, do you feel good enough that I can go below and get some paperwork out of the way. And I said, I felt quite comfortable. Matter of fact I was asked that twice." It was a simple maneuver. The course change was already established. All that remained was a ten-degree rudder right at Busby Island, which would take the ship back into the channel.

Hazelwood directed that the engine be placed on "load program up." The command put the engine under the jurisdiction of a computer program which would increase the engine speed from 55 rpm to sea speed full ahead at 78.7 rpm, or to a little over 14 knots. This command, too, would become the subject of a furor — another signal of Hazelwood's disarrangement — and yet it was, according to the testimony of officers both from the *Exxon Valdez* and other vessels, a routine practice. At the time the command was given, the *Exxon Valdez* would remain within the parameters of peak maneuverability as long as it was in the area of Bligh Reef and, ponderous as the tanker was, it would not attain sea speed for 45 minutes.

At 11:52, A.B. Maureen Jones relieved Radtke on watch and A.B. Robert Kagan relieved Claar at the helm. At about the same time, Blandford was taking over for Taylor at the VTS in Valdez and going downstairs to make his sandwich. Jones was directed to stand watch from the starboard bridge wing as opposed to the bow as specified under Condition C — yet another of Hazelwood's commands that would be questioned. Jones's primary duty at this point, however, was to keep watch on the red buoy light at Bligh Reef. Being on the bow would have given her no advantage, while being on the wing kept her in close physical contact with the bridge. Hazelwood directed Cousins to call him by phone when the turn was begun, and then at 11:54, he once again went below to his quarters. Hazelwood was 15 seconds away, down a flight of stairs and a few steps along a hall — so near that Cousins would say he felt Hazelwood "still had control of the vessel."

Hazelwood's departure left Jones on watch and Cousins and Kagan on the bridge. Though employed as a third mate, Cousins was licensed as a second mate. He had made the passage through Prince William Sound between 26 and 30 times, 3 of them on the *Exxon Valdez.* Half of those times, he had been on the bridge. His qualifications were not questioned by anyone, and Chief Mate Kunkel characterized his abilities as "exceptional." A.B. Kagan, on the other hand, who was at the helm, was not as highly regarded. In a previous trip, he'd had some trouble keeping the ship on course. Left to his own resources, he was likely to oversteer, or to "chase the compass." Of Kagan, Kunkel would say, "I felt that Mr. Kagan needed extra supervision when assigned a task. . . . If I told him to go paint a bulkhead, normally you can send a sailor to paint. Mr. Kagan, I would have to make sure that he used the right paint, that he was applying it properly, using the right brush, et cetera. As far as his tendency to drift off, that is, in his steering ability, in my opinion he needed practice." During testimony at Hazelwood's trial, Kagan would blurt out, "I get so confused."

Another element in play on the bridge may have been that since Cousins was extending his duty over into Second Mate LeCain's watch, he was working with A.B.s not normally under his command. It was the first time Cousins had had Kagan under him at the helm. Nevertheless, and presuming that the autopilot had not been left on, the first command Kagan would be given that night — ten degrees right rudder — was the most elementary of commands. It consisted of revolving the wheel until the ten degree turn was registered right in front of him on the rudder indicator, or put a bit more directly, of knowing one's right hand from one's left and being able to read a number. All agreed that Kagan was quite capable of executing the maneuver.

At 11:55, Cousins took a sighting on Busby Light, which was abeam of the ship, then moved to the chart room, apparently to double-check his orders. The lookout, Jones, reported seeing the flashing red light for Bligh Reef on the starboard side. There's a phrase that anyone with any experience at sea has had driven into them: red right returning. It means always keep red buoys and red channel markers on your right when returning to port or harbor, and keep them on your left when departing. The *Valdez* was departing. Jones had sighted the buoy light on the right side of the ship. Cousins, who had seen the same thing on the radar, was not alarmed for the moment because of the exception to the rule: At a given point, and at sufficient distance from the marker, an outgoing ship by virtue of the angle of a maneuver may well find the marker on its right side. There's a follow-up rule: Make sure the ship is turned well before you reach the marker. This was the right rudder Cousins was about to order.

He returned to the bridge and gave the ten-degree right rudder command to Kagan, then called Hazelwood to tell him that it looked as though they might get into the leading edge of the ice. Hazelwood asked if it looked like a problem and Cousins said no. Reassured, Hazelwood responded that he would be back up in a few minutes. During the minute-and-a-half conversation, Cousins had his back to Kagan. When he returned to the port radar and looked at the rudder indicator, he saw that it read between six and seven degrees right rudder. He immediately ordered the ten-degree right rudder again, then — in a fateful move — stepped out to take a visual sighting on the Bligh Reef light. Once again, for a moment, he was not watching Kagan. According to a computer mockup presented by Peter Shigume at the trial, if the right turn had been decisively executed at this moment, the ship could still have cleared the reef. The *Exxon Valdez* was still not far off the course of the ship that had preceded it out the channel, the *Arco Juneau*, which in its deviation from the ice had successfully executed a far closer and more dangerous maneuver than the one Hazelwood intended. When Cousins returned, he ordered a 20-degree right rudder because, as he put it, "We hadn't turned." Somewhere in here, too, the ship's automatic recorder indicated that an inexplicable counter-rudder might have been made — perhaps another gesture of confusion, perhaps a desperate effort to slow the ship down (for which the counter-rudder, as it directs the ship against its existing trajectory, could be used), but it was now too late for anything. There was no way to either stop or turn the ship before it reached the reef.

Sensing the depth of his trouble, Cousins moved back into the chart room and "in haste" marked a chart, then returned to the bridge. It was an odd gesture — like a person falling and groping for the ripcord to the parachute he doesn't have. Maureen Jones appeared in the doorway in a state of alarm over the position of the Bligh light — red right returning. Cousins would testify, "This is the time when I'm becoming very concerned about the movement of the vessel toward the reef . . . I gave the hard right command." This was, according to Cousins's testimony before the NTSB, at 11:56 P.M., though the course records kept on board the *Exxon Valdez* indicate that the turn wasn't begun until 12:01 A.M. Robert LaResche, the Alaska oil spill commissioner, compared the five-minute gap to the eighteen-minute gap on President Nixon's Watergate tapes. At Hazelwood's trial, however, Cousins suggested that his NTSB testimony might have been mistaken.

At the trial, Cousins went on to say, "I called the captain, told him that I thought we were getting into trouble. He said, where's the rudder? And I said it's at hard right. I turned. It hadn't moved to hard right, it was still at twenty. At that point we suffered the first shock, and within a matter of seconds we were hard aground. . . . There was a, you know, a mutual hang up of the telephones." It was now, according to Cousins, 11 or 12 minutes past midnight.

Because of its mass, the tanker plowed into the reef with extraordinary softness. The rudder was finally angled for the hard right and the ship pivoted, swinging its stern to the left. Cousins, fearing that the engine room would be hulled, and fearing for the people in it, ordered a hard left to correct the swing. When Kagan hesitated, Cousins himself grabbed the wheel and turned it. He switched on the exterior floodlights. Over the edge of the ship, oil was visible, bubbling up from deep beneath the surface. By that time Hazelwood had returned to the bridge and ordered Cousins to take a fix on their location. Hazelwood had been gone for 15 minutes. The "mundane" thing, or things, may have been, first, Kagan's confusion; second, Cousin's failure to observe the rudder angle indicator after his commands; and third, and perhaps most fatefully, that Cousins was, as Captain Portillo of the *Arco Spirit* put it to me, "lost in the charts." What Portillo meant was that Cousin's behavior in the closing moments was like that of a person driving in a city, searching for a street, and while looking down at a map at the same time, going right by the desired street. The 30 seconds or so that it took Cousins to move to the chart room for the final time, to mark the chart and come back to the bridge, were likely the last 30 seconds available to avoid catastrophe. The fourth possibility, obscured by clouds of testimony, is that through miscommunication and unfamiliarity between Cousins and Kagan, or through simple error, the autopilot was left on, or turned back on and not observed to be so until too late. The early questioning of crew members by the FBI and later by the NTSB, much of which was directed toward the autopilot and general lighting conditions on the bridge and adjacent chart room, strongly suggest suspicion on the part of interrogators of an autopilot warning light mis-observation or misfunction. My own surmise is that the cause of the grounding was a combination of miscommunication regarding the autopilot and as the closing seconds ticked by in the confusion of the Third Mate's becoming lost in the charts. But finally, of course, the failure is the captain's — that early on he gave the rather unusual command for the autopilot to be put on at all in close waters, however temporarily, and then most tellingly, that he was not on the bridge. When he gave his account to the NTSB, Hazelwood would say, "I should have been up there."

Hazelwood ordered the engine shut down at 12:20 A.M., and sent Cousins and Jones down to wake people up, preferring that method to sounding the general alarm, which might have caused panic. He would be questioned for that, but later Kunkel would say that considered in retrospect it was the correct decision. Kunkel had been awakened by the sound of the grounding. He in turn awakened the pumpman and LeCain, announcing, "Vessel aground. We're fucked." Kunkel then went below. In the cargo control room, Kunkel saw to his alarm that a large quantity of the "product" had already escaped, that "there was movement in all the center and starboard tanks." The gauges were hard to read. He called the bridge, and Hazelwood directed him to take stability and stress tests. The radioman, Joel Roberson, saw oil shooting up 40 or 50 feet into the air from one of the tanks. Also, inside the cargo control room, LeCain saw oil spouting out of a tank. They managed to shut it off. Kunkel calculated that they'd already lost in the vicinity of 100,000 barrels of oil — in less than half an hour.

At 12:26, from the bridge, Hazelwood called the VTS in Valdez to report the grounding, and added, rather dryly, "Evidently, we're leaking some oil." When Blandford, who had taken the call, switched on the radar, the *Exxon Valdez* came right up on it, perched on the reef. The on-duty officer assigned to the VTS was not on the premises, but at home. Blandford called the Coast Guard commander, Steve McCall, who went immediately to the VTS. Alyeska's top Valdez executive, Chuck O'Donnell, was awakened at about 12:30 by a call from the terminal and informed that a tanker was possibly aground on Bligh Reef. O'Donnell ordered a subordinate to go to the terminal, then rolled over and went back to sleep.

At the ship, the fumes grew stronger as the oil continued to bubble out. Kunkel took a computer readout up to Hazelwood and reported that as best as he could determine, the stress level on the tanker was too high, but the ship seemed stable. Hazelwood replied, "Okay, we can't go out to sea." Kunkel then asked again if the captain wanted the general alarm sounded. Hazelwood declined, but ordered the lifeboats and rescue gear readied. Kunkel would testify that Hazelwood gave him "the impression that he had command of the situation and I felt comfortable that he would be taking charge."

Hazelwood sent Kunkel back down to the control room to get more information. The pumpman and engine crew were also sent down to assess damages.

At 12:40, Hazelwood ordered the engine up from stop to dead slow ahead, and then gave a succession of engine commands over a 40-minute period: "Half ahead, full ahead, full ahead, slow ahead, dead slow ahead, stop." At the same time, he gave rudder commands to Kagan, who was still at the helm. This action would produce one of the more puzzling episodes in the story. A few minutes after 1:00 A.M., Commander McCall radioed from the VTS and asked for an update of the situation. Hazelwood told him that the ship was in "pretty good shape . . . stability-wise" and that he was "trying to extract her off the shoal."

Hazelwood's account of the ship's stability was accurate enough, but if his report that he was attempting to get her off the shoal, or reef, were true, it would, first, very likely have been a dangerous maneuver. Some would argue that if the ship had been freed of the reef, it might have capsized.[20] Secondly, it appeared once documents were examined that no matter what he said, Hazelwood had not in the least attempted to free the ship, but on the contrary, tried to drive it deeper onto the reef. Even some members of his crew, including Cousins and Jones, indicated in early interviews with the FBI and NTSB that they thought the captain was trying to float the ship free of the reef, but later they would pull back from their impression. Hazelwood hadn't told them what he was doing.

In his testimony at the trial, Kunkel was especially clear in his argument that Hazelwood's efforts were directed at stabilizing the ship on the reef. One essential fact is that the engines were never ordered into reverse, which would have been necessary to extract the ship from the reef. Also, Hazelwood's commands to Kagan seemed intended to stabilize the ship and to successfully correct a list that it had developed. Finally, after Kunkel's second report — to the effect that the vessel was still intact but not fit to proceed — Hazelwood directed him below to monitor the ruptured tanks and to find a way to "ballast it [the ship] down" with seawater without opening any sea valves. He wanted Kunkel to find a way to make the ship heavier so that it would stay where it was. In Kunkel's view, Hazelwood's orders were prudent, and in fact "the only option we had." Kunkel said, "I felt safer. After the ship had listed to starboard . . . it stopped . . . and started to ease back to port, well, to zero list."

---

[20] Others, including the man who subsequently directed the salvage operation, said that the ship would have floated if it had been freed.

The question of what maneuver Hazelwood was attempting was critical both to his reputation for drunken wildness in the days following the grounding and in the course of his trial. Why he told McCall that he was attempting to get the ship off the reef is a mystery. He may have been confused, or still making up his mind, or expressing his disdain for Coast Guard authority. Perhaps he was unable yet to allow the outside world to come into what he knew, or maybe he still hoped for a retrieval that he knew otherwise, by his touch for the relation of a ship to sea and rock, was impossible. As it happened, the actions he did take to stabilize the ship and protect his crew — whether only hazily understood by him or perfectly understood — were the best actions that could possibly have been taken.

A little after 3:00 A.M., the ship was approached by a party consisting of Coast Guard Lieutenant Commander Thomas Falkenstein, Chief Warrant Officer Mark Delozier, who himself had had a couple of beers at the Pipeline Club before being unexpectedly called to duty, and the redoubtable DEC representative, Dan Lawn, armed with his videocamera. Oil was boiling along the entire starboard side of the vessel. According to Delozier, it was "spreading all around. The oil was coming out of the vessel at a very intense rate . . . bubbling up into the air, sometimes up to sixteen, eighteen, twenty inches high. Against the hull, it was a foot, a foot and a half deep."

They boarded the ship and found the captain on the bridge, standing near a window and looking out. He was drinking coffee, and had been smoking. He had his hand over his mouth. Delozier took these as signals that Hazelwood was trying to cover something up. When he came near Hazelwood, Delozier smelled alcohol on the captain's breath. When Delozier asked what had caused the accident, Hazelwood said, "You are looking at it."

At his criminal trial, which was held in Anchorage between February 5 and March 23, 1990, Hazelwood was charged on four counts under state law: criminal mischief in the second degree, driving a watercraft while intoxicated, reckless endangerment, and negligent discharge of oil. He was found innocent of the first three counts and guilty on the fourth, and given a $1,000 fine, an additional $50,000 reparations fine, and sentenced to 90 days in jail. The jail sentence was suspended in lieu of 1,000 hours' community service on projects designed to eliminate environmental damage caused by the spill. The guilty count has been twice successfully appealed on the grounds that by reporting the oil spill to the Coast Guard in a timely fashion, Hazelwood should have received immunity from this charge. The appeals have been twice reversed, and as of late 1998 Hazelwood stands convicted of the class B misdemeanor. His attorneys at the Manhattan firm of Chalos and Brown are seriously considering an appeal of the standing conviction in federal court on the same grounds, although in December, 1998, I was advised in conversation with Tom Russo of Chalos and Brown that a firm decision on the matter has yet to be made.

In a July 1990 administrative hearing before Coast Guard officials, charges of drunkenness and misconduct against Hazelwood were dismissed. Hazelwood pleaded no contest to charges of violating Coast Guard policy by drinking liquor less than four hours before taking command of a vessel and of improperly leaving the vessel's bridge while it was headed for Bligh Reef. The result was that his license as a ship's master was suspended for nine months, with consideration given for the time that he had already undergone without his license. His license has since been restored. A court date for an appeal of the monetary judgment against Hazelwood in the 1996 civil trial, in which his defense is linked to an Exxon defense, is expected to be set early in 1999. Joseph Hazelwood is presently employed by Chalos and Brown as a claims adjuster and consultant on maritime matters.

In August 1989, some five months after the spill, the U.S. Coast Guard undertook another study of tanker traffic in U.S. waters. To a large degree, the study was prompted by the *Exxon Valdez* grounding. The study was completed in October 1989, and though not intended for public scrutiny at that time, a copy of it was obtained by the *Seattle Times* through the Freedom of Information Act. The study was wide-ranging in its field of scrutiny and surprising for the frankness with which it presents Coast Guard deficiencies, particularly in regard to its undermanned, undertrained, underequipped, and sometimes demoralized corps of inspectors. This trend has occurred, the study notes, simultaneous with a decline in construction and maintenance standards for U.S. tankers, and with an increase in the number of 700-foot-plus vessels, which experience more wear and cracking than shorter ones. Discharges at sea through cracks are commonplace. The study observes that during recent years there has been increasing pressure upon shipping companies to compel their masters to drive ships hard in order to meet schedules, including operating vessels at maximum speed in rough seas. "The game rules now," the study says, "are for a professional investor to move freely within the marketplace spending as little as is necessary. Today's adage is to do more with less, make two tankers do the work done by three previously." This may be why the *Exxon Valdez*, and immediately before it the *Arco Juneau*, and before that scores of other tankers, diverted around the ice at full maneuvering speed rather than slowing to go through it. Doing so saved them at least a half-hour and as much as four hours in transit time.

The Coast Guard study is especially critical of reduced manning levels on tankers, the effect that it has upon crew fatigue, and the excessive reliance placed upon new technology both in and of itself and as a means for reducing crew sizes. "Coast Guard manning standards are primarily intended to ensure that the vessel is adequately manned for the safe navigation of the vessel," the study reads, and then, without naming the *Exxon Valdez*, nor Kunkel, LeCain, or Cousins, it goes on: "The standards do not adequately take into account other duties that the ship's officers and crew are required to perform when not on watch."[21] The study questions the over-reliance on technical systems, their maintenance, the expertise of crew members to deal with problems in technical systems when they occur, and the tendency of officers on watch to experience "information overload." Again without mentioning the *Exxon Valdez* or, in this case, Cousins by name, the study observes that the bridge design — which places the chart room off to one side, where Cousins went to look at his chart, and to scratch a pencil mark on it, at the very moment his last opportunity for making the course adjustment had passed him by — should be reexamined.[22]

Perhaps most tellingly, the study asserts that the Coast Guard itself "cooperates with the owners and operators of the tankers by allowing ships to be unprepared for inspections by using the old excuse that we are facilitating commerce. . . . Inspectors are, in many instances, acting as quality control agents for the owners." The study recommends that owners again assume responsibility for maintaining quality and regular inspection schedules, and for assuring safe conditions for crews, and that the Coast Guard put the bite on the failures of the companies by refusing to certify them. At present, such

---

[21] As late as 1998, in response to my question on this matter, Exxon media officers stated, "Sleep problems are not an issue in the *Valdez* accident. Operations aboard the *Exxon Valdez* were in full compliance with the Coast Guard rules. In fact, Coast Guard Commandant Admiral Yost testified that working conditions on the *Valdez* were comparable to 'normal operating practices on every Coast Guard ship, every Navy ship and merchant ship in the world,' and that he was 'not aware that fatigue was a factor in the ship going aground." This statement, in my view, is legalistic in nature and still does not contradict the "other duties," particularly those of the First Mate during loading and unloading.

[22] Again in 1998, Exxon stated that the chart rooms in its shipping subsidiary's vessels remain unchanged, and that the NTSB marine accident report on the *Valdez* incident "did not identify the position of the chart room as a contributing factor." Interestingly, though, since then improvements have been introduced to some ships, such as "electronic chart display(s) added to the wheelhouse to reduce the dependence on the use of the chart room."

refusals are virtually unheard of, or about as likely as shutdowns in the pipe-line system for its violations.

The Coast Guard study articulates a basic question about the relation-ship between government and private enterprise. If private enterprise will not regulate itself, if government will not reasonably regulate private enter-prise, or even itself, even when it comes to soiling our sustenance, and if money managers are allowed to drive the conduct of commerce, then our society becomes dangerously compromised to private power. Not wishing to face that, not wishing to face our role as the final arbiters in the matter of oil consumption through our purchase of it in excess, it is no wonder that we hung the weight of disaster upon a single human head and, filled with self-righteousness, refused to carry our share of it, standing back to watch as it grew heavier and heavier like the head of John the Baptist, severed from his body after Salome's dance to satisfy the manipulative spite of Herodias.

Hazelwood's voyage took on an imaginary dimension for a host of rea-sons. The external safeguards that surrounded it were outright fabrications or so faulty that they functioned as fabrications. The Alyeska contingency plan that had promised to handle what was termed the 200,000-barrel-spill scenario was based on a plan, formulated in 1986, which projected the likeli-hood of such a spill occurring as once every 241 years. The Coast Guard-administered Vessel Traffic Service in Valdez, charged with monitoring tanker traffic in Prince William Sound, had downgraded its radar system. A quietly executed change in Coast Guard pilotage requirements allowed officers with-out endorsements for navigating Prince William Sound to be at the bridge, and before the change the opposite regulation hadn't been enforced; even ships' officers were confused about what the regulations were and how much radar coverage the VTS had. The Exxon Shipping Company policy forbid-ding the use of alcohol by crews was not consistently enforced. Oil shippers had reduced manning levels on tankers. An underfunded Coast Guard failed to properly maintain tanker inspection schedules. The level of quality in tanker construction had fallen, and oil companies subordinated all aspects of oil transport to profitability. All these things and more do not absolve Hazelwood of responsibility, but they did make the continued exercise of safe operations imaginary. A catastrophic breakdown, as Riki Ott had predicted, was merely a question of time.

For Hazelwood, the journey became imaginary in the sense that once the *Exxon Valdez* struck Bligh Reef he would be propelled into a version of his life that was hardly his own; from master mariner to a drunk held on a million-dollar bond in New York, his deed compared to the bombing of

Hiroshima, to a fool who tried to refloat his dangerously crippled ship, the one upon whom blame must be fixed, to an inside-out Earth First! hero who finally ruptured the oil industry's seal of secrecy, and through it all a media wonder, the butt of jokes on talk shows, his face on T-shirts, his name in headlines, and a made-up story about him drummed into the living rooms of every other house in the country for days on end. The theatrical culture could fix its sense of outrage and guilt upon him.

Through it all, Hazelwood, for legal reasons, maintained silence on what occurred on the *Exxon Valdez*. At the end of his criminal trial, he thanked the jury for their care. The judge chastised him for failing to apologize. He had apologized when he first came to land from his wrecked ship. He would be asked again and again for his apology through ensuing years, but, taciturn and self-contained, he inclined not to add the weight of servility to the wild weight already placed upon him.

5

CITY LIFE

On April 8, two weeks after the spill, I flew to Prince William Sound. In Seattle, I asked for a window seat on the right side of the plane in hopes of having a view of the coastline, but the plane entered the clouds above the southern end of Vancouver Island and did not drop beneath them until, over the Gulf of Alaska, it began its descent for Anchorage. In a few minutes, Prince William Sound presented itself — an expanse of gray-green water rimmed by jagged, snow-covered peaks. We passed above Hinchinbrook Island, and then above the eastern portion of the sound. The mountains were the section of the Chugach Range that extends between Cordova and Valdez and beyond them north and easterly as far as the eye can see, white peak upon white peak vanishing into the white sky. In a moment, the pilot announced that we were passing over Naked Island, where the *Exxon Valdez* had been towed on April 5, and he tipped the 727 deeply to the right. It was down there, a tiny, toylike dark thing anchored in Outside Bay. It looked like a token to a gameboard. The two arms of the island made a backwards C to embrace it. A portion of the slick, a harmless appearing shine darker than the water, surrounded the tanker and extended before it in long fingers and down, out of sight beneath the fuselage of the jet.

A hush fell over the passengers and everyone craned to see. There was the sense of unanimity to the silence as of prayer, and as if the tiny thing down there were a terrible icon. The silence held sway for a moment after the pilot righted the plane and continued the descent, and then the conversations started up. The snatches I heard had to do with the tanker, with how much oil it had spilled, with the latest on Hazelwood, with the gasoline price spike in California. Everyone had a story. By then I'd come to understand that the better part of the passengers were headed for Prince William Sound. Among them were scientists, technicians, and fishermen heading home. The man seated next to me, Max Stone, said, "The objectives have to be clarified." It was a simple but singularly prescient remark, and he was speaking as much to himself as to me. He had a sheaf of papers on his lap and was staring at one that was filled with numbers and small diagrams.

Max was in his mid-sixties, a retired chemist who had worked in the oil industry for years, mainly for Arco and Richfield, and most recently for Global Environmental Systems out of Bakersfield, California. He was a work-hardened, slightly bemused-looking man, disarmingly soft-spoken and kind. He had worked spills and seeps off Santa Barbara and was proud of his work and, I gathered, pleased to be called up out of retirement.

Before the pilot had dipped the plane for the view of the tanker, Max had been telling me that he thought his job here was to help build and operate a plant to salvage water-saturated oil and clear the water. I asked if I'd understood him right — "build a plant?" Unfazed, he said yes, but that he wasn't sure if it would be stationed on land or on the water. He'd said that Exxon had called his company, then given him 24 hours to get here. I suspected he'd been offered a good deal of money. I would learn that Exxon was culling the ranks of recently retired oil specialists, just as it was combing the West Coast for boats, barges, and equipment to bring to Prince William Sound. Although Exxon had taken over responsibility for the cleanup from the woefully unprepared Alyeska Company, the furor over who was truly in charge was raging full tilt at the very moment we were in the air. According to the newspapers, the state of Alaska had pleaded with President Bush to federalize the cleanup. Bush had initially declined, but then just the day before, on April 7, he had reportedly relieved Exxon of control, put the Coast Guard in charge, and promised to send troops. Actually, the question of who was in charge, of what was the proper relationship among the four institutional entities that came to the fore — Exxon, the Coast Guard, the state of Alaska, and various agencies of the federal government — would never be resolved.

By this time much of the oil had formed what was euphemistically called mousse, a water-saturated mixture, and Max had told me that in his job the whole trick was to separate the oil from the water. Once that was accomplished, the water would be returned to the sound and the oil would be salvaged. In principle, it was simple enough, like Alyeska's water ballasting system, but of course the scale of oil out there, and the extent to which it had spread, presented formidable obstacles. The water-saturated oil might be heated, Max said, and run through a series of tanks and filters to separate it. He thought it possible that they could use a centrifuge, but he doubted it. He didn't know where he was headed. All he knew was that somebody would meet him in Anchorage. He said, "If we're not trying to get perfectly clear water out of the salvage operation, then we can recover a lot of oil. We might make a macro-change that way. But if they want clear water it'll be a very long haul. That's why you have to clarify the objectives."

Although I didn't fully appreciate it at the time, Max Stone had touched upon two critical matters. His uncertainty over what exactly he was supposed to do proved typical of the confusion of efforts that went on for weeks. The question he raised about what degree of water clarity was desired would persist indefinitely. Indeed, it would make impossible what Exxon would come ardently to desire — the sense of an ending to the cleanup. When was the water clean? When were the beaches clean? What was clean? Where was the uneasy margin between pure enough and not pure enough? For some — but not Max Stone, who was a practical man — the question of purity and of its sullying would assume visionary proportions.

Back on March 24, late at night on the fateful Good Friday, Captain Hazelwood had been relieved of his command of the *Exxon Valdez* by Exxon Group Commander William Deppe. Hazelwood returned to Valdez. On Sunday, he met with members of the NTSB, but on the advice of his attorneys declined to cooperate with the NTSB inquiry. On Tuesday, the twenty-eighth, the news media broke the story of Hazelwood's drinking record and the national uproar began. That same day, Hazelwood again refused to cooperate with the NTSB. He shaved his beard to evade recognition and left

Valdez without the knowledge of either Exxon Shipping or investigators for the state of Alaska (under the laws of which he would be charged on the four misdemeanor counts). For a week, he dropped from sight.

On March 30, NTSB announced the results of the blood tests, which appeared to show that Hazelwood had been too drunk to legally operate a ship. On the same day, in an action it might well have come to regret (since the charges of drunkenness did not stand up in court), Exxon Shipping responded by firing Hazelwood. Hazelwood resurfaced at his home on Long Island, and on April 5 he turned himself in to New York police. In court, an assistant district attorney referred to him as "the architect of an American tragedy." His bond was set at $1,000,000 and his bail at $500,000 by New York Supreme Court Judge Kenneth Roth, who himself came from a maritime background. Roth said that "these were misdemeanors of such magnitude that had never been equaled in this country." He compared Hazelwood's deed to the bombing of Hiroshima. The next day, April 6, bail was reduced to $25,000 by another New York Supreme Court justice.

The tanker remained perched on Bligh Reef until April 5, when it was floated and towed to Outside Bay on Naked Island for temporary repairs. From day one, there had been two priorities for officials to address: contain the spilled oil and pump out the oil that remained on the ship — what was then reported to be 42 million gallons. Both things had to be done quickly.[23] Pumping out (or "lightering") the *Exxon Valdez* clearly fell under the jurisdiction of Exxon Shipping, and by the time its president, Frank Iarossi, arrived in Valdez early Good Friday evening, arrangements were well under way. There were problems, such as locating fendering material to put between the *Valdez* and the first of three lightering tankers, the *Exxon Baton Rouge*, which had been diverted from taking on cargo at the Port of Valdez. Mainly, there was the problem of determining the sequence for pumping oil from the *Valdez's* tanks, both ruptured and unruptured, and of reballasting the ship in the process so as to avoid its collapse or capsize. It was an extremely delicate and dangerous operation that would preoccupy not only Captain Deppe and his crew of over 20 but Exxon officials on land, as well. After several setbacks, including pumps that didn't work, additional spillage from hoses, and weathering a storm that spun

---

[23] In fact, a substantial portion of what was claimed to be oil remaining on the *Valdez* was water, placed into an emulsion with the oil in the ruptured tanks through the surging action of the sea and its heavy tides. Exxon would report that 4.6 million gallons of water was recovered from the *Valdez*, but later inquiries would reveal the actual amount of water to be 19.2-million-gallons. Straightaway, this raises questions about the true amount of oil spilled. See text and footnote immediately following.

the rafted ships — two tankers and four attending tugs — 12 degrees, the operation continued through to April 4.[24]

The spilled oil was the other matter. By Good Friday evening early (and probably inaccurate) estimates had the quantity of oil on the water at 10.1 million gallons. As it happened, this was the first of three unusually calm days for the season. Nevertheless, the slick slid over itself and spread by force of gravity until by Friday evening it occupied an area of 18 square miles, and the four entities that might take responsibility for controlling the slick — Alyeska, Exxon, the state of Alaska, and the Coast Guard — had quite different visions of who was in charge and what should be done.

Alyeska, it was understood by the state, was to provide the first line of action on spills in Prince William Sound. For spills in excess of 200,000 barrels, its written Contingency Plan assured a response within two to five hours and that 50 percent of the oil would be ultimately retrieved. As it turned out, Alyeska didn't reach the scene for 15 hours and then with woe-

---

[24] In addition to the *Baton Rouge*, the *Exxon San Francisco* and the *Exxon Baytown* performed lightering operations. It's worth emphasizing that all three vessels were Exxon vessels, and for good reason: Exxon could bring them expeditiously to the scene, and also control their operations and records. Once loaded, and due, feasibly, to the limitations of ballast water treatment resources and storage capacities at other sites, each of the three vessels separately undertook quixotic voyages to Honolulu, Richmond, and Long Beach, California, and back to the Alyeska facility in Valdez Harbor. The *Baton Rouge*, for example, left Prince William Sound fully loaded on March 29, discharged most of her cargo at Honolulu, but retained 9.2-million-gallons of oil and water emulsion, which were later discharged to a storage tank at Alyeska. The emulsion was estimated by observers on board to be in the vicinity of a 60:40 ratio of water to oil. In this instance, the meaning was that approximately 5.5-million-gallons of what was reported as oil was, in fact, water, and that roughly another 5.5 million gallons of oil in addition to the 10.8 were somewhere out in Prince William Sound. Later yet, in the San Francisco Bay Area, the *Baton Rouge* lightered 6.6-million-gallons of emulsion in a 70:30 ratio from the *Baytown*, and returned it to *Valdez*.

The effort was intended to deliver as much recoverable oil as possible to "outside" facilities for refining, and the emulsion and water to Alyeska to be treated in the Ballast Water Treatment Plant. Finally, the water pumped ashore from the three vessels and passed off as oil totaled 19.2 million gallons. Therefore, while accounting for the approximately one million gallons of oil recovered during later stripping operations on board the *Valdez* in April and May of 1989, the total amount of oil spilled is brought, it would seem, to 29 million gallons, or given a margin of error of 20 percent, somewhere between 23 and 35 million gallons. This is roughly three times what Exxon reported. At the time the original edition of this book was being researched and written, I, along with thousands of other observers and workers in the region, assumed that the 10.8-million-gallon figure was more-or-less correct. At the same time, a greater quantity of oil spilled would immediately explain the intensity of its effects. Why Exxon, while the state of Alaska looked the other way, might allow false figures to persist makes for a compelling question about the moral dimensions of information as it is passed from corporations and government to the public.

fully insufficient gear. Equipment had been buried under piles of boom in warehouses. Some had to be dug out from under several feet of snow. A damaged equipment barge had been unloaded for repairs and left for two months. Loading it took ten hours. Other Alyeska employees in Valdez waited by their phones to be called to work. An oil container barge that Alyeska had been trying to get since 1988 still hadn't arrived. Eighteen hours into the response, no boom had been deployed around the tanker or slick, and only two small skimmers were operating. The skimmers, boats equipped with devices to draw the oil from the surface of the water, were full within a short period of time but had no barge in which to unload the oil they'd collected and, so, no further function.

For the next few days, Alyeska maintained a slightly enlarged but essentially token presence and at the same time declined to respond to calls from fishermen in Cordova and Tatitlek, who stood ready to throw dozens of boats into the recovery operation. Riki Ott, who twice flew through the haze above the spill on the morning of Friday the twenty-fourth, said, "I was stunned. There was no boom, no containment. Just a tanker on the rocks with two fishing boats coming up to it. Where was everybody?" Rick Steiner, an assistant professor with the University of Alaska's Marine Advisory Program, and stationed in Cordova as the marine equivalent of a county extension agent, flew over on Friday morning and saw the same thing, and also a group of Steller sea lions trapped in the slick. Chuck Monnett, a marine mammal scientist stationed in Cordova, flew over once with Riki Ott, and then again with fellow marine mammal scientist Lisa Rotterman. Monnett and Rotterman were alarmed by the increasing reach of the slick and by the menace it presented to marine life, sea otters in particular. The lumps they saw in the oil were animals. They flew some 20 miles southwest to Naked Island, a prime otter habitat, and found a tongue of oil there. When they dipped for a closer look, the plane's engine faltered. The fumes from the oil were making the engine run dangerously rich. Later, when Rotterman and Monnett informed National Oceanic and Atmospheric Administration (NOAA) representatives in Valdez that there was oil at Naked Island, they were told that it wasn't so.

According to its plan, Alyeska should have recovered 100,000 barrels of oil by the end of the third day (Sunday), but it recovered only 3,000 barrels. Its woefully optimistic projection of a 50 percent oil recovery rate was far beyond the standard of between 10 and 15 percent for previous big spills worldwide, and twice as much as the 25 percent experts posed as the absolute top performance under ideal conditions. As it happened, conditions for mechanical recovery were ideal for three days, but a few weeks later, Alyeska's public relations officer, Tom Brennan, would beg off Alyeska's failure by saying, "I myself flew over at 8:30 A.M. [on the first day], and yeah . . . I expected to see booms surrounding the ship, but that just wasn't what was called for. No one envisions anything like that. . . . It was obvious we weren't going to be able to contain it. . . . We knew that from the first."

Even without seeing the spill, Exxon Shipping's Frank Iarossi apparently suspected the same thing, and probably also understood that Alyeska's ability to undertake any mechanical measures was next to nil.[25] Before leaving Texas for Valdez, he'd begun making arrangements for spraying the slick with dispersant. There were several problems with this. Iarossi thought he had received permission to spray from the On Scene Coordinator (OSC), Coast Guard Commander McCall, but DEC Commissioner Dennis Kelso, by then the state's chief representative in Valdez, thought otherwise. There were not sufficient quantities of dispersant in Valdez, Anchorage, or anywhere in Alaska to do any good. Nor were there airplanes with which to spray it (before departing for Valdez, Iarossi had ordered shipments of dispersants and two C-130s and a DC-8). Finally, the use of dispersants was a highly complex and controversial issue and would persist as such through the summer and into the next year. It would become a critical point of dispute in litigation between Exxon and the state of Alaska.[26]

---

[25] In his testimony before the NTSB, Iarossi said, "I don't think there was a power on earth that could have removed that oil from the water prior to those winds blowing that came up Sunday night, Monday morning. . . . The only technology that could have worked or had a hope to work was chemical dispersant."

[26] In 1988, a U.S. federal court decision concerning damages stemming from the 1978 *Amoco Cadiz* spill had penalized the French government for restricting the use of dispersants to waters deeper than 50 meters. The presiding judge, Frank McGarr, observed that the imposition of the 50-meter limit "seems to have been solely the result of pressure from ecology and nature groups." Exxon apparently took this as a signal that if they could show that the use of dispersants was impeded by Alaskan or U.S. officials, the company would fare much better in the damage suits that were certain to come. Consequently, much of Exxon's early effort was directed at creating a paper trail to document impedance at actually using the dispersants to good effect.

In October 1989, Exxon filed suit against the state of Alaska for opposing dispersant applications in the early stages of the spill. The Exxon complaint stated: "The state knew or should have known that its vigorous and active opposition to the use of dispersants would cause the Coast Guard to delay granting permission for the use of dispersants."

Tapes of conversations between officials from Exxon and Alyeska during the first days of the spill, which were released in 1992, well after Iarossi's NTSB testimony, confirm both the likely ineffectiveness of mechanical remedies and Alyeska's woeful state of unpreparedness, as well as the darker side of industry manipulations of perception from the get-go. In the tapes, Exxon's Don Cornett tells Alyeska officials, "Get that stuff [the response equipment] out there. I don't care if it picks up two gallons a week. . . . It behooves us to have everything flapping in the breeze, whether it's catching oil or not."

Applied under the correct conditions (moderate turbulence, so as to mix with oil), dispersants were then considered the best existing quick fix for oil spills. The key components are "surface active agents" (surfactants), or high-powered versions of what are otherwise loosely known as detergents. Surfactants break up the natural cohesiveness of oil, causing it to fracture into tiny droplets that cease to float on the surface but instead sink down into the water column. The fracturing of the oil into droplets increases the total surface area of the oil and therefore hastens the process of degradation and bacterial breakdown. Dispersants make oil do what oil normally does, only much faster. They work best when applied very soon after a spill when the oil has weathered as little as possible, preferably, according to experts, within one to eighteen hours (judging from his testimony, Commander McCall understood the window to be twenty-four hours). After that time, the effectiveness of dispersants drops off sharply, and in any case they would work on only 5 to 30 percent of the oil. Their main attraction is that when applied under favorable conditions and in open water, they reduce the amount of oil that reaches the shores. A second attraction, and a very important one from a public relations standpoint, is that they make the oil seem to go away. It would have made a huge difference to Exxon's image if the oil hadn't hung around to be photographed.

The problem with dispersants is that unlike washing machines, natural systems don't come equipped with drainpipes, and so the use of dispersants involves trade-offs. Dispersants themselves have "low to moderate" levels of toxicity — much lower in 1989 than the notorious dispersants used in previous spills, such as the 1967 *Torrey Canyon* spill. Even so, by forcing the oil into the water column, dispersants would cause for a brief period — six hours or so — a severe toxic hit by virtue of the rapid release of hydrocarbons from the oil itself. The hit would be much greater upon the immediate marine environment than if the oil were left alone, floating on the surface. This is why it is far preferable to apply dispersants to open waters as opposed to near shorelines where life is much denser. The exception would be when there is something like a phytoplankton bloom or a heavy fish migration, which can make even deep waters extremely sensitive.

It presented a classic high-tech dilemma, like chemotherapy or insecticide applications: Do something destructive in hopes it'll make things better. And if one considers massive oil spills and chemical responses as late-twentieth-century extensions of the "horrid beauty" of our great machines that William Carlos Williams articulated in 1925, there were also elements in dispersant use of another dangerous notion — nearly as indiscriminate in its effects as the oil spill itself, and also hostile to life — the presumption that the natural world would behave in the way we wanted it to.

The choice was this: oil by itself or oil with dispersant. Even practically speaking, the choice presented complexities over which there was genuine scientific disagreement and doubt — partly because there had been very few field studies of dispersant use prior to the *Exxon Valdez* spill, and partly because of the presence of a host of highly discrete variables, the combination of which take the ability to predict results well off the end of the graph. The success of dispersants depends not only upon water conditions but upon water temperature, too, and salinity level, the thickness and specific chemical makeup of the slick (crude oils vary widely in their composition) and of the dispersant itself (there are many formulations and Exxon wanted to use its own), upon the carrier, or solvent, with which the dispersant was applied (the carrier for Exxon's dispersant, Corexit 9527, is kerosene), upon the ratio of dispersant applied to the oil, and upon the method of application. In short, even given the rather limited range of their optimum effectiveness, dispersants might work a little or they might not work at all.

Riki Ott would emphasize the fact that dispersants introduce to the water column quantities of the toxic lightends (hydrocarbons) of oil which would otherwise have evaporated, and that once lodged in the marine food chain the toxic molecules are persistent. All, including the panel of scientists under the chairmanship of one oil spill guru, James N. Butler, who co-authored the National Research Council's *Using Oil Spill Dispersants on the Sea*, agree that dispersants should be used in combination with an effective retrieval operation, at which Alyeska had so thoroughly failed. Everything considered, and knowing in retrospect what happened once the oil got away from Bligh Reef, it probably would have been a good idea to use dispersants, had they been available. But taking the same sort of logic to its extreme, it might also have been a good idea to evacuate the nearby villages of Ellamar and Tatitlek, even Valdez itself, and the *Exxon Valdez,* and firebomb the holy hell out of the slick. That would have abbreviated news coverage. Otter and bird bodies would have been hard to locate, and once the oil remaining on the ship took to the torch, the obstruction Bligh Reef presented to marine commerce might have been eliminated forever. Ultimately, fewer animals might have died.

The truth is that the decision on dispersants was never made. As it happened, Alaska, the federal government, and the oil industry had agreed earlier in the year, on March 1, on yet another state-of-the-art plan, the Alaska Regional Contingency Plan (ARCP). It mapped out Alaskan seaways into segments and, in the interest of facilitating speedy response, gave the OSC (in this case, McCall) permission to approve dispersant application in certain areas. Initially, the bulk of the spill was near Bligh Island, or in what the ARCP designated Zone 2 — an area that required consultation with the Regional Response Team (RRT) and approval from the EPA and the state of Alaska prior to dispersant use. Additionally, McCall may at first have been unaware of a provision in the plan stipulating that the preapproved area, or Zone 1, into which a portion of the slick would begin to enter — the deep water of the tanker channel — was Zone 1[27] only from October 1 to February 28. During the rest of the year, because of fish migration, spawning, the phytoplankton blooms, even this Zone 1 was considered too sensitive for automatic approval of dispersant application. The eggs left by spawning fish were especially sensitive to the toxic elements in crude oil and dispersants.

The ARCP also included provisions for stockpiling equipment and supplies, and a Decision Matrix, or flow chart, intended to help the OSC take prompt action. James Butler and his National Research Council group had questioned Alaska's Decision Matrix, observing that, "The user must assemble a significant amount of information prior to making a dispersant-use decision, including a comparison of the effects of dispersed oil and untreated oil on populations at risk. . . . However, this system gives no guidance as to how to make the comparison and appears to assume a fairly high level of expertise by the user."

They were right. In addition to the Zone 1 conundrum, and the necessity for him to seek out approvals and scientific advice, McCall immediately found himself subjected to intense pressure and infighting from and among Exxon, the state, the fishermen, the environmentalists, the press. The interim solution was to conduct a series of test applications. The first was run at 6 P.M. on the twenty-fourth (18 hours after the spill) and made use of the only available aircraft equipped to spray dispersant, a helicopter with a 300-gallon bucket called over from Anchorage, and drew from existing dispersant stores (a total of 364 drums spread out between Valdez, Homer, and Anchorage).[28] The first test, according to McCall, showed "no positive ef-

---

[27] For the remaining designation, Zone 3, dispersant application was not recommended since it was defined as the area in immediate proximity to sensitive resources (usually shorelines). Application required the same consultation and approval as Zone 2 and also that decisions be made on a specific case-by-case basis.

[28] Each drum contained 55 gallons of dispersant, for a total of about 20,000 gallons. Dispersant is applied at a rate of 1 to 20, so the dispersant on hand on March 24 was enough to treat 400,000 gallons of spilled crude. Had all other factors fallen in place, including the weather, the 5 to 30 percent effectiveness rate (McCall and Exxon claimed 35 percent) meant that between 20,000 and 120,000 gallons of the total oil spilled would have been dispersed.

fect," and the several tests run over the next few days were repeatedly characterized as "inconclusive." McCall had by then enlisted the advice of Gordon Lindblom, a field dispersant specialist and former Exxon employee, who, according to McCall, agreed with all his decisions throughout the test period. McCall and others connected with the response team (including the EPA's Carl Loutenberger) would observe that the state of Alaska did not in any way impede dispersant application, but that the weather and the lack of supplies and equipment had. A later dispersant test run on Tuesday, March 28, included the accidental spraying from a recently arrived C-130 of a Coast Guard contingent on the deck of the *Exxon Valdez*, which raised questions about the ability of aerial personnel to hit their targets.

The net result was a standoff between the state, Exxon, and the Coast Guard, deepening a paralysis that would become one of the central features of the spill response and that would enrage the public, especially the fishermen. Alyeska in the meantime was withdrawing farther and farther into the shadows, and with it, incidentally, went the other six oil companies, which naturally wished to minimize their association with the spill, even though as co-owners of Alyeska they had collective responsibility for the failed remedies. Exxon had taken over the response, and yet three days into the spill, well beyond the optimum application period, the original 364 drums of dispersant had increased to only 900 drums, and by that time rising winds had made aerial application hazardous. A full week after the spill, Exxon had on hand only about 2,000 drums of the 5,000 drums they needed. Later, Exxon Chairman L. G. Rawl would use the supposed obstruction to the use of dispersants Exxon didn't have as a means of browbeating the state, and perhaps of laying the groundwork for Exxon's coming legal position. In the May 8 issue of *Fortune* magazine, Rawl flew in the face of every known fact about dispersants and the events in Prince William Sound by stating that "we could have kept up to 50 percent of the oil from ending up on the beach."

After the oil had laid there for three days in a state of relative docility, nature stepped in. At dawn on Monday morning, a storm blew down from the Chugach Mountains. Planes were grounded. Boats were confined to the harbors. The winds blew the slick by the Naked Island complex of islands and into the southwestern portion of the sound, down to Knight Island, past Chenega Island and Green Island, and through the channels between Bainbridge, Evans, Elrington, and Latouche islands, up Resurrection Bay toward Seward, and on along the Kenai Peninsula. Twenty-five-foot waves slopped it up on the rocks. Everything was different now. The quick fix was gone, and the oil had to be dealt with on a new level of detail. To that end, the call-up of equipment and personnel that had begun on the first day in-tensified. Max Stone was one of hundreds.

Max Stone and I parted company when the plane landed in Anchorage. I did not see or hear of him again. I boarded a flight from Anchorage to Valdez. Forty-five minutes later, the Convair jet prop slipped between two ragged peaks, dropped precipitously, banked steeply, and landed in the Valdez airport. The plane was loaded to the gills with men and equipment, so loaded, in fact, that our departure from Anchorage had been delayed while several crates were taken off the plane to bring it within legal weight limits. In Valdez, the runway was lined with military helicopters, and flights passed in and out on top of one another. I would learn that what had once been a schedule of 8 to 12 flights a day had gone up as high as 600. The small terminal was jammed with confused people. They were looking for their luggage, or waiting for the next flight, or they milled about, searching for whoever was supposed to pick them up.

There were men and women in National Guard uniforms. One man, who was headed out to Naked Island to work on the *Exxon Valdez*, wandered around with a steel diving helmet hanging from his hand. Television crew-men carried cameras over their shoulders. On the floor were mountainous stacks of luggage and gear in duffel bags and hard, protective cases. There were scientists, consultants, and electricians, plumbers, carpenters, a heavy dose of the press from all over the world, bureaucrats, politicians, insurance adjusters, scam artists, and scavengers. There would be high-tech medicine shows, people coming in with their schemes and inventions — super steam-cleaners and anti-crude chemical elixirs. Word had it that the whorehouse was hiring.

A merchant seaman, whom I'd met in the Seattle airport, had arrived before me. He'd been called suddenly to duty. In Seattle he had told me in no uncertain terms that the grounding was the Coast Guard's fault, that Hazelwood had his drink after the grounding. He'd said, "Of course they drink on the tankers. After three days at sea, we're climbing the walls." The press, at this point, had the story otherwise. News of Hazelwood's drunken piloting was still spreading across the country. Now, the seaman was working the telephone, trying to find lodging. A line built up behind him.

Finding a place to stay was a problem. The churches had people sleeping on the floors, and the once dignified bed-and-breakfast industry had run out of control. Some, including myself, would pay over $100 a night to sleep in a living room in the company of two or three others, and the landlords, I would soon learn, wanted to be paid in hard cash. There would be two or three of us there each night. At that rate, the income came to a tidy unreported $7,000 a month. I learned that the place was 15 miles out of town, and tried to rent a car. Those prices had gone through the roof, too; moreover, all the agencies were out of cars. If I put my name on the waiting list, the people said, I might get a car in a few days. There were trucks hauling rental cars from Anchorage. It was not just the airport, but the road to Anchorage, too. The road was fundamental to what Valdez was becoming. Cars loaded with tents and people looking for work were coming down it, vans and buses filled with people who had work, and semis loaded with gear, refrigerator trucks filled with food, trucks hauling equipment, supplies, computer systems, reams of paper, boom, boats, hosing, engines, compressors, Caterpillar tractors, more modular buildings, cases of rubber suits, bales of absorbent pads, digging tools, snacks and coffee machines. By then, eight skimmers had been hauled from the North Slope to Valdez.

Eventually, I caught a ride out to my place, and then another back into town. The overtaxed services, the general practice of gouging, and the scams that were being run were the downside of the situation. One part of the upside was that many, including Valdez residents, would give anyone a lift. After trying and failing to talk to somebody at the temporary Exxon office and otherwise cruising the downtown, I went into a restaurant called the Totem Inn. The place was as crowded as the terminal had been. As I waited for a seat, I asked the manager, a large, florid-looking lady, what she thought of the crowd. In my innocence, I expected her to betray weariness at least. She said, "It's not bad," then smiled knowingly. "But it's not near as good yet as when the pipeline came in."

Service took an hour. The telephone in the entryway also had a waiting line that stretched outside the double doors. When I got a seat, I discovered that the customary sense of boundaries between tables had completely dissolved, that the general atmosphere was somewhere between a church camp and a dog pack. There was an endless din, and shouts across the room. Two disaster reporters who hadn't seen each other since the Union Carbide incident in Bhopal thumped each other's arms. The waitresses had trouble keeping track of who had ordered what and could be seen wandering from table to table with lost expressions. It didn't matter. You ordered and then ate what you got. People found themselves sitting with strangers. Eavesdropping was acceptable behavior, even expected, and any conversation was open for entry. All conversations were rivulets leading into the one conversation, anyway: the tanker, Hazelwood, President Bush, the crowd, the press, the closed herring season, the otters, the death, the money, the cleanup wages ($16.69 an hour, 12-hour shifts, seven-day weeks, and time-and-a-half for overtime), and the oil, which was off Hinchinbrook Island and down along the Kenai Fjord National Park, 175 miles from Bligh Reef and covering an area over 2,500 square miles.

"We're a boomtown again," said Gari Norman, a Valdez schoolteacher who was seated across from me. Gari was concerned about the destruction in the sound, and especially concerned about the lag between that and what was going on here in town. There was a distinct fatalism to his attitude. "But the boom's built on a disaster, and it'll make us into a company town." He was referring to the fact that Exxon was leasing warehouses, buying up buildings to house its specialists and managers, constructing camps for the workers, running the city planning office ragged, and generally spending money hand over fist. The bill was already well into the millions, and even the accountants brought in from Houston, I would learn, were getting white knuckles over the level of the flow. The evidence of the bottomless bankroll was everywhere in Valdez.

Exxon had taken out ads in newspapers and magazines across the country and apologized for the spill. L. G. Rawl had repeatedly assured the public and the U.S. Congress that "Exxon takes full responsibility and has done so from the start." The apologies, though, had a hollow sound, and many felt doubt over just what "responsibility" amounted to. Exxon was clearly capable of calling up millions of dollars' worth of equipment in reasonably short order, that is, of poising itself for action, but there was continuing confusion over just what the action would be, and according to what guidelines, with what devices, and for what purpose.

The fishermen of Cordova and Valdez, who had protected their hatchery sites and begun recovering oiled otters and birds essentially with their own resources, were finally invited by Dennis Kelso into the inner sanctum of the tripartite authority (now Exxon, the Coast Guard, and the state), where they were consulted on such matters as the patterns of currents in the sound, about which no one knew as much as they. They came back with more tales of confusion.

Coast Guard Admiral George Nelson had been in Valdez for several days, having come to assist the overwhelmed Commander McCall, but there remained at the heart of everything an ongoing dispute over who had final authority. At this point, the state of Alaska was still begging President Bush to federalize the cleanup and to establish clear control. Bush finally declined on the day I arrived in Valdez. Admiral Paul Yost, commandant of the U.S.

Coast Guard, explained that federalization might leave an opening for Exxon officials to "close their checkbook" and force the government into assuming costs. Yost was also worried about his own thin budget. In a clear echo of the blurring of the line between economic power and regulatory authority that had created the inadequate response capability in the first place, the question of who now was in charge and who was to pay continued to clog up the bureaucratic channels.

In Valdez, it was hard to get much in the way of explanation from Exxon. Having taken repeated beatings from the press, local citizens, and fishermen, Exxon now refused to send representatives to press conferences. With justification, no doubt, Frank Iarossi would later explain that the press conferences, which were initially held twice a day, were also taking too great a toll on the stretched resources of himself and other managers. Soon, Exxon would muster a complete onsite platoon of what the company referred to as the Communications Group, but for now daily written press releases were passed out. These painfully upbeat announcements reasserted the company's intent to take "full responsibility," told of what equipment was arriving, and gave overly optimistic assessments of where the oil was, what it might do next, and how much of it had been recovered.

Exxon and the city of Valdez had invested heavily in security guards. Besides the airport, there were guards at the Exxon offices, guards at the Civic Center, and increased security at Veco, the largest of several oil service companies that would be hired out as cleanup subcontractors by Exxon. There were guards in all the public buildings. It had been clear to me from early on that considering the degree of confusion and the heat with which rumor was generated and passed, it might be a good idea to talk to a few scientists. I began what would be a long and often frustrating quest for hard information by seeking out a marine biologist a mutual friend had referred me to — Kathy Frost of the Alaska Department of Fish and Game (DFG). Along with her husband, Lloyd Lowry, Kathy is a highly regarded specialist in marine mammals. When I went to the Fish and Game office, I found guards. They had constructed a barrier in a hallway made out of cardboard boxes. There was another line here, in this case a dozen or so men sprawled along a wall. They were looking to be taken on by Fish and Game. I gave my name to one of the guards, told him who I wanted to see, then moved down along the hallway to wait. In a moment, two electricians were called up to the barrier, and the other men in line cursed under their breath. There were a couple of carpenters there, and an X-ray technician who had quit his job in an Anchorage hospital and driven here in expectation of making $7,000 a month working in the DFG morgue.

There was a guy with a grizzled, wild look. His hair sprayed out from under his dirty stocking cap and his eyes glared fiercely when he talked. He said he was sleeping in his boat down in the harbor. He hit on everyone who passed by in the hallway on the chance that he might find a lever, any kind of lever. He made a special point of the location of his boat — slip 52. He was from Anchorage and he wanted a job right now, any job. He had an aluminum-hulled boat with a six-cylinder, 175 horsepower jet-prop engine. He claimed that it was the fastest boat in the harbor. He'd hauled it here down the road from Anchorage. His frank rapacity was arresting. He was one of the few people operating with complete clarity. He knew the money was floating free, and he wanted some.

He got me to thinking about the food chain as I waited for Kathy Frost, who it turned out had left for the sound early that morning. I thought about the position of scavengers on the food chain, of the adventurers. Out there on the water, the oil slick slid along, breaching the habitats in place after place, touching its leading edge to barnacles and anemones, to the delicate, pearlescent herring eggs spawned over ribbons of kelp, overcoming the birds and otters and leaving them as waste for the bears and eagles to eat. Here on the edge of land, a surfeit of human nature had gathered in a pack. The situation on either side of the shoreline was an expression of the likelihood that had been in place for years: one of the ecologically most productive and richest places in the world had spawned colossal greed and heedlessness whose predictable after-effects now drew citizens in droves, pulled up close to the dark table, eating deeply, lost in the last dark petroleum dream that had made the American twentieth century possible. It was unsettling to consider that the guy with the boat in slip 52 was merely continuing on to the end in his own very defined way.

Several things had become evident to me in the twenty-four-hour period I'd been in Valdez. One of them was that the beleaguered "experts" were going to be hard to reach, and that little would be revealed in the arranged Exxon press conferences, which by then had been taken over by the Communications Group, consisting of facile stone-wallers and side-steppers — unlike Frank Iarossi, who, I would later learn, had inclined to be uncomfortable and truthful in such venues. Another realization which grew in me was that since I was operating on the very thin *Village Voice* expense line, I was in no way prepared to compete with nationally and internationally based news teams in terms of resource. I was a novelist who happened to have a very strong sense of the difference between fact and fiction, and a passion when it came to environmental despoilment, and without even yet forming it clearly in my mind, since the outward confusion of Valdez moved readily to the interior, I had begun almost instinctively to draw upon the novelist's methods — the eye for wayward and telling detail, the distrust of any pronouncement, the interest in the edges of action and in the way trouble could be expressed through the character of a person (it was so that the fellow with the boat in slip 52 intrigued me as much as Kathy Frost herself might have). I had also begun to know that I was on the cusp of a gigantic personal struggle with the meaning of what was appearing before me, this, too, instinctive and *felt*.

It was so, I think, that instead of going to a scheduled press conference on my first full afternoon in Valdez, I made my way to the Animal Rescue Centers that had been established. Exxon had hired professionals to manage the centers, among them Randall Davis and Terrie Williams from Sea World Research Institute in San Diego and Jessica Porter of International Bird Rescue and Research Center (IBRRC). Porter and her associates, however, had the advantage of the established, field-tested organization founded by Alice Berkner. Every oil spill creates oiled birds, and by 1989 IBRRC had standardized techniques for cleaning and determining the birds' readiness for release. Porter was contacted at 6:30 A.M. the morning of the spill and was setting up shop in Valdez by Saturday morning. Randall Davis, who was put in charge of the Otter Rescue Center, did not arrive until after the oil had been blown through the sound, and had to create procedures on the spot for diagnosing and treating oiled otters. At the same time, he had to assemble his staff, build a facility, and otherwise handle the complications that developed around what he referred to as "the most political of marine mammals." The otter would become the intensely scrutinized, international symbol of the Alaskan spill.

The creation of the centers had been ordered by the U.S. Department of the Interior at the time when Exxon's attention was riveted upon lightering the *Exxon Valdez*, but in a parallel development to the federal government's approach to cleanup, the Interior agency normally charged with primary responsibility for protecting wildlife, the U.S. Fish and Wildlife Service (USFWS), had refused to take an active role in the process. Further, questions about the Service's role in actually obstructing both animal rescue and scientific research were about to break surface.

In the early days the centers had been staffed largely by volunteer towns-people, whose care for the animals offered a little different take on human nature from what Valdez otherwise offered. To these as time passed were added volunteers from the lower forty-eight. Many of the volunteers would say that their work was an exercise in penance. For Exxon, it became a form of damage control. Here, too, Exxon paid all the bills. Suzanne Stolper, public relations officer for the animal centers, said that the funding was sufficient, that Exxon was not interfering in the least with operations. Although such statements invited suspicion, this one was by and large true. Stolper herself was forthright, skilled, and remarkably patient even with TV crews that had come expressly to get a few shots of death for the homefolks.

The Otter Rescue Center was located in the old Growden-Harrison Elementary School, which had been closed down after the pipeline boom. A front-end loader worked the parking lot, clearing huge piles of snow left over from winter. In the open space carpenters were constructing holding cages. As of that day — April 9 — 103 otters had come in. Half of them had died. Here, the dead were hustled out the back door to avoid the press. Out in the sound, a quarter of the 10,000 or so otters were considered either dead or imperiled, and they were found floating in the water, or writhing in torment, desperately attempting to groom their fur. Thick ribbons of oil hung from their recta. As I passed the carpenters, a van pulled up and several otters were carried inside. They were inert, coated with oil. If still alive, they would be tested, warmed, and cleaned, and if they continued to survive they would be attended to with great solicitude.

Most of them arrived hypothermic because of the oil's effect on their insulating underfur, upon which they depend for warmth, unlike whales and seals, who have layers of blubber. Otters' fur has to be kept clean and arranged just so. For this reason, they groom continually. Many suffered from chemical pneumonia. R. V. Chelan, a veterinarian and toxicologist from California, explained to me that the pneumonia caused gasping, which in turn created air sacks in the lungs. After a brief exposure to the toxic fumes in the crude, many of the otters developed emphysema and it progressed rapidly to an advanced stage. If they ingested the crude, which they did as a matter of course while they groomed themselves, their livers would go. Compounds were also absorbed through the skin, producing the same effect on the lungs and liver. The benzene in the crude caused bone marrow depression, immune deficiency, and neurological breakdown. Those that died, Chelan said, would usually do so in agony.

Two blocks down at the Prince William Sound Community College, more carpenters were hard at work on the Bird Rescue Center. I spent the afternoon and next day there, learning the process. The birds came in hypothermic, too, because of the way oil breaks down their natural oils. They also suffered from various forms of toxic shock. They were warmed, tested, washed with Dawn detergent, then rinsed and put in pools to see if they floated. If they floated, they were sent to the drying room and fed a mash through a tube until they recovered to the point where they could eat fish. From there, in the case of both birds and otters, there was a question as to what to do with them — send them to the lower forty-eight, release them back into the oily sound, or what? This, too, would soon provoke a bitter controversy. By the time I'd arrived, eight birds had been released back into the sound.

"The Procter and Gamble reps have been here," my partner said as we washed an Arctic loon. I held the bird and she worked with a toothbrush and Water Pik. We had been advised that the loons and pelagic cormorants were dangerous, that the cormorants could slash the flesh with their beaks and that a loon could put a hole in your chest. I held the loon warily, keeping it low in a small plastic basin. It was a large bird. "They came to check out the Dawn," my partner said. She was cleaning, stroking each feather with the toothbrush, squirting on the Dawn, then working under the feathers with the Water Pik. My partner was suggesting the possible Procter and Gamble ploy: a high-toned ad, a bird, maybe, standing off to the side of the picture and a bottle of Dawn in the center. I never saw such an ad and in fact Dawn was remarkable stuff — a domestic surfactant. We rinsed the loon and cleaned it again, and then again, going through the process four times. It seemed strange, and in a way wonderful and calming to work on the wild things with such implements — Water Piks, toothbrushes, small plastic basins — and then check to see if they floated. The loon felt docile in my hands, as accepting as a baby. The melodic, mournful cry of another loon echoed through the hall from the drying room at the far end of the building. The loon I held didn't move a muscle.

A Valdez couple had rented me a car for $20. This was more of the upside of human nature, and an expression of the Alaskan cordiality to strangers. The couple hardly knew who I was, and did not ask for identification of any sort. They had merely heard from someone else that I was stranded. At sunset, as I drove toward my bed in the living room, I stopped alongside the highway to look at the Alyeska terminal across the bay. It was bathed in bright sunlight. To the right of the terminal, to the left, and behind it were the snowy mountain slopes, brilliant in the sun. The concrete holding tanks and control buildings began about three-quarters of the way down from the mountain peaks. I had already been over there, and the holding tanks were very large indeed. There was a sign every 50 feet that said, "Don't Litter. Keep Alaska Clean," and the ditch on the shore side of the access road was black with sludge.

From the highway, a distance of a couple miles, the tanks looked small, and it was then that I was struck by their Third Reich-like appearance, the extremity of function in their design. I counted the 18 of them. Beneath the tanks was the power plant, beneath that the vapor recovery facility, the metering building, and then the overtaxed ballast treatment facility, the maintenance building, the control center, and the impound basins. Long pipes stretched to the water where three tankers were loading up. The traffic was gradually coming back up to capacity. The ships looked small and precisely silhouetted in the sunlight. The whole business, set off against the tremendous slopes, looked like a slightly larger toy than the version of the *Exxon Valdez* I'd seen from the 727.

The next evening, I boarded the ferry from Valdez to Cordova, a fishing town with a fast-developing reputation for outrage and activism. In the Valdez harbor, a couple of fishing boats with oil-encrusted hulls were being steam-cleaned. Helicopters and seaplanes flew incessantly back and forth over the harbor. In the distance, two more tankers were docked at the Alyeska terminal, taking on crude.

The atmosphere on the ferry was as different as it could be from the atmosphere in Valdez. Here, too, the conversations revolved around the oil spill, but the voices were muted. It was partly the calming effect of being on the water, the sense of patience and deliberateness that comes with that, and partly a sense of grim expectation. Most of the people on board were Cordovans, heading home from often far-flung places. What they had heard was bad. What they expected to hear and see would be worse.

Among them was Tom Cumming, a fisherman who had been crabbing off Washington State and had driven 3,000 miles in 55 hours to get here. We were up on the third level of the ferry, standing outside the solarium. The water we'd been passing through and the shorelines were clear of oil. I had yet to see the oil, as a matter of fact, except on animals, boat hulls, and rubber boots worn by workers. This roundabout approach to the oil was a function both of my being yet *lost* in this place, and of the instinctive, barely understood method of coming very slowly into the heart of the killing. Tom was in his thirties, blond and bearded. He wore one tiny, bright earring. He spoke softly and had the name for every island, inlet, mountain peak, and point. We passed Potato Point, a hump of land on our right as we came out of the Valdez Narrows and entered the arm. A few minutes later we passed Rocky Point, the place where Pilot Murphy had disembarked. Tom pointed out Ellamar Mountain to our left. We then saw the first sign of the bergy bits that had drifted into the channel from Columbia Glacier. Their color was extraordinary, white, and pale blue, and sometimes an intense deep blue, the result of their density. Some of them were indeed as big as houses. It was at this point that Hazelwood had informed the Vessel Traffic Service that he was changing lanes.

"The Native village of Tatitlek is in there," Tom said. He nodded toward an opening in the shoreline, the Tatitlek Narrows. "They could be wiped out by this. The spill was in their backyard." I gazed at the inlet, into the intricate, winding darkness there of water and rock, and saw a sheen of oil, a long, thin shine. The water was that blue and green and milk color. The shine was dark gray.

In a few days, Gary Komkoff, the Tatitlek council president, would tell me that nearly everybody in Tatitlek had lived in a white town for a while. "But we chose to come back. We don't like the city life." On the day after the spill, Saturday, Exxon had conducted one burn test, but hadn't informed the Tatitlek people. The villagers found out about it when they saw the flash of flames leaping 300 feet into the air, and then smelled the fumes drifting their way.[29] I would see Tatitlek later, a neat row of houses with blue roofs, a Russian Orthodox church with a blue parapet, more scattered houses with red roofs, a landing strip, a community building, a dock with a few fishing boats and a float plane. One hundred five people lived there. Many fished commercially for income, but their main concern was over the damage to their subsistence resources.

"We fish, hunt, and trap," Gary would say, speaking evenly and with remarkable calm. "We eat deer, fish, clams, urchins, almost anything that tastes good. It's been our lifestyle for years. To have it suddenly jerked out from under us like this by an oil company causes a lot of hurt. This is the way we live, and now it's taken away." He would tell me that North Pacific Rim, an organization that serves Native villages in the Chugach region, would sue Exxon for damages, but then he would add sadly, "What the effects will be is

---

[29] In this test, a bit of the spill was drawn off within a fire-resistant boom and ignited. It was estimated that between 15,000 and 30,000 gallons of the total spilled oil were eliminated and that close to 99 percent of the isolated oil had burned off.

unknown." I would take him to mean not only the effects of the spill itself but of engaging in the lawsuit, as well.

From the ferry, Bligh Island came into view, and before it the illuminated buoy — red right returning. It was on our left. It was okay. We were going out. Now, three sea lions were resting on the base of the buoy. They lay close together, touching each other, and their heads came up to watch the ferry. Tom smiled and said, "They never let up." Then he fell silent and I could sense the anger rising in him. He repeated what Admiral Nelson had said, what many had come to say — that a child could steer a tanker through the channel, the Valdez Arm, which at this point was ten miles wide. Tom said, "Exxon's gonna get it." I'd heard that in order to avoid the ice and save time, the ferries used to take a similar shortcut that the *Exxon Valdez* had attempted. Not surprisingly, this ferry stayed within the channel.

"Most fishermen wouldn't be sorry to see the sea lions bite it," Tom admitted. They are profligate eaters of commercial fish. "But it's not so with the otters. I catch otters in my nets and throw them back overboard. They don't eat that many fish." Tom had a passion for the sea, a hunter's sense of the earth, and now a great, quietly held anger.

"I don't know what'll happen," Tom said. "The oil will drift around for a long time. It'll get the crustaceans and coat the eel grass and popweeds. The deer will eat the eel grass. The bears will eat the deer carrion. The pop weeds will get in the nets, and then we'll have a little oil coming off the net onto the fish. Is the fish contaminated, then? What is contamination?"

By the time we began the turn around Knowles Head, Bligh Island had fallen away from view. Five tankers were anchored off Knowles Head, though, awaiting their turn for the run to the terminal. These ships, too, looked oddly tiny at first. As we neared, they became huge. They flickered in and out of their bigness and smallness. A nasty silence fell over the people on the upper deck. Near the tankers was an oil slick. It had a dark shine, as if polished, almost the luster of a patent leather shoe. It came from one of them, not the *Exxon Valdez*. We had still not seen any significant portion of the main slick, and our route was now taking us farther away from it. At that time, the reports of what happened on the Valdez were still obscure and loaded with contradictions, and Tom shook his head and said, "I have a real hard time figuring it out. That tanker was miles off course. Way inside the buoy. From the buoy it's two miles to the reef."

At twilight, the sun sank in the west. There was a wide, white wake behind the ferry. On either side of the wake, the water was lead-colored, and further to the sides were the black crags. In the distance the tankers were alight like tiny cities. They could well have been independent cities with their own sinister codes of conduct that set them apart. Beyond were the jagged snow-covered peaks, turning a luminous pink, and above the gray clouds, the same color as the sea had now become. Tom said, "It looks just the same to me here, but all the tidal grounds out in the sound are finished." He fell silent, then gestured to the right and said, "I shot my first black bear on that hill."

Later, after the lights of Cordova had come into view, I saw Tom standing over in a front corner of the solarium. He was gazing at the lights of Cordova, watching as we came near. His body was slouched against the wall and his head touched the glass.

CHAPTER
6
CORDOVA

"It tore up its own face," Richard Newman, a photographer from California, said. He was talking about a sea otter. The day before, Richard had been out on a float plane, and had seen the general slaughter by air and from the shore. His first response when he stepped to shore was to throw up, a reaction that came in part from disgust, but in the main from the effect of fumes. It was a common enough reaction, but striking for its occurrence two weeks after the spill. The bulk of the most toxic aromatic hydrocarbons should have evaporated off the crude oil within the first 48 hours.

"Knight Island is thick with crude," Richard had told me. "Green Island is gone." That was just the beginning of the gruesome litany. The latest reports had the slick splitting out in the Gulf of Alaska, one finger curling around the corner of the Kenai Peninsula and headed into Cook Inlet and the other finger pointed at Kodiak. In the meantime, by the action of tide, wind, and twirling currents, the islands in the sound had been smeared and resmeared with oil. Knight Island, which lay directly in the path of the oil, was among the hardest-hit places. Knight Island was considered by many to be the heart of the sound, the wildest, richest, most exquisite, complex, and magical of places.

"The fishermen say the area normally swarms with birds," Richard said, "but now they're simply not there. Maybe they're dead and washed under. Maybe they flew away. There are places that are completely covered with crude." Huge pools of crude sloshed up onto the beaches, he said, and made oil-filled lagoons that seeped into the crevices. He had taken his Hasselblad camera with him, but couldn't focus it. "There was nothing to focus on, no rocks, no bushes, nothing, just crude oil."

We were in Cordova, a town as different as it can be from Valdez. It had a population of about 2,600 that swelled annually to about 5,000 during the peak of fishing season, when cannery workers and Prince William Sound fishing permit holders who live elsewhere during the winter arrived. Valdez had a steadier population of about 3,500, and a city budget at least six times the size of Cordova's, thanks in no small part to the property tax levied against the Alyeska terminal. In Valdez, occupations were apportioned among education, small business, fishing, tourism, the Coast Guard, and Alyeska. A good percentage of the people put in their hours and went home to their climate-controlled houses. Valdez was a microcosm of the sharp occupational tensions one finds in most American cities. Tourism and fishing had long been at odds with oil shipping. With the oil spill, the differences became conflicts.

In Cordova, everything was directly or indirectly addressed to fishing. Before the oil spill, divisions in the community tended to take the form of close-in body punching followed by clinches, as if among relatives. Although Cordova itself, protected by the sound's prevailing westward currents and Knowles Head to the northeast and Hawkins Island just across the bay, had not been struck by the slick (nor had the nearby, prolific fishing grounds off the Copper River Delta, the home territory of the famous Copper River red salmon), the town depended upon all of the sound for its sustenance. In response to the spill, the townspeople formed a solid wall of protest. On the Tuesday after, the first of several town meetings found the high-school gym packed with upwards of 2,000 hissing, hooting, contentious people, furious over the lack of action. The Exxon and Alyeska representatives arrived late and wanted to leave early. They couldn't.

Through loss, Cordovans' feeling for the beauty of their place and for the way their lives were entwined with the sound had taken on new force. Fishermen have a not always deserved reputation for being roughnecks, or cowboys of the sea, who dump their trash and pump out sewage into the water, who catch all manner of things besides fish, and who sometimes cut loose their damaged nets and let them float to the bottom, where they became ghost nets. Made of plastic, they trap fish forever. Now, it was not uncommon to hear the crustiest among them say, "We should have been paying attention," or "The environmentalists were right." They also resented the way Exxon, especially at the beginning, had treated them as incidental. The question, finally, would be to what extent Cordova and its fishermen could form new alliances or renew old ones with other fishing interests, environmentalists, tourism interests, and independent oil shippers, such as Chuck Hamel, and what steps they could take to counter the inherent imbalance in power between themselves and the oil companies.

At the moment, Richard Newman and I, each of us outsiders, were becoming aware of what Cordova already knew. We sat in the loft of the Killer Whale Cafe, a delicatessen-style restaurant that operated in the same building as the Orca Book and Sound. Valdez had no bookstore, and this one in Cordova, though small, had a stock that ran from bestsellers to esoteric literature, philosophy, and natural history. It bespoke the community. The store was also a center of oil spill response in the town, one of many private establishments where the margin between the conduct of business and community action grew so thin as to be invisible. The owner of the deli, Jeff Bailey, and the owners of the bookstore, Kelly Weaverling and Susan Ogle, husband and wife, were involved in the response. Ogle had been the first director of Cordova's Oil Spill Disaster Response Office (COSDRO). Since the fifth day of the spill Weaverling had coordinated an effort to rescue oiled wildlife — first birds, then birds and otters. While Richard Newman and I were talking, volunteers were busy pounding together plywood bins to make what Kelly hoped would be the Cordova Otter Rescue Center just across the street, a place to treat the animals Valdez could no longer handle. Paths had been beaten by the steady stream of people between the bookstore, the prospective animal center, and the offices of CDFU and the Prince William Sound Aquaculture Corporation (PWSAC — pronounced pizzwac) a couple doors down, the city hall down around the corner where COSDRO was located, and below that the harbor where because of the storm and the closures by then of herring, shrimp, sablefish, and crab seasons, the better part of Cordova's fishing fleet was docked against its will. The salmon season remained in doubt.

Richard had purchased the store's last navigation chart of Prince William Sound and we had it spread out between us. Richard touched the places he'd been to. I let the map emblaze itself on my mind, especially Knight Island, which had the shape of a very ornate palladin. To one side of us were windows that overlooked the harbor. Beneath us on the other side, a window faced First Street. People passed by. A clump of them had stopped and were engaged in intense conversation. One burly man in an orange coat thumped his palm with his fist as he spoke. A pickup jerked up against the curb and the driver jumped out and lurched up the sidewalk. Outside, it rained steadily, but the atmosphere on the street was electric. The rain was the tailing of the second major storm that would move the slick during the otherwise unusual period of calm for late March and early April.

Richard said that he'd seen a blacktailed deer trapped in the crude, and a sea otter that had scratched its eyes out. He made a motion with his hands, scraping down from his eyes across his cheeks, and it was then that he said, "It tore up its own face. It scratched out its eyes because of the hydrocarbons. It died with its paws folded on its chest, where they stopped from the scratching. Another otter had chewed off a paw. There was a starfish, still alive, but half-eaten through by crude."

Richard had felt sick since he'd got back, as if he had the flu or a cold. As time went by, similar symptoms among beach crews and workers in the animal rescue centers would become the subject of dispute. Some would argue that it was the effect of the fumes. Others would say that it was merely an influenza passed among people working long hours in sometimes close quarters. I was never able to learn the truth about that, but my suspicion was that the answer was not simple. Nothing about the oil, from its chemical makeup to the manner of its mobility, and nothing about the response of stressed organisms to it, whether that of humans, animals, or vegetation, was simple. As we spoke, the slick was out there roving around in all its complication. Driven by wind and current, it was an infinitely malleable, elastic blob that could vary in thickness from a couple of feet to a hundredth of an inch. It picked up sediment and grew heavy. It coated the birds and sea otters. It was death, possibly, to the microscopic lower reaches of the food chain, and to fish. It might cancel the fishing for the year. Richard's chair creaked as he leaned back. He got a hollow look in his eyes, and said, "The place was devoid of life. Ever since I've felt a weird detachment from life."

I would see him several more times in the next few days. He couldn't shake his sore throat. Each time I saw him, he looked gaunter and more hollow-eyed.

The corner of First Street and Council Avenue, a few steps away from Orca Book and Sound, offered a view of the town. Above, up on lower slopes of Mount Eyak, was a residential section that the earthquake had left intact. There was a dense quiltwork of walls, and of roofs set at crazy angles to each other. The houses were sometimes large and sometimes tiny, sometimes filigreed and sometimes plain. Among them were vestiges of narrow boardwalks from way back to the early part of the century. The boardwalks passed between the boundaries of adjoining lots to reach landlocked homes. In the yards and driveways were bicycles, old cars, turned-over skiffs, and heaps of fishing net. The residential tangle expressed the history of the place, recent and old. The colors were blue, white, rust, and the deep silver of weathered clapboard made luminous by the steel gray sky. Spruce trees fringed the upper edges of the neighborhood. Between their trunks you could see the dark gray rock of the mountain.

Down toward the water was Railroad Way and a line of new buildings erected since the 1964 earthquake, which had damaged the waterfront: metal equipment outlets and drydocks, a new post office, and city hall. Much of the traffic, the cars that careened between First Street and Railroad Way, came from the harbor. Directly beneath the corner where I stood was the Reluctant Fisherman, a popular motel and restaurant that overlooked the harbor.

First Street runs parallel to the shoreline, and strung out along it to the northwest are the canneries, the ferry terminal, and at the old New England Cannery, the offices of the Chugach Native Corporation. In the opposite direction is a road that leads out of town, past Eyak Lake to the airport, and then northerly and inland over a series of concrete bridges that span the Copper River Delta. There, the country grows harsh. The silt-laden river is white with froth, and the land around it, the sandy banks and muskeg, the bush and gaunt, windblown trees, have the look of a tremendous and repeated scouring.

The road is the Copper River Highway, built on an old railbed. It represents another boom. Copper, discovered in 1900, brought an influx of Guggenheim money, and a railroad was completed in 1911 between the Kennecott Mine and the Port of Cordova. In those days, Cordova had been what Valdez was now, a major terminus for raw materials. The mine closed in 1938 due to the collapse of copper prices, and the town began the long process of reconstituting itself as a fishing port. Much of the rail was pulled out as salvage during World War II.

Practically speaking, the highway stops about 60 miles out of town at the Million Dollar Bridge, a four-span steel and concrete railroad structure completed in 1910. The earthquake had dumped the end of one of the spans into the river, but the bridge had been pieced back together, the fractures in the standing spans strapped with steel plate, the collapsed span judged to be stable enough even in its wild tilt, and reconnected to the adjacent span by a big steel stairway, lashed with U-bolts, turnbuckles, and inch-and-a-half cable. Over the stairway were laid two-inch planks which made a bridge upon the bridge and rather tenuously permitted single-file vehicle traffic to the shore across the river. Beyond that point, the road gradually dwindles to nothing.

The question of upgrading and extending the road to the point where it would connect with the Richardson Highway, and thus to Valdez, Anchorage, and points beyond, had been controversial in Cordova for years. The absence of a road made the town an island of sorts, accessible only by sea and air, and eliminated the incursion of certain classes of traffic — the casual traffic of tourists and the insistent traffic of truckers. Road advocates bemoaned the fact that Cordova could not be a cleanup staging base, which reduced the amount of Exxon money that came into town. Others were grateful that Cordova could not become another Valdez. Too much Exxon money was coming in as it was, they said. As much as anything else, the absence of the road contributed to the town's integrity. It defined motion, reduced interruption, increased continuity, and encouraged reflection. It made relationships different, because it was not easy to just go away. One could drive only so far, then one had to turn around and come back.

When I moved away from the corner and headed back along First Street, past Orca Book and Sound and toward the CDFU and PSWAC offices, Tom Cumming appeared. He moved quickly across the street, stopping for a moment to talk to a group of men out in front of the grocery store, then ducked into the alley that led to the Club Restaurant. I'd had breakfast there. The place had been filled with fishermen who would have been happier to be out fishing for herring. Instead they'd been stopped in their tracks, which in itself was frustrating enough, never mind that they also didn't know whether they would fish at all that year, for anything, or how, in many cases, they would survive the loss of livelihood. Fishing was a precarious business, anyway, dependent upon the whims of nature and the stringent regulations applied by the Alaska Department of Fish and Game (ADFG), whose job was to control the pressure of fishing upon a run. Fish now, Fish and Game would say, and then order a stop five days later, or two days, or 12 hours. Exxon had announced that all losses suffered by closures would be compensated, but given the circumstances that seemed a chancier thing than fishing itself, and in all respects far less desirable. The fishermen were unsure how or when or to what degree that compensation would appear. In the restaurant, the word Exxon rose repeatedly and cut through the rest of the low, swirling talk like a curse. One man said, "Exxon's already made eighty million off the spill by raising the prices at the pumps. It's a damn tax."[30]

[30] The figure is probably mythical. In April, L.C. Kumins of the Environment and Natural Resources Policy Division of the Congressional Research Service observed that between the beginning of March and the first week of April 1989, there had been a little over a ten-cent average increase in per gallon gasoline prices at the pump. In certain West Coast locations, the jump went as high as twenty cents. This was due partly to gradual price increases prior to the oil spill caused by then newly installed EPA regulations governing the volatility specifications of gasoline, and by a slowly developing shortage of crude supplies relative to demand for refined products following the raising of prices by OPEC at the end of 1988. As of March 1989, pump prices had not yet caught up to the rising price of crude. To all of this was added the brief shutdown at the Alyeska terminal, and then the 11-day slowdown, which resulted in approximately a 16-million-barrel delivery shortfall, two-thirds of which was to be refined on the West Coast. Since the Alyeska terminal operates all the time at capacity, the shortfall could not be made up. The shortfall and accompanying doubt over when full-capacity operations would be restored precipitated allocation assignments by refiners and then a rash of speculative spot-buying by wholesalers. The 16-million-barrel shortfall from Alyeska constituted about one-sixtieth of the daily 975-million-barrel crude oil working inventory needed at the time to keep the nation's fuel supply system in operation. The effect of the Alaskan shortfall upon the market was analogous to what an ecologist would call a perturbation.

The lesson to be learned from this applies not so much to a specific instance of profit-taking (profit-taking as a general practice is another question) as it does to the heavy lever which the Alyeska consortium *could* apply to the fuel supply system. At the time of the spill, public scrutiny upon the oil industry was quite sharp. In fact, many West Coast Exxon dealers held their prices below par in order to placate their customers. In another scenario, the consortium might reduce the flow in the pipeline for profit-taking or for political reasons. Over a year later, in July of 1990, in a walkdown with the EPA and DEC, the consortium threatened to shut down the pipeline and did reduce the flow for one day as a protest against being held liable for violating state and federal air pollution laws. A federal judge intervened with the result that the matter once again was thrown onto the negotiating table. The cost of a shutdown or protracted slowdown would be felt by the federal government and Alaska state government in the form of lost tax revenues, and then by the public in the form of increased prices at the pump. By the summer of 1990, Alyeska was well back on the offensive again, and the American public's insatiable demand for cheap gas, especially when it lacks an oil spill to serve as a reminder of the tradeoffs that are at stake, is finally the consortium's most valuable bargaining chip. To this attenuated set of circumstances would soon be added the 1990 late-summer Iraqi invasion of Kuwait, and then the ensuing Persian Gulf War of 1991.

I reached the doorway leading to the PWSAC and CDFU offices and stood there for a moment, reading the notices that had been taped to the windows. The burly man in the dirty orange coat and Greek fisherman's cap that I'd seen through the window of the bookstore stood next to me. His name was George Velikanje. I asked what he thought of what was going on. He turned it straight back, asking what I thought. It was not in the least necessary for us to name what we were talking about. I said I guessed the people were pretty angry.

"Angry!" George said, turning to me. His broad, bearded face had hardened and his eyes turned steely. He lurched toward me and stopped about four inches away, close enough for me to take on a little spit. "Angry!" he said. "Do you know what rage is?"

He pulled back and lightened up a bit. "Some of the people here are shy, but if you went into the living rooms at night, you'd see that this thing's tearing them up. Pretty soon the rage will spill over.

"There are a lot of Vietnam vets among the fishermen, and they damn sure don't want to get wasted all over again," he said. "They've been through that." He said the vets had brought weapons home with them and that some of them were talking about loading up the Cordova fleet with guns and explosives and blockading the Port of Valdez. He paused, waiting to see the effect of his words, and smiled. "The right wing and the left wing have met in this town, the oldtimers, the vets, the ex-hippies. Look," he said. "This is a small town. We know who you are. Let the lower forty-eight know, because when that happens it's time to watch out."

His notion was fairly compelling — the new union, a project for revolution — but just exactly how seriously George meant it was a bit hard to read. I'd seen him working the street with admirable energy, buttonholing one person after another. He was an operative, a catalyst. Loquacious, articulate, and theatrical, he'd been called to that, as others in Cordova had been called to do other things. Later on, David Grimes, who at this time was in Valdez serving on the ad hoc citizens' advisory committee, would explain to me that one of the striking things about the oil spill was the way it called people beyond themselves, and made them rise to find their own necessary roles.

As I would learn, that process had begun two weeks before on the morning of the spill. When Riki Ott and acting CDFU president Jack Lamb reached the CDFU office at 7:30, Marilyn Leland, CDFU executive director, was on the phone, making and receiving call after call. Shortly thereafter,

Riki made her flyover with the marine biologist, Chuck Monnett. They saw the slick, the *Exxon Valdez*, the *Exxon Baton Rouge* pumping ballast into the sea,[31] and no cleanup activity. They then flew on to Valdez in search of information. There, Monnett was cornered in a restroom by a reporter who'd heard he was a biologist. Monnett sent the reporter to talk to Riki Ott, and Ott, who would tell me that she'd "left professional science because of the numbers of scientists who wouldn't come out from behind closed doors to speak to the public," found herself cast into the role of the conscience of science. During the first Exxon press conference, she stood up from the audience and offered a lone, dissenting voice to the optimistic account Exxon's chief environmental scientist, Al Maki, was giving of the way oil dispersants would make the oil "disappear." The effect of Ott's objections to industry science's version of this and other issues had an immediate and decisive effect upon the attention of the press, and thus upon what would grow into a national public outrage. Later, Frank Iarossi would say that one of the reasons he stopped giving press conferences was because Ott took up half the time.

Chuck Monnett was then in the sixth year of an otter population study project run under a contract with the U.S. Fish and Wildlife Service. Knowing that he and his colleague Lisa Rotterman were more informed than anyone else on the otters in the sound, fearing for their study, and for the animals themselves, who represented the most diverse genetic stock of sea otters anywhere in the world,[32] Monnett had wanted to get out ahead of the oil spill's path and do a full count, to firm up a baseline on the population against which damage to it could be measured, and to track individual otters. Since no one knew at that time where the oil would flow or how much more would be released from the ship, it was also not known how imperiled the entire otter population was. Monnett and Rotterman were seeking a way to protect a portion of the population. On Good Friday, Monnett secured "unlimited funding" from the Minerals Management Service (MMS). Three days later, the Fish and Wildlife Service threatened to cancel Monnett and Rotterman's long-term project and quarantine all their equipment. Then they were al-

---

[31] This observation is otherwise, to my knowledge, undocumented. Presumably, it was the *Baton Rouge's* own ballast that was being discharged, which would not affect the quantities of oil and water drawn from the *Exxon Valdez* as discussed in preceding pages. Discharge of ballast, in any case, in the open waters of the sound is illegal.

[32] As the oil spill wore on, the damage to the genetic stock of several sometimes highly localized species or subspecies was, from a scientific point of view, among the most serious possible consequences. Also, and as with the otters, the lack of pre-spill baseline counts often made it difficult or impossible to accurately assess the effect of the spill upon many species of birds and animals.

lowed to continue with their surveys. Two weeks after the spill, Monnett and Rotterman were shut down once more, and then again later yet they were put back into operation. For the duration of the summer, they were run through a gauntlet of bureaucratic machinations in which they found themselves at odds with their own agency, at odds with the Otter Rescue Centers, which they helped establish, and their work and careers jeopardized. Monnett would tell me, "Early on, we felt like Fish and Wildlife was trying to control damage, that it was ANWR. Two weeks later the ANWR bill was dead and the agencies turned around and started taking samples of otters, but it was too late."[33]

On the morning of the spill, Rick Steiner, the Marine Advisory agent in Cordova, had been awakened in his home at 7:00 by an alarming telephone call, telling him of the oil spill. He went to his office at the harbor where he worked the phone seeking information. He also tried to get two Fish and Wildlife agents stationed in Cordova to go out and assess the spill, but they wouldn't move. Steiner then walked up the hill to the CDFU office, where he found Jack Lamb, David Grimes, Jeff Guard, and Marilyn Leland, who was still on the phone, taking calls and otherwise trying to get word on what was going to be done. She called Exxon, Alyeska, the Coast Guard, the DEC, EPA, and Fish and Wildlife. At 9:00 A.M., she informed Exxon that she had 30 volunteer boats ready to assist with containing the spill. At noon, she informed Alyeska that she had 75 boats, including 15 from Tatitlek. What she eventually heard from Alyeska and Exxon on Saturday was that they were "reluctant to use the boats because of the liability connected to using amateurs."

As Steiner, Grimes, Guard, and Lamb talked in the CDFU office, they were joined by other fishermen. The place was loaded with confused, worried people. Lamb pulled out the Alyeska contingency plan. It said that any spill within 50 miles of the terminal could be contained within 12 hours. The

---

[33] The bill was wounded, at least. Legislation that would have approved limited oil drilling in the Arctic National Wildlife Refuge had passed through the Senate's Natural Resources Committee and was expected to receive congressional approval during the 1989 summer session. Although President Bush continued to advocate the bill, the consequence that oil companies feared most, that the oil spill would change the thinking of senators previously supporting the legislation, had happened. By early April the bill was moved to the back burner — for a time. It is, of course, resurrected at regular intervals, either as a direct possibility or as a bargaining chip played by the petroleum industry to gain other advantages. In 1997, Alaska's Democratic governor, Tony Knowles, advocated opening ANWR for exploration to Congress and to a Democratic president, Bill Clinton. ANWR again remained protected, but offshore sites to the west of Prudhoe Bay were opened for bids.

group knew a few things from the reports they were receiving: first, that the spill was much less than 50 miles from the terminal; second, that so far, eight or nine hours after the spill, nothing at all had happened; and third, that no one had any idea what was going to happen except that the spill would spread. They talked of the threat to the imminent million-dollar herring fishery, and the likely effect of a storm upon the slick. Steiner decided to take a flight out to see for himself what was going on, and he saw the same thing that Riki Ott and Chuck Monnett had seen: the spill, the *Exxon Valdez* listing on the reef, the *Baton Rouge* discharging ballast, and no boom, no barges, no skimmers, and nothing coming, and lumps in the oil that were sea otters, and sea lions swimming in it.

Steiner returned to Cordova and spent most of the night talking to fishermen about what they could do. Many of the fishermen had already geared up their boats to fight the spill. A tall man, blond, bearded, lean, pleasant, and smart, Steiner has a way of listening closely that inspires trust, and — as his role would develop over the next year and a half — a way of maintaining effectiveness and hopefulness even in the densest tangles of power politics and litigation. He held the fishermen's respect not only for his knowledge of the sound as a biologist but also for the fact that he was a fisherman, too. His knowledge had been trued by reality.

The next day, Steiner flew over the spill again and found that it had expanded toward Naked Island. He went on to Valdez in hopes of getting information there to pass back to Cordova. Like Riki Ott, he found chaos, the national press installed, federal scientists who had come more to monitor than to take action, the DEC completely lacking in the equipment to do anything, Exxon keeping people out of its makeshift headquarters in the Westmark Hotel, and Alyeska not answering its telephones. Steiner called his friend, David Grimes, and told him to get over to Valdez. Grimes, himself a fisherman, an accomplished musician and poet, a natural historian, and a man possessed of an uncanny ability to bring diverse people together, would become the oil spill's metaphysician.

The Cordova contingent in Valdez came to consist of Steiner, Ott, Grimes, Lamb, and Guard. Their forces were augmented by, among others, Doris Lopez, a Valdez fisherman, Ray Cesarini, a Valdez cannery operator who provided temporary living quarters, Jim and Nancy Lethcoe, Valdez tour boat operators, historians, and activists, and Theo Matthews of Soldatna, the president of United Fishermen of Alaska. By the third day of the spill, Sunday, the twenty-sixth, the population of Valdez had almost doubled, and at a press conference that afternoon, the group heard Frank Iarossi announce that the oil spill had progressed beyond the point where it could be contained mechanically, and that plans were being formulated to use dispersants and laser-ignited burns. To the group, the news was chilling.

They stayed up all Sunday night, even as the first gale blew the oil slick around, and put together what Grimes referred to as the "educational press conference" in which several of them presented various subjects — fisheries, ecology, oil pollution, dispersants, local history. The press conference was held the next day. It built on the ground Riki Ott had first taken in the Exxon press conferences and resulted in wide national coverage and yet more pressure placed upon Exxon. The interests of those concerned with wildlife and fisheries had been permanently lodged as a factor in the battle. Afterwards, DEC second-in-command, Larry Dietrich, who had been ordered by Governor Cowper to "do something," arranged with his boss, Dennis Kelso, for members of the group — Steiner, Grimes, Ott, and Lamb — to join the brass at a meeting of the oil spill triumvirate that night. Jack Lamb was the only one among the group with a family. He was by nature more conservative than the others, more patient, more given to working within regulations, and a bit uncomfortable at being cast in the role of a rabble-rouser. He was the best at talking to the brass. Unassuming, clean-cut and square-jawed, Lamb looked like a high-school football coach. David Grimes would tell me later that Lamb "was brilliant, a pillar. Though he took some heat for it later back in Cordova, he became the de facto spokesman for fishermen."

At the meeting, the group found that the brass knew very little about the currents and tidal patterns of the sound. The result, thanks largely to Kelso's insistence and Iarossi's willingness to listen, was that they were heeded and, then, to their amazement, given the power to order equipment and formulate plans. Considering that the oil spill was completely out of control, they decided to focus their attention on protecting selected natural spawning streams and the hatchery system. David Grimes said, "When it looks like everything's lost, you're freed from limitations. You can go for it."

Back in Cordova, many of the fishermen were vacillating between blockading the tanker channel and continuing to marshal volunteer forces to fight the spill, first more or less independently of the group in Valdez, and then in tandem with it. Some, such as Tom Copeland, preferred independent action. He outfitted his boat with a pump and five-gallon buckets, then went out looking for oil. Near Knight Island, the first day they pulled out 1,500 gallons, and on their best day they drew 2,500 gallons, while Exxon's best skimmer collected just 1,200 gallons a day, which raised questions about what might have happened if the authorities had turned the "amateurs" loose to begin with.

What came to be known as the mosquito fleet, a small armada of seiners, bowpickers, long-liners, skiffs, and the ferry *Bartlett*, commandeered by the DEC from the Alaska State Ferry System, eventually made their way to the Koernig Hatchery at Sawmill Bay on Evans Island. Despite Iarossi's initial receptivity, battles with the Exxon system continued. There were unending complications, shortfalls of equipment, and lapses in communication. Steiner would say, "The disaster was unfolding minute by minute. None of us had gone through anything like this before, so we were winging it. . . . The fishermen needed stronger boom, more skimmers, and better logistical support. . . . Exxon's people were trying, but the company was still our biggest hassle. . . . We'd say we needed something and they'd say, 'Yes, we've ordered it. Yes, it's on the way.' Then it took days. At first we believed them. Then we realized they were just trying to get us off their backs. There were so many people in the chain of command that if one link goofed, nothing got done." Finally, the hatcheries were saved from the main onslaught of oil, but questions of lingering damage to the salmon fry and to the hatchery grounds awaited returns from the 1989 release, which would not begin until 1991.[34]

George Velikanje moved off and I went inside the doorway that led to the CDFU and PWSAC offices. I met Heather McCarty, the PWSAC news officer. In previous years, Heather had been the editor of the *Cordova Times*. She fished commercially with her husband, Max. An Englishwoman, both she and her husband had graduated from Whitman College, an elite liberal arts school in Washington. She'd majored in English. Max had majored in theatre, and they'd come to Cordova on a shoestring in the early seventies. They, too, were typical of a new breed of fishermen. Max, a rebellious man with a sharp wit, had described the first planeload of lawyers that flew into Cordova as the landing at Normandy. Heather gave an impression of intensity and solidity, and because of her position and the changed reality in Cordova, she had emerged as something more than the PWSAC news officer.

"Our seiners get the prime catch," she told me. "Our boats get the first, highest-quality catch of the run. Each boat takes in about a hundred fifty

---

[34] As to the herring fry, the extent of the damage would not be known for the four years it takes them to become reproductively mature and recruited as adults. Indeed, four years later, the herring populations in Prince William Sound (but nowhere else in Alaska) crashed. Virtually no young herring filled the ranks of the adults.

thousand fish a day." I stared at her for a moment. It was strange to imagine that many fish — a pile of them, silvery, mountainous. Heather pressed on, explaining that 20 percent of PWSAC's annual budget comes from a 2 percent tax the state of Alaska collects off the top of each fisherman's gross. Eighty percent comes from the contract seiners that are stationed at PWSAC's hatcheries at the beginning of the run. Once PWSAC makes its budget, she said, the run is opened to commercial fishermen, for whom $20 million is generated annually from the aquaculture's Armin F. Koernig (AFK) and Esther Island hatcheries.

Roughly speaking, the hatchery system works this way: Salmon returned from the ocean to spawn are captured. Females are electrically stunned and slit open, their eggs removed and placed in buckets. Male salmon are held over the buckets and squeezed, so that their semen squirts onto the eggs. The eggs are then placed inside warehouse-like buildings in trays, hundreds of them arranged in stacks. The stacks are lined up in rows through which water is pumped and percolated like a mechanical, perpetual-motion river going up, down and back around. The trays are designed with plastic gravel to simulate gravel beds. When the same water is recirculated as it must be during winter when the source freezes, or during times of drought, it is filtered and sometimes treated to remove the ammoniacs of waste.[35] The trays are checked daily and the dead culled from them. Up to this point, the process has been a form of interdiction and enhancement intended to increase dramatically the numbers of young salmon, or "fry," that will be released into open waters. The fry are kept in net pens in the bays at the hatchery sites until they are ready for release. By this time, their olfactory sense, or "chemical memory," has been "imprinted" with their place of origin, and those that survive will return after an ocean journey of between 2,000 and 10,000 miles and a lifespan of two, three, four, five, or seven years. The length and duration of the journey varies according to species. The enhancement process with eggs and fry simply improves the odds on substantial returns.

The remarkable and not fully understood ability of the fish to return to their home ground to spawn and to die, the regularity of their timing, and their food value have made salmon a staple resource of fishing cultures (and a staple of myth) for centuries. The relative predictability of their runs makes them especially vulnerable to being overfished, as they had been, but also capable of being managed toward recovery. There are definite hazards in the management process, too, including the pitfalls associated with mechanical incubation, the overstocking of a habitat with one species, and the huge num-

[35] At times the water has been otherwise treated, with malachite, for example, as a fungicide.

bers of identically imprinted salmon returning to one site as opposed to diversely imprinted wild salmon returning to various estuaries and streambeds.

What PWSAC and other hatchery systems in Alaska were originally about was to augment the overfished natural populations and to provide a buffer against periodic fluctuations in the numbers of wild salmon runs, that is, to stabilize a commercial resource, and to do this with pink salmon in particular which is the species with the quickest turnover. Most of the pink salmon catch is canned. As of 1989, PWSAC operated three hatcheries, one of which, Esther Island (later renamed the Wally Noerenberg Hatchery), was devoted to producing a variety of species in addition to pinks, including chum, chinook, and coho salmon, all of which are at sea for longer periods than the pinks, less abundant to begin with, more sensitive, and as sport and table fish more valuable per pound. Because of their locations off the main path of the oil slick, however, neither the Esther Island Hatchery nor the third, Cannery Creek, was under immediate threat.

Young pink salmon spend three to five months in the estuaries, inner bays, and channels, then begin a 2,000-mile migration in the Pacific. In the spring and summer of their second year of life, they move back toward their home streams. PWSAC's Koernig Hatchery, located on Evans Island, was thus under a threefold threat: first, to the pink salmon fry that were soon to be released; second, to the year's returning salmon; and third, the possibility of lingering toxic effects on future releases and returns. Potentially, the damage could be exponential. The result of the second of the threats — that to the annual run, and so to the 80 percent of PWSAC's budget Heather was speaking of, and to the year's income for fishermen — would not be known for two to three months, when the return runs began. As noted above, the results of the third threat — lingering effects — would not be fully known for years.

The first threat was immediate. As Heather and I spoke, 8 million pink salmon fry were in the net pens at the AFK hatchery and 600,000 more were emerging each day, their movement toward maturation as ineluctable as the oil that hovered in the bay. Heather explained to me what PWSAC, the canneries, the fishermen, and the town stood to lose. The hatchery system, though granted seed money by the state and the canneries, had been established and literally built by the volunteer labor of the fishermen themselves. The first and fairly modest returns from the system came in 1974, but it was hoped that during 1989 and the succeeding few years the success and viability of the system would be firmly established.

To the effort expended in developing the salmon run and the possible financial fishing losses in 1989 and succeeding years were added the $300,000 that a permit to fish with a seine net then cost, or the $50,000 to $70,000 that a gillnet[36] permit cost. The permits — regarded as real property, not unlike leases on Bureau of Land Management pastureland for cattle ranchers in the West — are bought, sold, and passed down through inheritance. "It's not unusual for a seine fisherman to be carrying three-quarters of a million in permit and equipment investments," Heather said. "On top of that come the annual fees and operating costs — fuel, labor, nets." The permit fishermen here had bought the farm, so to speak, and it became easy to understand their rage.

Heather thought there would be no fishing at all in the sound in 1989.[37] PWSAC's prime concern was to protect the fry in the net pens. They had received a million dollars from Exxon toward funding the effort to protect the hatcheries — in the form of a signed personal business card that Frank Iarossi had handed to PWSAC president Bruce Suzumoto.

There were two areas of concern in Cordova. One was money: the spilled oil's threat to the fisheries and hatcheries, and then the threat of Exxon money to community solidarity. The other area was that of place, home, the environment. Normally, the two concerns overlapped to varying degrees, but by this time they had collapsed quite completely into one another, just as the left and right wings that George Velikanje had talked about were merging.

Kelly Weaverling, who runs the bookstore with his wife, Susan Ogle, discovered his part as a preservationist carried to an extreme he himself would

---

[36] Prince William Sound seine nets are 150 fathoms (900 feet) long and set in a circle around a school of fish, then drawn shut, capturing the fish within. The vessels that deploy them are called purse seiners. Gillnets are also 150 fathoms long, but are set in a line and allowed to drift with the current. The vessels, gillnetters, are smaller than purse seiners and take smaller catches. Gillnetters primarily target the red and silver salmon runs of the Copper River and fish in the sound between river runs.

[37] As it turned out, the salmon fisheries were partially opened. Certain areas remained closed because of the oil. The total catch in Prince William Sound was slightly above the ten-year average of 20 million fish but well below the preseason projection of over 48 million. The lower than projected return was due in part to closures, but mainly to much poorer returns than were expected. The 1990 returns, which would still not prove or disprove oil effects in 1989, did reach record levels. The 1991 returns also came in record numbers, which Exxon promoted in national advertisements as evidence of the success of its cleanup, but the credit might as well be given to the inventiveness and resolve of the volunteer "mosquito fleet" of fishing vessels that protected the Koernig Hatchery. The wild salmon runs in the western portion of the sound and which went essentially unprotected in the early stages of the spill, were severely affected.

never have expected. A tall man with aquiline features, long black hair, and a beard, incisive, opinionated, and given to wearing sandals, baggy pants, and dark sleeveless sweaters — yet another one in whom the combination of articulateness and offbeat appearance would give the brass pause — Weaverling had been a submarine navigator during the Vietnam War. With Ogle, he had toured the sound by kayak every summer for years. Quite possibly, no one knew parts of the sound better than they.

Over in Valdez, the bird rescue people, Jessica Porter, Alice Berkner, and Jay Holcomb, had encountered a surprise as they set up their center. No arrangements had been made to retrieve the birds, which were usually out there in remote, hazardous locations. They had expected that the Fish and Wildlife Service would at least administer the retrieval operation. Traditionally, responding to wildlife damage fell under federal purview, although since the eighties Fish and Wildlife had been backing away from oil spill cases because in its view the limited number of animals rescued did not justify the expense. And in this case, since the spill had not been federalized, Fish and Wildlife felt that the agency had no obligation to involve itself with bird rescue. It was a bind of the sort that was becoming familiar: the Department of Interior had ordered Exxon to rescue animals, while an agency of Interior, the Fish and Wildlife Service refused to cooperate. The bird center was desperate to find someone who would take charge of a rescue fleet. Jay Holcomb of IBRRC had heard about Weaverling and contacted him. This was on Wednesday, the sixth day of the spill. Weaverling agreed to manage the operation, which would be funded by Exxon, and immediately set out with Holcomb to Knight Island to learn the techniques.

The next day Weaverling went to work, beginning with five boats. They brought oiled and injured birds back to Valdez. However, since they were encountering otters at the same time — lying in the water next to the birds — they began collecting them, too. It was an understandable response, driven by compassion, the urge to redress pain. Soon, there were 21 boats bringing in animals, and then 45 boats, mainly from the Cordova fleet. The Bird Rescue Center had trouble keeping abreast, and in the Otter Center animals were stacked up in cages in the hallways. The retrieval operation had become too efficient.

Randall Davis, who was in charge of the Otter Center, concluded that even the newly completed Valdez Otter Rescue Center, which I'd just seen there, would be filled to capacity in a day at the rate the otters were appearing. Davis encouraged Weaverling to open an otter center in Cordova, and Weaverling received approval to do so from an Exxon spokesman, Don

Cornett. This was the center in which the carpenters were pounding pens together across the street from the bookstore. They had assured Weaverlng that the center would be ready in five days.

At the time, there were several particular causes of outrage in Cordova. The fate of Weaverling's rescue project and the otter center would soon be added to them. Another had to do with 70,000 feet of boom that had been ordered from Florida to protect the Koernig Hatchery. Exxon, it was thought by Cordova people, had intercepted the order for other purposes, and it would take two weeks for a replacement to arrive.[38] Exxon had representatives in town offering short-term financial relief for those immediately affected by the disaster, but only two persons had as yet signed on. The Cordovans remained wary, offended, and deeply divided over the capitalization of what had begun as a volunteer effort. Exxon now was offering $3,500 and more a day for leases on boats from Cordova's fleet, but the contract came equipped with a gag clause. Fishermen were not to express their opinions to the press. Most of the fishermen absolutely refused to have anything to do with such a contract.

A community information meeting was held each day. Sometimes the meetings doubled as a press conference, but their purpose was to disseminate information about the spill and spill response to citizens and local organizations. Some of the meetings were conducted relatively quietly. Others were volatile, especially when Exxon representatives were present. Monte Taylor, the chief Exxon liaison to the communities of the sound, came to one on April 10. Retired now, Taylor had once been Exxon's Alaska manager. He was white-haired, a bit heavy around the jowls, and he looked tired. During the meeting, Ken Adams, CDFU second vice president, said that he had flown the sound the day before and had seen no active oil skimming. Taylor didn't seem to understand the point. He said, "There is a skimmer in Valdez, not Cordova." In fact, there were about ten skimmers stationed at various points out in the sound, awaiting instructions. Adams asked Taylor for a list of what materials, what boats were in the sound, where they were located, and what their instructions were. Taylor said, "We're organizing a list."

He was asked by a town council member about the superskimmer, *Vaydaghubsky*, that Exxon had contracted with Russia to bring into Prince William Sound. He said, "It left yesterday and should arrive within ten days." He was not certain where it was headed. He asked the group for suggestions.

---

[38] When I later asked Fred Davis of the Exxon Communications Group in Valdez about the mislaid boom, he referred me to Les Rogers in Houston. Rogers said that he could answer the question if I produced a copy of the purchase order.

When they gave them, he took no notes. When he was asked in turn what he did with such suggestions, he said, "I call around." When he was asked what was to be done with the sludge once it was skimmed off, he said, "It's not timely to know that." I thought about Max Stone and wondered if he had figured out yet what was to be done with that sludge. Taylor was asked what plans there were to test water quality near Cordova. There were oyster farms there, and the proprietors were worried. They feared that if oil were to come their way it would poison the oyster beds. Taylor said, "Water quality should be a high priority."

It was hard not to feel a little sorry for Taylor. The Cordova people, though at this juncture polite enough, were not swallowing run-arounds. Heather McCarty sat at the table behind Taylor with a searching, intense expression on her face. Taylor clung desperately to the obscure language of the bureaucrat. He spoke in a monotone, taking care not to give anything away by a show of emotion. He used all the half-answers and distracting asides at his command to hold his position and yet appear friendly, but finally it was apparent that there would be nothing forthcoming, only the blockage to communication and the same lack of precision and decisiveness that was encountered repeatedly with Exxon representatives.

Immediately following Taylor's appearance, Kelly Weaverling came into the room. There was a blackboard up against a wall on which a flowchart of the animal recovery operation had been drawn. Weaverling had intended to discuss that, I gathered, and perhaps to report on the progress of the new otter center. Instead, he told the group that he'd just come back from the water, that the bird people said this was the most difficult terrain they'd ever worked with. He said his group had begun collecting otters, too, and that there was trouble. He looked bad. His face was drawn, and he spoke in bursts, and paused and looked down at the floor, then spoke in another burst.

Fish and Wildlife officials had just told Weaverling that there would be no otter center in Cordova. There would be one in Seward, instead, the advice of Randall Davis notwithstanding. Moreover, they informed Weaverling that he had to cease and desist from capturing otters because his fleet was unauthorized, untrained, and had been operating without inspections. Since the otter was a federally protected species, Fish and Wildlife had stepped in. There was an uncomfortable silence in the room. The irony was not lost on anyone: the federal government would shut down a citizens' response group, but not a faulty oil delivery system. Later, Weaverling told me that at that moment he felt "so low they could have driven a snake over me."

Fish and Wildlife officials had feared — perhaps with justification — that otters that might survive on their own were being unnecessarily stressed. Nevertheless, Fish and Wildlife officials, who would decline to be identified, later said that they regretted that the rescue operation had been shut down. In an indication, perhaps, of the kind of basis upon which many choices were being made, they said the decision caused them a lot of bad press.

A few days after the Fish and Wildlife shutdown, Exxon, which still had charge of the bird rescue operation, ordered Weaverling to stop rescuing birds, but he continued anyway. "I was never personally paid by Exxon or Veco," he said, "so they had no control over me." In early July he was fired, though reports circulated that he had resigned in protest. He told me, "I did not resign. What happened was I worked on a verbal agreement and a handshake with IBRRC. You'd think the chain of command would be Exxon, Bird Rescue Center, me, my fleet. But at that point Exxon didn't want any of this stuff done, because they wanted the bird problem to go away . . . because if the birds weren't being brought in, then the birds out there must be okay. They started directing the vessels themselves and letting me and the Bird Rescue Center know later. I became a supernumerary. I did not resign."

Weaverling went on to organize an observation project at Perry Island, which had been heavily oiled. His objective was to create a record of the impact of oil and of humans engaged in cleanup. The project was staffed by volunteers, or what Weaverling called "vertical citizenry," and funded by donations channeled through the Alaska Conservation Foundation. "I'm unaffiliated," Kelly said. "I'm an independent voter. I came here to get away from society."

"Most fishermen are fair," said Belen Cook, a slight, dark-haired woman. Belen and her husband were gillnetters who fished for herring in the sound and for salmon off Cordova in the Copper River Flats. "If they see that Exxon is fair, they may be satisfied, but Exxon has proven that not everything they say is true." Belen believed that Exxon should pay punitive damages, in addition to paying for the losses. "The unknown is frightening," she said. She said she had cried, and that she would never have dreamed of seeing the men cry that she had.

We were in the CDFU headquarters. Ken Adams came quietly out of the office at my back and sat down, took off his hat and ran his fingers slowly through his white hair. He was probably in his early forties, intense and handsome, and had emerged as yet another of the forceful CDFU spokespersons. We faced each other on the long side of a particleboard table, which was up against the wall that separated CDFU from PWSAC. Beside us was an open area and in it were more tables loaded with heaps of photocopied material — fishing closure announcements, press releases, newspaper articles. People passed in and out. Adams told me that he'd awakened in the middle of the night and had three visions. The first was of David and Goliath. "Should the people of Cordova offer Exxon terms? Did David give Goliath a chance?

"Bush should be impeached," he said. "He's pimping big oil. Are we still a free people?" This was his second vision — the wimp transformed into a pimp. Adams had a message for the board members of big corporations: "I know you are good Americans, and so I personally invite you to come out on my fishing boat. I'll supply the gloves, boots, and chow. You supply the tooth-brushes. Do you know what work is?"

His third vision was of covering the Exxon board members with oil and letting them suffer the fate of the sea otters. "Then they would know." He glanced at my notebook as if to make sure I had that right, then added that most of what he was saying was personal, not necessarily a CDFU position. By this time, I understood a little more about what was at stake with the fishermen. I understood that Ken Adams, like many here, was caught in a terrific, mortal bind: his life, his livelihood, his home, his values, his family and friends, everything pitched against the oil slick. He was not a radical. Like Jack Lamb, he was well accustomed to working within the system.

Adams had an explanation for why it had taken so long for Alyeska and Exxon to begin cleaning up the spill: "They didn't want to clean it up. Who's accountable? Does accountability simply mean pay on the books? Exxon didn't understand responsibility. For Exxon appropriate measures mean confusion, manipulation, and deception. It's incomprehensible that they couldn't clean it up if they wanted to. We had phenomenally good weather until yesterday — day seventeen of the spill. Exxon can't say the weather made it impossible to clean it up. They were counting on bad weather to use as an excuse and they didn't get it."

It made sense. It was the same principle as running tankers until they broke down, of using a faulty delivery system. It was cheaper to keep things that way and sidetrack the regulators. Similarly, it was cheaper to figure that the spill wouldn't happen, and if it did, then to wait for the wind to come up, to hang tight and try to control the imagery. When I asked Exxon represen-tatives about this later, they denied it, even exhibited outrage at such a sug-gestion, but an examination of the events as they occurred — the lack of preparation, the indecision, the confusion, the foot-dragging, the impediments, the refusal to consult the knowledgeable until pushed into it — lent credence to Adams's accusation.

The next day, I met George Velikanje again down at the docks. He invited me into the cabin of his tender, the *Salmo Point*. The boat had a pleasant, slightly sweet smell, the odor of long use in the wet. Outside, rain fell steadily, and it was warm and snug in the cabin. George sat up behind the wheel while I sat on top of a storage trunk. The boat was 60 years old, one of the older boats in the fleet. George himself was 45, a fourth-generation Alaskan. "I'm free and clear," he said, which I took to mean that his boat and permits were paid for.

It was George who introduced me to the channel metaphor. "The only people in this town in favor of working through the channels are the people in the channels," he said. "But they don't know anything, or they forgot." George spent a few years down in the lower forty-eight when he was young but didn't like it. "I came home and told my father that they've got it all fenced down there." Once, he set out with a friend on a 200-mile hike here in Alaska. They almost starved to death. Near the end, as they were climbing a slope, his friend stopped and called out for help. He thought he'd ruptured something. George, who was in the lead, told his friend that he would wait, but he sure as hell wasn't coming back down to get him. They both made it up and at dark found an abandoned Native fishing camp. They saw the silhouettes of salmon hanging from a line, and tore down the fish, gorging themselves on it. When they awoke in the morning, they saw that the fish were infested with maggots. George said that he and his friend looked at each other, and laughed, and ate some more.

George rocked back in his chair and said, "That's what we know. We know about death. I've been that close to death and I know how to laugh in its face. Those Exxon fuckers don't know anything about that." He pulled off his boots and tucked his feet underneath his legs. "You know," he said. "The pipeline can't be turned off. If it's stopped up in winter it'll freeze. It'd take one hell of a snake to ream it out." Again, he smiled. "The monkey wrench."

Outside the cabin, a raven landed on top of a piling and cocked its head at us. They are smarter than dogs, some say. They are opportunistic feeders. They have powerful spirits. This one surveyed us closely, checking us out. George said, "This is a chance for us to force a little responsibility on the kings of capital, the robber barons of our society. They say, be realistic. I say, what the hell do you think is real?"

Exxon and the government, in George's view, were concerned only with controlling the damage to themselves. "It's fucking image manipulation, that's all," he said. He repeated the sentiment I'd heard from many: "The fishermen have a track record of seeing things correctly. Exxon has a track record of screwing us over. Now they've proven it to everyone. How come they're getting to make the decisions? How can I love my fucking country when it isn't real?"

7 SHOWTIME

I referred to Prince William Sound as one of the two most beautiful places on earth. I leave it to each of you individually to decide what the other one is. We all have a special Shangri-La in our hearts and minds. Think of yours when you contemplate what has happened to ours.

— Don Moore, Cordova city manager, in an appeal to the nation, 1989

KIMO, an Anchorage ABC affiliate, staged a televised town meeting in Valdez on April 11. It was held in the Civic Center, a capacious place made of bricks and nestled among rock outcroppings not far above the ferry terminal. At the entryways, security guards searched bags. They were checking for tape recorders, they said, but they were probably looking for weapons, too. Reportedly, some of the Exxon people had received death threats. The guard I got, a wiry man with bright eyes, bowed his head and murmured apologetically as his hand moved among my notebooks and socks. Inside, the plush auditorium was packed and swirling with talk. I found a seat near the front.

John Valentine, one of two KIMO moderators, informed the crowd that Exxon had initially agreed to send a representative to the panel but then reneged. A murmur rippled across the hall. Valentine, the size of a tight-end, was handsome and shiny-looking, a universal jack who could have been plugged into any news show in the country. He prowled the stage, which was still in the process of being set up, and spoke into a handheld mike. He said he had spent three hours negotiating with Exxon officials, a statement that left a perplexing aftertaste since its main import seemed to be that Valentine had been allowed access to the inner chamber where so few had ventured. When Valentine said that Exxon's condition was that there be no audience participation, a snicker broke from one of the back rows and the murmur in the hall increased in intensity. Valentine said he had declined to meet that condition. There was spotty applause.

This was to be a "Donahue" or "Oprah Winfrey" style show, and Valentine, no doubt, understood that a fair amount of serious network weight was in town. This was akin to combat duty for a man in his position. A highstepper could move up fast. The front row of the hall was a bank of cameras. The feel of the audience reasserted the difference between Valdez and Cordova. These people were more diverse, an internally fractious group that ran the gamut from out-of-town environmentalists to oil industry employees, from onlookers to bureaucrats and irate fishermen. Valdez was in a state of sensory overload, and the televised town meeting had promised to draw the chaos within the boundaries of ready-made theatre, maybe even to tap a little of the truth from the inner sanctum. The man seated in front of me, who turned out to be the city manager of Valdez, tipped his head toward the woman next to him and said, "I'm going to keep real quiet through this thing."

Valentine announced that Bill Allen of Veco International, Inc., had come in Exxon's stead. The contingent at the back of the hall hooted. Allen was over on the extreme right end of the group of men seated on the stage. He looked like a bear-wrestler, long-limbed and heavy. His legs were stretched out beneath the table, and he lounged against the back of his chair and communicated a sense of his apartness from the others. He was a classic Alaskan type: roughcut and sly, fathomless in his ambition, adept at damming up and diverting the streams of money that flowed through the state. The public version of his life took the shape of an exemplary fable: poor as a child and raised in the small town of Ione in north-central Oregon, he dropped out of high school when his mother moved with her children to New Mexico. Allen went to work in the oil fields of the Southwest to help support his family, and by the time he was in his early twenties he was supervising projects for corporations such as Bechtel and Fluor in southern California. He appeared in Alaska as an oil rig welder in 1968. Following a series of adversities and liaisons with big oil, he ended up the owner of Veco, a subcontracting company that managed equipment, supplies, and construction and maintenance crews for the oil principals. Alaska had long been a good place for subcontractors, for those who built the pillars that held up the expressway. It became an even better place when construction began on the Trans-Alaska pipeline.

Allen had said, "We bet everything on the North Slope." Veco prospered during the pipeline days, mainly through its association with Arco and British Petroleum. A union construction subsidiary, Norcon, was formed to meet pipeline requirements. After the pipeline days, Veco continued to diversify, and one investment into a Houston shipyard sent the company into bankruptcy court in 1982, but Allen surfaced and with the help of Arco, it was said, reassembled his company. A couple of years later, Veco was found guilty of illegally inducing its employees to make pro-oil political contributions, which increased Allen's notoriety as a front man for oil interests. By the late eighties, Veco International had essentially recovered from bankruptcy proceedings. It remained principally devoted to oil field service and construction, but entered the oil spill cleanup business in 1988 through a contract with the Cook Inlet Response Organization. In the same year — as if in an act of prescience that secured in advance a Veco marker in the environmental response business — Allen's company became involved with supplying equipment and personnel to the widely reported rescue of three gray whales trapped in ice in the Arctic Ocean off Barrow. By the time the cleanup from the *Exxon Valdez* spill was over in the fall of 1989, a new Veco subsidiary, Veco Environmental and Professional Services, had been formed, and Allen had institutionalized his role as a major player in the Alaskan information game by buying out the more conservative of the two Anchorage newspapers, the *Anchorage Times*.[39]

[39] Bill Allen's Veco International, would jump from the fifth largest Alaska-based company to the largest in 1989. Mainly through its nonunion and union construction and maintenance subsidiaries (Veco, Inc., and Norcon), the parent company grossed $960 million, nearly nine times its revenues of $110 the previous year. Of that amount $800 million came from Exxon, and $32 million showed as profits from Veco's 4 percent cost-plus cleanup contract.

With him on the stage were Rear Admiral Edward Nelson, Jr., commander of the Coast Guard's Alaska District, DEC Commissioner Kelso, John Devens, the mayor of Valdez, and Don Moore, the Cordova city manager. The man who was missing, and in whose stead Bill Allen had appeared, was Frank Iarossi. Iarossi, Kelso, and Nelson (later to be replaced by Vice Admiral Clyde Robbins) made up the private, state, and federal triumvirate charged with directing the response to the spill. Although Iarossi, according to reports, had asked Nelson to take command so that there would be a clearer framework for action, Nelson had declined because the spill had not been federalized.

At this point, the hope that the newly installed administration of George Bush would step in and take control was rapidly dissipating. Bush had dragged his feet on Governor Cowper's request for a declaration of a national disaster and subsequently decided against it, and so against federalization, but agreed to send troops to Prince William Sound. Now, that order had just been rescinded. As it happened, the Coast Guard Commandant Admiral Paul Yost would arrive in Valdez in two days, on the morning of Thursday, April 13. One of his first actions would be to give Exxon three days to produce its plan for cleanup operations, then a week late. Yost was there, as he put it, "to take names and kick butts." He came to be widely admired for both his humanity — his willingness to be affected by the damage and the pain of the people — and his leadership capabilities. For as long as he was around, things improved considerably, particularly in the upper echelons of decision making. Execution of decisions by private and public subordinates on the shorelines and in the communities or with, say, the otter and bird rescue operation was another matter.

The Bush administration's argument was that the oiling of the sound had been caused by private enterprise and that private enterprise should therefore be held accountable for corrective measures immediately, not sometime in the future. Legally, politically, and economically, this was an eminently defensible position. Also, there was absolutely no evidence from declared national disasters in the past to suggest that federalization would have improved the effectiveness of the response. The fact that the spill had occurred in U.S. waters, however, did make it possible to bring in the Coast Guard, and hence Admiral Yost. Eventually, Exxon managed and paid for the cleanup and supplied equipment while the Coast Guard made final decisions and approved and monitored the plans. In order to mollify Exxon's fears over government lawsuits, the Coast Guard streamlined the process of gaining approvals and permits under the labyrinth of regulations and laws administered by state and federal agencies. Belatedly determined, it was not an unreasonable solution.

The KIMO show was called "The Spill." John Valentine announced the commercial breaks by saying, "'The Spill' will continue," which provoked raucous, bitter laughter from the audience. Valentine roamed the aisles with his handheld mike. Questions concerning the lack of response to the spill were raised, and Admiral Nelson and Dennis Kelso were unable to agree on even the most fundamental matter. Admiral Nelson said that the first priority was to get the oil off the water, a proposition that by this time had come to seem fanciful at best since each passing day brought news of the oil slick's invasion of new territories, and somebody like Tom Copeland with his boat and five-gallon buckets could claim to pick up more oil than a skimmer. At this stage 800 miles of beaches had been fouled and observers were still trying to track where else the last storm had driven the oil. Kelso more reasonably echoed the conclusion that the CDFU people had arrived at, that the first priority was to maintain the boom defense, particularly at the hatcheries, and that getting oil off the water came second.

The primary cause for delay in shoreline cleanup was the lack of supplies and manpower. A second cause had to do with the question of standards, a complex and, politically speaking, heavily freighted matter that involved several issues. It raised again the question that would never go away, the question of purity: When was a beach clean? What was clean? How was clean measured? What did pristine mean? The state and Exxon would fight over this for the next several years. It also raised the question of what cleanup methods to use, chemical or mechanical, or both, and of the further damage to shorelines that might be caused by an invasion of workers and equipment. Admiral Nelson stated that cleanup standards had not been set yet because the islands in the sound were still in the process of being analyzed for their ecology, their sensitivity, for the presence of archeological material. Kelso stated that the standards for beach cleanup had already been set. Bill Allen, who had to be prodded to respond, said that there was a communications problem and that he was in the dark so far as standards were concerned.

Mayor Devens of Valdez, who among the men on the stage probably felt most acutely the need for direction since his town was under the siege of a human spill, derided the Bush administration and Alaska's congressmen for not declaring the sound a national disaster area. At the same time, he credited himself for talking the Bush administration into not sending troops. He was understandably very worried about the impact of the still-developing cleanup mobilization upon Valdez, but precisely what his vision was of the federal presence remained unclear. He was also worried about underwater oil, claiming that it was distributed at some depth under the surface — 15 to 20 fathoms. He was wrong about that, or basically wrong, although at the time there was talk everywhere of oil sliding beneath the surface and then reappearing as if from nowhere, of fishermen hauling up oil-coated anchors.

Jack Lamb was in the audience. He rose to his feet and asked that Exxon and Alyeska be required to hold a public conference to answer questions concerning their lack of response to the spill. As one of the group of fishermen ushered into the inner chamber, Lamb knew better than most what Exxon and Alyeska's answers would be and what they would not answer at all. He said that both Alyeska and Exxon were stonewalling, that they were offering no response to the public. He asked the panel to tell him when movement would be made on the cleanup. He wanted to be told who was running the cleanup operation. He was asking for what the audience wanted to hear. They had come in the vain hope that in a forum such as this a meaningful answer or two might emerge.

Admiral Nelson said that the Coast Guard command structure was running the operation, though effectively this was not true. Admiral Yost hadn't arrived yet. Nelson, knowing very well who Jack Lamb was and perhaps recollecting what the people in the inner chamber had decided to do, now said that the salmon hatcheries were the first priority. Otherwise, he did not respond to Lamb's questions, which were really a form of serving notice on Alaskan television in the face of an appalling misuse and concealment of information: Where were the skimmers? Where was the boom? Where were the barges? Where had Alyeska been? Where was Exxon? What about the beaches? When would they pay heed to the people who understood the currents of the sound? What about reparations? What about the animals? What was next?

Bill Allen of Veco was unable even to hear the questions. They had to be repeated for him, and more than once his catchall response was that there was a "communications problem." His company had been taken on as the primary contractor for cleanup services, and his deal with Exxon was on a "cost-plus" basis, which meant that he was guaranteed a profit on every dollar spent, but Allen was able to say only that he was "in the dark." The effect of his approach, whether intentionally or accidentally guileful, was precisely the same as the approach Monte Taylor used in Cordova — plead ignorance, blur the distinctions, misinterpret the questions, talk about something else.

Quite possibly Allen, the Exxon surrogate, was truly in the dark, and if so, his failure lay in agreeing to come here when he had nothing to say or, having come, in his refusal to explain the darkness. By not articulating the source of their confusion, both Allen and Exxon hung what was serious in the public's interest out to dry. Exxon kept repeating in its ads and press releases that it "accepted responsibility" for the spill, but it sounded more and more as though the purpose of the apology was to absolve the apologist of responsibility and that it knew nothing at all about the pain the apology should have addressed.

The grizzled guy I'd met outside the offices of the Alaska Department of Fish and Game a few days before reappeared here. He latched onto Valentine's mike and gave his pitch. His boat was still waiting in slip 52. His bottom line was that having exhausted his other possibilities, he wanted Bill Allen to tell him when Veco would hire him on. Allen didn't understand the question. The guy pushed the limits of decorum and Valentine, sensing the nearness of theatre, maybe, turned him loose. The guy's voice rang in the hall as he repeated his pitch, the whole garbled, frenzied thing: what kind of boat he had, what kind of engine, how fast the boat was, where it could go, where it was, and where he was from, which was Anchorage, and how he looked the way he did because he'd been sleeping in his boat for the last 14 days, long enough, he said, to make him an official resident of Valdez.

Bill Allen drew his legs up, leaned forward to listen, and smiled. The guy had Bill Allen's attention, and suddenly it became a moment when all the confusion, indignation, subterfuge, evasion, and even outrage were stripped away and the true meaning of the cleanup came out, burned clean to its nub. The guy wanted to make some money, that was all. Allen understood that. The audience fell silent. It was a moment in which the floor and walls of the hall seemed to atomize and drop away. Everything was suspended and into the weird, glassy, rapt space two sharks came and swam free.

After a time, Allen said that he didn't know when the guy would be hired, or for what, or how, or by whom, but that it sure sounded as though he would be hired to do something.

The next morning in the Totem Inn, I fell into a conversation with a correspondent for the Canadian Broadcasting Corporation. He told about stumbling upon a refrigerated semi trailer down by the docks that was stacked to the ceiling with otter bodies. It was the morgue to which the dead otters slipped out the back door at the rescue center were taken. The bodies were numbered and kept for the pathologists to dissect and test.[40]

The Totem Inn was packed again. There was a line at the telephone. A clump of people stood waiting for empty seats, and all around us was the noise of intense conversations. Everyone had news and rumor ran rampant. Two men seated next to the CBC correspondent and me joined our conversation. They were Charles Jurasz, who operated a whale observation station in Oregon and a consulting and educational operation in Juneau, and David Lonsdale, the assistant director of the John G. Shedd Aquarium in Chicago. Lonsdale had several reasons for being here, among them to encourage the establishment of an aquarium in Alaska for the rescued otters, and possibly to procure otters for his aquarium. There were disputes over everything, of course, and that included the disposition of otters once they were ready for release from the rescue centers. Public aquariums had joined the orbit around Valdez. The Shedd Aquarium would eventually send three staff members to help with the otter rescue project and take in four otter pups that for reasons unknown had been abandoned by their mothers and then cared for in the Seward Otter Center.

Charles Jurasz, whom I would come to know as the months passed, was a passionate, tendentious man. He said that the humpback whales were due to migrate into the sound any day now. "They're surface feeders," he said. To demonstrate, he craned his neck downwards, dropped his jaw, and cruised low over the surface of the table. He straightened up, eyed the rest of us fiercely, and said, "Oil floats. Can you imagine?" The best hope, he said, was that the whales would avoid the slick.

He and Lonsdale had just seen an otter die at the rescue center. Charles did the trick with compressed breath that I remembered from childhood playgrounds. He leaned back in his chair and sucked in air, then sucked in more, and more. His face deepened in color as he squeezed the air in his lungs, then suddenly he let it out in an explosion of air. The puff was as visible as breath exhaled in the cold. "It was like that," Charles said, "when

---

[40] The bodies would remain refrigerated for over three years until October of 1992, when following the resolution of the charges against Exxon, what by then had amounted to thousands of corpses of sea otters, birds, and other creatures were finally released. They had been kept as evidence of oil spill damage, that is, as a legal resource, in three refrigerated semi-trailers. The trailers had been pulled to an Anchorage parking lot. Although the bodies were in states of putrefaction due to the oiling, and to repeated thawing and freezing in the imperfect refrigeration technology, they were first apportioned out to interested researchers and museum curators, then what was left behind of them was burned.

the otter died. That was the pain it felt, and the constriction of its muscles. Its last breath came out like that."

At the rescue center in Valdez, the recovering animals were out in the sun. They were given ice in their cages. One of them, number 81, was dying. She had almost died an hour or so before, but had perked up after being given ice. Now, she was fading again. Two volunteer helpers, Jake Metulka and Dave Berrey, crouched by the cage. Dave said, "Alaska's been raped, but the question is, is it by consent or force?" He looked over at me to see if I was writing that down. I wrote it, though I could sense the shine of frequent use on the words. There was a troubling impulse among many here to assure that they were being memorialized along with the event. The press seemed to carry the power to do that. I'd been inside the building where otters were held in plywood stalls, and I had watched, aghast, as an NBC crewman shoved his way up to a stall, shined his lights on a startled otter, and began rolling the film. He was a big man with a taut, blunt face, and he had to be chased off.

Dave went off to find some towels to try to warm number 81. She lay on her back, moving her legs indiscriminately. She scraped at her face, bit at her paws, rolled over, and cut her lips by biting at the wire cage. The otters were readily anthropomorphized in the imagination: they were articulate with their paws. Their eyes expressed intelligence. The pain of number 81 seemed familiar and close. Her mortality was my own. She writhed in a slow, ceaseless frenzy, as if striving to locate the source of her trouble.

I headed down to the Bird Rescue Center to help with the evening feeding. Surgical tubes were inserted through the beaks of the birds down into their stomachs, and a sugar mash was forced in from a large syringe to rehydrate them after the diarrhea caused by the oil. I held them — a white-winged scoter, a common loon, a red-footed pigeon guillemot, a gray, white, and orange harlequin duck that looked dazzling in my hands. The head of a Barrow's goldeneye, seen close, had a rich purple sheen emerging from beneath the black. I was holding the birds gently, feeling the dryness of their feathers, and at the same time my mind was filled with the image of number 81, with white mountains, with Bill Allen awakening from his reverie and leaning forward to listen to the guy with the waiting boat in slip 52, with the Totem Inn, packed with people, with the raven that had so narrowly scrutinized George Velikanje and me, with the slick, the elastic thing that engulfed the beaches. I thought about Kelly Weaverling's frustrated rescue efforts.

A gray-haired woman in the Bird Center had had the side of her nose ripped open by a pelagic cormorant. She continued working, dabbing at her nose with a Kleenex, her blood dripping on her yellow slicker. My partner and I approached a cage of cormorants. Angular and quick, they had athletic necks and long, menacing beaks. They attacked in a pack any outstretched hand. I had to move fast to catch one safely, then gripped its head with one hand and pressed its body against me with the other. It calmed down. My partner inserted the tubing through its beak, slid it down, and slowly compressed the big plastic syringe. The cormorant's belly swelled intimately against my palm, then it crapped on my boot. My partner laughed softly. When we finished, I set the cormorant gently in its cage. It whirled suddenly in a rush of slate-colored feathers, its neck whipped, and its beak tore at my fingers.

The next morning, I climbed into a four-passenger red-and-white Cessna 180 at the Valdez airport. We flew over the Alyeska terminal where they were still skimming up a 168-gallon spill from an April 10 tanker-loading mishap. At another time, that would have caused a stir. Each of the three gray tankers moored at the terminal was encircled by a silvery boom in compliance with regulations. We headed out above Valdez Narrows and along Valdez Arm toward Naked Island. To the right, pale blue icebergs from Columbia Glacier floated in the dark water at the mouth of the arm. At Knowles Head, another tanker awaited permission to enter.

The sky was clear in this part of the sound and we flew at about 1,000 feet above the water until we reached Storey and Peak islands just north of Naked Island. Black oil bled from their rocky shorelines. The oil in the water had a milky tinge. We circled Naked Island twice, and the pilot banked the Cessna for a view of the *Exxon Valdez,* anchored in the bay. A repair barge was tied up to the tanker's side. The tanker was still leaking and the barge was engulfed in thick, black crude. The bay was filled with oil. All of Naked Island's shoreline was lost to the blackness.

In the five-mile stretch between Naked and Eleanor Islands was a large, oval oil slick. It had the rainbow appearance oil took on in the sun — gray, white, faint blue, brown, red. The brown or red color that indicates thickness is called chocolate mousse. When the oil is thin and light gray, it is called cloud. The euphemisms seemed outrageous. The longer the oil sat out in the water the more it would harden, making it more difficult to skim.

The natural color of the bottom in the shallows near the shoreline was emerald green, which came from the fucus beds. A few patches of the color flashed by as we passed over Eleanor and Ingot Islands and started down the

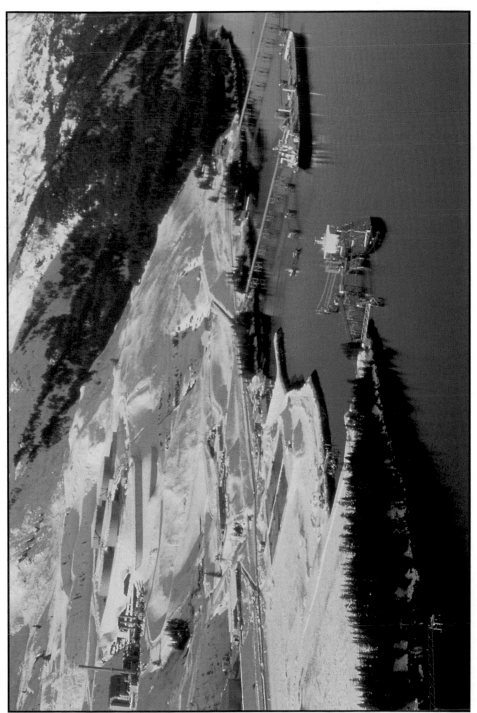

Ships loading oil at the Alyeska terminal in Valdez Bay, oil storage tanks on the slope

The *Exxon Valdez* on Bligh Reef and the spill

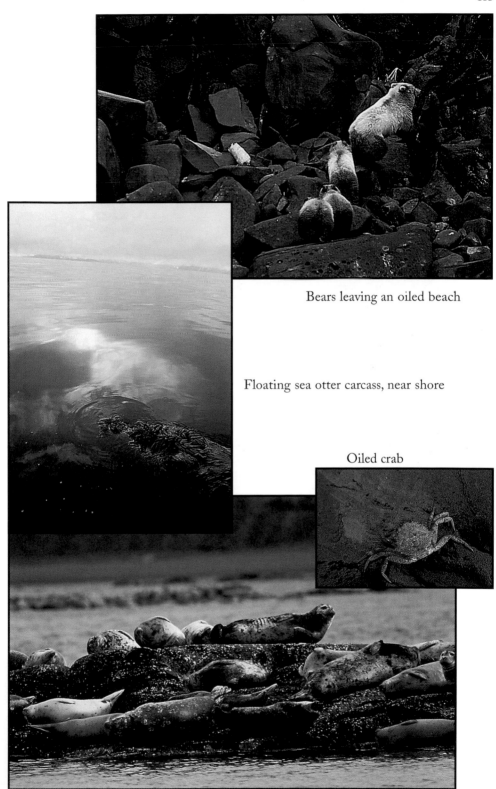

Bears leaving an oiled beach

Floating sea otter carcass, near shore

Oiled crab

Oiled seals on a "haul-out"

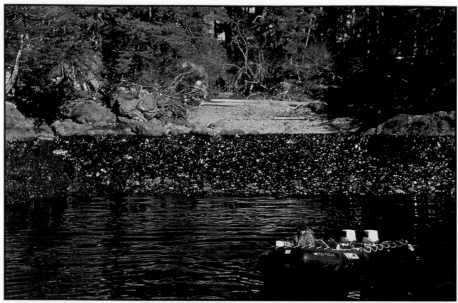

The "Bathtub Ring" of oil

Oil skimming in a boomed bay

High pressure hoses washing oil off a beach, skimming team in the background

Oiled bird, protective gloves

Fishermen setting boom from an inflatable, Eleanor Island

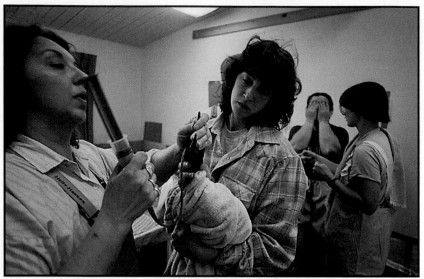

Feeding by syringe in the bird rescue center, Valdez

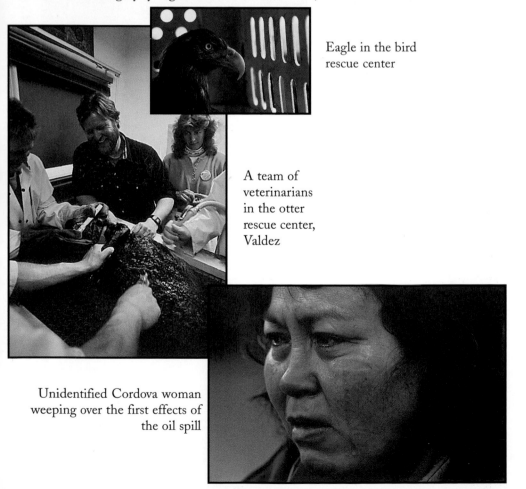

Eagle in the bird rescue center

A team of veterinarians in the otter rescue center, Valdez

Unidentified Cordova woman weeping over the first effects of the oil spill edge of Montague Strait along the eastern side of Knight Island. Then the color disappeared. A large portion of the slick was trapped in Montague Strait between Montague and Knight Island. The rocks along Knight Island were covered with oil. Pools of crude were locked in all the coves. I spotted several brown, rectangular shapes floating in an inlet and reached for the binoculars. The pilot dropped the plane to the level of the cliffs. The shapes were motionless in the murk. They were otters, eight or nine dead ones, washed into the inlet.

The coastlines are intricate. There are coves upon coves, inlets upon inlets, twisting jagged peninsulas and complex watery arms. All the shores on the eastern side of Knight Island were coated with oil. We were near low tide and the beaches, cliffs, and shrubs were black 20 feet above the waterline. Offshore, the oil floated in elongated ribbons and congealed around the rocks. From the southern tip of Knight Island, we cut west to Sawmill Bay, the site of the Koernig hatchery. The oil had crept within a half-mile of the hatchery and I counted 20 boats down there, frantically skimming, running boom, sopping up crude with the two-foot-square sponges that could hold a gallon of oil. The efforts to save the hatchery seemed frail and desperate.

The Cessna swung out and passed up along the western side of Knight Island. The normal colors of gray rock, the ocher of dried eel grass, and the green of the shallows were utterly gone. Everywhere, the water was rainbow-black from crude. At the northwest edge of Knight Island, Herring Bay, a deep, labyrinthine inlet, was clotted with black. Because of their intricacy, all the islands and shorelines looked like computer-generated fractals, fine, complex, and infinitely specific in their structures. The complexity of the ecology along the shorelines and in the estuaries, where the exquisite chaos of commerce between microscopic organisms, fish, plant, and land animals became most intense, appeared dead. By this time, two hours out and finally brought near to the thing itself, I had long stopped fooling with my binoculars, camera, and notebook, and instead held my head still against the window and stared down at the horror.

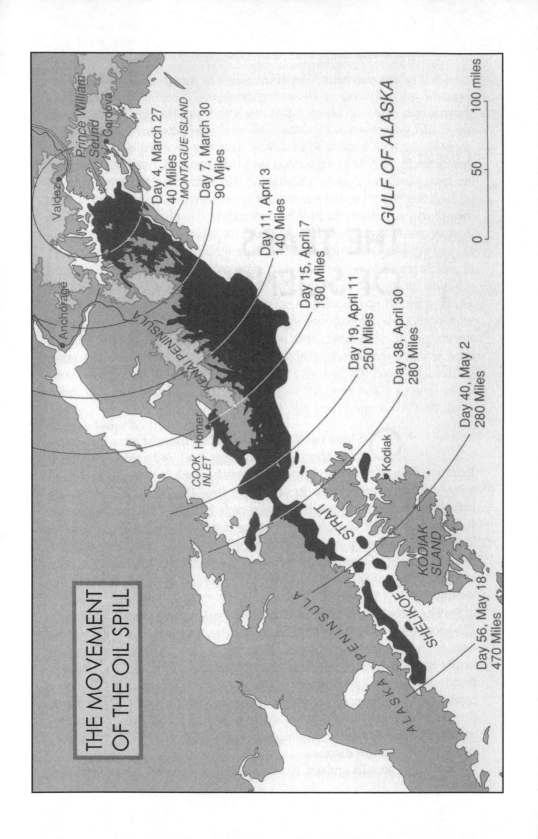

THE MOVEMENT
OF THE OIL SPILL

GULF OF ALASKA

Prince William
Sound

Valdez

Cordova

Anchorage

KENAI PENINSULA

COOK Homer
INLET

Kodiak

KODIAK
ISLAND

SHELIKOF

STRAIT

ALASKA PENINSULA

Day 4, March 27
40 Miles
MONTAGUE ISLAND

Day 7, March 30
90 Miles

Day 11, April 3
140 Miles

Day 15, April 7
180 Miles

Day 19, April 11
250 Miles

Day 38, April 30
280 Miles

Day 40, May 2
280 Miles

Day 56, May 18
470 Miles

0   50   100 miles

8   THE TEARS
OF SCIENCE

On June twelfth, two and a half months after the *Exxon Valdez* foundered on Bligh Reef and midway through Exxon's cleanup exercise, I stood on a rocky bank beside the mouth of a stream that emptied into Resurrection Bay. The bay is a narrow, 25-mile-long indentation into the eastern side of Alaska's Kenai Peninsula. Its mouth is about 50 miles west of the edge of Prince William Sound, and it is ice-free, protected from winds, and for a time was the principal shipping connection between the Pacific and the Alaskan interior. The town of Seward lay a half-mile to my left in the shadows of the mountains.

Between the town and the bank where I stood, the *Alpha Helix*, a 133-foot steel-hulled vessel operated by the National Science Foundation, rocked gently in the water alongside its dock. The ship's hull was bright blue. Its above decks and communications antennae were white. Beside it, the dock, damp from a recent rain, was a glistening gray. I could see the figures of the science crew as they hustled up and down the gangplank and passed down duffel bags and crates loaded with diving and laboratory gear to the ship's crew on the main deck. Their voices sounded thin in the distance.

Shortly, we would embark for Prince William Sound. I would spend ten days in the company of a team of natural scientists under the leadership of John Oliver. Their specialties were in benthics (sea bottom) and intertidal regions. Since I still embraced the well-acculturated trust in science and its methods, my hope was that I could come to understand, accurately and in detail, just how far-reaching the poisoning had been. There was the pitch of emotion in Valdez, Cordova, Seward, Homer, Seldovia, and Port Graham, the ever-rising din of claims, denials, and false information, the shrill and sometimes woefully misinformed response on the part of environmentalists in the lower forty-eight. And by this time science itself had become partitioned into adversarial camps (again, the state, the federal agencies, and Exxon), and into camps within camps. The otter centers competed for victims. Some specialists jockeyed to get the inside track on future research papers. There had been a shift in command, too. For the Coast Guard, Admiral Yost had stayed until the end of April, then to be replaced by Vice Admiral Clyde Robbins. Frank Iarossi, who some said had come to care too deeply, left his position at Exxon Shipping for one at the American Bureau of Shipping, and was relieved by Exxon's Otto Harrison, whose mission seemed at times to be to question every recommendation and protect Exxon against every possible legal twist. This sometimes had the effect of undoing Admiral Yost's work. The spill had by then covered over 6,000 square miles, but finding the truth about it in detail was like searching in the dark for a narrow ledge to hang onto.

Of the panelists on the KIMO show in Valdez, the one who stood most apart from the others was Don Moore, Cordova's city manager. A spare, balding, and thoughtful-looking man, Moore had given notice of his resignation in Cordova for personal reasons and had agreed to accept another position elsewhere before the spill occurred. The result was that he would soon leave the town. During the KIMO show, he spoke much less than his fellow panelists, but among them he alone had raised the question of the impact of the oil spill upon Native subsistence villages, particularly Tatitlek and Chenega, the latter of which had had its resources obliterated. When the sense of the paralyzing effect of infighting among interest groups had become especially strong on the panel, Moore said, "We should seize this moment to rise above ourselves. There should be a major research effort."

That was the first time I had thought seriously of the spill as a research opportunity. It had been clear from the start that science was to be an integral part of the cleanup and recovery — to take custody of the oiled otters and birds, to try and to fail to take custody of the oil slick itself, to observe and to monitor. What I hadn't appreciated was that extraordinary energy would also be devoted to research that ran the gamut from "applied" in the strictest sense (findings might inform the response to future spills and so be closely allied with technologies such as dispersants and bioremediation) to "pure" or "almost pure" (the response of organisms to toxicity might lead to inquiries that would bear upon, say, genetics). Calamity had come to be a staple resource for science-oriented government agencies and cottage industries across the nation, and the research process and its presumed results — that is, "knowledge" — would come to be heavily leveraged by the parties of interest.

At the beginning, I had visited several of the science meetings in Valdez, which were then gatherings of state and federal agency, Exxon, and freelance scientists. In some cases, they were scouting out contracts. At first, the meetings functioned as open distribution centers for information. Later, they became fractured, even useless some would say, as the state and federal agency scientists and Exxon scientists came to be pitched against one another in complicated ways, thus reflecting the fractious relationship of their employers. They would fight, for example, for proprietorship of the bodies of the dead that were to be examined and used as evidence in litigation.

I went to one early meeting in the company of Charles Jurasz and David Lonsdale. Previously, the Shedd Aquarium had been granted permits by U.S. Fish and Wildlife to capture several otters from Prince William Sound. Then the permits had been withdrawn because of the quite understandable uncertainty over the status of the otter population. Lonsdale's mission was to barter the lost permits and expert help for the four otters the Shedd Aquarium eventually received from the Seward Otter Center. It is not my intent to question Lonsdale's or the Shedd's motives (Lonsdale seemed a kind, compassionate man), but Lonsdale's presence was one more example of how the margins of the scientific community were being worked. Another, much more problematic skirmish involved bald eagles. The National Foundation to Protect America's Eagles wished to transport threatened eagle fledglings to Tennessee, but Fish and Wildlife impeded that effort, as well as other early attempts to care for stricken eagles in Alaska.

At the beginning, the conduct of the scientists seemed, by and large, exemplary. At the meetings, which were held in a large, well-appointed conference room of the same Valdez Community Center, reports were given by members of what was called the Oil Spill Assessment Team on the current location of the oil slick, on beach surveys and the numbers of birds found dead or captured and carried to the Bird Rescue Centers, on otters dead and captured, on the progress of the then newly opening rescue centers at other locations, on the condition — insofar as it was known — of the hatcheries, the fisheries, water quality, on the status of the expected migrations of birds and marine mammals. Arranged on a table at the back of the room were neat stacks of photocopied handouts available for the taking — maps of the latest NOAA overflights, summaries of reports, lists of contact persons, and animal counts.

The undercurrent of emergency could be heard in the voices of the scientists, in contrast to the coolness of manner with which they presented their data. Their faces sometimes looked stunned. They were fatigued. Due to the hours spent each day gathering and reviewing data, these meetings did not begin until ten at night. Nevertheless, statements were succinct and clear. The meeting itself was well organized. People awaited their turn to speak. Details were offered freely, questions were answered, and in accordance with the scientific practice of accuracy and skepticism the holes in findings were readily acknowledged — the problems with counts of the dead and the living, the question of whether or not humpback whales would see and avoid the slick, whether sea lions could survive swimming in it. The willing acknowledgment of such holes made them exactly what they should be to science — portals through which more light might eventually be shed upon mystery. This was a question of a quality of mind, of not rushing to fill all the gaps with enthusiasm, blame, and cant, and consistent with such a quality, there were no guards at the doors of the conference room at that time.

Aside from the dispersant fiasco and other initial misapprehensions about winds and currents, the early impression given by scientists in general was that they could be counted on to be calm, accurate, and forthcoming, that is, scientific. So far as the efforts of many of the individuals were concerned, the impression would hold. Many would remain scientific in the face of physical, intellectual, and professional peril. So far as the group of them was concerned, however, the spin on the impression would reverse direction and science would come to seem a refuge from the true damage and many of its practitioners the sometimes quarrelsome and often secretive high priests of disaster. This came later.

The scientists at the early meetings were invariably under 50 years old and usually much younger than that. Their clothing was neat. They were handsome or pretty, trim, fit, well washed. There was not a black face among them. A third of the Assessment Team were women. It was an upwardly mobile group of young professionals, adept at weighing hazard against advancement, and good with words and apparatus. They were well paid. They had the security of their expense accounts, most of them, and they, or their superiors, saw the opportunity to get bigger ones. They had all the advantages of class and position. In contrast to the sense of immediate peril and the will to action that the villagers and fishermen displayed, they were watchers, and many would decline to cross the line that separated their watching from action.

As time passed, as conflicts among the agency and private scientists deepened, the enlarging chaos out in the field ate at all the edges of their method. Kathy Frost was a member of the Assessment Team and told me in early May that oiled river otters and harbor seals had begun to turn up. Several premature harbor seal pups had been found dead, and the oiled adults seemed to be displaying aberrant behavior. Normally, they dive into the water when approached while sunning themselves on the rocks, but now they sat still, even when helicopters flew as close as 600 feet. She worried that the oil had caused some kind of systemic shock. Secondary and tertiary effects upon the food chain were unknown. She said, "Mussels and bivalves may get oil in their sediment, which would affect growth and recolonization, which in turn would affect the otters. The otter pups may not make it because of the food problem. We could get a double whammy on the otters." By that time, as many as 2,500 otters were thought to have died. Eagles, sick from having eaten oiled carrion, were appearing.

There was concern over the coming arrival of migrating humpback and transient killer whales, over the impending spring migration of sea and shore birds. It was said that in terms of the diversity of species and sheer numbers, Prince William Sound, together with the Copper River Delta, was the single largest stopping place for waterfowl in the world. Between April and June, gulls and petrels would arrive, three species of puffins, birds in flocks coming one after another and numbering in the thousands and tens of thousands, kittiwakes, murres, auklets, murrelets, oystercatchers, snipe, dowitchers, sanderlings, surfbirds, plovers, phalaropes, whimbrels, ducks, and geese to join the resident flocks, surf scoters, sandpipers, and shearwaters in flocks as large as 100,000. Because of the forbidding nature of the adjacent country — to the south the Saint Elias region and the Kenai to the west — Prince William

Sound with its tidal flats, snow-free estuaries, its islands and bays and its milder spring climate served as a feeding and resting habitat for the birds as they came north from their wintering grounds. As many as 20 million birds pass through Prince William Sound during the spring and summer months. They feed upon near shore life, invertebrate life of all kinds, clams, mussels, squid, lugworms, copepods, amphipods, schooling fish, flatfish, pollock, sand lance, capelin, and carcasses and marine mammal placentae. In April and May the outlook remained grim. There was concern not only over the effect of oil upon birds that happened to land in it but over its effects upon the food supply, how such effects would be measured, and by whom, and for whom, and to what use the findings would be put.

A scientist in tears was one of the insistent images of the early days of the spill. Charles Jurasz told me he had wept. As Belen Cook had seen hardened fishermen weep, Jurasz said he'd seen the most stoic of scientists weep openly. The grief was a response to the removal of a presence from a thousand miles of beach and thousands of miles of near-shore waters. The loss was felt most keenly by those whose daily life had been woven into the fabric previously, such as the fishermen, the villagers, and the scientists like Kathy Frost whose work had already put them on intimate terms with Prince William Sound. Lisa Rotterman, the otter specialist from Cordova, would say that something momentous happened "when Kathy Frost came back from Green Island and said, 'As a scientist I'm not supposed to feel anything, but it's overwhelming.'" That scientists could weep, especially the natural scientists whose business often enough was pathology just as killing, finally, was the business of fishermen, seemed to validate the loss. That the image of a scientist weeping passed so quickly among the growing numbers of people gathering around the event served as a kind of awakening to the fact that this thing had actually happened and that its substance consisted of something rather more than could be calibrated, weighed, or counted.

Between the dock and the town of Seward and around the curve of the shoreline was the Seward Otter Rescue Center. It was made out of conjoined mobile homes and garrisoned by a chain link fence. I had tried to get in earlier with Bruce Stewart, education director at the Monterey Aquarium and a member of the science crew on the *Alpha Helix*, but we were turned away by a portly, affable guard. No amount of expert talk and no display of credentials would convince him to change his mind. "There was no entrance without permission from Exxon," he said, but he was willing enough to serve as an informant himself. He said that up to that time 150 otters had passed through the Seward center and that there was now a 90 to 95 percent success rate — meaning that 90 to 95 percent of the otters brought in lived.

Considering what I'd heard otherwise and what I'd seen previously in Valdez, the figure seemed outrageous. I thought it was another lie. Bruce and I went on our way to dinner and as we walked I asked him if he thought it was possible. He shrugged. When I told him about the otters I'd seen in Valdez, he gave me a dark look, then said that if the guard here had his numbers right, the best explanation would be that the otters were arriving in a lot better shape.

It was a simple enough answer and, as it turned out, a perfectly reasonable one. By this time — June — a majority of the toxic aromatics were gone from the oil. The bulk of the otters that were hit hardest by the oil had been hit immediately, and those that remained out in the waters might have been situated in relatively clear areas to begin with. They might have learned to avoid the oil. Their main vulnerability by this point might have been to the secondary and tertiary effects Kathy Frost had spoken of.

I would eventually learn that by the summer months the success rate at all the otter centers was indeed in the 90 percent range. In October, Lisa Rotterman would tell me that as time went on, many of the otters brought in survived for just the reason Bruce had suggested, that indeed some were captured from spottily oiled areas, that whatever problems they had upon arrival in the rescue centers came mainly from the stress of being chased and captured. Some of the boat people, she said, were confused, or driven by excessive enthusiasm, or by greed. There was big money in "otter rescue," thousands of dollars a day. One reason Fish and Wildlife had proposed closing down Kelly Weaverling's rescue operation back in April — the stress upon healthy animals — had turned completely around. Otter rescue contracts had continued to be let. Randall Davis told me that there was disagreement among the veterinarians over how to judge whether or not an otter should be brought in. Some felt that any slightly oiled otter should be captured. Others felt that even moderately oiled otters should be left alone. From a boat, there was no way to tell a moderately or lightly oiled otter except by chasing it. It also became a technical question. There was no objective method for detecting oil in fur. In August, Fish and Wildlife issued a permit to capture 16 otters to test a spectrophotometric method for measuring oil. One of the 16 had detectable oil in its fur.

The lights of Seward glimmered faintly just beyond the otter center. It was 8:45 in the evening, almost time to go. There were nine days to solstice, and the pale, slowly deepening twilight had just begun. Across the bay, the mountains were dark blue, almost black. Directly before me, the pale blue water of the bay was tinged with green and the milk color of glacial silt. The green gave an appearance of depth to the blue and the milkiness gave it opacity. It was the extraordinary and changeable mineral-like color again for which I had no name. Down along the bay, the dark humps of small islands were visible. At the edge of the bank and along the mouth of the stream, eight men were fishing for pink salmon in the rising tide. Soon, the water would churn with spawning fish, and they would appear in the estuary, exhausted, dark, hook-jawed, and breaking surface with the humps of their backs. At the moment, the water was quiet. The men matter-of-factly cast and reeled in their lines, or fooled with their gear.

Seward had some 2,000 residents, although its population would temporarily rise by close to 1,000 before the oil spill summer of 1989 was over. The tsunami that followed the 1964 earthquake had destroyed its port installations. Through the succeeding years the town had broadened and stabilized its economy. Fishing and associated industries remained the chief source of revenue. There was a strong government presence, a maximum security prison, a vocational school, and a nursing home financed by oil-rich state coffers. In the last five years, 3 million tons of coal were delivered by rail, then shipped out of Seward's port to Korea. Rising out of the complicated ironies of the modern Alaskan economy, a timber industry was being developed by the Chugach Native Corporation, and soon a state-of-the-art mill would open. Industry practices, which were controversial both within and without the Native community, included targeting long-term production to the Asian market, old growth harvesting and clear-cutting[41] right down to the waterlines and along watersheds. Before the oil spill, fishermen here and in Prince William Sound had considered the timber industry their most immediate threat to the fisheries. In the years immediately following, this threat would emerge again from under the oil spill's shadow.

Like Valdez, Seward had a highway to connect it to Anchorage. Seward's population was opportunistic, quick to assess a changed situation, and to capitalize on it. Each of Veco International's cleanup subsidiaries, Veco Inc., and Norcon, would use Seward as a base of operations. Bill Noll, then a

---

[41] Old growth stands include centuries-old trees and sustain long-established and complex ecosystems. Also, because of the tightness and clarity of its grain, the wood in old growth trees is generally superior to new growth. Clear-cutting is a heavily mechanized form of logging by which, for the sake of efficiency, all timber growth is removed from a large tract of land.

member of the Seward City Council and one of the leaders of the oil spill response during the summer, and later to be elected mayor, would tell me in November that "Seward did not get involved with trying to pick sides. The reporters go back to New York. Sure, the spill was a national tragedy, but mooning and crying don't get it fixed. If Exxon's to blame, then pay up, Exxon. A lot of people in Seward feel like that."

Some distance out in the water from where I stood was a "sheen," a remnant from the oil that had filled Resurrection Bay and kissed the Seward shoreline on April 17, 24 days after the spill. I was surprised that so little was evident. I bent to catch the sunlight slanting against the skim and saw that there was maybe a quarter-acre or so of the stuff. On the water, the oily swirls were visible by their shine and changeable coloration — red, gray, blue, and white. On a larger scale it was the same as what one sees on an asphalt parking lot after a rain. The fish the men were jigging for would skirt the sheen.

The tide had begun to rise and suddenly the salmon were running in earnest. The surface of the water churned from their density. They could be heard, chopping through the water and slapping in the shallows of the stream. The activity of the men at the water's edge intensified. They cast repeatedly into the roil. A Native man in jeans, plaid shirt, and high rubber boots hooked one, reeled it in, netted it, and walked up the bank and dumped it out not far from where I stood. He picked up a stone and hit it over the head, then returned to the water's edge to recast his line.

I eyed the fish, looking for some sign of oil, but saw none. A five-year-old boy, the man's son, clambered down the bank and stood over the fish. He picked up a stick and hit it, circled it and hit it again. A younger brother came down. The brother found another stick and hit the fish in the head. The two of them circled the fish and struck it repeatedly. It was a two-foot salmon, a good one, silvery and scarcely mottled with decay: a wild run *Oncorhynchus gorbuscha*, known variously as pink, humpbacked, or humpy. The pinks were the staple of the salmon crop, like brown-skinned potatoes or field corn, the most abundant of the species and the primary product of the hatcheries and commercial canneries. The canned salmon for sale in the grocery stores is almost invariably pink salmon. These men were catching them to take home to be smoked, dried, or canned and stored for winter.

Soon, the fish lay still where the boys' father had lodged it between two black rocks. Down at the edge of the bank, the other men were catching fish, one after another, and helping each other land them. The storm cloud had come near to us and the light turned to a radiant gray. A white seiner cruised slowly toward the docks across the bay. The blue, green, and milk-colored water took on the gray of the cloud. The oil sheen became almost invisible. The bending figures of the fishermen were dark against the darker rock and the bright fish flashed one after another as they were pulled from the water.

I understood what the boys were doing, hitting that fish — mainly because I had been a boy, once, and had three children of my own. It was a form of play or ritual that had to do with making capture and death familiar. It was akin to setting fire to an ant hill, but touched with exquisite and complete directness upon these boys' knowledge of the world, for to them death and the taking of quarry was a daily thing. They stood above the fish and looked at it, seeing its silver against the black rock, the incipient hump behind its head, the darker curve of gill, the hook of the open jaw. They prodded the fish and found it tensile, still filled with the tautness of life. They were engaged in an inquiry, asking — *What is this?* And maybe having been told that the fish had left this stream and returned a year or more later, knowing that it would be eaten, their inquiry might become layered with spiritual and moral dimensions and so extend into their own risky time. They might also ask for rightness of mind and thought. In their looking, they asked all the questions.

I returned to the *Alpha Helix*. As we set out, a group of us stood on the foredeck to watch. I looked at the white seiner a pair of binoculars. Two men dressed in yellow slickers were on the deck, hoisting plastic garbage sacks to a third man on the dock. The sacks looked heavy. Their contents shifted around, making them unwieldy. The man on the dock loaded them into a pickup. They were oiled birds, I suspected, brought in from the sea for the count. After that, they would be stored in the freezer trucks to be kept as evidence. The boat and three men passed from view as the *Alpha Helix* headed slowly down the long bay.

The rattle of the anchor chain playing out against the hull of the *Alpha Helix* was usually the last call for action. By the time the anchor hit bottom, one of the three inflatable Zodiacs or the wooden whaler had been lowered by the crane from the rear deck to the water alongside the ship. John Oliver, a compact bundle of energy, would be there, urging on the lowering of the next Zodiac and directing traffic . . . that gear bag into that Zodiac, that set of tanks there, those weights there, and these people together in the red Zodiac, you four in the gray one, you in the whaler . . .

His graduate students, of whom there were five among the thirteen-person science crew, would spin around, apportion the gear, drag the oxygen tanks across the steel deck, quickly secure the zippers and gauges on each other's diving suits, and then, once he was sure everybody was pitched in the right direction, John would be gone, the first one out with his team, down the ladder and behind the controls of the Zodiac with the biggest engine, the red one. He would cry out, "It's a good place to die," jerk back the throttle and slam through the swells at top speed toward his diving site.

A highly regarded benthic marine biologist, John Oliver was about five feet nine. He had light red hair and a complexion inclined toward pinkness. His students referred to him as "science in motion." He had been described to me by a mutual friend before I met him as "the bandit scientist." I was finally unable to resist raising the matter with John. When I did, he grinned and said, "Oh no, we're way beyond that, now." Just what he meant, whether he'd gone so deeply into banditry that he'd come out the other side burned clean, or if he'd adjusted his course, was not clear to me until much later.

On the night of the twelfth, as the *Alpha Helix* made its way from Seward to Prince William Sound, several of us sat in the galley, the principal gathering place on the ship. It was kept clean and snug. It had white walls, fixed chairs and tables. The tables had ledges and little corrals at their heads to hold things — a precaution against the roll of the ship. It was a place of comfort, inviting aromas, and conversation, a refuge against the rawness of the outside. Back in a corner, a pot of coffee was always on. Between the dining area and the kitchen stood a serving bar and beneath it a set of stainless steel coolers that were kept stocked with drink and food, most notably ice cream, which seemed to be a staple in the diet. The ship's cook, Trish Kaminsky, who knew the habits of John and his crews from previous voyages, and probably a few things about sugar and high-velocity activity, as well, had already announced that she'd loaded her freezers with extra quantities of the stuff.

We were eating strawberry ice cream on the night of the twelfth, big bowls of it, and talking desultorily about the ship, the weather, the sound, the oil. John said that what was required to chart the effects of oil were scientists who were familiar with the area and able to follow a project over a period of time. Also, he said, they should be "the sharpest possible scientists, who are also generalists, people capable of seeing things at the edges of vision."

There were others on more intimate terms with Prince William Sound than John, but he was experienced with oil spills and his own ability to use the edges of vision was excellent. Although ecological or "whole earth," and even "indigenous" thought have made an energetic entry into the biological sciences in recent years, the use of closely defined parameters to create a controlled research environment is still, and understandably so, the principle means of research. The universe is vast. Human capabilities are small. The trick, it would seem, is to scrupulously exercise the tools of controlled research and at the same time to retain the ability to look up, or away. There might be something in the air or out in the peripheries of the water column that is affecting the grids. There is really nothing new about this necessity of science and existence — to see what is before one, to see or even to imagine what is not before one. It's a function of intelligence, but not necessarily of formal education. The failure to see what lies beyond the edges of scrutiny — including, perhaps, the reason for tears or to carefully register what is felt, may be caused by a preexisting structure, either an external one that is exerting leverage, such as a government agency, or an internal, inflexible mind set.

As it happened, this voyage had been in the planning stages prior to the oil spill. It was originally intended as a part of a research project directed toward the feeding habitats of sea otters. John Oliver and Rikk Kvitek, of the Department of Zoology at the University of Washington, were seeking otter feeding sites and samples to use as a basis for comparison with other sites in Glacier Bay and along the coast of Washington, Oregon, and California. The buildup in recent years of the otter population in Prince William Sound (due to federal protection), and the resulting pressure upon otter food (clams, urchins, mussels, crabs, and fish) made the region interesting to them.

The oil spill had several effects upon their work. It came to be a part of their proposal to the National Science Foundation and therefore guaranteed their funding, but also increased the pressure upon the crew. There were now two major planes of observation — otter predation, oil — and each was to be approached through a form of survey. This suited John Oliver. To pretend that any occurrence, natural or otherwise, was discrete would have been contrary to his nature, and this, I would ultimately conclude, was where his banditry had come to lodge — in the freedom of his spirit, the steadfastness of his trust in inquiry, and his resistance under at times difficult circumstances to being driven by a predetermined system.

The ship did have a basic itinerary, or a floating plan, which John arrived at and amended through consultation with the captain of the ship, Tom Callahan, and other principal parties. Principal seemed to mean whoever had the most specific requirements at a given time or place, and usually included Rikk Kvitek and, in the initial stages of the trip, Gordon Robilliard, whose San Diego-based environmental consulting company was doing shoreline survey work for Exxon by virtue of a contract let by a Seattle-based consulting firm, Dames and Moore. Gordon had been added to the crew in the later stages of planning.

The basic itinerary, however, did not preordain what exact sites were to be examined from one anchorage to the next, nor did it necessarily seem to mean that anyone — even at times John Oliver, or Rikk Kvitek, or the captain of the ship — knew exactly what the plan was. In response to my own sometimes befuddled attempts to grasp what was going on, John would several times say that we would look at "whatever was interesting." It was not unusual to see him in the red Zodiac heading off full tilt in one direction, then slowing, rising from the saddle behind the wheel and peering off in a direction tangential to his course, and settling back down, throttling and swinging the Zodiac around in a wide arc toward a previously unanticipated objective . . . a rock or small island, maybe, a shoreline with an inviting-looking escarpment.

That was the method. No electronic monitors here, and not much in the way of chunks of habitat cordoned off for extended observation, but mainly just people looking and counting, making records, scratching the bottom, digging up shell debris left by otters and prying urchins loose from rocks. By the time we were done, the diving teams would have examined and taken samples from between 40 and 50 sites. More than 20 shorelines would have been inspected. The trip was a very aggressive survey undertaken by a posse of marine range riders. John communicated the sense of everything out there in the world being ephemeral, forever on the verge of slipping away. One had to be quick to get at it. There was a definite predatory quality to all of this, the electric buzz of preparation, the demands on the students, the dives themselves probing the deep, the booty brought to the lab, and the ice cream afterwards used to jack everybody back up. But at the outset, especially, John's joy in the pursuit of ephemerality, even of joining it, was contagious. In the beginning, when he appeared on the deck before a diving sortie in his red-and-black diving suit, replete with hookups and gadgets, he looked like an impish road warrior, ready to engage in battle with the eternal Proteus.

The path of the *Alpha Helix* would be approximately backwards along the direction the oil had followed. We would enter the sound at the southwestern edge, move toward the center, then swing clockwise. In the early afternoon of June 13, the ship set anchor just north of Point Elrington at the extreme edge of the sound. Once the diving teams were off, the last group of five of us made the first shore party. We donned our blaze orange float jackets and set out in the wooden whaler for North Twin Bay. Besides myself, the group included Bruce Stewart, Gordon Robilliard, Peter Slattery, and Kathy Conlan.

The bay was deeply indented into the island. On a map it looked like a mouth agape, turned away ever so slightly from the gulf. As we entered into its protection, the chop of the sea against our left, or on the northern side of the bay, a sea lion slid off a rock and vanished into the water. Up above, tufted puffins flew in and out of their rookery in the cliffs. There was a passage in the air filled with them. They were stout, betasseled birds that had a determined aspect like small, antiquated bombs. They fed by diving, or "flying underwater," and so had been thought to be especially vulnerable to the oil. The birds were passing back and forth between a feeding ground out at sea and the young in their burrows. The sky was gray. They disappeared out there. They were soundless, as is the way with puffins, who make only a guttural noise in the vicinity of their nests.

The water around the whaler was clear. We landed and the five of us spread out. The beach was composed of cobbled rock. There was no immediate sign of oil. I followed Gordon Robilliard along the northern arc of the bay toward the cliffs. A harbor seal poked its head up about 40 feet from shore and looked at us. In the curve of its skull and in the way its head lay low just above the water, it was unmistakably seal, the fur brown, the snout and eyes dark. In the equipoise of its position and its bodily address to us there seemed to be intelligence, an inquiry into our presence: *What is this?* It disappeared. Overhead, the puffins flew back and forth, as intent as small fullbacks.

Gordon found a chest-high patch of oil on a rock, and it became easy, then, to locate more oil at the same level along the outer rim of the beach. The oil had been carried in by a high tide and had left its traces like a bathtub ring. Gordon marked it down in his book. We turned and walked toward the southern half of the beach where Peter and Kathy had gone. The footing abruptly grew uncertain. I looked down. The stones had taken on a sheen. The farther we went, the darker the sheen became until it was the amber color of engine oil. The rocks grew steadily larger as we moved around from the center of the beach, and the footing became precarious. Kathy Conlan, wearing green hip boots, had waded into the shallows to search the oiled rocks. She stood in the midst of an oil sheen and called out her findings to Peter Slattery, a stout man with a red beard, who was at the edge of the shore, crouched over Kathy's Zip-Loc specimen bags, helping to organize them.

The bags contained amphipods, mainly, the tiny shrimplike creatures that Kathy planned to take home to Ottawa. The amphipods were alive.

She'd found barnacles and periwinkles alive on the rocks, living in oil. Kathy returned to shore and showed us a gum boot chiton she'd found. The gum boot was a good eight inches long and flatly built. Its eight cream-colored plates were coated with oil like the rock it had been found on. Chitons fed by grazing rocks for algae and detritus. Kathy turned this one over. Its long, peach-colored foot was smeared with oil. Now, two harbor seals poked their heads up to look at the four of us from just beyond the edge of the oil sheen. They were watchful, and seemed calm. They ducked out of sight, then reappeared to look from a different vantage point. The sea lion had not reappeared. Over on the other side of the beach, a column of puffins still flew out. Another column flew back.

We all moved back to the center of the beach and then up and across a quarter-mile of densely overgrown land bridge. There were birds here, sparrows and thrushes that scuttered ahead of us and rattled sideways into the brush. It was then, because of the whip of their wings and their alarmed chirps, that the silence of the beach we'd just come from struck me. We broke out into the open at the top of another beach on the opposite side of the island, facing Elrington Passage. The scientists scattered. No one said anything. This place smelled of oil. Kathy immediately carried her net and bucket into the water and began searching a group of large rocks just offshore. Bruce and Peter poked at the algae. Gordon moved along the beach, then sat down on a log and began writing in his book. In terms of impact, he would say, this beach was maybe a four or five on a scale of ten.

The upper wrack of algae was lightly coated with oil. Below it a fresh set of deer tracks approached a line of eel grass, then stopped and broke back toward a clump of alders. It had been startled away by our approach. Fifteen feet or so down, the lower algae wrack was so heavily oiled that when stepped on, it gurgled and emitted a sharp stench. Below that, oil covered the rocks and lay in pools in the crevices and depressions. Out in the water, dense ribbons of it slipped around the protruding rocks and undulated slowly with the motion of the ebbing tide. As Kathy moved, it swirled around her boots.

A fishing boat, no doubt leased out as a cleanup vessel, was nestled some distance away against a small island. Behind it was another shoreline. It made a vista — dark rocks, green spruce trees deepening almost to black on the slopes, and gray, luminous sky. My feet were in oil. Before me the water was black with oil, then further out it took on the dreamlike color of blue, green, and milk. Overhead, first one bald eagle, then a second appeared. They flashed in and out of sight as they circled in overlapping arcs. They were looking for food to carry to the young they had nested in a snag on the land bridge between the two beaches.

On either side of the land bridge was a microcosm of the entire chaos: on the other side a half-clean, half-oiled beach, and on this side a heavily oiled beach, over there harbor seals that would become oiled if they hauled out on the wrong rock, a somewhat less imperiled sea lion, and puffins that seemed to have so far avoided the risk of diving into oiled waters, and over here one line of algae that might survive, another line that would not, a deer that might ingest oiled eel grass and die, and eagles that might tear into that fouled carrion, and no doubt a bear in the woods that might also feed on the carrion or lick the oil off its paws after walking across the beach, and in the intertidal region wildly varying levels of damage for the clams, mussels, shrimp, starfish, urchins, kelp, and chitons. Kathy found surviving barnacles, mussels, and amphipods around those rocks on this side, but the far greater hazard lay here, no doubt because this bay faced one of the channels down which the oil had flowed. The beach on the other side had more wind, more exposure, and perhaps was in its presently bisected state because of an eddying effect as the currents drove the oil around the tip of the island. The oil had less opportunity to settle over there. Some of it had already been scoured off by the wave action.

Along with Bainbridge, Evans, Latouche, and Montague, and to the north Knight Island, Elrington is one of the group of islands that form a broken barrier to the south and west of Prince William Sound. At the approximate geographical center of Prince William Sound is Naked Island, to which the *Exxon Valdez* had been towed on the twelfth day after the spill. The predominant currents move counterclockwise, although this basic directional tendency is complicated not only by the irregularity of land masses on the surface but by the like irregularity beneath the surface. There are crosscurrents. The water moves in contrary directions and shears against itself. Due to the extreme differences of depth, stream flow from the land, and glacial outlets, the temperature of the water varies. Again, because of outflow from land, the density of the water changes. There are differences in the levels of salinity or sediment load.

The Japan Current, or Kuroshio, swings clockwise by the gulf. The Alaska Current, a big, powerful eddy of Kuroshio, flows counterclockwise just off the continental shelf. Within the sound, there are underwater eddies, highly variable tidal patterns, and unpredictable winds (these the intricacies of the water known most intimately by fishing people). Some of these irregularities are minor. Others, such as prevailing currents (also counterclockwise in the sound) and the wind, are significant. Taken together, they create a mosaic of forces which are in a constant state of interplay and flux. Since oil is lighter than water, it is somewhat less affected by its own inertia than water. In a wind it may shear from the surface of the water and skim. In calm water, it spreads laterally. In the presence of surface currents, it will move at their speed, and it is otherwise affected by waves.

Over time, the oil changes its nature, seeking stability. The bulk of the lighter-weight aromatic hydrocarbons — benzenes, xylenes, etc. — evaporate within 48 hours after a spill. These are also the most toxic elements, and through inhalation and absorption were the primary cause of the first, devastating loss of animals. The heavier aromatics, which are chronically toxic, may enter into temporary solution in the water, though in much smaller quantities than the evaporated aromatics. Their dispersion in water may be effected in part through metabolism by bacteria and other organisms over a relatively long period of time. These metabolic processes introduce toxic elements into the food chain.

If the oil has a concentration of waxes and asphaltics, as does Prudhoe crude, it may mix with water and form mousse, at which point weathering of the entirety can be dramatically impeded because of the sealing effect of water. Cleanup also becomes much more difficult. Most skimming machinery is designed to pick up oil, not heavy concentrations of water. As time passes, the oil becomes heavier. It may collect sediment, thus becoming heavy enough to sink, or it may adhere to beaches. Eventually, Prudhoe crude becomes asphaltic. The oil has its own complex set of internal forces. It simultaneously follows its own dynamic and interplays with whatever it touches, deepening the complication of the mosaic. There are no computerized models that come close to replicating the complexity of the movement and gradual decay of oil in a place like Prince William Sound, Cook Inlet, or the Gulf of Alaska.

This is one reason why the oil industry is so actively interested in a fast-acting remedy, such as dispersants which, if effectively applied, would have the real advantage of drastically increasing the rate of the oil's weathering, and the public relations advantage of making oil seem to disappear. It is also why it was hoped that the oil would exit to the Gulf of Alaska and keep going out to the open sea where it would disperse on its own — that is, gradually break up into increasingly smaller and less visible packages, ultimately transferring the last of its discrete droplets into the water column. It may also be why Exxon flew in the face of the physical evidence and repeatedly exaggerated both the likelihood and the facts of dispersal. A month after the spill, Exxon still clung to the vestiges of its hope and told a *New York Times* reporter that 66 percent of the spill had been eliminated: 13 percent by cleaning, 35 percent by evaporation, 8 percent by burning, 5 percent by biological breakdown, and 5 percent by disintegration. Every one of the figures was preposterous. The figure for evaporation represented a physical impossibility since no more than 22 percent of Prudhoe Bay crude can evaporate — the March 25 test burn eliminated at most 30,000 gallons of the slick, or about one-third of one percent of the reported 11 million gallon total,[42] and the figures for biological breakdown and disintegration were both exaggerated and blurred. When I quoted the figures to Kathy Frost, she laughed and said, "What's the difference between biological breakdown and disintegration? And how did they measure it?"[43]

By March 28, the oil had moved by both the eastern and western sides of Naked, Eleanor, Ingot, and all of Knight Island. By the thirtieth, it had ricocheted off the inside shores of Montague Island and hit Latouche Island. By the thirty-first, it had entered Elrington and Latouche Passages on either side of Elrington Island. During the first few days of April it had touched all the channels in the group of strainer islands and parked itself off the coast of the Kenai Peninsula. Parts of it would wash back toward the sound, and then wash out again, and go back-and-forth repeatedly. Other parts would go up Resurrection Bay, Cook Inlet, and by mid-May reach out to Kodiak Island and slip behind Kodiak to the Alaska Peninsula.

Those central and southwestern islands were the same ones I had seen on my overflight in early April. The channels between them vary from narrow to wide, deep to shallow, but the overall pattern as the current and the oil moved nearer the edge of the sound is one of increasing constriction, as of a funnel. The visible edges of the islands are infinitely complex, and so they provided a variable and gradually tightening obstruction to the oil that flowed by them before it was released from the sound. The effect of tidal movement works in sympathy with the irregularities of land. For these reasons, what we saw at North Twin Bay on Elrington Island and the bay across the isthmus was a primer for the diversity of damage that was in store for us. While the

[42] And a yet much smaller percentage, of course, if the total spill amounted to 25-30 million gallons.

[43] In another of the many contrasts with Exxon's April figures, Steven Provant of the DEC would estimate in mid-September that somewhat over 6 million gallons, or a little over half of what was thought to be the original spill, remained, much of it on the shorelines. Once again, if the true figure of the spill was 25-30 million gallons, the amount of the residual at that time would be increased.

basic course the oil would follow might have been known, the detail of its impact could never have been predicted.

During the evening of the twelfth, the *Alpha Helix* edged toward Knight Island. It has the most intricate shorelines of any island in the sound and after the boundary islands, Montague and Hinchinbrook, the largest land mass. Its bays are so long that at several points they cut almost completely across it. We anchored for the night in Snug Harbor, a large bay near the southeastern end of the island that would be used as a site for research on dispersants and bioremediation.

Diving teams had been out to the island. They had grim tales of oil on the shorelines. Knight Island had taken the brunt of the hit. Their reports of conditions beneath the water, however, were much more hopeful. Rikk Kvitek was normally dour, but even he seemed buoyed by what he'd seen. In the galley, he said, "Things are carrying on as normal. It's business as usual. The barnacles are alive. The algae is still working. The polychaetes are alive." I went to the deck after dinner and gazed out at the island. It was about nine o'clock and we were still well within the long, luminous twilight. The *Alpha Helix* was parked in an oil slick. The stuff lapped and stuck to the hull. Three fishing boats were anchored near to shore. The edges of Snug Harbor glistened with oil. Beyond the beach was bush, then trees, then the snow-capped mountains. It was utterly quiet.

The next morning, the *Alpha Helix* cut back south. A party of us went to shore at Sleepy Bay on Latouche Island. Sleepy Bay is at the northern tip of Latouche, a big cavity, an opening like a waiting embrace. There was oil at least a foot down. When I tried to walk, I slid around on the rocks. When I stepped on an algae wrack, my boots sank deeply into the slime. Each step broke the seal of oil and the stink came out — oil, carrion, and decay like shit. At times, I had to reach down and grab the top of a boot to extract it. Pools of oil hung on in the depressions and crevices in the rock. It swirled thickly in the water and clung to both sides of a line of boom. Gordon Robilliard said that this beach was about a six on a scale of ten, which left hanging the question of what a ten would be like. There was no sign of life here, not a single bird. Kathy Conlan waded out into the murk, then came back and searched the algae wrack for amphipods. Here, she found nothing.

9

THE
RAPTURE OF
MACHINES

Alaska Falsejingle
Alaska Volute
Amphipod
Ancient Murrelet
Arctic Fox
Arctic Loon
Arctic Surfclam
Bald Eagle
Barrow's Goldeneye
Beaver
Black-legged Kittiwake
Black Rockfish
Black Scoter
Black-tailed Deer
Black Turnstone

Bonaparte's Gull
Broad Snow Crab
Brown Bear
Bufflehead
California Armina
Canada Goose
Canary Rockfish
Chinook Salmon
Chum Salmon
Clay Pipe Sponge
Coho Salmon
Common Eider
Common Goldeneye
Common Merganser
Common Murre

Coonstrip Shrimp
Coyote
Crisscrossed Yoldia
Dall's Porpoise
Double-crested
  Cormorant
Dungeness Crab
Eel Grass
European Starling
Feathery Shipworm
Fuzzy Crab
Glaucous Gull
Golden Eagle
Great Horned Owl
Gray Whale

Gray Wolf
Hairy Cockle
Harbor Porpoise
Harbor Seal
Harlequin Duck
Hermit Sponge
Herring Gull
Horned Grebe
Horned Puffin
Horsehair Crab
Humpback Whale
Humpy Shrimp
Kelp
King Crab
Kittlitz's Murrelet
Knobbyhand
Hermit Crab
Ladder Whelk
Limpet
Longhorned Decorator
  Crab
Magistrate Armhook
  Squid
Mallard
Man
Marbled Murrelet
Milky Venus
Mink
Northern Crow
Northern Goshawk

Northern Horsemussel
Northern Pintail
Oldsquaw
Orange Bat Star
Orange-pink Sea
  Urchin
Orca
Pacific Halibut
Pacific Herring
Pacific Sea Lemon
Parakeet Auklet
Parma Sand Dollar
Pea Crab
Pelagic Cormorant
Phalarope
Pigeon Guillemot
Pine Grosbeak
Pink Salmon
Porcupine
Red-breasted
  Merganser
Red-faced
  Cormorant
Red Fox
Red-necked Grebe
Red Sea Urchin
Red Squirrel
Red-throated Loon
Rhinoceros Auklet
Ridged Crangon

River Otter
Robust Clubhook Squid
Rusty Moonsnail
Sablefish
Sea-clown Triopha
Sea Otter
Sea Raspberry
Sei Whale
Shrew
Slender Seawhip
Sockeye Salmon
Sparrow
Spot Shrimp
Steller Sea Lion
Steller's Eider
Surfbird
Surf Scoter
Tanner Crab
Trenched Nutclam
Tufted Puffin
Vole
Warped Whelk
Weathervane
  Scallop
White-winged Scoter
Wolverine
Yellow-billed Loon
Yelloweye Rockfish
Yule Grass

— Partial list of species affected or killed by the *Exxon Valdez* spill,
compiled by Jody Morgan, *Equinox*, July/August 1989

For two days the *Alpha Helix* remained in the vicinity of northwestern Knight Island and the group of islands just off its northernmost tip — Disk, Ingot, Sphinx, Block, and Eleanor. Besides Knight, two of the islands — Ingot and Eleanor — are sizable bodies of land. The others are small. On a map, the group of them look like morsels broken away from the big chunk. At close range, they seem separated from Knight Island only by the merest happenstance of water level. A shore party I accompanied would find two of them — Eleanor and Block — joined at low tide by a land bridge.

Night was a squint of darkness that closed briefly and then reopened. We retired at midnight and rose at four or five in the morning. Throughout the night, the befuddling light seeped through the portholes to the cabins. During the day, the skin absorbed the light. The body took the light into its darkness and felt oddly large and soft. The mind seemed to compose itself within — in a pool of radiant white. The diving teams, driven by light, worked from six in the morning to nine or ten in the evening.

We had passed across the verge into the heart of the oil's blackness, and were close to the source of the original slick. Great fields of oil had passed here. "Knight Island is the heart of Prince William Sound," David Grimes would say to me several months later, and by then his words would strike a chord in me. There is something decidedly mysterious about Knight Island, a primitive power that has to do with its size, irregularity, and the line of its peaks, two, three, and four thousand feet high, that make a jagged spine visible from great distances. "It's the lodestone. It's appropriate that it was the hardest hit," David would say, and then, veering toward animism, he added, "It opened its arms to the oil. The oil was surprised to be taken out of the earth and released from heat and pressure. It was homeless, and sought stability, and went to Knight Island."

The *Alpha Helix* was less than ten miles from the bay on the western side of Naked Island where the *Exxon Valdez* had been anchored for over two months for repairs, and where, despite the company's repeated claims to the contrary, it continued to leak oil. The ship was still there, since the authorities in Portland, Oregon, had strongly discouraged the company from sending it to their harbor for repairs. Given the political cast of Oregon, to have sent it there would have been to court a local display of outrage. The Coast Guard took it a step further and indulged itself in a romance of law and order when it raised the possibility of sabotage by what Captain James Calhoun called "radical elements." Exxon backed off. Calhoun's phrase provoked the public question as to just what was meant by "radical elements."

Although those of us on the *Alpha Helix* weren't aware of it, since we had been out of touch with the news, a two-million-dollar plan had just been announced to tow the *Valdez* to San Diego, where it would be repaired by the company that had built it, the National Steel and Shipbuilding Company. In another of the relentless and mind-boggling expressions of optimism by Exxon officials, it was announced by Exxon Shipping that the entire ship had been cleaned of crude oil and would not leak. When the ship was towed out of Prince William Sound on June 24, it trailed a mile-long oil sheen.

At the time of my voyage on the *Alpha Helix*, the cleanup activity was centered in the area of Knight Island, and what for the crew had been previously a nearly private witnessing would now add machine and man to the picture. Early in the morning of the fourteenth, I heard the thudding sound of a helicopter. I moved out from the *Alpha Helix's* galley to the deck to look. In the pale light a large gray shape loomed up, a navy vessel that Exxon had leased out. The *Alpha Helix* as it swung around the northern edge of Eleanor Island came nearer to the navy ship. Secured to the ship's starboard side were two barges that made a dock for three fishing boats. The barges also had shelters erected on them to form a cover for supplies. Overhead on the ship's deck stood a crane, used for loading. One helicopter rested on a landing pad at the foredeck. The other helicopter approached across the pale blue sky, then circled and hovered above the pad. In the distance beyond the ship was the dark outline of Naked Island. The helicopter descended to the pad. Its rotors slowed to a stop and four men in dress slacks clambered out. They were observers, presumably executives, politicians, or reporters.

An hour later, Kathy Conlan, Kim Kiest, a graduate student from Moss Landing, and myself put ashore on Eleanor Island near what is called Upper Passage, a channel between Eleanor and Ingot Islands. We were not far from Block Island. The bay we came into was shallow and nearly ringed by land. There were traces of oil in the water, bands of it that encircled the protruding rocks. We cut our outboard motor and tipped it up to protect the propeller blades from the bottom, coasted to land, then waded ashore. The beach was composed of a coarse sand and it had at first glance an inexplicable pale beige color, a whiteness.

Before me was the small bay, and at the intersection of water and earth a line of greenish, gummy matter — diatoms. To my right, the beach gave way to a line of rock faces. Kim moved that way. At my back, Kathy worked her way up a small stream, upending rocks and digging into the clumps of growth. She had her tools with her — the net, the bucket, the plastic Zip-Loc bags. To my left and separated by a line of rocks was a tidepool. Its water was dark and its far bank drenched with oil. Above it was a long, narrow landform, dense with growth. I moved that way. From the distance, the high noise of a two-cycle engine slipped in and out of audibility. Scattered all across the beach were bits of broken shell. The wrack of brown algae appeared to be alive, if discolored, but when kicked even lightly it broke free. I crouched and picked up a handful of sand. When I dropped it, a thin, clear sheen was left on my palm. What was wrong here had just begun to dawn on me when Kathy said, "It's been cleaned."

I looked up. Kathy was on her knees at the edge of the stream. "It's barren," she said. "It's like a desert." It was true. The sand was the color of the Mojave. It lacked the deepening hue of organic debris and of the plethora of tiny living things that normally flourished on its surface. This color was wrong. The beach, we would learn, had been cleaned by the "hot-water wash" method a few days before. "It looks like a sewage-polluted beach that's been taken under protection," Kathy said. "It's only the really hardy stuff that's survived."

The "hardy stuff" she referred to consisted in this case of two species of amphipods that she found in the stream. She speculated that they might have survived because of the presence of freshwater runoff. Amphipods had come to intrigue me because of their strong capacity for survival, and because they were near the bottom of the food chain. They are commonly known as beach hoppers or sand fleas, the tiny creatures found on beaches that sometimes bite and that have the ability to suddenly straighten their backs and leap. Some species are microscopic. Others grow quite large and are a food source for salmon and (the gammarid) for gray whales. The ones Kathy found were usually about a third of an inch long. Nearly flat on their two sides, they lay on the tip of a finger and wriggled.

Reproduction is triggered by "carrying," a process by which the male attaches itself to the female, sometimes for long periods, and Kathy was concerned about the lack of reproductive activity among the specimens she found but finally reached no conclusion on the matter. Amphipods are primarily but not exclusively marine animals, and many tolerate radical changes in salinity. They are usually but not always bottom feeders. Many are strong swimmers. They may be herbivorous, carnivorous, or both. They are voracious and opportunistic. True marauders, they eat what presents itself to them. In a way, they are the coyotes of the intertidal zone because of their capacity to live almost anywhere, to eat almost anything, to thrive in the face of any menace. Long line fishermen sometimes find their lines stripped of bait by amphipods. Several nights before, Kathy had shown me one under the microscope in the lab of the *Alpha Helix*. It lay on its side and wriggled its many appendages — legs, antennae, and a set of powerful graspers clustered near its mandible. Kathy explained that museums use amphipods to clean specimens for skeletal displays. A pit is dug, filled with water, and the specimen — a seal, say, or a whale — is dropped into the pit along with a good dose of amphipods. Before long, the skeleton is clean. On the dish beneath the microscope, the amphipod looked like a shrimp. Its body was nearly transparent, luminous as a chip of moonlight. It was possible to look right through the creature to its other side.

Peter Slattery had told me, "They're not that important, probably," by which he meant that they would probably recolonize. In his opinion, their power of survival was so strong that they would come back even if they were wiped out of a certain site. In the great debate over what happened to fouled shorelines, the power of certain creatures to survive or return was critical. Peter and Kathy had found amphipods living on oiled rocks. Generally, they found two species of amphipods on oiled beaches, and three species on the unoiled. The first beach we'd visited — North Twin Bay on Elrington Island — overlapped with an amphipod survey a colleague of Kathy's, Dr. Ed Bousfield, had conducted in 1961. She found two species there where he had found one. This was hopeful, if the flimsiest shred of a comparative finding.

In my effort to understand, it seemed important to find survivors capable of containing hydrocarbon doses lethal to others, of surviving drastic changes in the chemistry that surrounded them. What if the species lost on oiled beaches were genetically discrete? If so, the amphipod gene pool would be interrupted. What if the species that survived suffered sublethal toxic effects from the heavy aromatics that might affect its reproductive capabilities or be passed on to its predators?

On Eleanor Island, I stepped into the stream to cross to Kathy's side. A dark cloud rose from the bottom and swirled around my boot. I stepped again and raised another cloud. I dipped my hand into the stream. Water and oil droplets separated from each other in my palm. The oil must have percolated to the stream bottom from the subsurface elsewhere. I turned back and dug through the sand with a stick, creating a small hole about four inches deep. Quickly, the bottom of the hole filled with oil. I dug another hole in the beach, and another, and a small trench four inches wide and six inches deep. Each time, the black oil seeped into the bottom and rose to its level a couple of inches beneath the surface. Except for the amphipods and oil-fouled diatoms at the edge of water and sand — which, Kathy and Kim would surmise, had washed in with the tide after the cleaning — the beach was dead, and for the time being, deader than any beach that had been merely oiled. Aside from the amphipods and diatoms, there was absolutely nothing alive on it, and it had the oil still in its substrate.

The hot-water wash, like many of the cleaning methods, had been questioned from the start for precisely the reasons we were witnessing — its destructiveness and its inefficacy. The method consists of heating seawater, putting it under pressure, then blasting the beaches with it. It was one of several related approaches that included spraying water at various temperatures and pressures by fire hoses, hand-held wands, and sprayers with eight high-pressure nozzles mounted on cranes (omnibooms). Here, the force of the wash had been sufficient to shatter clamshells into bits and to penetrate a couple of inches into the coarse sand. The heat increases the liquidity of the oil and thereby causes a portion of it to run down the beach and into the water, at which point it might be skimmed. However, the wash subjected the plant and animal life with temperatures well beyond the range of their experience. Brown algae wilted on contact, hence its pale color and the fragility of its hold. The argument used to promote the method is that on heavily oiled beaches it impedes the formation of tar mats (asphalt), which, through their sealing effect and persistent toxicity, might retard successful recolonization by plant and animal life.

A test beach in Knight Island's Herring Bay, not far from where Kim, Kathy, and I were, would be hot-washed in mid-July. The test was conducted by Exxon scientists and scientists from various federal and state agencies. The lead agency, NOAA, struck an agreement with Exxon to keep the data secret. Months later, in February 1990, following an application by the *Anchorage Daily News* under the Freedom of Information Act to NOAA, the data would be released and reported in an article by Charles Wohlforth. The results showed that on the upper part of the beach 86 percent of the plant life hit directly by hot water was killed, and that some species of plant and animal life, for example, snails, sea lettuce, and brown algae, were completely wiped out. In all, 13 species of plants and animals were lost completely from the site. In the water where the hot water and oil flowed, dead starfish, crabs, and small fish were found. The magnitude of this secondary effect, according to Jacqui Michel of NOAA, was unexpected.[44]

The machine used in the test discharged 500 gallons a minute of 130-degree water. It was estimated that 1,300 gallons of oil lay on the beach before treatment and that half of that remained afterwards. Some 300 gallons of oil were picked up by the waiting skimmer. What happened to the remaining 350 gallons, no one knew for certain, although roughly speaking, the answer was obvious. It was dispersed in the water, or it washed back onto the beach, or onto another beach, or it mixed with sediment and settled to the bottom. The 300 gallons the skimmer picked up was probably offloaded into a bladder or into a storage barge, then transferred to a central site, probably run through a water separator, perhaps shipped by barge to Tacoma, and

---

[44] My requests to both Exxon and NOAA for "white sheets" that would include specific data on the test sites were ignored.

trucked to the toxic waste dump in Arlington, Oregon, where it would be stored or recycled as asphalt. Cleaning spilled oil was like trying to whitewash a red barn. No matter how many coats are applied, the red always seems to show through.

It should be noted that there was (and is) a general scientific consensus that there have been very few rigorously conducted field tests of cleanup methods for any oil spill. In the case of the hot wash test beach here, Jacqui Michel would assert that cleaning heavily oiled beaches by whatever method was preferable to simply leaving the oil and allowing it to harden into mats. This was an activist position, a triage, and it was supported with even greater vigor by Exxon's senior environmental advisor, Al Maki. In a March 2, 1990, letter to the *Anchorage Daily News* following Wohlforth's article, Maki wrote:

> The extent of the impact of hot-water washing was weighed against the alternative, which was, to leave the heavy oil concentrations on the beaches, posing a greater threat to shoreline species. Data clearly indicated that while hot-water washing caused some incremental localized impact on these species, the removal of heavy hydrocarbon concentrations stabilized the shoreline and will likely speed overall recovery of biota.
>
> The finalized report on the test results show a considerable variety of organisms still present on shorelines treated by the hot-water cleanup method. Although the numbers of several species were reduced significantly, enough remain to strongly suggest the ability to reproduce and the return of a viable shoreline ecology. This trend has been observed in several studies of other spills worldwide, showing that shoreline biota recovered in impacted areas within two or three years after the event.

With both Michel and Maki, it was a judgment call, though Maki's assessment seems overly optimistic. By "shoreline" biota, he presumably meant intertidal life — crustaceans, bivalves, diatoms, plant life, etc. — indigenous to that shoreline, and not, say, the migratory birds whose numbers might be depleted first by the oil spill itself, and secondarily by the lack of food during the succeeding two-to three-year period. The possibility of exponential effects through the reduction in food sources for predators, such as birds, is glossed over. The decision to clean any beach by the hot-water wash was a selection from an array of forbidding choices, which included the various means of flushing, the various means of mechanical and manual removal (from excavating beaches with backhoes to wiping rocks with absorbent pads), using dispersants, vacuum pumping, skimming, burning, and sandblasting.

The conundrum with which decision makers were presented was absolutely resistant to full solution. At best, the hot-wash method, when compared with other methods of interdiction, merely reduced the amount of time required to achieve what Maki called "viable shoreline ecology" (what is meant by "viable" would seem to be open to interpretation) by a factor which is beyond accurate prediction, and which, everything considered, remained a great deal more than two or three years. Some experts put the recovery period for cleaned beaches that had some oil left in the substrate at 30 years, or as long or longer than if the oil had been left alone. At its worst, the method severely damaged species diversity and made the recovery period longer than if nothing at all had been done.

Kathy, Kim, and I walked across the isthmus to Block Island, situated nearly in the center of Upper Passage, between Ingot and Eleanor Islands. Like the other interior land bridges, this one was verdant with growth. The green and yellow plant life and the dark tree trunks and the dark, humus-heavy earth came at one in a startling rush. As we began our descent toward the water, our vantage point brought to our eye birds flying in and out of a rookery. They were black-legged kittiwakes, the most common gull of the Arctic, named after their cry. They were to our left, coming away from a cliff and flying into the trees and then around, out of sight. Their pattern of flight had an intentness to it, quite unlike the whirl and hover one customarily sees when gulls range the water for food. No doubt, they were headed out to locate food for the fledglings situated on the ledges of the rock. It was the first sign of bird life we had seen for some time, and for these birds in this place the search for food could not have been an easy prospect.

We swung rightwards along a narrow trail, and down, moving toward the smell and the noise, the shoplike stink, the sound of engines, then we clambered down the face of a rock and into what had become a recurrent vision: a beach or, in this case, a line of several shallow beaches separated by jutting rock formations like knots in a rope. Everything before us was inundated with oil. The detail of it all provoked a morbid fascination, this rock six feet above the water level and yet drenched with oil, and this twisting, glossy line of algae, and this fish body cast upon the edge of the beach, and these fissures and crevices and little bowls and indentations filled with oil the consistency of mayonnaise, and this small cove aswirl with chemical colors — gray, white, brown, and rust — and that rock out there in the water, a tiny island, to which Kathy Conlan, following her ritual of inspection, waded. Her scrutiny sought once again the durability of certain creatures, for here among the oil she found sculpins, a common fish of intertidal regions, amphipods, mussels, and what she referred to as "scads of hermit crabs."

With the fascinations, however, came the inescapable blunting of what grew into a repetitious horror, a customary deathliness. Our fascinations, or the high and low points of a day, came to reside in the detail of abuse and the detail of amazing survival. The acceptance of the pervasive reality of abuse caused despair. As our despair deepened, we all found it increasingly difficult to speak of its source. It was there, everywhere. Oil was the landscape and so in its viscous, glossy darkness it was drawn within us, even as we knew that science, once distanced from the immediate, referred to such assaults as mere "aesthetics." I found myself sinking into the world of symbology in hopes of finding a way to grasp what I saw. . . . It was like the *Inferno* where the very substance of Dante's landscape, of exterior form and of the interior acceptance of that form by the condemned, was made out of evil. Even Kathy gave up her chores for the moment, and neither she, Kim, nor I spoke, but looked in appalled silence, and turned away to look at something else, and then at this, at this bulb on a popweed streaked with an eerie red, at that steel-colored streak in the water.

The water in the cove directly before us was closed upon itself by a stretch of blue plastic boom. The boom's purpose was to hold in what oil was here until a cleanup crew arrived. It had failed in its purpose, for even then in slack tide ribbons of oil passed from one side of the boom and under it to the other side. To our left, a second length of boom lay draped across the rocks, and 30 yards and a couple of coves farther down, a group of college-age people — two young men, two women — were building a pair of shelters out of two-by-fours, plywood, and fabric. A skiff ferried back and forth from a boat out in the channel to the young people, who were there to conduct a kittiwake census under the auspices of the Fish and Wildlife Service. There were other crews scattered throughout the sound doing bird censuses, one of the young women told me when I walked down there. Her broad face was filled with intentness and purpose, like the kittiwakes flying out to look for food. She said there was also a Fish and Wildlife cruise ship roving the sound to do counts. She and her comrades had their building supplies ashore and one man had the first shelter almost constructed. At the edge of their beach was a growing stash of fuel cans, food, and equipment. A lime-green portable latrine stood at the edge of the woods.

From there, I could see that beyond the Fish and Wildlife supply boat was a large, bright blue and white cruise ship, a fancy vessel with big, recreational decks. It was owned by a religious organization with a reputation for swinging, and had been leased out as a work crew hotel boat. Off its bow, three large, black bladders floated in the water. They looked like dead, finless whales. They were used either as repositories for recovered oil or as storage for fuel to run the machines. The water in the channel was still and dark. The sky was clear. Downwards and across the channel lay more of the dark, the darkness of Ingot Island across the way, and the darkness of the water and the shine on it glinting in the sun. Beyond the cruise ship were a barge and several more fishing boats, and beyond them, small in the distance, a shore crew ran high-pressure hoses on Ingot Island. A small skimming vessel waited just offshore. The crew's yellow hardhats looked like buttons. The milk-colored ricochet of spray from their high-pressure hoses arched against the dark slope of the island.

I worked my way back toward Kim and Kathy, past them, and then out onto a point of land. Another bay came into view, an anchorage. In the bay were over 25 fishing boats, also leased out for work. Occasionally one of them, answering a radio call, would start up and ease out into the channel. There was the noise, the noise of this boat or that, the distant hum of the engine running the hoses across the channel, the noise of the Fish and Wildlife skiff coming and going, the racket of the hammer the young man used to put together the shelters, and yet what we saw here and heard was nothing compared to what the diving teams were seeing in Herring Bay that day, or to what I would see there later. We caught a glimpse of it that evening as the *Alpha Helix* passed down along Knight Island, retrieving the diving teams: big ships floating in the open water, smaller ships and barges crammed into all the inlets, and makeshift constructions along the shoreline, shelters, latrines, and bulldozers, backhoes, cranes, generators, compressors, a barge loaded with an omniboom. The omniboom had six oil-fired burners that heated 100 gallons of 40-degree water to 160 degrees in a minute and then shot the water out at the rocks and beaches under 80 pounds per square inch of pressure. Later, a floating incinerator would be brought in to Herring Bay because the landbased incinerators couldn't handle the waste being generated at the rate of 250,000 to 500,000 pounds a day.

In some places, everything was thrown into the incinerators — oily logs, rock, gravel, sludge, broken shovels, spoiled containment booms, absorbent pads, rain suits, boots, shit from the latrines. When the DEC began strictly applying air pollution regulations, a way had to be found to ship out the oily debris. At its peak, the cleanup effort would involve 14,000 vessels, 80 aircraft, better than 500,000 feet of boom, boom dragged out of every corner of the world. There would be 11,000 workers who consumed 330 tons of food and had 10 million gallons of water delivered to them, who wore 31,000 hard-hats, 600,000 pairs of gloves, 73,000 pairs of rubber boots, 53,000 lifejackets, and 167,000 rain suits. They were ferried from one place to another, herded onto the hotel boats and then back on shore into temporary camps. To fulfill their needs, maritime and cleanup equipment pulled off the shelves of supply houses all up and down the western United States, and huge quantities of food were shipped in. In order to monitor the cleanup, the Coast Guard itself had deployed 7 major ships, 20 aircraft, and more than 1,000 personnel. The lists go on and on.

Vessels became unavailable on the West Coast. The price of gasoline out on one Aleutian island rose to six dollars a gallon because there were no transport barges left to deliver it. It had to be flown in by light plane. The lists were late twentieth century, computerized versions of the now seemingly quaint lists one might find in the journals of explorers, Colnett, Cook, Vancouver, Fidalgo, Lewis and Clark, lists that served as ironic mirrors of the lists of damaged species. A supplies list, excluding food, for *one small response vessel*, for example, looked like this:

750	Ft. Expandi 4300 Containment Boom
1	Each GT- 185 Skimmer
1	Each Pharos Marine Hydraulic Power Pack w/Spares
1	Each 1000 Gallon Oil Water Separation Tank
2	Each 16' Rigged Hull Inflatable w/50 HP Outboard Motor
1	Each Spare 50 HP Outboard Motor w/Spares Kit
2	Each Fish Totes
20	Each Bundles Sorbent Boom (800')
20	Each Bundles Sorbent Pads
10	Each Bags Viscous Sweep (1000')
1	Each Roll Nylon Reinforced Visqueen (20'X100')
1	Each Steam Cleaner
1	Each 4kW Generator
1	Each 2" Pump (Diesel Driven)
100	Ft. 2" Suction Hose
100	Ft. 2" Discharge Hose
2	Each Response Boxes (Storage Containers)
12	Each Boom Lights w/Batteries
12	Each Anchor Buoys
12	Each Mustange Float Suits (to be sized)
12	Each Sets Carhartt or Refrigewear

2	Cases Rain Gear (1 Lg, 1 X-Lg)
12	Pair Rubber Knee Boots
12	Pair Insulated Arctic Pack Boots
24	Pair Felt Boot Liners
12	Pair Safety Glasses
12	Pair Ear Protection (Peltor)
2	Dozen Rubber Gloves
4	Dozen Glove Liners
4	Dozen Cloth/Canvas Gloves
5	Cases Plastic Bags
1	Case Ear Plugs
1	Set Hand Tools (Rakes, Hoes, Shovels)
2	Sets Mechanic's Tools
2	Tool Boxes
4	Coils ½" Poly Line
4	Coils ¾" Poly Line
2	Coils ½" Nylon Line
2	Coils ⅜" Nylon Line
12	¾" Shackles
24	½" Shackles
1	55-Gallon Barrel Hydraulic Oil
2	Cases Outboard Motor Oil
5	Five-Gallon Gas Cans
1	Set Spare 2" Camlock Fittings
1	Fully Equipped First Aid Kit
1	Drum Motor Oil (30 Wt)

When he arrived in early April, Admiral Yost had said, "This spill is a war. I intend to fight it as a war." It became an event on the order of a military call-up, marshaling platoons of people and incorporating immense quantities of big things and tiny things — the navy frigate, the ¾-inch shackle, a box of Ritz crackers, ear plugs. By the time the cleanup was in full swing, on-scene Coast Guard commandant Vice Admiral Clyde Robbins would say, "As far as my actual authority over the cleanup, I have none, unless I take over the spill. My only hope is to get Exxon to do what I want to get done through jawboning and coercion."

Exxon was called upon to do what it did best: organize and transport equipment, position that equipment, call up the specialists and the work force, make arrangements with a host of subcontractors, and keep track of the money.

It tended to use three basic approaches to beach cleaning — various kinds of washing, chemical applications, and bioremediation. Bioremediation, which used fertilizer to "spike" the populations of resident oil-eating microbes, proved promising, but generally the early predispositions were for massive, systemic remedies applied by armies of workers and hundreds of machines. To a degree this was an inescapable condition of the situation, and not entirely Exxon's fault. The state of Alaska and the public generally were applying intense pressure to remove all possible unsightliness, even beyond reason.

In another time, only 30 years before, Americans would have eulogized the display of machine and muscle, but that time seemed gone, even for Alaska. Instead, what we were faced with was the deep confusion of an awful detritus, oil on the beaches, and then of the whitened, steam-cleaned beaches, pale as the whiteness of Melville's "transcendent horror," and beneath the surface of those beaches the oil still there, thick in the substrate, and the intrusion of the workers, the graffiti carved on the rocks, the trash, the beaten-down growth, the dance pounded out to the beat of thousands of internal combustion engines small and large, running day and night, upon "pristine" environments.[45] The culture was locked inside a loop, an infantile solipsism on a massive scale.

The culture that perfected the mechanized way of being, then spilled the oil, kept true inside its loop, seemingly proposing by its action to redeem itself through the very mental set that had caused the spill in the first place. In the process it consumed yet more of the raw material as it drove itself to and around the site and reasserted its way of being, than it had spilled in the first place. Eighteen million gallons of refined fuel (gasoline, diesel), or in volume about 160 percent of the reported 11 million gallons spilled, were used to operate the cleanup machinery, and this says nothing of the fuel that

---

[45] Just what constitutes "pristine?" The waters of Prince William Sound were already heavily affected by fishing and, historically, by the fur trade. The landforms are somewhat less heavily affected than the waterways, although there was a history of mining, a growing timber industry, the tourist industry, and in general the new rage for adventure as hobby. Practically speaking, Prince William Sound is (or was) relatively pristine. On the other hand, the Alaskan historian, Morgan Sherwood, argues in his essay, "The Wilderness and Alaska," that any place accessible to modern transportation, which all of Alaska, indeed all of the world, now is, no longer constitutes a wilderness. It logically follows, therefore, that there is no longer any such thing as wilderness. The Exxon call-up, for the potential it displayed, and the pressure from the Alaskan government to advance that potential, would seem to validate Sherwood's point quite completely.

Exxon and the state of Alaska waged a war of semantics over when a shoreline was environmentally stable and this became a pivot in the ensuing litigation. Exxon proposed that environmentally stable meant capable of supporting viable life; the state, actually supporting that life — two different views of damage.

was used to manufacture and ship the equipment, or to bring the workers here. There was and is a large leak in the system, which would be a great deal less troubling if the oil spill and cleanup were a discrete event, which it was not. The parallel systemic leak occurs across the land. Despite improvements in the efficiency of motor vehicles, American consumption of petroleum has continued to rise. In the meantime, the culture lives within its own mythology of machines and world proprietorship. At that time, Exxon was the second largest corporation in the United States and the world's third largest energy supplier,[46] but to have asked it to stand apart from the grand illusions of the dominant world culture, or to give up its own culture, would be to ask a great deal. In Prince William Sound, the alternative — once the oil had been spilled, then churned into mousse, once it was clearly beyond control, once the initial retrieval and dispersant strategies had failed — was to come in softly, discreetly pick up what oil could be picked up, employ what beneficent means were available, rescue what was truly rescuable, and leave the rest to succeeding winters, and then delicately rehabilitate. Once the oil was there, the die was cast. To have accepted this required full acknowledgment of one's own impurity and complicity.

As the *Alpha Helix* passed Herring Bay that evening, I stood on the deck and looked into its broad, inviting opening. I knew that it penetrated deeply into the island. Its mouth was conveniently cocked in the direction the oil had come from. Its ragged shores were a series of coves and inlets. It had its own small islands and peninsulas. A favored haven for seals, otters, sea lions, and migrating birds, it was like a Prince William Sound in miniature.

We were in the heart of the long twilight. I could see the rigging lights of small boats, pale in the mist, and the outlines of large boats and barges, the sometimes resplendently illuminated hotel boats. Laughter wafted across the water from the bunches of vessels crammed together like small towns floating just off the ghettoes of the beaches. The power of despoilment was making its next visitation. Soon, it would pass on with its rattling head. These places had never heard such engines, or felt such high-pressure spray, such heat, such chemistry, nor been stripped bare, as they sometimes were, of gravel and rock. They had never been walked upon by so many feet, had never been left this way, black with death, white with death.

[46] In 1989, according to rankings by *Business Week*, only IBM was larger than Exxon among U.S. corporations. In 1980 Exxon was the world's largest oil company, but by 1988 it had fallen behind the state-owned Saudi Aramco and Royal Dutch/Shell. The rise of OPEC and increased nationalization of oil sites and concessions during the 1970s and 1980s heightened the competition among members of the old oil trust, including Exxon. This, together with the American demand for low fuel prices and shareholders' demand for high revenues, is a factor in the cost-saving measures applied to petroleum production and shipping.

THE
CHAPTER
10
RAPTURE OF
SCIENCE

The *Alpha Helix* drew away from Knight Island, then passed Ingot and Eleanor Islands. I stood outside on the rear deck and gazed down along our wake through the legs of the crane mounted on the stern. The clusters of lights faded slowly from view. We passed the same navy ship we'd seen early that morning. It was a gray outline resting on the dark water. In the distance were the ragged peaks of Knight Island and over to the west the mainland. Bruce Martin, the ship's Able Bodied Seaman, came out and began checking through the whaler and Zodiacs, the engines, lines, tanks.

He moved fast. He was a Yup'ik Eskimo from Nome up on the Seward Peninsula. A small man, hardly over five feet tall, he had a times an explosive personality. Quick to anger when his deckhands screwed up, or when he felt pushed by the science crew, but just as quick to laugh, he was trusted implicitly by the captain, Tom Callahan. He called me over to the rail of the deck and pointed eastward. "Tanker," he said. We had now come into the open water between Eleanor Island and the Naked Island complex and had a good view across the tanker channel. A tanker had come into sight from behind Naked Island as it steamed toward Hinchinbrook Entrance. I stared at it, impressed by its tininess in the distance.

A few days earlier, I'd asked Bruce how he felt about the spill, and he'd spat out his response, "It's another bullet!" According to Bruce, it all began with the forced relocation of Eskimos by the Russians for the sake of the fur trade in the eighteenth and early nineteenth centuries. When the Russians sold Alaska to the United States in 1867, the Russians asked the United States if it wanted the Eskimos as part of the deal or if it wanted Russia to move them out. "That tells you everything," Bruce had said.

Prior to the 1971 passage of the Alaska Native Claims Settlement Act (ANCSA), the controversial resolution in law to the question of Native land claims, Bruce said he'd traveled around to the villages to tell them not to vote for acceptance. The primary impetus for the legislation was the push to open oil production on the North Slope, to which the Native land claims were a legal impediment. By turning the land over to Native corporations as private land (as opposed to the "trust" or reservation system), Congress presented the Native people with a host of legal and economic problems that they were not initially prepared to deal with and that would change their lives forever. Bruce said he'd told his people to send their children to school to become lawyers so they could defend themselves and not pay out all the money to corporation lawyers. He'd said, "At first a village would think it could hire one lawyer, then they were told they had to hire a firm, so the villages ended up paying ten lawyers. The village elders who were put in charge of negotiations were picked by the government, not by their own people. So the elders were put in a very bad position. How could they decide all these things? The settlement act was just a way for the outside corporations to get their hands on the land."

Bruce said he'd got disgusted and had gone down to Seattle to live, that he'd joined the Seattle Native Corporation. "But then finally I had to come back," he said. I had the definite impression that he'd had a hard time in Seattle, that he'd nearly lost his life there, that he'd passed directly out of the crisis of his people and into a personal one.

In the few minutes we'd stood side by side at the rail, looking out, the tanker had grown abruptly larger. They had that capacity to appear small, to appear to be barely moving, and then suddenly to seem huge and fast. Fishermen told of seeing a tanker in the distance and of starting to cross the channel, but then discovering before they were in the clear that they were barely going to make it. The *Alpha Helix* altered its course northward. In a few moments, the tanker grew smaller again. Members of the science crew began to drift out to the deck, then work their way up the gangways toward the foredeck. We were going to pass the *Exxon Valdez*, one person said. At times, the science crew transformed itself into tourists.

Out of the blue, Bruce said, "It's all lost now. Only a handful of the Eskimos still believe in the old way." Then he fell silent. I leaned out, looked toward the bow, and caught a glimpse of the *Valdez*, its long slender shape on the water. Bruce and I stayed where we were, our bodies rocking gently to and fro with the motion of the ship on the water.

"The Eskimos believed in dimensions," Bruce said. "This life is lived on one dimension. If you do well, you will pass on to the next dimension, but you'll still be here. If you do bad, if you commit suicide, then you have to do this dimension over again."

The *Alpha Helix* made an arc and now we had a good view of the *Valdez*. There were smaller boats scattered around it, and a large work barge pulled up to its side. In the water, strips of boom and patches of oil sheen caught the fading light. The ship was still being cleaned and welded back together to make it seaworthy. By then, I felt as though I'd seen it a thousand times. Bruce said, "Everything considered, it's a positive way of looking at things."

Many times after that, I would think of what he'd said of the idea of dimensions as opposed to the remote afterlife I'd been raised to believe in, and of the fluidity of the relation between ethical behavior and the several levels of life as opposed to the rigid dualism of heaven and hell, and most of all of the idea of the other dimensions being here as opposed to somewhere else. It seemed to me that to have the potentials of the other worlds of one's life bound up inextricably with where one happened to be now was at its very foundation a less fractured and more adult way of seeing.

Later, a group of us gathered in the galley. John Oliver came and dawdled over a bowl of ice cream, then disappeared. There was a reflective air among us, probably because we had pulled away from Knight Island. For the scientists, the most demanding and the worst was over. Some of us were still finishing dinner. What had begun on the first day out as a set schedule for meals had by then dissolved into shifts that stretched into the evening. Trish Kaminsky accommodated the crew by working irregular hours herself. I gathered that she liked this group, as opposed to some of the other officious science crews she'd cooked for.

Trish was in the kitchen now. It was after nine. She was a big woman, well over six feet tall, well read, and given to conversations that took a spiritual drift. When I'd first met her, I'd thought — *basketball*. She had told me that she was considering writing a novel about living an entire life under the threat of nuclear war. The remains of the night's dinner — broiled chicken, potatoes, green beans, potato salad, green salad — still lay in the deep pans between the eating area and the kitchen. We ate extremely well. Rikk Kvitek and Diane Carney, an M.A. student from Santa Cruz, came in to eat, and Rikk, who rarely paused for anything, sat for a while and talked. Finally, Dan Reed, a kelp forest ecologist who had recently completed his Ph.D. at the University of California at Santa Barbara, Gordon Robilliard, Bruce Stewart, and I remained at one of the tables. I could see straight ahead through the doorway to the lab. Another of the graduate students, Stacey Kim, was entering the day's findings into a computer. Beyond her at a bench against the far wall, Kathy Conlan was busily cataloguing her specimens. To my left, Trish thumped around in the kitchen.

The three scientists at the table were probing what they'd seen. Gordon said, "In the intertidal community we've got pretty much what we'd expect." He meant that what had not been killed by the initial onslaught of oil was still there, and remained reasonably healthy. This reinforced what the rest of the crew had been seeing in the intertidal communities and put the onus on the massive cleanup effort.

Hunter Lenehan, another of the Moss Landing graduate students, came in and searched the cooler for something to drink. Hunter wore a pair of sweats and a red T-shirt with a black picture of Che Guevera. "I always dive with Che," he'd said. Of all the crew members, it was Hunter who had been the most clearly thunderstruck by what he'd seen at Herring Bay. He'd come back to the *Alpha Helix* expostulating and cursing and John Oliver had shushed him down. The shushing, I suspected, had something to do with my presence. I had been sensing a certain tension on the part of some over the insertion of a "reporter" into the ship's activities, and indeed, despite my several requests, the scientists had declined to take me with them to the interiors of Herring Bay. For a long time I puzzled over the precise cause of my exclusion. Surely, it was not the prospect of my seeing the next and worst grotesque of the oil's effects. I had seen plenty of that, and I would see Herring Bay eventually. My suspicion was that the cause was in some part the likelihood of my observing responses like Hunter's, in some part the result of the scientists' wariness over having an observer leap to conclusions from incomplete information, and in larger part the cautious confidentiality of conversations the ship's crew would enter into with other scientists. This was the period of time that nearly all research was being converted to a litigation-driven protocol and therefore sliding out of sight under the shrouds of government and corporate secrecy. Since I had boarded the ship in hopes of achieving knowledge and understanding, it was troubling in this instance to find it denied me not because of the subject's difficulty but for political reasons.

The ship's engines kept up a low, steady growl. Over in the kitchen, Trish ran a mixer, then opened an oven door and bent to look inside. Bruce Stewart said, "The cold water may have something to do with it. In more temperate zones, we'd see things like tumors on the coral."

Gordon said, "Coral is truly stationary, but that sort of thing could still happen here over time. The oil will probably affect the algae and so a lot of the herbivores."

Algae and anemones are nearly stationary. Bivalves, starfish, sea slugs, and crustaceans are less so. The migratory fish and marine mammals — salmon, say — and killer whales, travel great distances. The degree of a creature's mobility, combined with other factors, made them more or less vulnerable to various types of what scientists rather euphemistically referred to as "perturbances."

The more stationary creatures in intertidal habitats that might be washed and rewashed repeatedly with oil would often be the most vulnerable. There are exceptions, mobile creatures such as otters, who have their own peculiar vulnerabilities of physique and habit. It was not clear whether mobile creatures were altogether avoiding the oil or swimming into it. The seals we had seen at North Twin Bay on Elrington Island, popping up, disappearing, and popping up again just beyond the margin of the oil slick, would seem clearly to have been avoiding the oil. Scientists who had observed marine mammals swim directly into the oil from open water, or flocks of birds landing in it, would argue that animals had no such avoidance capability. That such conversations, which presumed the superiority of human sentience, took place in proximity to beaches soaked with oil as a result of human error seemed peculiar at best.

"The point," Gordon said, "is that we're not seeing dead communities. It's going to take a lot of looking before we're sure of anything, but for now the communities are not dead. They've been perturbed, but at five to seven feet below the waterline, we're still seeing communities that have certainly not come back in the three months since the spill. They were there before, and they're still there now."

Because of his experience, knowledge, and his association with Exxon, Gordon's view quickly became the focus of the conversation. Earlier, he had told me that even the chief accountant Exxon had brought up from Houston had been staggered by the amount of oil spill response money — something on the order of $10 million a day — that poured out of the company coffers. Gordon had added that so far as he could see the large-scale cleanup would accomplish two things: it would employ Alaskans, and it would get the deepest pools of oil picked up off the beaches.

Now, Bruce Stewart said, "The other thing would be reproduction rates. The effect of the oil on reproduction would be subtle and hard to track. The clams' reproductive reaction would affect clams first, but we might not be able to see it until it moved farther down the line. Then when we did see it we might not know where it was coming from."

This was the issue that would preoccupy oil spill observers and much of the scientific work for months and years to come. How much damage? What kind of damage? How far-reaching? As Bruce had put it, the issue bore upon the effect reduced numbers in one species might have upon that species' survival, and next upon the effect reduced numbers in one species might have upon another, predatory or otherwise dependent species. It bore upon the lasting effects toxic exposure might have upon survival and genetic make-up, and upon passing toxicity on what is commonly known as the food chain, though the image "chain" evokes in the mind — a linear system of interlocked links — is hardly accurate. It's more like a convoluted, three-dimensional net, the far edges of which are well beyond apprehension. Computer-driven models on the order of Mandelbrot fractals come nearest to representing the ever-widening domain of the net and the simultaneous ever-diminishing, microscopic detail of the linkages.

Butter clams live in fine gravel or sand and feed upon tiny bits of food gathered willy-nilly from the bottom by ciliary action. A primary food source in the sound, these clams may be dug out of the sand, drawn from their shells, and ingested by sea stars. Sea stars range the bottom and rocks for scallops, too, and for urchins, nudibranches, sea cucumbers, dead fish. They will cannibalize other sea stars. Urchins graze algae for food. Crabs, fish, otters, ducks, and sea gulls eat urchins. They are also a traditional food of Aleut people. Sea stars are eaten by the dominant sea floor species, the tanner crab, and by the less abundant but larger king crab. Larval crabs feed on plankton, diatoms, and barnacle larvae. Juvenile tanner crabs eat diatoms, algae, and hydroids. Juvenile king crabs eat diatoms, algae, sponges, copepods, polychaetes, small clams, gastropods, and sea urchins. In addition to sea stars, adult king crabs will eat algae, mollusks, polychaetes, and fish. Leeches may live and lay their eggs on king crabs. They are eaten along with the crabs by walleye pollock and halibut. People eat butter clams, fish, king crab, and birds. Octopuses eat adult king crabs. Octopuses are eaten by halibut, sea lions, and people.

Otters eat butter clams by the method that has endeared them to aquarium visitors all across the country. An otter dives, scoops up clams and a small rock, returns to the surface, lies on its back and sculls the water with its tail. It places the rock on its chest and cracks open the clam shells by striking them against the rock. Sometimes sea otters develop an affection for a certain rock. After primates, the sea otter is considered the most adept user of tools in the world. It will also tie itself with seaweed to keep from drifting while it sleeps. It is a voracious eater, consuming 25 percent of its weight each day. Sharks and some killer whales eat sea otters.

Though far from an exhaustive portrait of the near tidal zone, this may suggest the scope and detail of the exchange, all of which is further influenced from location to location by physical conditions — the density of the flora, the topography of the bottom, the nature of the surface, the degree of exposure, the energy of the wave action. An oil-caused genetic defect picked up initially by, say, clams in polluted sand or by urchins grazing oil-coated algae, and perhaps reinforced by doses from other sources along the line, might be discovered many steps removed from its source, in a sea lion, say, or a killer whale, and it would then be virtually impossible to trace it back with precision.

Gordon's response to Bruce was measured. "Clams are free spawners," he said. "Even a substantial reduction in reproductive capacity probably wouldn't show up because of larvae recruitment and resettlement from the outside." He was met with silence. After a moment, he said, "Look, my whole thing is community response. In a situation like this it's either going to be real dramatic in a small area, or else you'll have a small-scale response spread over a large area. But typically, man, creating an oil spill like this, can't touch the effect of something like a hard freeze, or an earthquake, or a change in currents like El Niño."

Some of the bite in Gordon's observations derived from his position. John Oliver, an old friend of his, would later tell me that Gordon, like many of the experts Exxon had brought in, found much of his energy directed at conflict resolution. John would say, "Gordon can't produce truly accurate results because they may not be accepted by Exxon. His work is defined by the conditions of his employment, so as a biologist he mainly finds ways to design research programs that will resolve conflict."

I understood John to mean not that Gordon's findings themselves would be inaccurate, but rather the results that followed the findings — this a consequence of conflicts between the findings and Exxon's response to them, and with the balancing off of what Gordon found with what others had found, with determining which findings would be shared, and when, and with whom, and how his findings meshed with the needs of other departments in the company and with the needs of individual managers, whose first function was to protect their position. Finally, his findings would have to accommodate Exxon's purpose, which was to minimize and resolve its own conflict with the state of Alaska, the Coast Guard, the American public, and Congress. In that contest, the scraps of information Gordon would produce likely had very little potency.

At my side, Dan Reed, who had so far been quiet, said, "We don't have any control over freezes and El Niño. To have a disturbance caused by human error is different. For one thing, human disturbances are often recurrent and you have to consider not only the severity but also the frequency. And here, it's really obvious that there's damage."

Bruce said, "But maybe it's impossible to prove long-term damage."

Dan said, "That's a different question. What sort of damage is acceptable?"

Bruce got up to put his plate in the dish bin, then came back and sat down. "I suppose that's the dangerous thing about the research," he said, "that when they're done, they'll have to say it's no big deal."

The research he was referring to had evolved from the original scientific meetings in Valdez. An umbrella organization called the Damage Assessment Project (DAP) had been formed. It was headed by a board of trustees made up of representatives of the state of Alaska and the federal government, including the Secretary of the Interior. Federal and state agencies, such as the Alaska Department of Fish and Game, NOAA and its various sub-agencies, the U.S. Fish and Wildlife Service, etc., sponsored or contracted out research activities by a host of scientists. Frequently a private contractor, such as Dames and Moore, was involved.

Among the papers in the briefcase at Gordon's elbow were some 60 scientific Project Files outlining research undertaken under the auspices of DAP. On our first day out from Seward, I had sat at this table with Gordon and John Oliver while John looked through the two-inch pile. As he had moved deeper into it, John's initial businesslike approach began to flicker into a kind of wonderment. He sat hunched over the pile with his elbows on the table, looked sideways at Gordon, and frowned quizzically. He began to laugh and, in an allusion to the Mad Hatter's advice to the March Hare, said, "We're buttering our watches." He thrashed through the papers, snapping them down one after another, and looked up again and said, "But it's the best butter." He meant that the quality of the scientific work that had been contracted had little relation to the mechanism to which it was being applied.

At his side, Gordon chuckled. I looked through the files later. Some of the projects were in principle fairly rudimentary, involving counts such as the kittiwake census we'd seen in its initial stages, but many were highly technical and involved extensive field and laboratory work — tissue samplings, for example, and the numerous water column studies. The projects included studies of flora — eel grass, algae, kelp — and analyses of creatures of all descriptions: diatoms, marine worms, amphipods, shrimp, oyster larvae, herring, salmon, pollock, river and sea otters, seals, whales, migratory birds, resident birds, deer, bears. One not atypical study of salmon (Fish/Shellfish Study #11) proposed to study the occurrence of herring spawn in oiled and unoiled inlets and to chart lethal and sublethal effects, such as fin erosion, neoplasms, lesions, and the accumulation of hydrocarbon concentrations in bile and roe.

Even the simplest was open-ended, allowing a vent for future study. A relatively straightforward otter mortality study (Marine Mammal Study #6), for example, included a plan to "instrument" otters with radio transmitters so that their mortality and distribution following the spill could be followed. Such provisions made for good science, of course, but they also made for continued funding. The above-mentioned salmon study had an initial budget of $1,943,400; the herring study, $374,500; and the otter study (with which Chuck Monnett of Cordova finally became involved), $763,000. All those figures were projected through February 1990 only, and the bulk of the projects were subsequently funded for continuation. As of February 1990, the total allotted for the studies conducted under the State and Federal Natural Resources Damage Assessment Plan came to $35,330,000. In a sense, the entire undertaking was an exact analogue to funding granted otherwise to subcontractors, government employees, engineers, marine equipment outlets, communities, beach workers. It began as a maelstrom of money and would continue so for years to come.

At the time we were on the *Alpha Helix* the figures were not known to us, but John certainly read in the level of funding. He bent over the files again, then looked up, wide-eyed, and said, "This is incredible. Everybody is doing something. We're managing the shit out of this spill!"

Gordon rocked back in his chair and said, "A good scientist never passes up a good boondoggle."

Now, in the galley with Bruce, Dan, and myself, Gordon said, "You have to separate the ecological effects from the effect on people — from the economics of it, from philosophy, aesthetics."

By economics, I gathered he was referring to effects like that upon the fishing industry, whose seasons were at times shut down completely, not because the fish they caught would necessarily be hazardous to people's health but because the slightest intimation of the presence of oil on a catch had a devastating effect upon the perception of the market, and so upon prices. By philosophy, I suspected, knowing his predilections, that he meant in particular what he regarded as the sentimentally driven "opinion" of the environmentally disposed population. He had already introduced me to the concept of what he called "the Bambi effect," that is, the public reaction to the death of otters, those apparently cuddly creatures who were regarded — usually in a photograph or from the other side of an aquarium glass — as a symbol of the fallen. By aesthetics — a term I often heard used by scientists in its pejorative sense — he meant how things looked on the surface (the extraordinary ugliness of an oiled beach), and not as an artist might intend — how things looked as a consequence of structure or underlying form.

For my part, I had to wonder at what point the separation of the appearance of destruction from the measurement of destruction allowed the measuring, or the scientific romance with quantities, to obscure the reality of destruction. The interest of clarity was served well by separating fields of study and thought into categories, but left unassimilated with other forms of knowing, the compartments of science were ripe for misuse by politicians, journalists, private corporations, scientists themselves, and true believers of all descriptions, to say nothing of the broken sense of being that living within a fractured world produced.

"If there's a synergism going on," Bruce said, "there's a point where you say this system's maximally perturbed, like a human body with drugs. If the system's lined up just right, or if the addict's chemistry is critically loaded, you can tweak it. If the synergism is on the upsurge, you could knock the system out. If you pollute it only once in a while, maybe it'll be okay. But if it's repeated, there's no question but that you're going to have a disturbance. Sometimes you have to avoid what you can't know for certain."

Dan said, "It's really obvious that there's damage here. That is certain. You don't have to look very hard to see that."

"But you still can't prove long-term damage," Bruce said.

"That's a different question," Dan insisted. "What level, or what kind of damage is acceptable?"

Although Dan's response was directed to Bruce, the real opposition in the exchange lay between Dan and Gordon. The heaviness of Gordon's bearing expressed the weight of the obligations he carried, and the years of experience and frustration. I liked Gordon and respected the rigor of his mind. I liked his self-containment. After he finished his paperwork in the evenings, he would go out to the deck and stand alone for hours, fishing. A couple of days later, as we approached Cordova, he expressed his disappointment at having to get off the ship and go back to the bureaucrats. He had a feel for the world. He was the type of person who could lay down a hand firmly but gently and make things move. It was the touch of a farmer. When Gordon spoke to you, though, he often looked away, which I took not to be self-effacement but the sign of a sadness he held close to himself.

Dan was filled with promise. I had even heard John Oliver suggest to Gordon that Dan might be somebody Gordon would want to take into his consulting company. When he spoke, he looked you directly in the eye. Dan had qualities equal to Gordon's, but the application of those powers upon the world had yet to break down his idealism. He retained a faith in remedies that Gordon seemed to have lost. I empathized with Gordon, and yet I agreed with Dan and put my hopes in him.

"It's a risk-analysis game," Gordon said. "How much are you willing to pay for the privilege of driving your Cadillac around?"

Dan, holding to his point, said, "The effect on otters and birds is obvious, while the intertidal community is more resilient. That's all."

Bruce, who was playing the role of the trigger in this conversation, said, "Look at DDT. Could you have proved there was a problem before the effects started turning up? There may be an incredible effect happening here that we can't see."

"It'd be a lot easier to track the effects on humans who bathe at sea," Gordon said. "They drown."

Dan said, "Man and society have a responsibility for their effect on the environment."

"Concern has nothing to do with ecological effect. That's a smoke screen. Look at the newspapers," Gordon said. And again, though it was the subterranean despair that he expressed as contempt for the meanderings of public information, Gordon's point was accurate enough. For all the play the Alaskan oil spill had been given in the media — even bracketing the massacre at

Tiananmen Square — and for all the eagerness with which the latest eco-logical horror stories were lapped up, for all the noise and furor, there were only the faintest indications of any attempt to realistically address the root causes of the oil spill, which might have come in the form of a mass petro-leum fast, or the acceptance of, say, a dollar-per-gallon surcharge on gasoline to be used to research alternate energy sources and to effectively police oil production and shipping. Gordon was avoiding the question both Dan and Bruce were putting to him, about dealing with what might not be proven and therefore not predicted but was clearly manifest — the destruction.

"Of course, we've got to stop spilling oil," Gordon said. "Regulations will probably get tightened up. The Clean Water Act will probably become law. Better traffic systems for tankers, double-hulled tankers, etcetera, will be in-stituted. In the case of the *Exxon Valdez,* though, a double hull wouldn't have made any difference.[47] It's hard to legislate against human fuckups."

Bruce returned to his tweak theory, which was a version of the final straw on the camel's back — the last ounce of poison that threw a stressed habitat into havoc, or the one confused helmsman who put a tanker from a strained shipping system on the rocks. "So far as error and contingency backups are concerned," he said, "if you get all the conditions lined up just right, some-thing will happen."

"Maybe," Gordon said. "But on the other hand, if they'd had ships from the North Sea and thousands and thousands of feet of boom, maybe they could have controlled the spill. The North Sea has ships dedicated to oil spill cleanup. If you had one of them, and then a way to pick up the oil, you might have been able to get most of it, but then you would still have the economic problems with the fisheries, and the outcry, and also the tendency of people to become indifferent again. Oil coming out of a tanker, at three to four feet high, then moving over itself downhill, it's a tremendous amount of energy and very hard to contain. The viewpoints need to be balanced in discussions such as this."

Dan still held tenaciously to his point. "Regarding the otters," he said, "first think that they are a separate population, and endangered."

Gordon said, "It's never been clear to me that we have to protect isolated species as opposed to protecting the species in general."

---

[47] Gordon was right with virtually all of his prophecies but wrong about the *Valdez.* Following assessment of the damage to the tanker, experts, including the Coast Guard, reported that a double hull could have reduced the spill by as much as 60 percent. The Clean Water Act had become law in 1972.

"You have to protect the gene pool," Dan said, "and you have to begin somewhere and stop somewhere."

Gordon said, "One of the problems with an oil spill is that certain species cannot adapt genetically." He meant species like otters, with their near-shore feeding habits, their specialized insulating fur, their 670,000 hairs per square inch, their need to constantly groom that fur, their peculiar vulnerability. When exposed to oil as they had been, the effect was mass death. For them this was Bhopal.

Dan said, "Right, and if spills are repeated, other organisms will adapt and become over-evolutionized. They'll adapt to oil. This produces a new kind of vulnerability both in those that have adapted and in those that haven't."

Gordon smiled at Dan. "Yeah, as soon as the animals get up on the learning curve, we'll run out of oil. If petroleum were radiation, we'd really be in trouble. Something definitely toxic, both short- and long-term would be very different." Though still shot through with cynicism and irony, it was Gordon's peace offering, a kind of salute to Dan.

Late in the voyage, I would try once again to learn from John Oliver exactly what he and his crew had found. This was two days after Gordon Robilliard had left the ship.

"It's a mew," John said.

He was referring to the emotionally indeterminate sound of a kitten; he judged that the findings would be soft and inconclusive. He spoke of the failure of the Fish and Wildlife Service to put scientists in front of the spill to gather what data they could before the oil hit. "Without evidence from immediately before and immediately following the spill, you have nothing," John said. "It's a wipeout. There are no baselines. The evidence is gone."

My mind flashed back to the question that I had carried onto the *Alpha Helix*: What, truly, is the damage? And more specifically for the scientists on this ship: What about the damage to the kelp, the starfish, mussels, worms, and to the shellfish the otters required, what about the effects of the wholesale removal of the keystone predator, the otter, and what about the likelihood of long-term toxic damage to the lower reaches of the food web? What about the evidence that only science could provide? Although the days spent on the ship had certainly eroded my innocence, I retained enough of it to hope that simple persistence might still yield the answers to some of those questions. I had begun spending a lot of time in the company of Dan Reed and had enjoyed the benefit of his positiveness. Dan was with us now at the table. He didn't speak. I was stunned by John's answer.

"This is a garbage can," he said. "We've got this garbage can full of shit, and we're playing it just outside the lip. We're no different from anybody else." He was angry. He was talking about how scientists get their funding. His anger was in part directed at my persistence, and perhaps at my foolishness as he perceived it, but also directed at himself. He stared at me again and waited. Normally, he waited for nothing and nobody. He was usually irrepressible. He loved his work. His life was bound up in science, in the "stories," as he put it, that it told.

Two days before, after a series of dives off the eastern side of Naked Island, we'd beached two Zodiacs on the small Storey Island, the northernmost of the Naked Island complex. A group of us had climbed up a 20-foot rock abutment from the beach and entered a glade. It was morning and light fell in shafts upon the ground. The shadows were dark. In the light, the tall, green grass that grew between the rocks was bright. There was a muskeg, dotted with large rocks. Lichen covered the rocks. Green moss blanketed the lower trunks of the huge spruce trees that grew around the muskeg. There were big skunk cabbages and small, pastel-colored mushrooms — lavender, mauve, and pale yellow. We found a heap of bear scat at the foot of a tree, still steaming in the cool air. It was a strange wonderland, made to seem stranger by the fact that we were well under ten miles from the *Exxon Valdez'* anchorage. John came into the glade, filled with electric delight. He moved this way and that, looking, then nearly running, extending his survey, and bending to look down, and leaning back to look up, then vanishing over the top of a knoll. In a moment, he came back, eyes gleaming and his face filled with the pleasure of the world he loved.

At this moment in the ship's galley, though, his face was drawn taut, and the rapture had been turned inside out to its equally compelling opposite — disgust. I stared back at him. I had also suddenly become angry, and at him — for not taking me to Herring Bay, for the arrogance of science, and in response to his anger — and I felt a terrible cold despair entering my belly. Only later would I think that my despair was a commiseration, that the despair he felt over the unanswerables and the opportunism was more informed than but fundamentally akin to my own. The outrage he felt over what was perfectly obvious, the wanton death caused by the oil and the sense of self-compromise and helplessness the money triggered, was exactly the same as my own. Though more specifically directed, perhaps, more confined, he was telling me the same thing that the University of California's Todd La Porte would tell the Oil Commission in August — that the consequences were greater than the value of the lessons, that in this particular scenario we had already passed through the veil to the other side where what we learned didn't matter anymore.

"Look," John said. "We don't want to get too close to the dump. We hold out our cups underneath the rim of the can to catch a little of the shit that's trickling over the top. That's all. We want to get enough of it to do our work. But we don't want to get any dirtier than we have to."

After leaving the Naked Island complex, after I had been on the beach just off Flent Point with Gordon, Peter Slattery, and Kathy Conlan, and had seen the plover and the brown bear, Tom Callahan, eased the *Alpha Helix* up Glacier Bay to within several hundred yards of the face of Columbia Glacier. The ship seemed much closer than that, but as with all things pertaining to size and distance here, the reckoning was tricky. In fact, the front of the glacier was 300 feet tall. Its width was four miles. The ship lightly bumped the growlers and steered clear of the bergy bits, those big ones that might drift out from behind Glacier Island and across the tanker channel. We had come very near to one source of the calamity. The icebergs were blue and white. The front of the glacier was white streaked with blue. On it were huge mounds of black earth. The water was pale blue, laden with cream-colored silt. There was no oil here.

On the icebergs were harbor seals, sometimes one or two on one iceberg, sometimes as many as twenty. The seals pup on the icebergs and haul out to rest. One seal, curious, perhaps, or playful, or perhaps running point for the others, swam back and forth in front of the ship's bow. I leaned over the prow to look at it and wondered again about the sentience of animals. Tom Callahan cut the engines and let the ship glide silently. There was the sound of icebergs cracking, like huge ice cubes in a glass. It was as if we were inside the glass. At times, a huge chunk would fall off the face of the glacier and make the roaring sound like thunder. A couple of minutes afterwards, a wave would wash by and the ship would rock.

The entire crew had come out on the foredeck to look, everyone. At first, there was excited talk, but then gradually everyone fell quiet. The ship, a blunt, benign probe, slipped past icebergs that rose above our heads. The seals were dark, as if etched against the ice. They were acutely watchful of the ship. The icebergs came in shapes as various as clouds. Some had ledges for the seals to gather on. Others had tunnels for them to dive through. We edged nearer to the dangerous face of the glacier. The place was still just as it should have been. The sight was eerie and wonderful, the silence, the cracking, the white and blue and black, and light-blue water and pale gray sky, everything huge. The air was cold and white.

2 MONEY

11
GUESTS

... it is to symbols they are reacting when they believe they are acting upon reality ... The irrational system rules political life no less ... The criterion of maturity: the ability to resist symbols. But mankind grows younger all the time.

— Milan Kundera, *The Art of the Novel*, 1986

On September 28, 13 days after Exxon had officially closed down its cleanup exercise for the year, the *Orca II* came out from behind Glacier Island and crossed Valdez Arm. As we approached the lee side of Busby and Bligh Islands, David Grimes pointed out a line in the water. "Out here," he said, "You can see exactly where the wind chop is and where it isn't." On one side of the line the water had a ragged look. We were in that, and the *Orca II* pitched as it cruised. The water was blue and green and chalky with glacial sediment. On the other side of the line, the water appeared smooth, viscous, and darker, almost like gelatin. We crossed into the calm water, shaped a course around Busby Island and into the Tatitlek Narrows between the mainland and Bligh Island. The navigation charts showed reefs all around the island and a solid bank of them within the narrows. David located the channel and guided the boat along it. It was midafternoon and the three of us — David, Lynn Schooler, and myself — stood in the wheelhouse, looking out. We'd been on the water for five days. We were headed for home port, Cordova.

Following their work on the ad hoc citizens' advisory committee to the Valdez triumvirate (Exxon, Alaska, the Coast Guard), David and Rick Steiner had traveled to Sullom Voe, a marine terminal on the Shetland Islands that ships 6 million barrels a day of North Sea crude oil. There they found a very different situation from the one at Valdez, even in what might be yet harsher conditions. Sullom Voe is located just 30 miles south of the same latitude as Valdez, but 6,000 miles to the east in the North Atlantic. Sullom Voe's majority owner is British Petroleum, and Exxon holds an interest in it. Several key Alyeska figures, including its then president, George Nelson, and James Hermiller, who was appointed to run day-to-day operations during the summer and would replace Nelson as president in October of 1989, were also BP executives. Interestingly, BP essentially vanished from sight in Valdez, along with Alyeska, following the *Exxon Valdez* spill. At Sullom Voe, where there had been a big spill a dozen years ago, Steiner and Grimes learned there was an oil spill contingency plan in place that looked very similar on paper to Alyeska's. The difference was that it had been put into practice. Unlike the Alyeska terminal, Sullom Voe had reels of boom permanently deployed at sensitive areas, random helicopter surveillance of tanker traffic, full radar coverage, a permanent on-site pollution response team, regular drills, pilots who rode tankers to the open sea, regular inspections of tankers, more tugs used for berthing, and backup assistance for major spills available within 24 hours. Sullom Voe has not had another major spill since instituting its plan.[48]

David and Rick returned with a clear sense that, as David said, "It was the delivery system that was at fault," and the contingency plan in place at Alyeska was "laughable." It was quite evident to them that the oil companies

[48] Since 1991, there have been North Sea spills outside the immediate confines of Sullom Voe, including the 1993 24.6 million-gallon spill from the tanker *Braer* off the Shetland Islands and the 1996 65,000-tonne spill from the *Sea Empress* off the coast of Wales. Because of the lighter grade of spilled oil and harsh weather conditions, each of these caused considerably less damage to wildlife and habitat than did the *Exxon Valdez*.

had cut their costs and allowed procedures to become sloppy where they could get away with it, as in Valdez. From there, Rick and David set off on separate but sometimes converging paths to redress the wrong. Their paths would also entwine with those of many others . . . Riki Ott, Marilyn Leland, Jack Lamb, Kelly Weaverling, Larry Smith and Marge Tillion of Homer, John Mickelson of Seldovia.

The two, Rick and David, would finally become deeply involved in an attempt to resolve the tangle of civil and criminal proceedings by proposing, through a new group called The Coastal Coalition, that damages be immediately settled out of court and be paid by establishing a restoration fund for, among other things, acquiring and placing in trust Prince William Sound timber rights so as to quickly minimize further harm to the wounded environment. Following his return from Sullom Voe, David had followed his gift for binding people together. He co-produced a documentary video, *Voices of the Sound*. He then acquired the *Orca II* under what he described as an almost magical convergence of circumstances.

He had wanted to put an independent vessel in Prince William Sound — one not bound up with Exxon or the government. Because of the completeness of the vessel call-up for the cleanup, this would make the *Orca II* a rarity, maybe one of a kind. It became known as a "spiritual cleanup vessel." David had said, "Spiritual cleanup was what we needed. Physical cleanup would not address the underlying problems." Although David himself seemed often filled with doubts over his effectiveness, his approach displayed both the artist's vision of the way the sound, the oil, the turmoil, and distant political forces were an interconnected and fundamentally spiritual webwork, and the activist's sense that at times the best way into the heart of trouble would be found by patiently working the edges.

The *Orca II* is wooden, 38 feet long and 10 feet at the beam, with a 115-horsepower Chrysler gasoline engine that rumbles throatily and inspires confidence. A Jacobsen double-ender boat, it was built in 1946. Its hull is white above the waterline, trimmed with dark blue. The above decks are white trimmed with brown, its masts festooned with flags. Long and low, the boat has a graceful, canoe-like profile. It is a pleasure to regard from any position and a pleasure to be within — snug, clean, friendly. Through excellent craftsmanship in the first place and years of meticulous maintenance by several previous owners, it had taken on the quality of a loved thing, like an old family home. By its look and the touch of its wood fittings, the sliding windows in the wheelhouse that open readily when they are pushed just so, the wooden cabinetry in the galley, the brass lamps, the lightness of its carriage in the water, its two iron hearts — the Chrysler engine in the hold and the oil-burning cookstove in the galley — it has the power of engaging anyone who enters it.

To this is added the pictures, poems, feathers, beaded things, baskets, notes, and books inside, many left as mementos by those who had ridden the *Orca II* during the summer. These included David LaChapelle of Juneau, who had been instrumental in finding the boat for David, several Scottish members of Parliament, Earth First! people, Congressman Gary Studds of Massachusetts, Russians from the Soviet oil-skimming ship *Vaydaghubsky*, and Charles Hamel, the oil broker, James Naughton, the actor, Jean Michel Cousteau and several other members of the Cousteau Society, Greenpeace people, National Wildlife Federation people, the musician, John McCutcheon, Chris Moscone, the son of San Francisco's mayor, Mavis Mueller, the artist, as well as other artists, musicians, volunteers, and politicians from Prince William Sound and the state of Alaska. A portion of the densely inhabited orbit of activists that formed around the oil spill were transported by the *Orca II*.

We were in Tatitlek Narrows, cruising easily on the flat water. The three of us still stood in the wheelhouse, looking. Ahead of us, the bald, sheer, rock face of Copper Mountain rose from the mainland. David wore his brown hair in a ponytail and his feet were in thongs in all seasons. He had a clear, pleasant face. His good manners seemed ingrained down to the bone. Lynn was well over six feet, rawboned and powerful. Thoughtful, more taciturn than David, he was given to breaking his quiet with flashes of insight. He worked in Juneau as a carpenter and an expert small boat pilot. David had secured his help when the *Orca II* was first brought up from Juneau. They came through the Gulf of Alaska to Prince William Sound, but out of fear of the pain he would feel, Lynn had then flown straight home without looking at the oil. They had even approached Cordova through the tricky back door at the Copper River Flats so that he wouldn't see it. The voyage from which we were returning had been Lynn's first contact with the spill. We were now debating whether or not to stop at Tatitlek, knowing that there could be problems of decorum if we pulled in there unannounced.

We decided to put off the decision and to stop first at Ellamar, a tiny waterfront hamlet just west of Tatitlek, and to visit Susie Gill and Jon Rush. They had been the first people to see the *Exxon Valdez* on Bligh Reef, and had then seen it every day from their living room window for 12 days before the ship was moved to Naked Island. Their house, a fanciful-looking place built close to the water, sat high on the bank. Gabled, four stories, filigreed, turreted, and fronted by a rank of log pilings driven into the beach, it had a commanding presence. Its clapboard was pale and the trim blue. A sign on it read "Windsinger Haven." On one of the pilings was a large banner made of black petrofabric that had a picture of a hand giving the finger and the words painted in white, "Fuck Exxon." Because of the visual distraction of the house, the banner, and Jon Rush's boat — another, smaller double-ender — we nearly ran the *Orca II* aground on a reef. Lynn saw the rock shelf first, looming up toward the surface of the water. He shouted. David cut the engines and turned, and then backed out. It seemed an odd incident, alarming for a moment and then funny, an echo on a very small scale of the big one that had happened just around the corner.

We anchored and took the Zodiac to shore. Alerted by our antics with the rocks, Jon Rush had come down from the house to meet us. He was a tall man with brown hair and gray in his beard. He wore blue jeans, a blue plaid shirt, and thick glasses — the consequence of his work with scrimshaw. He'd had to all but quit scrimshaw for the sake of his eyes, he would tell us. He led us up a long stone stairway to the house. Susie, a thin, dark-haired woman with a page-boy haircut, met us at the door. We entered a capacious place. The kitchen, dining, and living rooms were open to each other and arranged in a line that led to the big bay window looking out on the water and Bligh Island. The house had the adventurous look of all such self-built places that were lived in and kept as clean as possible while they remained under construction — here the exposed plywood subfloor, and over there a partially finished wall. It had the unmistakable quality of an artist's home, of one who delighted in the visual. There were things on the walls, pictures and artifacts, things knocked into niches and hanging from the beams overhead — tools, odds and ends, a pair of rubber gloves, an old wagon. It was not unlike the inside of the *Orca II*.

Jon and Susie sat us down in the dining area. They were pleased to see us and treated us in the manner I had by then encountered again and again in Alaska — with cordiality and generosity. I supposed it was a function of what some would call isolation, the lonesomeness that pleasured in company. I thought of it as a balance struck with the world that allowed for space between people and thus for the proper value to be placed upon exchange and talk. At this time, of course, there was always the one big, ready-made subject — oil. The talk sought news of all its convolutions — where it was, where it wasn't, what it was killing now, and what further charlatanry it had provoked. Jon plied us with coffee and Sylvia put a bowl of dried salmon on the table. The three of us had difficulty not devouring the salmon, since by then our food stocks on the *Orca II* seemed to have narrowed to Fritos and salsa. Jon and Susie wanted to know where we'd been and what we'd seen. We told them: Knight Island, mainly, Snug Harbor, Mummy Bay, Lucky Bay, Herring Bay. We'd spent a day hiding from a storm at Disk Island. For David, the journey had been the last sojourn of the year in the place he loved, after the cleanup and before he put the *Orca II* up for the winter. We could say all that, but it was hard to speak of the luminous sense we held of water and dark land, of the mountain lake that perfectly reflected the trees and the clouds in the sky, of the way time had turned to liquid.

When we said that the sound looked better than we'd expected, Jon murmured and nodded. He knew David had been deeply involved in the response to the oil spill. For a time the two of them talked shop. Lynn and I sat quietly and listened. Susie moved into the kitchen and resumed what she'd been doing before our arrival. She was chopping vegetables with a cleaver. The rhythmic sound of her work formed a backdrop to the conversation.

Jon himself had tried first to join the volunteer brigade of boats from Tatitlek and Cordova, and then to organize a food lift to the Native communities whose beaches had been despoiled, what came to be called the Native to Native Assistance Program. The idea was that other Alaskan Native people would procure food and that it would then be distributed in the sound, particularly to the people of Tatitlek and Chenega. Chenega's shoreline resources had been destroyed, although the damage to Tatitlek remained something of a question. A ribbon of oil had entered the narrows and in the first few days of the spill the fumes had been almost overpowering. The extent of damage to Tatitlek's resources had raised the familiar bundle of claims, counterclaims, and denials from various scientific, political, ethnic, and economic quarters. Jon and Susie's efforts in those early days had sprung from the simple desire to do something, the reaction common to others everywhere on the sound and Kenai Peninsula. "But they shot the project down," Jon said. "And then Exxon took it over."

The insult he felt over having his efforts rebuffed was also common, though in my travels I had rarely seen a hurt as strong as his. He failed to get that project off the ground, and then was repeatedly frustrated in his attempts to be taken on by Veco, which had been put in charge of hiring boats and cleanup personnel in Valdez. Jon was told to apply in person in Valdez, but he was delayed by the closing of the channel, and then by a storm. When he got to Valdez, he was told that boats the size of his were no longer needed. He was told it might be needed later. Then he was told his boat couldn't be used because it was uninsured. He couldn't get insurance because the boat had fiberglass applied over the original wood, and when he inquired with other skippers as to how they had insured their similarly fitted boats he discovered that there were many uninsured boats under contract. He said there were people using boats far less seaworthy than his own — plastic boats, pleasure craft. He stayed in Valdez to fight the bureaucracy. He was told that Veco had priorities in its hiring preferences: first to local Area E (Prince William Sound) permit holders, second to Alaskan Area E permit holders, and third to out-of-state Area E permit holders. "But they didn't even stick to that," Jon said. "They lied about that, too. They asked me what fishery I was involved in. I said I was an artist and that we live in shouting distance of Bligh Reef. That was the end of that. They didn't want to touch me at all. They said, 'Tough, we're a big company and we'll hire whoever we want.'"

Lynn, David, and I were listening to a tirade. It had begun because we were here. As guests we gave structure to Jon's pain. He rolled one cigarette after another from his packet of Bugle tobacco as he spoke. At first, he directed his words mainly to David, who had managed to connect himself to the heart of the oil spill response in a way that had not compromised him. David's position, I thought, would seem enviable from Jon's perspective — because David had found a way to take action, whereas Jon had been left here, turning slowly on the spit of his own fury. Judging from the drawn look on David's face, he sensed this, too. It then came out that I was a writer and Jon turned to me. My role, the responsibility I had for translating his pain to the world, tightened the focus on his anger. As he went on, Susie's chopping in the kitchen grew steadily louder and faster until it sounded frenetic.

Jon told us how he had proof of instances of graft and payoffs, and how in the midst of the chaos at the beginning of the cleanup operation he'd spent an entire month and a half pursuing some of the hiring people. He also said there was a ploy on Exxon's part to maximize the public relations advantages of aiding Native people. He said that food had been delivered to Tatitlek but not to the Ellamar people, that as many of the Tatitlek boats as they could get had been hired, but not his boat. He said that he was a subsistence person, too, that he hadn't had time to cut his wood for the winter because of the spill. He told us how they'd had to put up with air traffic the whole time the *Exxon Valdez* was on Bligh Reef, and how even after that they found themselves in the flight pattern of the supply helicopters from Valdez. One had hovered right outside his studio window on the fourth floor.

In the kitchen, Susie abruptly stopped chopping and said, "We were ready to get a cannon. They all had to detour over here to check our place out."

"Some of my neighbors made a half a million dollars," Jon said. "All I got was a lost month and a half of work and the frustration."

This was the fracturing effect of the cleanup money, the ability it had to turn neighbor against neighbor, and even to come near to splitting entire towns in half. It had happened in Cordova, Homer, Seldovia, Port Graham, English Bay, Tatitlek, and most visibly in Valdez. It was the result of capitalizing the remedy to the spill, of the power of money, which drove the initial impulse to collective, voluntary action into a heavily charged predatory environment. Scruples fell away. The quick, the rapacious, and the well-equipped had the advantage and became what were known as spillionaires. Outsiders arrived. For Exxon, money was not an obstacle. Understanding that the public in the lower forty-eight, especially, had long been accustomed to accepting symbols in lieu of information, the company put its money behind symbology — the otter rescue centers, the machinery on the beaches, aid to Native people. Like all such symbolic campaigns, it had the effect of sweeping negative details away. Jon and Susie, who had found themselves out of the channel, connected neither to Cordova nor to Tatitlek, nor to the fishing industry, were negative details.

Jon said he was mounting a massive letter-writing campaign. His electric typewriter, in fact, had been disemboweled and was spread out on the floor beside his chair. When we'd arrived, he'd been repairing it for just that purpose. He told us how he planned to go to court to sue Exxon for invasion of privacy, trauma, stress, and loss of reputation. He told us how he'd asked the lieutenant governor of Alaska, Steven McAlpine, if he could expect any sympathy from him, and McAlpine had said, certainly. Jon told us how he'd typed up a bunch of information, and how McAlpine took it and never brought it up with anybody. "I had a shootout with the bigshots," Jon said. "As soon as McAlpine saw he might have to bump heads, he dropped it." Jon paused and looked between his knees at the floor, then said, "It's been an angry summer."

We were quiet for a moment. I got up and moved to the bay window in the living room. Jon, Lynn, and David followed. Jon pointed out where to look through a slot between the dark rocks near the end of the island. Beyond the rocks was an open space of pale water and sky. I imagined the ship in that space, listing ever so slightly, oil spewing from its holds.

"For the first four days," Susie said from the kitchen, "it sat there and they did nothing. I couldn't believe how ill-prepared they were."

"The screen got pulled away," David said. "And there was the Wizard of Oz."

Jon told us how he'd been up late working at his bench when he heard the steel grating against rock. He peered out his window toward Bligh Reef and saw the tanker's running lights. The ship seemed much too close. Then suddenly the sky went alight. The shorelines and hills around the reef turned bright. All the ship's lights had come on.

"Actually," he said, rocking back and turning away from the window, there was no surprise to it whatsoever. We'd been waiting for it to happen. We knew it was a question of time. They've been cutting that corner for years. I was almost run over by a tanker once near Jack's Bay on the right-hand side of the lane. He hung a turn and suddenly I was looking up at a steel wall. He'd mistook Jack's Bay for the narrows and turned into it. Can you believe that? Later, I saw the pilot in Valdez and asked him how that could happen. He said it never did happen."

"It makes you feel the oil companies have more power than the government," Susie said.

We moved back into the dining room and sat down. "The next thing will be the corruption," Jon said. "Wait and see. Susie and I finally ended up playing the role of watchers, not participants. Maybe we were lucky."

"It's economics," David said. In this were shades of what he would eventually become involved with, The Coastal Coalition, the ambitious attempt to knit together the detail of local economy and, in the form of reparation, the resources of an international petroleum superproprietor. "When it comes to economics, we're not really a community."

"That's right," Jon said. "Now, my main concern is how are we going to recover from this thing as a people. The whole thing is warped completely out of shape by the money."

David took a sounding: "What do you think would make you happy?"

Jon thought for a moment, then answered with a cold fury, "Exactly what my neighbors got. Not a penny more and not a penny less. Because I just can't live with the arrogance." He paused again, lit another cigarette, and said, "I debated really hard whether I should even bother with it, or if I should just sit at my bench and do what I always did. I wanted to help and I kept an open mind about what I would do until I ran into the arrogance."

We looked at Jon's paintings. He brought out a box and showed us his scrimshaw. Much of his work, he said, emulated Native techniques. He readily granted that, angry as he was with some of his neighbors in Tatitlek. The root of his outrage, I understood then, and the cause of the fracture in his views came from having been turned against himself by the cleanup money. He showed us a moveable sculpture called *Slow Dancing*. It was close to two feet tall and had a base made of four kinds of wood sanded down and varnished to a shine. Faces were carved into each side of the base. Inside the base was a clockwork. On the base, a man and a woman, carved out of a walrus tooth, made love. Above them was a carved snail shell. The clockwork in the base turned the couple and snail shell one revolution every 24 hours. Over the couple and snail shell was lantern glass, capped with a carved mushroom. The mushroom had a little battery-run spotlight inside it to illuminate the shell and the couple as they made love and turned ever so slowly. It was a wonderful thing, delicately carved, intricately conceived, and mysterious in the way the natural elements played against its mechanics. As we admired it, Jon's mood softened.

He came out to visit the *Orca II*. He and David went ahead in his skiff. Outside the house, Lynn and Susie talked for a few minutes about mutual friends and the garden. Susie seemed abruptly changed, happy to be out of the pressure cooker of the house. Lynn and I motored out to the *Orca II* in the Zodiac. When we entered the galley, Jon and David were talking. Jon also looked changed, as if he'd shed several years. "This boat's immaculate," he said admiringly. He gazed through a window back toward his house and said, "Ellamar. The community Exxon forgot. But they were over to Tatitlek the first chance they got."

"The people of Tatitlek don't really measure their life in dollars," David said. "If you screw up the environment, you've screwed everything up. If you make a cash settlement, you screw them up."

"Tell that to the kid who bought a Corvette with his cleanup money. What's he going to do with a Corvette in Tatitlek?" Jon stopped himself, and sighed, then smiled at us. "I've known those people for twenty years and lived next to them for eleven. Some of them are the best people in the whole world."

After he left, we went on our way toward Cordova. As we neared Tatitlek, the face of Copper Mountain loomed higher. Guggenheim mining money had been here, too. The village of Tatitlek had been relocated for the sake of the copper mine. Ellamar had been a mining camp. On a distant shore before us, we could see a swath of bare mountain, a timber clear-cut.

Lynn said, "There's a metaphor with Jon, the way the money like the oil goes in some places and not in others. A million dollars on either side of the man who was the first one to see the tanker."

CHAPTER 12

THE VALUE OF THE DEAD

War and photography now seem inseparable, and plane crashes and other horrific accidents always attract people with cameras. A society which makes it normative to aspire never to experience privation, failure, misery, pain, dread disease, and in which death itself is regarded not as natural and inevitable but as a cruel, unmerited disaster, creates a tremendous curiosity about these events — a curiosity that is partly satisfied through picture-taking. The feeling of being exempt from calamity stimulates interest in looking at painful pictures, and looking at them suggests and strengthens the feeling that one is exempt. Partly it is because one is "here," not "there," and partly it is the character of inevitability that all events acquire when they are transmuted into images. In the real world, something is happening and no one knows what is going to happen. In the image-world, it has happened, and it will forever happen in that way.

— Susan Sontag, *On Photography*, 1977

The storm that struck March 27, the fourth day of the spill, drove the oil slick south and west through the sound. Prevailing currents moved the leading edges past the islands in the southwest and into the Gulf of Alaska. By March 29, the oil had come near Resurrection Bay and Seward on the south shore of the Kenai Peninsula. The town of Seward declared a local emergency.

By April 3, day 11, portions of the slick had moved northward up Resurrection Bay and southwesterly along the Kenai Peninsula off the Kenai Fjords National Park to cover an area of 1,000 square miles. On NOAA maps, the slick was represented as long strips and patches in Prince William Sound and as a large oblong settled just off the ragged shoreline of the Kenai Peninsula. Two days later, the slick widened to cover 2,600 miles, and on April 6, it struck the Chiswell Islands in the Gulf, 35 miles southwest of Seward. The islands were a nesting site for 70,000 migratory seabirds, including auklets and puffins, and a haulout for thousands of sea lions. On April 10, the eighteenth day of the spill, the second major storm hit, and the oil moved ashore at the Kenai Fjords National Park and at the Alaska Maritime National Wildlife Refuge, a place that includes over 700 islands.

Well before this time, the residents of Seward and the towns clustered around the southwestern corner of the Kenai Peninsula — English Bay, Port Graham, Seldovia, Homer — had understood very well what the winds and currents would eventually bring to them. Although some of the authorities, including NOAA representative Hal Alabaster, continued to issue hopeful statements about the powers of wind and wave action to break up the slick, the residents of the Kenai towns thought otherwise and formed volunteer organizations in preparation for the defense of their shorelines. The day after the spill, Alabaster suggested that nature was succeeding in breaking up (or dispersing) the slick where man had failed, which was true enough, generally speaking, but at the same time chunks of the slick were being driven toward the shorelines. Bill Noll, who was to become mayor of Seward, said, "As soon as we knew a river of oil was headed for Montague Island, we knew damn well what was going to happen. We knew it was first going to hit the gulf and then come back our way. We started by borrowing and stealing boom anywhere we could get our hands on it. We were organized before anybody else got here."

In Homer and Seldovia a rift developed between NOAA scientists and residents who remembered what, outside Alaska, was a little-known incident in Cook Inlet — the 159,000-gallon spill from the tanker *Glacier Bay* in the summer of 1987. NOAA had the data from laboratory experiments, knowledge of previous spills, and the circumspection allowed by scientific distance. But as it turned out, the image evoked by descriptions of the oil breaking up and slipping away from sight somewhere out at sea was quite at odds with the developing reality. The image and the misapprehensions it engendered were due in part to what NOAA's Jerry Galt would later tell me was an over-reliance, especially by the press and those in charge of coordinating the response, on "anecdotal data," and to the fact that while NOAA had a good basic fix on the currents of the sound and gulf, not much was known about the winds. "We learned a lot about the winds," Galt would say.

On April 11, the oil moved around the tip of the Kenai Peninsula and was sighted just below English Bay, another Native village. By this time the utterly changed and astonishing reality of the spill and of the increasingly complex exigencies of cleanup were coming to be accepted, though in differing ways, by everyone. On the twelfth, Dennis Kelso said, "We are entering a new phase." On April 16, the slick moved up Cook Inlet. On the seventeenth, it finally hit the shores of Seward at the head of Resurrection Bay. On the eighteenth, patches were sited in the mouth of Kachemak Bay, near the village of Port Graham.

By the end of the first week of May, oil had been carried across the mouth of Cook Inlet to Katmai National Park, where large numbers of dead birds were sighted. It reached Wide Bay, which is on the mainland behind (west of) Kodiak Island. In some areas, the slick moved at the speed of 17.5 miles per day, and it was now more than 500 miles away from the original site at Bligh Reef. By the end of the next week, oil had drifted to Alinchak Bay on the Alaska Peninsula and washed ashore at Homer, Kachemak Bay, the southern and western sides of Kodiak Island, and Chignik Bay in Shelikof Strait.

Fisheries in Prince William Sound, Cook Inlet, and off Kodiak were rapidly being closed or threatened with closure. Over 16,000 dead birds and nearly 700 dead otters had been recovered, and thousands more dead animals had been sighted on and near the oiled beaches. Because of the rugged conditions and the difficulty of spotting oiled animals in an oiled terrain or on oiled water, however, it had become apparent that the majority of the dead animals would never be recovered or counted. They were often seen as black, bubble-like protrusions in the stick. An unknown number of them would sink from sight. Counting fish and other marine life forms was an even chancier proposition. How many sea stars? How many pounds of popweed? The count of the dead was important to the symbology of the spill. Here, where it came to be announced in daily meetings at the Oil Spill

Coordinating Office (OSCO) in Homer, the count took on the character of funereal litany. Elsewhere, and certainly in the lower forty-eight, the count took on a cartoon-like spin — violent, powerfully affecting to those predisposed to receive it, and yet remote from the experience of actual violence.

So long as the oil remained mobile, like an alive thing reaching up Resurrection Bay, Cook Inlet, and way back behind Kodiak Island, the story had an arresting effect on the public in the lower forty-eight. Even though the public at large but dimly understood where these places were and what they looked like, the story acquired a libidinous narrative drive not unlike a soap opera or science fiction thriller. Like soap operas and science fiction, it had strong intimations of a morality play. The story was followed in the same way the Watergate hearings of the seventies or the recent Clinton impeachment hearings were followed as they moved day by day nearer and nearer to their final resolution. Just what the resolution of the oil spill story was to be, or should be, however, was unclear. The stripping away of Exxon's assets, the permanent shutdown of the Alyeska terminal, the permanent closure of future drilling sites in ANWR and elsewhere? Or maybe the public burning of Joseph Hazelwood and upper-echelon Exxon officials? None of these conclusions would come to pass. During congressional testimony on April 6, the same day the oil slick hit the Chiswell Islands and Joseph Hazelwood was released from the Long Island jail, Senator Slade Gorton of Washington suggested to L.G. Rawl that he consider resigning as a result of the spill. Gorton pointed out that Japanese executives often resigned when their companies were involved in environmental disasters. Rawl said, "I don't know if I have to respond to that, but a lot of Japanese kill themselves as well, and I refuse to do that." In this exchange, Senator Gorton, known in his home state as a "moderate" at best, and at worst as an anti-conservation "opportunist" when it came to environmental questions, served as a conductor for the intense public desire for some conclusion to the story. Rawl served as a reminder that the story would never end, that the morally definitive action it seemed to require would never occur.

The pictures of the dead as they appeared in newspapers across the country, newsmagazines, and periodicals devoted to popular science, nature, and the environment at once tended to make the image of death excessively articulate and at the same time to gloss over the fact of death itself. Among the most memorable and common were those that zeroed in on an otter or a bird — often loons, murres, or pelagic cormorants, which were among the most striking because of their long, graceful necks and sharply defined bills. The animals were seen covered with oil and stiff with rigor mortis. Their lower bodies emerged from a pool of oil and their upper bodies were cast in relief against pebbles, sand, snow, water, or sky. In some cases, the animals had clearly been positioned for the sake of the shot. By a quirk of physiognomy, the otters often had their paws crossed near to their chests when they died, and in the pictures this seemed to echo human mortuary practices. Such photographs displayed a studied element of romance in the face of inescapable horror. When I raised this matter with Natalie Fobes, a remarkable, Seattle-based photographer who spent weeks in Alaska following the spill, she said that she considered it her obligation to get the images of the dead into the living rooms of the nation and to keep them there as long as possible. Hers was an eminently defensible position, and yet in the interplay between the photographer's craft and sense of duty on the one hand, and the public's response to such images on the other hand, lay the hazard of what Susan Sontag calls "the chronic voyeuristic relation to the world that levels the meaning of all events."[49]

Such voyeurism, Sontag says, has "a way of at least tacitly, often explicitly, encouraging whatever is going on to keep on happening," and even, or especially, when the event is painful, to continue going on forever without conclusion. Due to the nature of the press, much of its coverage, and due to the necessities of its capital investments, all of Exxon's public relations efforts were devised, first, to keep the story thin and to keep the public in it until the story faded from audibility like a top-forty tune on the radio, and second, to prevent the public from conceiving of what had actually happened. In my journeys to and from Alaska, I was struck by nothing quite so much as the lag between what I had witnessed in one place and the versions reported in the other. When I walked an oiled beach, I learned that the dead were not nearly so likely to be found posing for the camera as they were to be discovered as one picked one's way among oil-inundated rocks ... felt through the touch of a footfall upon something too hard to be liquid and too soft to be rock, a pliant thing down there, too solid to be wood or stone, a thing that still had the give of what had been a life and the integrity of lineament, skin, and bone, a thing that slithered away from the boot and when punctured gave off gas. The smell of rot mixed with the smell of raw petroleum. Death was everywhere, twined upon itself and not articulate, a teeming, inchoate crowd, suspended in oil.

[49] The reader will observe what might seem to be a contradiction in the inclusion of Natalie Fobes' photographs in this edition of the book. However, her work is in my view so telling and sometimes strangely beautiful — witness the patterns of oil on water in her pictures — that to make them herewith an addition to the written record was too strong an opportunity to be denied.

Marge Tillion was one of the early community response organizers in Homer. Later, she was a principal member of the Homer Area Recovery Coalition (HARC — also referred to for a short time as SPARC, the South Peninsula Area Recovery Coalition). Later yet, she would represent Homer on a citizens' advisory committee to Alyeska, as Alyeska reformed its contingency plan.

Larry Smith was another Homer organizer and activist, a man of rectitude and yet capable of talking amiably with anyone from any position on the political spectrum. He'd been working for years on forestry and timber harvesting practices in Alaska and had founded what he described as a "profit/ not-for-profit habitat type of thing" called the Kachemak Resource Institute. The institute was located in a low, gray, wooden building on the outskirts of Homer. The building mainly housed an attorney's office and an infant learning program. A set of dilapidated steps led to the deck on which rested a stack of firewood and a filing cabinet with a sign on it that said, "Property of Kachemak Resource Institute." Perhaps most tellingly, out in the chest-high weeds of the front yard was coiled a length of blue oil boom. Later, Larry would move into another building and have, as he put it, "a real office," but when I visited, that was it — the oil boom as memento of the oil wars, the filing cabinet on the deck, and inside a legal secretary who cheerfully took messages for Larry and allowed him to use the phone. It was enough.

Larry had sent me to see Marge Tillion, whom he described as "a formidable character and a hell of a boat woman." Through his interest in the use of timber resources, Larry would also come to be in touch with David Grimes and Rick Steiner. That's how things were. Contacts spun around and jumped out in long arcs.

Joined by highway to Anchorage and by ferry to Valdez and Cordova, built on the northern side of the mouth of Kachemak Bay, Homer fell away to the north and east into plateau country. Out on the edge of town is a group of recent Russian immigrants who follow a communal and conservative style of life. Known as "Old Believers," they came here first from Oregon, and before that from Turkey, and before that from Russia to escape religious persecution under the communist state. More than 300 years ago, they had splintered from the Russian Orthodox. The town of Homer has about 4,000 residents; the greater Homer area, over 11,000. The numbers of actual residents rise and fall according to the season, and over half of Homer's population had lived there less than five years. Fishing is the main economy, followed by government employment and tourism. Here, too, the divisive business of timber extraction, including enterprise on public lands, was under development. The Homer Spit, which stretches halfway across Kachemak Bay, is the center of commercial fishing operations and also the point of embarkation for tourists and sport fishing.

The town also has a fine small museum, the Pratt Museum, and a first-class public radio station. There is a leftward-leaning activist presence and a strong sense of community spirit. During the summer, there are a lot of strangers around, who are treated pretty well, and a great deal of money in medium-sized denominations pinging to and fro. Although tourism was said to have suffered because of the oil spill when I was there in mid-July, a section of the Homer Spit was nevertheless lined with recreational vehicles. Larry told me that what I was seeing was nothing compared with what it could be, and nothing compared with what it would be when the annual Halibut Derby got under way.

He took me to the spit. We looked at the huge steel ore carriers brought up from Skagway, which were to be used for hauling oiled refuse out to Anchorage. Added to the already boiling controversy over the disposition of oily waste was the fact that the tanks themselves had been found to have been contaminated with lead before they arrived. We looked at the log oil boom stacked up in a Veco lot. There were lumberyard-sized stacks of logs here and at other locations on the spit. They were ponderous and heavy, affixed with plywood to make a splash shield, draped with petrofabric to make the skirt, and festooned with cable and all manner of metal and concrete chunks to weight the skirts. At the time, since much of the boom had been oiled, it presented its own disposal problem.

Originally part of a project initiated across the bay in Seldovia in the third week of April and then taken up in Homer, the boom had become the focal point in the battle between the people of South Kenai and Exxon. As the oil had worked its way toward the Kenai in early April, Exxon and the government agencies were still groping to mount an appropriate response in Prince William Sound. Exxon had concentrated its efforts there, and its expertise, and what equipment it had so far marshaled. The result was that events on the Kenai echoed previous events in Valdez, Tatitlek, and Cordova: the growing public outrage as the oil moved ineluctably in their direction, the town meetings in the Homer high-school auditorium attended by hundreds and during which Exxon representatives, notably Wiley Bragg, would take public verbal beatings, the community frustration over the lack of action, and the confusion over what action to take and how to pay for it. As the time between the day of the spill and the arrival of the oil was wider here than in the sound, so too was the lag between "official" recognition that the oil was indeed coming and mobilization. Because of the lag, the sense here that Exxon and the government had given up trying to prevent it from washing ashore grew ever stronger. The distinct impression was left that Exxon still hoped the oil would disappear, or that ignoring it would somehow magically reduce its impact, although in all fairness it should be said that at this point Exxon's resources and its organization were so overtaxed in the sound that it was virtually impossible to catch up and mount a response elsewhere appropriate to the problem.

On April 14, the Coast Guard had approved Exxon's initial cleanup plan, but as the oil spread along the Kenai and toward Kodiak, the plan became instantly obsolete. Included in the plan was the creation of a Shoreline Cleanup Assessment Team (SCAT). The SCAT team passed its recommendations back to Exxon's Valdez office. From there, revised recommendations were passed to multi-agency coordinating groups (MACs, which included representatives from the community, the state parks, the Forest Service, and at times other agencies), who made site-specific recommendations and passed them back to the Coast Guard. Included in the process was the issuance of permits by such agencies as the EPA and the Fish and Wildlife Service. The Coast Guard approved (or disapproved) the recommendations and sent them on to Exxon, which then implemented them by sending word to their regional representatives. By the time the crisis was hitting the Kenai, this was the form Admiral Yost's plan to cut through the BS and "kick some butts" had taken. In the meantime, the Exxon crews had cleaned less than two miles of shoreline in Prince William Sound.

What hit the Kenai people was the same contradiction seen elsewhere. On the one hand, they expected Exxon to get here and do something, even to do the impossible. On the other hand, they resented the presence of Exxon once it did arrive. What emerged for a time was another public effort by residents of Seward, Homer, Soldotna, Port Graham, English Bay, and Seldovia. The Homer MAC was at first headed by Loren Flagg, a fisheries biologist appointed by burough mayor Don Gillman. The group sought to channel efforts and expedite communication, supplies, and money, but not surprisingly found the system close to immovable. For two weeks, very little got done. Moreover, Exxon seemed once again to be trying to impede efforts, repeatedly telling the Homer MAC that commercial boom in quantity was unavailable. Marge Tillion began to make her own list of suppliers and outlets and, incidentally, of fishermen and boats willing to fight the spill. In 48 hours she had 100 boats signed up. The Homer MAC put in an order for

5,000 feet of boom and had it within two days. It was a prime example, Loren Flagg would say, "of our frustration with Exxon's lies. They hadn't tried to get it. They deceived us."

Because of the almost complete absence of commercial boom, at first, and then because the quantities on hand remained insufficient, the log boom project went on. The boom was intended to be used to protect the most critical shorelines of the area — notably, the state salmon hatchery at Tutka Lagoon, English Bay Lagoon, Dogfish Bay Lagoon, and other spawning grounds and prized wildlife habitats. Boom experts from the outside advised that log boom would not be as effective as commercial boom, but the volunteers procured logs, at times cutting, limbing, skinning, and hauling them themselves. Various designs were tried. Crews worked through the night to build the boom, and finally thousands of feet of it were floated and hauled to critical sites. In some cases it alone was deployed. In other cases, it was augmented by commercial boom. In many situations, it didn't work especially well. In certain other situations its heaviness was thought to make it superior to the commercial variety.

Although Larry Smith acknowledged that the boom hadn't always worked, he was proud of the project, and of his part in it. His skills as a carpenter had been put to use. He pointed out how this material was scrounged up from what was available — a piece of iron, say, cut out of a crab pot — and how this type of skirt had worked and how that one had not, how the logs were joined with cable and weighted to prevent them from rolling. Once again, the project spoke well of the capacity of Alaskans to take action, of the meaning of action when it sprang from the root of a community, of the variety of talents and capabilities that could be called forth, and mainly of the profoundly different effect upon the spirits of people such an approach had in comparison with the alienating effect of the approach emanating from the Valdez headquarters, and at times from the borough mayor's office in Soldotna.

What followed, and what caused the deepest frustration, was the invasion of Exxon, implemented mainly by its contractor, Veco. I talked to Ken Broginoff that night on the Homer Spit. He was a partner in a fishing fleet and head of operations for a packing company, and so had been in a position to command an impressive array of resources — a warehouse, 78 fishing boats, supplies, and the distribution contacts that go with an outfit of that size. He said that he knew the oil was going to come to the Kenai, so he figured that his best course would be to start a cleanup effort. Exxon told him that it wanted his yard and building and fleet, and so he became a Veco subcontractor. Dark-haired and spare, Broginoff has a melancholy aspect.

He sat behind a desk in the warehouse office and leaned back in his chair as he spoke. He struck me as an admirable man who had found himself in a position to make himself useful, but as often as not in ways that were objectionable to him. He had little respect for Veco, and detested the fact that local people had been put out of work by what he called the pipeline syndrome. He'd had to lay off all his regular workers because they weren't union members. He worried about the effect Exxon welfarism would have upon the people. He said, "As soon as Veco got into the log boom business, five chain saws disappeared. For two weeks, no groceries were delivered . . . where they went, I don't know. The paperwork is incredible, but I'm keeping accountability with everything that's come through here. If there's a pump out there, we know where it is."

He was worried about sinking oil, which at the time I spoke with him — mid-July — had become the dominant controversy on the Kenai Peninsula and at Kodiak. Science said that oil couldn't sink. Broginoff, who had worked previously at Prudhoe Bay as an engineer and project manager, said, "The oil gets heavier and heavier and eventually sinks. It gets stuck on gear. You pull a shrimp pot and it's oiled, and you can't figure where it came from. It sinks because of the shearing effect of currents. At one point," he said, "there was no progress on the oil spill. It disappeared. It was shearing, then all of a sudden it popped up at Chugach, and at Kodiak. As fishermen we're skeptical of fishing. We don't want to contaminate our plant. If they find one oiled fish, they can close the whole area and our plant could be quarantined.

"The people running the operations are good supervisors from Texas, but they don't know a thing about our beaches. We're putting a hundred-ton crane out on the barrens tomorrow," he said. "It's a bird sanctuary. The barrens have maybe the highest bird mortality of any place. They're planning to hand-clean the north side and use the crane on the south side. I've told them, but they won't listen. The crane's going to sink on that beach."

After talking to Broginoff, Larry and I went out to the docks and watched John Glidden, a DEC inspector, examine a salmon catch as it was unloaded from a seiner. The silvery fish were lifted from the boat to the dock in large plastic totes. The totes are loaded to the brim. From the tote, they went into a large steel container, but first Glidden spot-checked them for oil. The rule was "zero tolerance" on oiling of the catches, taken from what areas were allowed to open.

Larry and I moved nearer to the edge of the dock. Glidden would select a fish, stroke it, peer closely into the gills, and then check the anus. He would squeeze the fish and examine the offal emerging from the anus. Our presence seemed to make him nervous. He glanced over at us, and then back behind us at the notebook I'd left on top of Larry's car. Its pages fluttered in the breeze. Glidden's face took on an alarmed look, and in an expression of the wariness many of the government people had over being watched, he said, "You're not taking notes, are you?"

From Marge Tillion I heard another version of what had become the main story told and retold by lower Kenai Peninsula people — the shock felt when Exxon and its contractors came to town. I sat on a couch in Marge's living room and she sat across from me on an easy chair. She and her husband were fishermen. She was also a fireman and licensed emergency medical technician. Her father-in-law, Clem Tillion, was an old-time Alaska legislator and close associate of former governor Jay Hammond. Marge had dark, short hair and flashing eyes and was deeply tanned by the outdoors. She was articulate and, as Larry had said, formidable.

She'd become involved with the response four days after the oil spill. "My immediate thought was that they were going to need boats to help them," she said. "I made a data base by feeding in the lists from fishing organizations." She got up and left the living room, then came back with a three-inch-thick stack of spreadsheet-sized computer printouts, set it down on the floor, and ranged through it, looking down at it at times as she spoke and then over at me. The data base had grown fast, she said. People began calling to get their boats and equipment on it. For its range and sheer voluminousness, her data base echoed the other lists that were everywhere. Hers included storage tanks, hydroblasters, shovels, five-gallon buckets, people, showers, skiffs, airplanes, and 800 boats.

Right away, she said, she and the other local volunteers arranged to use the high school as a Bird Rescue Center and the junior high swimming pool for the Otter Rescue Center (later moved to Jackolof Bay near Seldovia). The high-school teachers encouraged their students to help with the effort. An Exxon representative called from Valdez to ask if he could get access to her data base. She had so many calls that she added five telephone lines to her house, and a fax and photocopy machine. By the first week in April, her house had become the Oil Resource Center, and then she suddenly discovered that she was up to her nose in politics.

The people were calling from Valdez and Cordova, warning about inflated prices, housing problems, the press, lawyers, the ruthless takeover of the towns. "I worked for hours begging our mayor not to let them bring Veco in," she said. She wanted a local organization to work with Exxon. She remembered what had happened in Valdez when the pipeline came in. "I had the clearest picture of what was going to happen here. But I still wasn't paying close enough attention. I still didn't believe that we wouldn't be able to do something to stop it. I picked up the first two Exxon people at the airport and pleaded with them — 'Please don't bring Veco in.' I showed them my data base. They assured me all they wanted Veco for was to do the accounting. I worked for two or three weeks without a contract, just to watch them because I had a gut feeling they were not being straight. Sure enough, Veco came in and started up with the accounting. During a storm, I heard Veco was hiring skiffs to go out in heavy seas to pull boom. Suddenly it hit me that somebody might die out there and that if they did I might be liable, too, and I told the Veco people, and they said, 'You shut up. You do what we want you to do, and say what we want you to say.'"

She moved back to the chair and looked at me. "I will not be bought off," she said. "A guy from Exxon blocked off my car one day and said, 'Hey, what do you want? Six, seven thousand a day? We'll pay you.' I said, 'I can't work with you. This is my data base and I want control of it.' It was a tough spot. I wanted to take my data base out of there, but at the same time if I did I'd set the whole effort back several weeks."

At that time, the Homer and Seldovia volunteers' log boom project was well under way. Marge said that Exxon went back on its word and turned the entire Kenai Peninsula cleanup operation over to Veco. "Everything went bad then," she said. She said that Veco inflated figures, including counting boat people twice — once as a boat crew and once again as cleanup crew — in order to increase the margin on its "cost plus" contract. Marge, like many others, had become distraught and decided to go out with a science crew to "cool out." When she returned she found that Larry Smith and John Mickelson, the Seldovia MAC representative, had secured a million dollars from Exxon, which was to be channeled through the borough to run an independent cleanup crew. It was at first thought to be a replenishable million, that is, a million-dollar balance that would be sustained by Exxon, but as it turned out, by the time the million ran out the entire operation had been taken over by Veco. In Marge's view, this was how Veco took the town over — by gradually encroaching upon agreements and filling in all the gaps until it had control.

In the meantime, an 18-man crew had been hired and put to work. In an echo of some of the Cordova efforts, it picked up between four and five thousand gallons of oil a day. But then they were left out there, awaiting tankerage to take on their oil. When the money ran out, Marge tried — and, but for one boat skipper, failed — to get her crew taken on by Veco. The entire operation was stalled, she said, while the new manager, a real estate agent, took two weeks to develop a company to handle his business. At the same time, oil was appearing in Cook Inlet. When it was reported, it took between two and three weeks to get anybody to look at it. She claimed that the Veco workers went to absorbent pads for cleaning because the crews were always green, and anything else was too complicated for them. She said they hired 40 crew members, flew them to the beach to perform for a film crew, and then when the filming was over, let the entire crew go.[50] "We don't hold it against them that they don't know how to clean beaches," Marge said. "What we do hold against them is that they refuse to use our expertise. They could have benefited from us and at the same time left us all feeling good about oil companies by putting us to work.

"Salmon is my whole income," she said. "They gave us ten thousand for the Cook Inlet Drift Net Closure, and that may be all I'll see. In the meantime I can't leave, I can't get a job, and I can't fish. I've got three kids, and one of them is going to a school in Seattle for dyslexia. The contract for our tender boat makes two-thirds of the payments on the boat, and we've got to find the other third somewhere or lose the boat." Her voice had begun to shake. She paused, then told me I should get Larry Smith to show me the bird-burning video. Eventually, I did see it at his house. Rough and grainy, strictly amateur and not attempting to be anything else, a kind of accidental document, the video definitely delivers the weight of death.

Marge's disappointment, and her desire to do something, to be engaged, along with similar feelings by others, led to a project sponsored by HARC. A beach-cleaning project, it came to be centered at Mars Cove, not far from Gore Point on the southern side of the Kenai Peninsula — a heavily oiled area that Exxon had essentially abandoned to the elements. The project proposed to rehabilitate one beach. It would raise all its funding through contributions, apply the strictest methods of accounting, and employ an all-volunteer labor force. Begun in early July, and initially using shovels, buckets, and absorbent pads, the project later used a rock-washing machine invented by a young man named Billy Day. The process involved digging up a small section of oiled beach at low tide, running the rocks through a system of high-pressure hoses, vacuuming off the oil from a catch pond, then replacing

[50] On May 19, a *U.S.A. Today* production crew filmed cleanup efforts at Gore Point for national broadcast. Two hours before the production team arrived, as many as 53 workers were shuttled to a Gore Point beach and then filmed as they industriously mopped and shoveled the heavy oil. After the production crew left, the workers were shuttled back out. The next day 40 of them were laid off.

the rocks. The project was begun in late August and ran through September, after the Exxon cleanup operation had pulled out. When the volunteers were done, a small patch of the beach was clean.

Larry Smith lived about 20 miles outside Homer, in a house he built. Between the house and water are several hundred yards of dense growth, out of which Larry's son, Liam, and a friend abruptly emerged one evening with a moose hot on their heels.

We watched the video in Larry's kitchen one night. The television and VCR were balanced on top of the refrigerator. The video had been taken by Drew Scalzi, a boat skipper employed by the Fish and Wildlife Service. He and the beach crew had gathered 676 seabird corpses at Gore Point, and then awaited instructions for what to do next. They contacted officials in Homer and requested permission to destroy the birds. Their request was denied. They waited, and then, wary of the fact that the birds would soon begin to rot, and mindful of their job description, which was, as Scalzi put it, "to get this stuff out of the food chain," the crew took it upon itself to burn the corpses. Scalzi made the videotape, he said, in order to prove he wasn't trying to destroy evidence against Exxon. Marge Tillion had told me that she thought the action had the elements of a protest.

The tape, which had become an underground classic of the oil spill, was often blurred and ragged. Shots veered wildly from one subject to another. The heavily oiled birds were first laid out in a long line on the beach like death camp victims, and photographed. The crew then made a seven-foot-high pyre out of driftwood, ignited it, and began carrying the birds one-by-one to the flames and throwing them in. There is a nervous boisterousness on the part of the crew near the beginning of the video. However, as the tape continues, as the birds mount on the pile, their attitude changes. The initial buoyancy dissolves. The joking ceases. The movement of the crew members, carrying bodies to the flames, grows more and more ponderous.

The tape was true, absolutely unadorned cinema verité. The person holding the camera is a participant in the action. As the tape proceeds, the shots grow longer. The lens seems as close to the eye of a human as a camera might get. The tape is run without break, and the occasional dipping of the camera suggests the cameraman's own fatigue. The imagery becomes less and less trivial. The movement is toward complete involvement, an emotional sinking in. The line between the disengaged bureaucratic view of the world and being in the world is inescapably crossed.

The Fish and Wildlife Service wanted the bodies for the sake of the numbers. Scalzi and his crew wanted, quite reasonably, to remove oiled carrion from the beach. Scalzi was fired by Fish and Wildlife when he returned to Homer. When he showed his video, he was reinstated. For Scalzi and his crew, the value of the dead had come to reside in the weight it transposed to those who grew to be intimate with death itself. For those who merely counted, the dead had no intrinsic value.

The dead were of great importance to institutions likely to be involved in litigation — Exxon, Alyeska, the federal government, the state of Alaska, and various environmental and commercial organizations. Counting the dead meant money, although there would always be argument over how much the dead were worth. Estimating the value of the dead began with arguments over the accuracy of projected baselines and of the surveys. As this ensued, and as litigation commenced, those of the dead that had been gathered waited in their refrigerated trucks.

In their article, "Assessing Damages from the Valdez Oil Spill," A. Myrick Freeman and Raymond J. Kopp point out that in accordance with "provisions of the Clean Water Act of 1972 and Alaska State law, both the federal and state governments can sue 'potentially responsible parties' to recover the economic damages sustained by the publicly owned natural resources of the affected region." In a courtroom, the damage to resources lost (or not harvested) due to fishery closures may be relatively easily established, though never to the complete satisfaction of all parties. Similarly, the damage to chartered sports fishing or hunting may be approximated. The damage to subsistence villages or to the visual beauty that might attract tourists becomes rather more complex because in the first case the material value of, say, urchins, sea cucumbers, or fish is tied to community and spiritual values, to a way of life. In the second case, the majestic appearance of a place is tied to something like spiritual values, as well, or at the very least in Euro-American culture to a commonly held romance. It was the rupturing of this romance, which sometimes takes the place of religion in our country, that caused much of the outcry in the lower forty-eight. John V. Krutilla, covering similar ground in his article "Conservation Considered," suggests that any "grand scenic wonder or unique and fragile ecosystem . . . [is] a significant part of the real income of many individuals." Such individuals, Krutilla says, "are the spiritual descendents of John Muir . . . to whom the loss of a species or the disfigurement of a scenic area causes acute distress and a sense of genuine relative impoverishment."

Freeman and Kopp also discuss what economists in a mind-crunching phrase refer to as "lost non-use values," that is, intrinsic values that might be said to affect a large group of individuals who have no direct involvement with the place or thing of value. "The origin of these values," Freeman and Kopp say, "may lie in a desire to preserve the natural environments for the enjoyment of future generations or from a simple expression of stewardship. Economists generally place diminished non-use values on an equal footing with diminished use values and argue that failure to account for lost non-use values will understate the damage suffered by society."

Krutilla speaks of the values of potential use, such as the potential usefulness (or benefit to the world) of maintaining diverse gene pools and unique habitats, and the usefulness of a resource that might be employed more efficiently in the future. Many oil fields presently under use, including Prudhoe Bay, continue to produce beyond their expected yields because of previously undeveloped drilling technologies. Attempting to measure such values in the present, though they are again certainly real enough, is so speculative as to put them functionally in a category like non-use values.

The method of measuring non-use values is referred to as "contingent valuation." It's another curious term: contingent upon what? Freeman and Kopp point out that the contingent valuation is based upon society's willingness to pay as that is revealed in surveys. Gathering and assessing relevant data from surveys involves not only economic theory but the psychological and statistical sciences, as well. The answer to the question has to include: to a significant degree, contingent upon itself, upon the very concept of assigning economic value to projections, intangibles, and abstractions.

The notion that those who purchase cheap fuel and so affirm the system of production every minute of every day — that is, all of us — should bear a substantial portion of the cost of both cleanup and prevention of future oil spills through what is paid for oil and through taxation has its roots in the traditional principles of conservation in the U.S., and pragmatically speaking is inescapable. The alternative is to lay waste and leave it so. Yet the entire economic and legal procedure for determining the value of lost or damaged habitats, or of the dead, spins in a loop that finally sails crazily away from the true matter of loss and death, of endings. The system attempts to measure the immeasurable — that is, what Marge Tillion, Drew Scalzi, and Billy Day felt, what caused them to take action; as well as what those who worked in the otter and bird rescue centers felt, no matter, considering the general picture of destruction, how futile their efforts might be; and what the people of

Chenega and English Bay felt had been sundered when their subsistence resources were taken away.

The system of measuring non-use values is another venture at pushing the elements of rationality — quantifying, counting, numbering — toward irrationality. The system would become critical to litigation. By the summer of 1990, Rick Steiner and others (including Alaskan Natives, environmental groups, commercial fishermen, tour operators, recreationalists, and biologists), joining in the Coastal Coalition's proposal for a comprehensive settlement of all resource damages from Exxon, employed the concept of "contingent valuation" as a basis for their demands. As of August 1990, the coalition had a simple solution. Drop all litigation. Free the dead from refrigeration. In return, Exxon should establish a two-billion-dollar Alaska Restoration Fund to underwrite continued restoration of oil-damaged areas, research, education, economic development, and, most importantly, the acquisition and protection of resources *equivalent* and *adjacent* to those damaged, such as forest lands. Following intense legal wrangling and power politics, something not unlike what the Coastal Coalition envisioned would come to pass in 1991.[51]

---

[51] For further discussion of the *Exxon Valdez* Settlement and its results see "Conclusion: The Bubble Net."

CHAPTER
13 SELDOVIA

On July 20, I took a Homer Air flight across Kachemak Bay. The 20-mile hop carried me from one place, Homer, made accessible to the world by the road from Anchorage, to another place, Seldovia, accessible only by air or water. In a rough sense, the two towns have a relationship rather akin to Cordova and Valdez. Like Cordova, Seldovia is built on the mainland but has the feel of an island community. Seldovia is a much smaller town than Cordova. Its population is around 500, and by virtue of that and its nearness to Homer, it tends to fall rather more into the gravity of Homer's orbit than Cordova does to Valdez. This is a source of some resentment in Seldovia, but again, because Homer lacks the singular presence of anything like the Alyeska terminal, Seldovia's edginess toward the richer town seems subdued in comparison with Cordova's to Valdez.

As communities, Seldovia and Homer share a vulnerability created by the movement of chemical and oil tankers to and from Anchorage and the Drift River Oil terminal. Also, the two towns and other towns on the Kenai Peninsula had already been through the spill from the tanker Glacier Bay,[52] and the politically divisive controversy over offshore Kachemak Bay oil leases. In 1973, leases had been sold in Kachemak Bay, but following pressure from local groups and fishermen, and a timely accident with a jack-up oil rig stored in the bay which resulted in a diesel spill, the state legislature bought back in the leases in 1976.[53] After the oil spill, the two towns would experience the collective alarm triggered by the eruptions of the volcano Redoubt during the winter of 1990, and the danger the flooding Drift River and ensuing mudflows presented to the Cook Inlet Pipeline Company's Drift River terminal — yet another precariously situated and ill-defended oil installation. The terminal is located across the inlet from the town of Kenai, not far north of Homer. The mudflows threatened to undercut the foundations of holding tanks, and so to spill millions of gallons of oil into the inlet. Finally, the tanks were drawn down, the terminal summarily closed by the DEC, the mudflow diverted, the waters protected, and the people, as if they needed it, reawakened to the danger of oil. Such circumstances of location may explain the degree of cooperation Homer and Seldovia forged during the *Exxon Valdez* crisis.

There were three of us in the six-seater Cessna — myself, the pilot, and a solid-looking man in a white shirt and suspenders. The two rear seats were folded down to accommodate our luggage and the overflow of parcels the flight was delivering to Seldovia. The pilot circled before landing, a common practice hereabouts. It is a good idea to check for obstructions before putting down, for vehicles, pedestrians, other planes, moose, or, in the case of English Bay, where I would land several days later, the logs that the sea regularly deposits on the runway. The crosswinds buffeted the Cessna. I took out my notebook to record what I saw: the town built up just off the runway, and just west of town the long, five-mile finger of water, Seldovia Bay, and running northward through the trees near the shoreline, a narrow road. The Cessna

[52] The 1991 $51 million damages award in the *Glacier Bay* case presaged what would follow for the Exxon corporation. In the *Glacier Bay* civil trial many of the same actors and issues were in play — the same federal judge, H. Russel Holland, many of the same attorneys, including the lead attorney, Brian O'Neill, and a similar group of plaintiffs, including fishermen in particular.
[53] Using the same line of reasoning, and following the 1989 spill, Alaska Governor Cowper would urge Congress to buy back the Bristol Bay oil leases that the government had sold in 1988. Bristol Bay is the site of the richest salmon fishery in the world.

dropped precipitously and landed neatly on the strip. I was seated next to the pilot and got out first. As we waited beside the plane for our luggage, the other passenger turned to me. Up to that moment, we had exchanged nothing more than pleasantries, but he said, "I hope you write something about how this has changed everybody. We knew twenty years ago it was going to happen. But we didn't know what it would do to us."

He had known that I was a stranger. The notebook must have told him the rest. He said, "We'll never be the same again, and the others need to hear."

I thought about that as I walked the mile or so from the landing strip. I had regularly experienced the sense of expectation the oil spill writers created in Alaskans, and even as I struggled personally to understand the meaning of the spill, I also felt the weight of an almost overwhelming sense of obligation to the Alaskan people. The roadway took me along a lagoon, the Seldovia Slough, where kids were fishing, and then into the trees and out again and down a slope to the town. It was a warm, sunny day and the sea air felt luxurious. The buildings in the main section of town seemed equally divided between strictly functional and quaint. The quaint addressed the tourist trade. The town otherwise addressed the bay and docks.

Frank Monsey, Seldovia's fire chief, found himself in a position rather like the one Marge Tillion found herself in over in Homer. Frank had a high regard for Marge. Of her troubles with Exxon and Veco, he said, "Nobody has a male ego problem like a bureaucrat. Here we had more women than men in leadership positions."

Frank had been trained in the Incident Command System (ICS), an emergency management structure that evolved from fire fighting. On paper, the system is represented as a series of boxes, each of which describes a duty and which as circumstances arise may be broken up into more boxes, or eliminated, or replaced. At the heart of the system is the emergency manager, Frank's position. The manager's responsibility is simply to facilitate the response. The system's emphasis is on decentralization of structure, and autonomy in the various positions. Since it was designed to handle situations in which sudden change occurs, such as a fire moving overnight out of the hills to a suburb, or an oil slick, the object is to maintain basic structure and at the same time maximize fluidity. Ideally, it addresses the objective, which is to quell the emergency, and nothing else. When the emergency is over the structure shrinks or even vanishes.

Frank Monsey waxed eloquent on this subject, and on Exxon's and subsequently Veco's inability to take control, which he ascribed to their centralization. "Exxon has all the managers, but everything is always falling apart on them because it's all so centralized. The first people they send out are the PR managers and the lawyers. Usually, they have no idea where they've come to, so they can't make a decision without routing it back through headquarters. If they'd had the correct people out here, and organized it right, and given those people authority to deal directly with us, a lot of the oil would have been cleaned up. They don't have their shit together. The company is running itself. It's a juggernaut.

"And then you get the agencies, and Veco, and you've got one huge cluster fuck. For Veco and Exxon, this is an industrial cleanup. For us, it was our life. Exxon's first concern is PR and Veco's managing the money. For us, the main thing became, first, be ready for anything, and second, never believe the assholes. The Coast Guard couldn't get Exxon to move. The Coast Guard supposedly has all the power, but they haven't used it. The Coast Guard keeps saying, Exxon has the resources, but the Coast Guard's job is to lead and manage, according to the law, and while they're screwing around, not cleaning up oil that could be cleaned, federally protected species are dying out there."

Frank stopped and settled back. We were inside the fire station, sitting in folding chairs on opposite sides of a steel table. To one side stood a red fire engine, next to it another engine, and stored all around and hanging from the walls were firefighting supplies. I guessed that Frank was in his early sixties. He wore a red cap, a gray pile vest, and an aquamarine-colored shirt. The strength of his language notwithstanding, he was actually soft-spoken and gracious, a grandfatherly type. He was given to smiling and, judging from the upwardly curved lines around his mouth and eyes, had been so for a long time. He'd lived in Alaska since he was three.

Frank Monsey had put his finger on something, what for me was a piece of the puzzle. It had to do with the government's and Exxon's inability to mount a structure of response sufficiently flexible and sufficiently direct to deal with a disaster that had the unpredictability of an oil spill. Something like the Incident Command System — the contingency plan — had existed in an underequipped, understaffed, and poorly maintained state at the Alyeska terminal. The state-mandated decision matrix for the use of dispersants had a flexibility analogous to ICS, but with a fatal flaw — no provision for expert decision making at high speed and very little provision for the use of local expertise, such as fishermen's knowledge of tides and currents. The Exxon system of management as it came to be instituted was hierarchic, and so structurally contrary to ICS. To it was added the state's involvement, the sometimes politically motivated state and federal agencies, and the Coast Guard, and the introduction of Veco and other contractors whose primary interest — making money — was at odds with controlling an oil spill. In addition, I would learn, the Kenai borough government had imported its own two ICS teams (one from Anchorage and another from Denver) which as often as not were at odds with Homerites and Seldovians. It was as if the system that arose had been designed for conflict rather than the reverse, and then for the inevitable decay through adversarial relationships toward the approval loop that made decisions ever more remote from the communities and their necessities. The failure of that system to respond to the oil spill raises serious questions about our capacity for dealing with another type of disaster, one, say, that might threaten human life on a massive scale.

Before I left, Frank sallied into a tirade. I had heard the like repeatedly, but it seemed the more surprising coming from a man of his demeanor. "The basic problem," he said, "started with Exxon's inability to see the world. They're concerned with PR, not cleanup. The little people getting screwed over by these companies have to start thinking big. Arrest the whole damn company. Run an air force strike on the Exxon offices. Organize a boycott. Block the channel. Hell, block the Suez Canal. Think big. We have to protect ourselves with power, otherwise the financial harassment will go on forever."

Frank looked down at the table, then took off his cap and ran his fingers through his gray hair. He looked up at me and chuckled softly. "Now see? I'm all excited again."

Others recounted for me the events in Seldovia. They included Annie McKenzie, owner of the Annie McKenzie Boardwalk Hotel, Tim Robertson, who with his wife, Debbie, was the owner of a lodge outside town, Sandy Elvsaas, who in July had become Veco director in Seldovia, and John Mickelson, Seldovia representative to the Homer area MAC and later a leader in the volunteer group, the Oil Reform Alliance. On day six of the spill, March 29, the townspeople — like the people in Homer, and the people in Seward, like the Park Service people at the Kenai Fjords National Park — realized that the oil was headed their way. When contacted, however, the Exxon office in Valdez disputed the likelihood. If anything, the situation was worse at Kenai Fjords, a 1,145-square-mile tract with a series of deep fjords and over 40 glaciers. Located on the southern, gulf side of the peninsula it was more in the track of the oil.

Park service people had been told previously by a NOAA representative that no more than 50 barrels of oil would escape Prince William Sound. As with the Fish and Wildlife Service, there were intimations in that case, too, of the upper echelons of the park service in Washington, D.C., trying to minimize the severity of the threat and deliberately stalling action. Eventually, Anne Castillina, the superintendent of Kenai Fjords, bucked authority and took action on her own by ordering boom through the Seward MAC, deploying it, and retrieving oiled animals.

In Seldovia — as in Homer, Seward, and a little later, Kodiak — the townspeople set out to organize their own response. They put the ICS into action and set out to design, fabricate, and then deploy log boom at the mouth of Seldovia Bay, even though they had doubts about whether or not it would be effective. Between two and three hundred people became involved, or, as Tim Robertson would put it, "the entire adult population of the town." The high school closed its doors. Logging people donated logs and equipment. Volunteer food and child care services were set up. Exxon's Wylie Bragg promised to send technical help for boom construction, but it never materialized. Money was promised, but it came in amounts insufficient to cover the supplies, and it was initially earmarked, the Seldovians were told, to fund setting up an office, not to purchase boom material. While they were building boom and trying to secure materials, the Seldovians reached a point, according to Annie McKenzie, where they realized that booming the bay was going to cost half a million dollars and that they only had $15,000.

I talked to Annie in her hotel apartment while she was preparing to fill out the claim forms needed to secure compensation for the loss of business she said her hotel had suffered during the summer. It was nearly four months after the spill. The forms, scattered across her desk, filled her with anger and frustration. They were the bitter tailings — money, financial exigency; and then there was the memory of what Annie called "the thrill" of being a part of the community's initial mobilization. Annie became Seldovia's first oil spill coordinator. Formerly a women's rights activist in Washington State, a pretty, vivacious woman in her forties, her dark hair speckled with gray, she several times nearly broke into tears as we spoke. "But for a solid week," she said, "we worked at a peak. We really produced, and it made us realize what our capacity was. We'd get mad at each other once in a while, but the intimacy among us as a group was exquisite."

That was the first week of April. The next week, Veco, operating out of its base in Homer, came into Seldovia, and brought with it Exxon money and the expectation that it would manage the response both for Seldovia Bay and outlying areas. There was confusion over the dispensation of funds to the volunteer effort — whether or not to route funds through local city or borough government. There were suggestions of graft that turned on the city's use of Exxon funds to order items that many believed had nothing to do with the oil spill — a computer, for example. A proposal, supported by the mayor, Jerry Willard, was floated to rebuild an old logging road through Native property to Port Graham, which by the extended access it created, it was hoped, would have tied in Seldovia more firmly to cleanup money. In Annie McKenzie's view it was an attempt to gouge Exxon, and to create an avenue for future logging development, which in itself was a controversial matter. The money tended to do that, to move out laterally and find pockets it could fill, and then to exponentially increase confusion and distraction. After Veco's arrival, the log boom project continued. It still needed supplies, such as industrial drills. Annie said she convinced the area Veco supervisor, Ray Springer, to order drills, and as he did so she heard him say over the phone, "Yeah, the chipmunks are running." She took it to mean that the community effort was being patronized.

Fishing and tourism were and are important to Seldovia. Even setting matters of environmental principle aside — which most Seldovians decidedly did not — it was inevitable that local people would be concerned with waterways and shorelines beyond their immediate environs. Simultaneous with the boom project, action was undertaken to protect fish, wildlife, and shorelines by collecting oil. Tim Robertson, who was to become a new city council member and then, for a time, acting mayor of Seldovia, and whom I had met previously in Anchorage, was instrumental in putting together the plan for oil collection.

Tim has a master's degree in fisheries biology and had worked six years for the Alaska Department of Fish and Game and eight years as an engineer for a North Slope service company. He took a rather more benevolent view of Veco supervisors, such as Ray Springer, than others did. Tim believed that the real problems were in the higher echelons of management and that the local supervisors were left in the difficult position of managing the cutting edges of controversy. Ray Springer had felt, according to Tim, that he had no problem with Seldovians. Springer had hired eight of the original volunteers as foremen, among whom Annie McKenzie was not included. Annie had told me that she preferred to operate as an independent voice. "But in Seldovia," Tim said, "we became Veco."

As it turned out, the oil never entered Seldovia Bay in quantity. The oil collection operation, however, performed in collaboration with Homerites, met with the same type of frustrations that all locally based operations did. Tim said, "Once we saw that oil wasn't coming into Seldovia Bay, we started preparing to go out and get it." The group secured and modified boats, and then Exxon called and ordered the operation shut down. Senator Ted Stevens intervened and the group went back to work. They had secured a float plane to spot oil. When they were ready to take off, a storm stopped them. By the time they did take off, according to Tim, Ray Springer himself had grown frustrated with Veco and resigned. The group had Veco funding, but they were running at cross purposes with the system. The new supervisor, Bob Warren, called the group on the radio and said that Exxon had ordered them back. The group refused and, having located oil, began to deal with the technical problems of recovering it on their own. They couldn't pump it because it was too thick. They finally used modified dipnets and buckets to gather it, techniques that would also be used at Kodiak. Two people, Tim said, could pick up 200 gallons an hour.

For their first load, the group captured 8,000 gallons of oil and oily debris, but then they had nothing to do with it. A tankerage ship had been in their vicinity for ten days, but the ship previously had been given orders not to take their oil. The group nevertheless towed their oil and debris to the ship, the *Alaska Husky*, but when the ship threw its pumps into it, the pumps plugged up immediately. Tim said, "We told them, 'We've got thirty-five guys with shovels and buckets. Where do you want it?' They said, 'Wait a minute. This is a union boat.'" Robertson's group, still intent above all else upon getting oil out of the water, no matter how tedious the process, did shovel the oil into the *Alaska Husky*. The boat, which had a 30,000-gallon capacity, took off, and the group had to find another for their next load. Tim said that they made three trips. "But each time it got more frustrating. We went down to pump it and found that you have to physically move it. We were worried about the toxicity. I asked for help with that and a guy said he would come out. He never made it. All the time, there were helicopters everywhere. Exxon and Veco were in control and they are not efficient. Fishermen aren't like that. They just go to it. They have the heart to get a job done."

Tim came to the same conclusion that Billy Day and Marge Tillion had, that it was better to go independent. At the time I spoke with Tim in early July, he, Mei Mei Evans of Homer, Marge Tillion, John Mickelson, and others were working to get their beach-cleaning project off the ground, and Billy Day was putting his rock-washing machine together.

Sandy Elvsaas was the Veco director in Seldovia in July. Veco had taken hold but had placed her, a local person, in charge. She managed 17 boats and 63 people who were rotating in and out of Picnic Harbor, the Barren Islands, and Port Chatham — all down around the corner of the peninsula. She also had a Veco boss, an Exxon boss, and five other people checking on her all the time. Her predecessor as Veco director, Jennifer Dilley, had left her position in a fury that was tied, in part, to the lack of support given to the oil collection enterprise. Sandy Elvsaas was a fisherman. Her husband, Fred, an engineer and fisherman, was president of the Seldovia Native Corporation. Sandy seemed to have a circumspect view of events in Seldovia.

She knew that there was bitterness in the town and was frustrated by the failure of cleanup in her area. She felt that Exxon still hoped the oil would break up and disappear and that compared to Prince William Sound, the Kenai Peninsula had been given short shrift. "If we hadn't screamed and hollered," she said, "we'd never have gotten anything. And it's true that if they'd let us go our own way, just funded us, we'd have got the job done better than they did." She disliked the peremptory way orders came down to her from her superiors. Earlier on the very day I talked to her, Veco people had come in and fired six of her workers. "This morning there were four people in this office," she said. "Now there's one. Me. I wish they'd allowed me to pick the six people, and prepare them and lay them off myself."

Her inclination, though, was to emphasize the positive. "Good things happened," she said. "Long-lasting alliances have been formed in Seldovia. Incredible things were accomplished, but now there's a letdown. Basically, everybody's tired. People need to refocus on the great things they did because you're never going to get all this oil out of here. The women designed the fabric to make wave skirts for the log boom. They helped build the boom. We had ten thousand feet of it. We shoveled oil off the beach and deployed the boom and felt really protected.

"And a lot of new technology has come out," she said. "We developed some things ourselves. The scientists are developing a fertilizer to break down the hydrocarbons in the oil."

She was talking about bioremediation. She said they were working on it at the NOAA station just down the road, where James Payne was. This was the same James Payne, the oft-quoted expert I'd heard of in the science meetings in Valdez. I'd been trying to reach him for months. It was his work that had been cited in the early science meetings as a corrective to Exxon's figures for the evaporation rate of crude oil. He knew as much as anybody about the nature of Prudhoe crude and how it interacted with a marine environment. Over the previous several weeks, the controversy over "sinking oil" had picked up energy, mainly because then, four months after the spill, oil still seemed to be arriving off Kodiak from unknown places. The issue was acquiring mythical proportions. Fishermen there and in Cordova claimed that oil was coming up with their nets. Frank Monsey had talked about sinking oil. Tim Robertson claimed that on one of his flyovers during the oil collection project, he'd seen a patch of oil shearing underwater. Back in Homer, Ken Broginoff had claimed that oil sank. Marge Tillion had said that oil had come upon anchors from four fathoms down at Picnic Harbor and that divers' bubbles pushed up oil near Home Cove on Nuka Island. Lee Glenn, the head Fish and Game biologist in Homer, had acknowledged the possibility of underwater oil. To discount these claims and questions, James Payne's research was always cited, principally by NOAA. The question of whether or not oil sank had become critical for one central reason, which carried with it all the usual political, economic, and legal baggage: if it sank, then its toxic effects would be expanded in area and extended in time, and the numbers of affected creatures would be enlarged.

John Mickelson agreed to drive me out to the NOAA lab at Kasitsnu Bay. We set out in the evening in his pickup truck and drove along the same narrow gravel road I'd seen from the Cessna before I landed in Seldovia. The lab was located about 15 miles away, halfway between Seldovia and the otter center at Jackolof Bay — where holding pens had been constructed as a place to care for and then retain healthy otters until a decision was made as to what to do with them.

Besides being deeply involved with all phases of the oil spill response, John worked as maintenance supervisor for the city of Seldovia. He was a tall man, powerfully built, and wore a baseball cap all the time. He was outspoken, passionate, friendly, and there was something in his bearing that suggested dangerousness, as if of a pirate. On the way to the lab, John recounted his story of Exxon, Seldovia, graft, greed, intrigue, and oil. He drove with one hand draped over the steering wheel and leaned toward me, talking as the stiffly sprung pickup lurched and swung through the potholes in the road.

As maintenance supervisor, John had begun at the heart of the action, and as Seldovia's representative on the Homer MAC, he remained at the heart for the duration. He had practical knowledge of equipment and of the channels of local government. He told me that by mid-July the city budget had a $300,000 surplus, while before the spill it had been running a $60,000 deficit. There had been an 8 percent increase in the city budget due to purchase orders run through the local store, and to such things as dock fees and leases for Veco offices. Port Graham, John said, had done "even better" than Seldovia. He said that with irony, though his voice remained even.

John's main complaint, as with many in Seldovia and Homer, was not so much with Veco as with Exxon, with Exxon's continued focus upon Prince William Sound, where the white lights of the media were trained, and its failure to respond to the presence of oil on and off the Kenai Peninsula. Exxon's slow response was compounded by its policy of shifting supervisors in and out of position. Exxon had a furlough system by which many of the supervisors and managers working on the oil spill would stay in a position for several weeks, then rotate out. The approach worked well on remote drilling sites and made some sense here in terms of the personnel themselves, who in many cases had left homes and families behind in the lower forty-eight, put in long hours, and were subjected to high stress.

In Homer, where the Exxon office was located, public appearances by Exxon's Wylie Bragg, John Dean, Dan Jones, and Dean Peeler, were sometimes occasions for merciless barrages of criticism from all quarters — citizens, local leaders, state and federal agency representatives. The furlough system further aggravated the situation and for local people heightened the sense of Exxon's colonialism — a foreign power that had pushed its way into a locale through foolish-looking representatives. The newly assigned Exxon people often had very little familiarity with the area to which they had come, and less than adequate familiarity with oil spill procedures as they had evolved. Everyone who came in had to "get up to speed," and it was not uncommon to see Exxon supervisors being educated by agency representatives or reporters. Because of the bureaucratic decision-making "loop," supervisors were encumbered with paperwork and also had very little real authority. Finally, everything was further exacerbated by the fact that the oil spill remained a rapidly shifting, quirkily evolving reality, or what Exxon's Dan Jones referred to in early May as "a moving target."

Public and private meetings in Homer produced tangles of contradictions and raised emotions to the boiling point. Back in the first week of May, for example, Dan Jones, then the newly arrived chief spokesman for Exxon, had asserted that boom was not being sent to the southern Kenai because headquarters kept diverting it to Prince William Sound, where, presumably, it was needed more. He had been contradicted by several MAC members, including a Coast Guard commander, Richard Asaro, who said he understood that Exxon's decision not to send boom to Homer was based on cost-saving considerations, not on environmental ones. On the lower Kenai, commercial boom was still needed at that time to replace the log boom that was in position at several critical locations. Jones had also said that boom and other support need not be sent by Exxon to boats in Port Chatham — a bay near the southernmost tip of the Kenai Peninsula that was acting as a catch basin for passing oil — because that was not an Exxon operation. In fact, however, boats under contract to Exxon had been anchoring at Port Chatham every night.

Jones had said that there would be no more skimming off the Kenai because at that time oil was not present in sufficient quantities to justify the procedure, and then two days later he had reported that that very day, the fifth of May, had seen the best skimming day yet on the outer peninsula. He had said that it was federal and state agencies that put the brakes on Exxon's offshore work at Gore Point — the narrow, heavily oiled protrusion of land just east of Port Dick. He had said that prior to an April 26 memo from Vice Admiral C. E. Robbins, the Coast Guard ruled that Exxon should not clean up outside Prince William Sound, and that that was a cause of much of the delay, but representatives of the state Department of National Resources (DNR), the DEC, and the Coast Guard stated that mechanical cleanup had been requested at Gore Point long before April 26, and that an Exxon official previously in Homer, John Dean, had said he couldn't order cleanup because Exxon headquarters had directed him to stay off the Gore Point beaches. Jones had also asserted that Exxon had not anticipated that shoreline cleanup would be necessary at all off the Kenai, this in contradiction to the advice of fishermen and to projections for the course of a major oil spill in the sound that were in existence long before the grounding of the *Exxon Valdez*.

These meetings in May took place while the retrieval project with which Tim Robertson had been involved was still under way, about two weeks after the bird-burning incident at Gore Point, and two weeks after a high-level delegation that included Alaska Representative Don Young, Alaska Senator Frank Murkowski, and Secretary of the Interior Manuel Lujan was presented with oily pom-poms and bottles of oil by Larry Smith as proof that oil was indeed in Kachemak Bay, contrary to Coast Guard reports and Exxon assumptions. The May 5 meetings were held three weeks after Marge Tillion resigned her volunteer capacity as a community liaison to Exxon and Veco, a full month after the oil had washed ashore at Kenai Fjords National Park. During this time, the various government and private parties continued to jockey for control, including control over the groundswell of effort and anger. Vice Admiral Robbins several times publicly chided Exxon for lack of action and state and federal officials repeatedly attempted to establish a clear chain of command, and in reaction, perhaps, Exxon staged the above-mentioned *USA Today* media fiasco. For awhile, recognition of the response was a weekly ritual.

Also during this time, the crews stationed on the beaches, some of whom were assigned to shovel oil into plastic bags, were complaining about fumes and lack of support. Some fell ill. They lacked tankerage for oil and storage for oily debris. They lacked facilities for cleaning themselves up at night after wallowing all day in oil. Back in town, John Mickelson and others, still using Marge Tillion's lists, were locating boom supplies for Exxon and generally trying to deal with the confusion. At its essence, it was a recapitulation of events in Prince William Sound during the first weeks of the spill, but in slow motion. It took more time for the oil to get to the Kenai, and, it should be granted, there was rather less of it and it was somewhat more weathered. The command structure in Valdez was preoccupied with Prince William Sound and even more hopeful that the oil would disperse and disappear off Kenai than it had been in the sound. It certainly didn't want to face a second front, nor a third, over in Kodiak.

While the command structure was attempting to handle the Kenai, it had also grown rigid. The response from within the Kenai communities was more organized, but so was the political infighting. Exxon money was more clearly a factor from the outset than it had been in either Valdez or Cordova, and therefore more of the Kenai people, including local politicians, were prepared to chase it. The subcontracting companies were more firmly established. The result was that, if anything, the local people were left even more out in the cold and more subjected to bureaucratic machinations than they had been in the sound. The fracturing was more immediate and more brittle.

"Ultimately, the truth is that we couldn't have done it," John said. "There was too much oil for fourteen people with shovels, or even ten times that many. The log boom didn't really work. It was all too heartbreaking to consider. Fourteen people on the first offensive. Two boats. But I told Wylie Bragg, 'Look, the people need to do something. We gathered a hundred thousand gallons of oil and Exxon didn't know what to do with it.' He said there were no barges. So, we went back to the boom again. We found them twenty thousand feet of boom and then some storage tanks, and said, 'Here it is. Just get it off the damn beach.' But nothing happened.

"Finally, I got fed up with the whole goddamn deal," John said. We were continuing in the pickup along the road toward the Kasitsnu Lab. The sky was beginning to darken, and the woods along the side of the road deepened. "The Exxon people cared less about what we said, though they were always pleasant. They just kept luring us on." John veered to avoid a pothole and my body swung inward and then back against the door. "I went into the legal library and started jerking books," he said. The force with which his presence seemed normally to bristle had diminished. He'd allowed the pickup to slow down, and he went on, speaking softly of what he'd done on May 5, the same day as the chaotic sequence of meetings described above. "I wanted to make a citizen's arrest of Dan Jones. I found federal code thirty-four ten. It was illegal to knowingly convey false information with reckless disregard for human life.

"We were just playing this fucking game," he said. "I got a declaration of arrest from the police. I arrested Jones, then I tried to get a park ranger to take him into custody. The ranger called the attorney general. I ended up talking to the attorney general [Doug Baily], who tried to talk me out of it. I had called the networks. I'd loaded the MAC meeting with everybody I could think of. The bottom line of the deal was that the networks never showed up and the attorney general instructed the ranger, Roger MacCampbell, not to take the guy into custody. So, then I understood that the government would refuse to enforce its own laws."

We turned off the road and John goosed the truck up a steep, deeply rutted lane. When we rode out into a parking area nestled between sturdy well-kept buildings, he pulled to a stop and we sat for a moment. I felt a great sympathy for John's daring action, and for the sense of loneliness with which the result had left him. He had hoped to enforce the letter of the law when the very arms of the law were entwined around the other entities in a lawless dance. To accomplish this, he'd merely tried to take one of the leaping maskers into custody, to make him stand still. John's had been an existential act that expressed his feeling about the engulfing perversity of the power that had gathered around him.

As we sat there, staring through the windshield at the wall of a building, he said, "Later that night they had a party at the Homestead Inn. I went up, but somehow hearing them all in there laughing, the Exxons and the Coast Guard, and all your agency people, and some of our own people who were making money hand over fist, all the permit people making jokes out of things that were crucial to the guys on the beach . . . it turned my stomach. I refused to go in and have a beer with them. The next day they had another party and invited everybody but me."

14 THE TRUTH ABOUT OIL

Outrage animated the oil and transformed it into myth. As myth, the actual multifariousness of oil was often reduced to a single, all-encompassing thing, an overwhelming pestilence, a horde, like the mythical plagues of locusts, snakes, and bees, or like the film versions of all-consuming forces of devastation, such as hoards of birds, man-eating ants, or uncontrollable magma as in The Blob. Natural occurrences of geology and weather, such as floods, earthquakes and tsunamis, and volcanic eruptions carry many of the same qualities — utter inescapability, wanton destruction, and a certain apocalyptic aspect. In natural disasters, the acceptance on the part of survivors that mankind is incapable of countering the force of nature is not unlike the stage of acceptance that terminal cancer patients reach. It grants the presence of a power beyond one's own control.

Marauding armies, particularly when they are considered barbarian, or subhuman, acquire the character of myths of pestilence. Coincidentally, in the American mind these armies have lately come from oil-producing states like Iran and Iraq. They are sometimes linked to visions of Armageddon and seen as corrective emanations of the overriding sentience of God. If any sentiment was universally expressed by those close to the oil spill, no matter what their persuasion, it was this: "We brought it on ourselves. We let down our guard." In the early days of the spill, much was also made of the fact that the oil spill occurred on Good Friday, 25 years after the Good Friday earthquake. Such sentiment is seeking a reason and tacitly acknowledges a source of wisdom behind the event, but in the case of the oil spill this was complicated by the fact that the spill was a quintessentially twentieth-century scourge of our own human nature, and so a small-scale model of the ultimate such feasible scourge — the atomic searing of all the earth. Thus, it became difficult or callow-minded to look to God in the expectation that all the provisions of the teaching would be provided.

The human inclination to use symbolic thought as a way of giving pattern to the inexplicable seems inescapable. The shapelessness and devastation of the horde as it is represented in film and literature is a barely defined version of the true, indecipherable, shapeless thing we carry in our subconscious — death, the unknown ending. Our foreboding of this thing is sometimes assisted by events. In the ninth chapter of Revelations, a recurrent Middle Eastern scourge, the locust plague, is transformed into an instrument of revenge that strikes only the ungodly. Following the sounding of the Fifth Angel, the locusts come, shaped like horses with gold crowns on their heads, hair like women, teeth like lions, and tails like scorpions. They will hurt men for five months. It's a powerful, beguiling, and fanciful vision, but hardly more fanciful than heaping all of the blame upon Joseph Hazelwood's head, or transforming the oil into a plague that carried in its wake men with briefcases, Stetsons, and Texas boots, hauling carts loaded with money and commandeering and equipping an army of 11,000, 14,000 vessels, 80 aircraft . . .

In what was the ultimate pro-development fraud, James Watt, President Reagan's first Secretary of the Interior, had used his purported belief in the Second Coming as a means of justifying the pillaging of resources — use it all up quickly before the final scourge arrives. His vision was animated by earthly greed and merely housed as a convenience in religion. In a similar manner, but with the animating force of despair, or fear of a dark, dangerous future, some environmentalists use their belief in the motherly beneficence of nature (the Gaia hypothesis) or presumed natural patterns as a means of leaping to blanket "preservationism." While gratitude and respect for the organism of the earth, and humility for the human place in it are essential, to deny its tumultuousness or the violence of some of the engagements it keeps, and that we must keep with it, seems as untenable as Watt's position.

Often enough, seeing the oil on the beaches and the machinery devised to trick it away from sight, I felt that I'd been dropped into a hell, a place of death, unending in its endings. To see it so shook me to my bones, but also made it possible for me to hold it in my imagination even when I did not understand it. That metaphor became for a time my guide for conduct and caused me to walk lightly, shadow-like. I would never fully clear away the shade in my interior, but I knew that the metaphor would need to be broken out into something more closely aligned with the reality, as best it could be perceived. The answer was in the oil itself. John Oliver and others on the *Alpha Helix* had taught me something about the true nature of Prudhoe crude, as had Riki Ott. Now, James Payne led John Mickelson and me into the NOAA lab — a clean, amply lit place decked out with long benches, computers, and exotic machines, and overlooking an exquisite bay that was visible through a line of plate glass windows.

Prudhoe Bay crude, like all crude oils, is a complex mixture of organic (carbon-based) and inorganic (noncarbon-based) compounds. The chemical make-up of crude oils drawn from different sites, or even from differing locations within one formation, may vary widely. Due to processes during petroleum formation that result in what is called molecular scrambling, crude oils contain thousands of different chemical compounds. Each variety of crude oil carries the traces of specific plant or animal precursors. Each bears individual molecular markers, or fingerprints of a sort, by which its source can be identified. One of the tasks performed at the Kasitsnu lab was to check samples of recovered oil to determine whether or not it came from the *Exxon Valdez*. There were other possible sources of spilled oil in Cook Inlet and the sound.

Of the types of molecular compounds in crude oil, hydrocarbons are the most abundant, varying from 50 to 98 percent of the whole. In Prudhoe crude, hydrocarbons constitute a little over 60 percent. The hydrocarbons are the concentrated residuum of the detritus of life that entered the formation and made the oil. It's a remarkable substance, crude oil, the chaotic, chemical essence of the North Slope's chaotic biota. Through their use of oil, humans have entered into an exchange with their own natural history that extends back through the millennia. This makes for another disconcerting metaphor:

we are consuming our natural history faster than it can replenish itself, and as we do so pressurized compounds previously contained in geologic formations have been released back into the world in the form of fuel and sometimes dangerous molecular junk, such as carbon monoxide and carbon dioxide.

The inorganic compounds are grouped into six classes, including sulphur, nitrogen, oxygen compounds, and trace metals. The organic compounds, or hydrocarbons, fall into two categories, or fractions — the aliphatids and the aromatics. The aliphatids are nontoxic, biodegradable, and do not persist in the environment. The aromatics come in two types — single ring compounds (they include BETX: benzene, ethylbenzene, toulene, and xylene) and multiple ring compounds. Single ring compounds have low molecular weights. They are light, highly soluble, and acutely toxic. They dissolve and suddenly evaporate. Multiple ring compounds persist in the environment. These are not acutely toxic but are long-term mutagens with the capacity to penetrate deeply into the food web, to enter on the cellular level, to be carcinogenic, to warp DNA.

The aromatics may otherwise be known as light ends, which refers to the relatively low temperatures at which they reach boiling point. In the process of refining, crude oil is heated and the compounds, based on their differing boiling points, are separated, or "cracked." The components made into fuel (gasoline, diesel, kerosene, etc.) are composed primarily of hydrocarbons and, of course, are highly toxic and explosive.

The refining process provides a rough picture of the rate at which the various compounds partition into what are termed the natural compartments — the air, the water column, the sediment, and the organisms. In the last category, organisms, there are potentially as many subcompartments as there are species within affected areas. Through feeding interrelationships the hydrocarbons (especially multiple ring) lodged in bodies pass from one species to the next. This is the way in which persistent compounds have chronic effects upon life, and such effects are most likely to occur in places that are repeatedly exposed, such as the Port of Valdez, Galveston Bay, and New York harbor. The words used by scientists — "partition" and "compartment" — imply an orderly process, as if of pantries and cupboards. In fact, the leading edges of molecular exchange are quite disorderly.

Generally speaking, compounds with boiling points below 488 degrees Fahrenheit, the light ends, are the only ones subject to partitioning into the atmosphere (evaporation). This process caused much of the first, acute wave of marine mammal mortality: animals, especially otters, inhaled the fumes and developed respiratory failure. The fumes also caused sickness among beach workers. Some of the compounds are the same as the ones we inhale when we put gasoline in our tanks. They go straight into the lungs. They are also the most subject to rapid dissolution in the water column.

As I had already learned, the single most obvious and most compelling fact about crude oil in its relation to water, and one that James Payne emphasized, is that it floats. Its specific gravity is less than that of water. This is a truth, and therefore a thing to be held closely. In the racket of claims and counterclaims, even among scientists, even concerning the behavior of oil, there were precious few things that could be said with certainty. Everything else seemed to plummet in the direction of paradox. But it is certain that oil floats. All matters connected to the oil spill are derived from this truth: the visibility of oil on the surface of the water, the visibility of affected animals, the propensity of oil to ride the tide to the shorelines, the possibility of retrieving it, or burning it, dispersing it, or biodegrading it. It would not sink unless enough matter, such as sediment, adhered to it to make it heavier than water, unless it was driven temporarily beneath the surface, or unless it stuck to something beneath the surface. These derivatives of the true nature of oil

Boiling point range of fractions of crude petroleum.

Source: John H. Steele et al., *Oil in the Sea: Inputs, Fates and Effects* (Washington, D. C.: National Academy Press, 1985), p. 27.

are important as things that happened in various places, but it remains true that crude oil floats on water.

Once crude oil is introduced to water, it immediately begins to weather. In all its peculiarities, weathering is also a function of the fact that oil floats. It occurs in several different ways, including spreading and drift, evaporation, dissolution, dispersion, water-in-oil emulsification, adsorption onto suspended particulate material, and shoreline interactions.[54] It should be noted that in no sense does weathering mean that oil disappears, but rather that its components are transferred into one compartment or another. Matter does not cease to exist.

Once oil has entered the sea, it spreads. Its lateral movement is affected variously by forces of gravity, inertia, friction, and surface tension, and by its own volume and the rate at which it is spilled. Eyewitness accounts of the *Exxon Valdez* spill reported that the oil came out of the ship so fast that it backed up on itself. Even presuming that the surface of the water is relatively calm, as it was in Prince William Sound on March 24, the oil will spread in an infinitely random combination of thick and thin patches. This is due in part to the chemical interaction between oil and water. It has not yet proved possible for laboratory scientists to model in detail the pattern of spreading.

Drifting occurs independently of spreading and is controlled by wind, waves, and surface currents at all levels of intensity. The center of an oil slick moves at roughly 3 percent of wind speed, with a 20- to 30-degree shift eastward in the northern hemisphere due to the Coriolis effect. These forces and others that occur simultaneously — the perturbation of secondary currents, the obstruction of land masses — add new factors to the already scientifically unpredictable destiny of oil. Both spreading and drifting increase the surface of the slick and therefore enhance transfer through evaporation and dissolution.

Evaporation is the most important process of weathering during the first 24 to 48 hours following a spill. This is the most acute phase in terms of damage to wildlife. Over a period of 12 days, between 15 and 20 percent of the total mass of the crude oil may be lost through evaporation alone. The rate of evaporation, however, is affected by such things as air flow, and air

---

[54] These categories and explanatory material are largely derived from conversation with James Payne and from his and G. Daniel McNabb's report, "Weathering of Petroleum in the Marine Environment." My presentation, of course, is far less detailed than is Payne and McNabb's. Two additional categories mentioned in the report but not covered here are the weathering effects of ice in arctic environments, which had little or no application to the *Exxon Valdez* spill, and photochemical oxidation, about which little is known.

and water temperature, which in south-central Alaska tend to be low. Ultimately, Prudhoe crude loses between 21 and 22 percent of its mass through evaporation.

Dissolution or the dissolving of hydrocarbons into the water column generally does not represent significant numbers in terms of the overall mass of an oil spill, but again the biological effects are potentially damaging because of the propensity of light-end hydrocarbons to partition into organic compartments and thus to enter the food web. Most dissolution occurs within 8 to 12 hours after the release of oil to the water and then falls off exponentially. Dissolution is heightened by the spilling energy of oil into the water and by wave action, which stirs the oil into the water.

Dispersion is the tendency of crude oil to break up into pieces or droplets within the water. This increases surface area and allows further dissolution and evaporation of the light-end hydrocarbons. Although most of the dispersed droplets will return to the surface of the sea, some will be ingested by organisms at depth, then redeposited as fecal pellets and enter the food web as a chronic source of toxicity. This phenomenon, in addition to the presence of toxins in chemical dispersants themselves, which speed up the natural process and for a time increase the amount of hydrocarbons in the water column, was the source of the controversy over the use of dispersants immediately after the spill. Science remains genuinely divided over the use of chemical dispersants because of persistent questions over their long-term effects. Thus, protocols for their application are controversial.[55]

A side effect of natural dispersion, dissolution, and evaporation is that the proportion of waxes and asphaltics in the oil that remains will have increased dramatically — in 12 days from 34 percent to approximately 50 percent. The formation of water-in-oil emulsions, or mousse, depends upon the presence of these materials, and Prudhoe crude happens to have them in high levels to begin with. Within a short time (following the first storms) much of the oil spilled from the *Exxon Valdez* had formed a mousse composed of up to 55 percent water. This made it impossible to burn off the oil and seriously compromised other strategies, such as skimming. Also, the formation of mousse, because of the sealing effect of water, significantly impedes evaporation, dissolution, and microbial degradation. Therefore, emulsified tarballs that appeared at shorelines on, for example, the Kenai Peninsula and Kodiak Island (they continued to do so at various locations for

[55] In a full-scale oil spill drill staged in Prince William Sound by British Petroleum and the Coast Guard in September, 1998, a policy confrontation developed over dispersant application. Except for one other issue — citizen input — the drill was generally considered successful.

months) tended to retain toxic compounds at serious levels. The transformation of the original oil slick into mousse following the initial period of calm weather and the failure to either mechanically retrieve it (the most desirable scenario) or chemically disperse it was one of the most critical developments in the history of the oil spill.

The adsorption of oil onto suspended particulate material, or in other words the tendency of oil droplets to adhere to the surfaces of minute particles suspended in the water, creates the possibility of oil sinking to the bottom because of the weight of the object to which the oil has adhered. Prince William Sound does have significant quantities of glacially powdered rock in the water. Oil adhering to rock would sink. Again, Payne's findings suggested that this process was not significant in terms of the total mass of crude oil but potentially significant in certain locations, usually those heavily hit by oil, or hit repeatedly through tidal action. In such places the load of oiled particulates could transport itself on a massive scale to the bottom and affect the food web. Although John Oliver and the *Alpha Helix* science crew reported very little apparent damage to life systems in the intertidal habitats they surveyed, their work was done in early June, and so they were looking at first effects. Long-term damage would not have been evident yet.

The final category — shoreline interactions — was easily the most serious development from the *Exxon Valdez* spill, and one for which nobody was prepared. The near-shore waters received many of the unpredictable variables of weathering, such as adsorption and dissolution, and the shorelines themselves added their own unchartable complexities: plant life and sediment to which the oil might adhere, surfaces of varying degrees of porosity through which the oil might sink to varying depths, and tides that delivered the oil sometimes repeatedly, sometimes forming asphaltic mats. More than any other compartment, it was at the shorelines that crude oil in its complexity assumed the proportions of an out-of-control pestilence.

As he spoke to us, James Payne de-emphasized the effects of oil at sea. His view was of the whole of the slick. If you took all the water from Valdez to Port Graham, a distance of 400 kilometers, he said, then went offshore 200 kilometers, and assumed for the sake of argument that the water was 100 meters deep (a low estimate), the oil concentrations would be three parts per billion, and effects on fish larvae will probably not occur until concentrations reached ten parts per billion. His point was that the water column concentrations were extremely low. He also de-emphasized the likelihood that oil could have sunk in appreciable quantities — the controversy into which his work and his name had entered. Contrary to much of what I had heard about him, however, even from other scientists, he did not downplay in the least the seriousness of either the adsorption of oil onto particulates or the interaction of shorelines with oil, nor did he deny that oil might submerge. He said, "Oil could be entrained into a rip, but it would be a transient, short-lived phenomenon. Reports of submerged oil had yet to be confirmed in the samplings."

That was clear enough. It was science, and it depended upon evidence. Later, I asked Dexter Chan, a NOAA scientist stationed in Homer, about sinking oil. He looked at me warily. Since he worked out of the Homer OSCO office, he'd been receiving his share of the brunt of the controversy. He said, "Every instance of sinking oil is in the intertidal areas. There's nothing in deep waters."

Some time after that, in late July, I spoke to Robert Tworkowski, a Woods Hole geologist working for Alaska DEC in Kodiak. He regarded the sinking oil question as unresolved because, as he put it, "of the complexity of the water systems off Kodiak." He said that he could see oil still washing up around Kodiak, and that the question was: How was it getting there? He offered underwater channeling, underwater eddies, and a huge underwater reservoir as possibilities.

Later yet, in November, still puzzled by the question, I spoke to Jerry Galt in the NOAA offices in Seattle. Galt had worked on the oil spill. He had a certain exasperation, even a disdain for the question. He said, "You can't repeal the law of gravity. Oil floats." Of Kodiak, he said, "Of all the oil that got there, the amount that might have been entrained would be in the 1 percent range." Throughout all that time and extending into the spring of 1990, fishermen reported oil showing up on their lines, crab pots, and anchors, but Galt referred to such reports as "hearsay."

James Payne was far more willing to grant the possibility of exceptions and variations. Trim, with something of the bearing of an assured surgeon, he has eyes as clear as any I have ever seen, like water. He spoke forcefully and rapidly, in the manner of one accustomed to holding forth. The company with which he was associated, Science Applications International Corporation (SAIC), had begun testing Prudhoe crude for NOAA back in 1981 with the 2,100-liter flow-through tanks located outside. They were designed as models of marine conditions. It was through this work that Payne had arrived at most of his conclusions concerning the behavior of oil in water. He was careful to have us understand that SAIC had never done work for a private company, including the oil companies. In the political climate of the time and place, this was a matter of significance.

There were certain things, he said, that he couldn't tell us. The court-ordered rule of silence placed upon scientists connected with any oil spill litigation included all research activity supported in any way by Exxon or state and federal agencies. It included the 60-odd projects I'd seen among Gordon Robilliard's papers. The effect since so few independent scientists (of which John Oliver was one) came into the oil spill region, or could afford to (Oliver and his crew came in on a National Science Foundation grant), was that beginning several weeks after the spill virtually no scientific information tied to damage was available to anyone. The order had provoked an outcry. It fueled the perception of science as an arrogant fourth estate and raised serious questions about the privatization of science and the apparent willingness of government agencies to allow themselves to be levered into joining that privatization. It raised the same kinds of questions associated with government-sponsored science generally — that it would be politicized. It raised questions about the validity of the scientific work itself, since all of it had become litigation connected and put in the hands of lawyers. Being secret, it was not subject to open review. Science is merely data and not science at all until it is reviewed by peers.

Millions of dollars were being spent on science: the $72 million so far budgeted through state and federal agencies, and the additional millions Exxon had budgeted to counter the government findings.[56] Within the adversarial attitude toward information were more loops from which the public was also excluded. Riki Ott said that Exxon had tried to contract all the private scientists. "So who does that leave as the public defender?" she asked. "It's the EPA," she said. "But through the Technology Transfer Act, the EPA and Exxon have a joint agreement to share patents." These patents included new dispersants that were being tested on the oil spill. Another effect of the secrecy, Riki and Heather McCarty of PWSAC pointed out, was that information critical to determining the condition of released salmon fry from the hatchery system was not made available. "It's creating tremendous problems for PWSAC," Heather McCarty would say. A part of the truth about oil was that the court system had so far not permitted those who knew the most about it to speak. James Payne declined to offer an opinion on the gag order.

[56] Exxon spent $2.5 billion on the oil spill during the first two years following the incident. My 1990 request to Exxon to break their expenditure figures down into categories (legal fees, research costs, cleanup costs, administrative costs, etc.) was declined. Further scores of millions were allocated for scientific purposes by the trustees from the 1991 $1.025 billion settlement, and as of the end of 1998, Exxon estimated its full expenditures on the oil spill to be $3.5 billion, a figure that includes settlement payouts but not the still outstanding civil trial award. See conclusion for further discussion.

In the NOAA lab, James Payne and I stood before a long bench where one of the lab's two gas chromatographs was located. The chromatograph is an instrument designed to calculate the compounds present in oil samples. It takes the fingerprints of oil and measures the quantities of compounds, including hydrocarbons, that remain in the samples. The cost of such an instrument, the computers, and the facilities at the NOAA lab generally were one reason why independent scientists were so rare. John Mickelson had wandered off, and I'd glimpsed him in a side room, talking to someone. The gas chromatograph abruptly went into action, as if by its own volition. It was loaded with tiny vials rather in the manner of a slide carousel. The vials contained samples. They rotated around the machine, and one by one an armature picked them up and entered them into an aperture. The contents spat into the instrument for measuring. Beside it, a printer fed out the results in graph form. The exact results of the measurements the machine was making were one of the things Payne could not talk about.

Payne brought John back and showed him the instrument in operation. He explained to us how it worked. He explained again how few of the aromatics remained in the oil, how little of the oil there was on the open water, how unlikely it was that the oil would travel underwater. He knew who John was, and he wanted him to understand. John stood still, listening.

Payne said, "Water column processes are not a concern. We knew this from other oil spills, and what we're seeing here so far is confirming it. The beach processes are another matter. It's a two-dimensional problem, as opposed to a three-dimensional one."

Some would disagree with Payne's inclination to de-emphasize water column processes. Riki Ott had questioned it all along, and she would tell me later that water column samples taken in the sound at five different depths by Exxon scientists showed hydrocarbon readings of 16 to 28 parts per billion. "You didn't get a reading like that until after the spill," she said. In April two marine scientists, Usha Varanasi and Byron Morris, reported finding rockfish, a bottom-dwelling fish, with evidence in their viscera of sublethal effects of hydrocarbon poisoning.

Payne went on talking about the two-dimensional problem: "The subsistence people have real troubles if it's their beach that's been hit. It's the same with the fisheries. All the aromatics are essentially gone. You're not going to be able to measure them. It's all the people walking around the salmon beds that are messing it up. Skimming doesn't work. The booms don't work. The futility of the cleanup exercise is awesome. They should have focused on protecting certain places at the beginning."

John Mickelson still didn't speak. There would probably have been little disagreement on Payne's last point, though, from John or anyone else. Riki Ott would have added, however, that the problems went beyond the mere presence of the gruesome stuff, the machines, and the footfalls. They also included those hydrocarbons that were persistent in the environment and that over a period of time could reduce the reproductive capacity of organisms. The metabolism of aromatic hydrocarbons can result in their activation to toxic forms. They are then in the food web. The existing literature almost universally states that the long-term effects of oil upon organisms are unestablished but that, from such spills as the *Amoco Cadiz* in France, there are definite indications of mutations.

Payne told us about the work they were doing on what he termed bioremediation, a process by which the naturally occurring assimilation and dispersion of oil by microorganisms (oil-eating bacteria) may be enhanced by fertilizer applications. Payne said they were seeing microbiological degradation in the lab at a rate five times higher than what normally transpired — up to one part per thousand. By adding nutrients to the oil (nitrogen and phosphorous), the fertilizer spiked the natural process. It was another speed-up mechanism, but maybe a good one. The project was being cooperatively pursued by Exxon and the EPA's Office of Research and Development (ORD). It was the same project that Sandy Elvsass had talked about back in Seldovia, and at the time seemed to be the single most promising development from the oil spill. Even Riki Ott would say, "It's a great technology."[57]

By way of explanation, James Payne said, "Oil is the result of bacterial degradation of living matter to begin with."

His was the circumspect view, taken from the vantage point of distance, and of definite advantage — his high-tech machines, his staff, his respectability — and yet there was a definite touch of the cosmic to that statement. Bioremediation seemed almost a form of alchemy in which the natural tendency of a prime matter to turn back into its own circle was merely acceler-

---

[57] The positive early signs from tests on bioremediation in 1990 were not conclusively borne out in field tests through 1993. Exxon scientists tended to emphasize the positive, while EPA analyses were more guarded. Following what appeared to be one successful application of fertilizer with a liquid carrier (Inipol EAP 22) in which a patch of beach turned white over a two-week period, later tests proved less conclusive and did not affirm the effectiveness of bioremediation to the same extent as laboratory tests had. The cause of the early success at Snug Harbor remains unexplained (it may have been in part an additional "surfactant" effect of Inipol), and the variation of the conditions under which the field tests were conducted (beach-to-beach, site-to-site, tide-to-tide) introduced a complex set of shifting elements. The tentative conclusions following 1993 suggest that enhancement via bioremediation may increase naturally occurring biodegradation by a factor of two.

ated. The leading edge of one disorder met another, the spiked bacterial rapacity locking onto the disintegrating veer of oil toward entropy. This was the metaphor I had been seeking.

John Mickelson held his silence, taking it in as he stood impassively with his arms folded across his chest.

CHAPTER

15

CRAPS

Never in the millennium of our tradition have we thought it possible for the water to die. But it is true. We walk our beaches. But the snails and the barnacles and the chitons are falling off the rocks. Dead. Dead water. . . . We walk our beaches. But instead of gathering life, we gather death. Dead birds. Dead otters, Dead seaweed. . . . We are in shock. We need to clean the oil, get it out of our water, bring death back to life. We are intoxicated with desperation. We don't have a choice but to take what is offered. So we take the jobs, we take the orders, we take the disruption.

— Walter Meganack Sr., Port Graham village chief, 1989

The barge was about 70 feet long. Near its stem and mounted side by side were two 5,000-gallon tanks used for water exchange. One held clean water. The other held dirty water. Between them was a filtration system. This was a cleaning barge, set up to wash boats, skiffs, nets, and fish totes in accordance with Exxon's policy of zero tolerance — no oil whatsoever released to the water. Near the center of the barge were engines and a compression system hooked up to the tanks and pressure hoses, and next to that was a container from Korean Shipping Lines, used as an office and storage space. The barge itself was licensed in Portland and leased out to Veco, Inc.

Toward the bow was a large pile of absorbent pads, bale upon bale encased in plastic, and drums to hold waste, and then an open area at the bow where the fish totes were cleaned. Off one side of the bow a wooden dock was attached, into which the boats could be pulled. Overhead lights illuminated the barge. In the time I was there, the better part of the swing and graveyard shifts over three days, no oiled boats or skiffs appeared, no nets, and only a few totes. The entirety — barge, docks, buoys, and skiffs — was surrounded by two rings of boom to hold in any oil that might be spilled.

During only the first of shifts that I visited was any work done at all, and that meticulously — a stack of a dozen or so totes left by a fishing boat that departed just as I arrived by skiff from the Native village of Port Graham. A villager named Martin worked the totes over with great care. He scrubbed with large scouring pads, steam cleaned and rinsed them, then spread out absorbent pads to soak up the oil from the deck. The pads went into the drums. He rinsed the deck and skimmed up the oil off the water with a fine net. Martin was a fisherman with a reputation for being a "highliner," the best commercial fisherman in the village, but since the fishing was closed he was working on the Veco barge. There were three other crew members on board, three young women from the village, as well as the barge's night supervisor, George Hiller, and Paul Katroscik, who worked for the Environmental Pollution Claims Service of the Crawford Insurance Company. Exxon had brought the Crawford people in to monitor cash flow.

The three young women sat on the bales of absorbent pad and talked as Martin worked. Occasionally, one got up to spray while Martin scrubbed, and even more occasionally one helped scrub. There wasn't enough work to keep one person busy for long, and Martin seemed content to carry that small portion. I fell into conversation with the women. Just beyond the line of boom were two otters. Periodically, one or the other would dive, then reappear in a different spot. One of the women, Anna Sue, was pretty and talkative. She said that the pair of otters had recently moved into the bay.

"They came away from the oil around the corner," she said. By around the corner, she meant down at the southern extreme of the peninsula where the oil was heavy.

"Now, they're eating the shellfish. They eat all the big clams," she said. "We eat every animal except the otter."

When I asked her why, she said, "The meat is bad."

Struck by her answer, I later asked the same question of another, older woman from the village, Fiona Sawden, who said, "We don't like them because they eat our seashells. But we don't eat them because they're our brothers."

The village of Port Graham is located southeast of Seldovia, on the next finger-like bay down on the peninsula. The bay goes by the same name, Port Graham. From the barge, anchored halfway across the bay, I could see the village. At the beginning of a shift it was visible as a line of lights backed by a dark space, and then another, more distant line of lights. The dark space was a landing strip around which the better part of the village pressed like a doughnut. As the night shift on the barge progressed, the lights of the town went out, and early in the morning they came on again. On the barge, evening dwindled to twilight, and there would be a pause in which the overhead work lights would be surrounded by dark. Soon, the light in the sky started back again.

At the western edge of the doughnut a cluster of houses extended to the woods. Beyond the houses, a small hydroelectric project was under construction. The project was a source of pride, as it promised greater self-sufficiency. Just to the north were the recently constructed Port Graham School and the old Russian Orthodox Church, a carryover from the Russian fur trading days. All the old Native villages and many of the predominantly white towns on the Kenai, in Prince William Sound, and out on the Aleutians, as well, have Russian churches. They are plain on the outside — white with blue roofs — and filled with elaborately framed portraits and gold icons. Services are at once heavily ritualized and casual. People wander in and out, and children are attended to as services go on. The churches are the vestiges of another imperialism, and yet they have become a part of the grain. They've been here for nearly 200 years. They replaced shamanism, but now exist side-by-side with the old ways of subsistence living.

From the church, a narrow road dropped down to the town store and the cannery operated by the Chugach Native Corporation. Everywhere, lying in the yards or standing in the road, were large, rawboned dogs. At the intersection of the narrow road and the main road that encircled the landing strip lived the village chief, Walter Meganack, and his wife. At all times during the day, it seemed, either he, his wife, or both of them were outside their two-story house, sitting on the porch, working in the front yard, or conversing with neighbors. They maintained a watch. Their house overlooked the main roadway, the narrow road that led down to the store, and the landing strip. Walter was a tall, imperious man in his seventies, a man of reputation, known by Native people throughout Alaska, proud, conservative, and at times uncompromising. At no time did the presence of oil on the water and of the money that pursued it seem so revolutionary as when it was cast against Walter Meganack's figure.

Off to one side from the Meganacks' house stood the remains of a dwelling from the old days, a small, chest-high, elliptically shaped dugout with sod walls and a corrugated tin roof. The rough typology of the village's history runs this way: dugout and tin roof, and then elsewhere the cannery, landing strip, the store stocked with all manner of supplies — food, paper goods, tools, hardware, clothing, fishing gear. In every driveway stood a three-or four-wheeled ORV (outdoor recreation vehicle) — Yamahas and Hondas. The ORVs buzzed up and down the road, scattering the dogs. Behind the houses were fishracks. Not far from the town was a natural coal seep that had been a signal to early white arrivals of the potential mineral riches in this part of the world. From the village, I could see the barge out in the water, encircled by its two loops of boom. Walter Meganack had said, "We fight a rich and powerful giant, the oil industry, while at the same time we take orders and a paycheck from it. We are torn in half."

In June, Elenore McMullen, the village health aide, had said, "Veco came in one day and literally took over the country. It was really strange. Telephone people were here putting in telephone lines. People were everywhere. It was unreal. Our people are very excited about going to work, but there also was a lot of fear about losing our subsistence. And we have. We haven't been able to collect our clams, seaweed, herring roe, halibut. . . . This is something that has affected us emotionally, and I expect it will affect us physically. It has affected us spiritually. Our spiritual leaders have gone off to work on the spill, making $16.69 an hour. . . . I don't know if Port Graham will ever be the same. People don't have time to visit. They don't have time for tea. They're too busy. Even the children look lost."

Cleanup work was done around the corner at Windy Bay, a large indentation at the bottom of the peninsula, cut into the landform and placed at such an angle as if designed expressly to accept the oil that floated by. One young villager, Neal Hedrick, told me that he and a co-worker had cleaned a square yard of beach one day on Windy Bay. "The next day," he said, "we cleaned the same square yard again. We were working the shovels. The third day we were given trowels instead of shovels because we were going too fast."

Another villager, who asked that his name not be used, told me that he'd made over $10,000 in two months on the beach crews, and that the only workers who'd survived much longer than he were the ones who didn't speak out. "If you work hard, they tell you to quit working," he said. "As soon as you feel like you've started to do something, Exxon shuts the crew down. You fill your bags with debris, then sit around for three days because there's no tape to close the bags with. The only time they want you to work is when the helicopters are coming. 'Incoming.' That's the command to get busy, and then when the helicopter leaves, everything goes back to normal."

Such stories were so common everywhere on the Kenai and in Prince William Sound that they became undeniable. They were the most wrenching when told by people who cared deeply for the natural world and would have worked for nothing to restore it. Walter Meganack had said, "The land and the water are our sources of life. The water is sacred. The water is like a baptismal font, and its abundance is the Holy Communion of our lives. Of all the things that we have lost since non-Natives came to our land, we have never lost our connection with the water. The water is our source of life. So long as the water is alive, the Chugach Natives are alive." Out of the hell of oil on the water had come the assignment of the people to a Sisyphean circle, where the penalty for the loss of their innocence was the ceaseless, meaningless labor of shoveling, troweling, and wiping, what Robert Engler described in *The Nation* as the spectacle of "hundreds of young people wiping oil-soaked rocks with absorbent pads . . . like a scene from a mental institution."

I was in Port Graham nearly a month after Meganack's remarks were delivered to the Conference of Mayors.[58] By then, Exxon had already begun dismantling its cleanup effort, and it grew increasingly clear that the company was placing its hopes for the future on bioremediation. Though it was not stated publicly, all signs seemed to indicate that the company regarded further efforts at mechanical or manual cleanup as an exercise in futility. Considering the circumstances as they had evolved to this point, such an attitude was understandable. The cleaning barge at Port Graham was but one indication of a futility that had passed across the line from despair to

---

[58] Some observers have questioned the fact that Walter Metanack's remarks were partially "ghosted" for him by another villager, and delivered by Elenore McMullen. Such questions fly in the face of the communal nature of village reality and that Meganack as chief gave the words his imprint in order to lend credence to the feeling the words expressed.

ludicrousness. At first, I'd had difficulty understanding why the barge was there at all, way up here, so far from the action. Relatively speaking, only moderate amounts of oil remained in the waters of Port Graham itself, and there was no sign of continuing beach cleanup. Neil Hedrick's father, Larry Hedrick, had taken me around the bay in a skiff. There was evidence of oil, but not a great deal of it — enough to justify watchfulness so far as food supplies were concerned but probably not enough, considering shutdowns elsewhere (Gore Point, for example) and the standards of futility by which such things had come to be measured, to have maintained a serious cleanup effort. Some of the villagers here had resumed fishing and gathering, avoiding the bad places.

Fiona Sawden told me that at first the barge was to be stationed on an island out near the gulf, but that the people complained that they would get sick if they had to travel so far out to sea. This suggested that the purpose of the barge was, first, to employ villagers, and secondly, to serve in the cleanup effort. George Hiller, the barge's night supervisor, said plainly that Exxon had "set up the Port Graham barge so that the people would get something." He said that he and Jim Perry, the day supervisor, "were sent here for PR." George also echoed Gordon Robilliard's assessment when he said, "The time to make money is when there's chaos." Later I told Dean Peeler, the Exxon spokesman in Homer, that I'd been on the barge and that virtually nothing at all was happening on it. A tall man, Peeler smiled down at me and said, "So, now you know."

What I knew was that the barge was stationed there for reasons quite apart from the cleanup itself. At that stage in that place, cleanup mattered only to those who lived there and yet who had given over what powers they had to execute the cleanup to outsiders. In return, they received money.

Port Graham is a transitional community — not as faithful in its adherence to traditional life as English Bay or Chenega but more strict than the urban villages located within Seldovia, Seward, or Cordova. There was a story making the rounds in Port Graham about an initial meeting between Exxon representatives and the villagers. When Walter Meganack entered the community hall, he found the Exxon people stationed at a table in the front and otherwise poised along the walls and near the doorways. Meganack immediately directed that the chairs be rearranged into two groups and that the Exxon people sit on one side of the room and the village people on the other side. He took his place at the head of the room. The story was told to me by George Hiller. He said, "It was a master stroke. It completely changed the dimension of power in the room." It's an exemplary story, at once indicative of Meganack's wisdom and canniness. The money spilled into Port Graham, nevertheless.

Exxon's solicitous approach to Native communities stemmed from several causes. No doubt there was genuine concern for those whose resource would be most directly and immediately affected by oil on the beaches. Exxon must have been aware, also, of the intense sentiment felt by a large portion of the American public in the lower forty-eight for Native people — the hazily formed romance of the "noble savage." From Exxon's perspective, such strong, potentially inflammatory sentiment must have posed a distinct PR hazard, and so put Native people almost in the same class as sea otters. The best way to snuff out such a hazard, Exxon seemed to have determined, was to inundate the victim with money. Most importantly, probably, Exxon managers were aware of the potential power Native people held as collective owners of 10 percent of Alaskan lands, including lands in which oil wells might yet be sunk, or across which more pipelines might yet be built.

In the view of Carl Pulliam, whom I spoke to only a few days after his resignation as the Veco area supervisor for Port Graham and English Bay, Exxon's plan had been "to buy out public relations in the villages and to divide the villages from Homer and Seldovia by creating tension between them." As time passed, Carl said, "the first idea among the people of cleaning up as much oil as possible changed to the idea of making as much money as possible."

Carl and I had met early one morning in his mobile home on the edge of the town of Seldovia. It was a few days before I traveled to Port Graham. Carl was still feeling ragged from his tribulations as Veco supervisor. I sensed that he also felt compromised by his role in an enterprise that had become loathsome to him. Even speaking of it made him uneasy, but we sat in his living room and spoke softly for two hours, while his children and wife, a Port Graham native, slept in adjoining rooms. Carl was a tall, lean man who fished commercially and taught high-school science and basketball. He spread out a navigation chart on the floor and sat next to it, hugging one raised leg. He leaned over the chart occasionally to point out the places of his former domain as he spoke: Windy Bay, the heavily oiled site of controversy over failed cleanup methods; Koyuktolik Bay, just down the peninsula from English Bay and, in Carl's opinion, the westernmost of the heavily oiled locations, the point from which the current spun off and carried the oil toward Kodiak; the Chugach Passage, where Exxon had ordered out the oil capture crew that Carl had felt needed to be stationed there to intercept as much oil as possible before it worked its way around the peninsula; and Perl Island, where some Exxon people had maintained what he considered basically a party house. He'd seen the stacks of beer cases outside, a direct contradiction of Exxon's stringently worded policy on the use of alcohol.

Carl spoke of the difficulty of accomplishing anything because of the competition that developed between the villagers and townspeople, between Veco and another subcontracting company, Martech, between Veco and Exxon because of Exxon's inefficiency and its refusal to listen to local people. "When Veco came in back in the spring," he said, "greed entered the picture. We were doing things that didn't make any sense. We'd send a boat with a six-hundred-gallon water tank to water up a boat with a twelve-hundred-gallon tank. We had a boat that needed a part. It took a week to get the part because Exxon refused to let boats cross the lines between Veco projects and Exxon projects. There were two sets of contracts. Exxon paid three thousand for a thirty-two- or thirty-six-foot gillnetter, while Veco paid fifteen hundred. We were always getting caught trying to work for one or the other, and they'd envy each other. One group got steaks. The other got beans. There'd be disputes over hours, Sometimes a crew would get paid for eighteen hours even if they only worked six. While I was working, I saw probably two hundred thousand dollars in wasted wages."

"It was like Cinderella. Everybody knew the story. But we all got thrown into Cinderella's part, anyway. We believed we were Cinderella, coming out of the ashes, but at the same time we knew there was never going to be a ball at the end."

At about eight o'clock on my second night in Port Graham, Paul Katroscik and I took a skiff from the village to the cleaning barge. We unhooked the first line of boom and motored inside it, then waited for a skiff from the barge to pick us up. When it came, as a safeguard against releasing the virtually nonexistent oil that might be inside we stepped from one skiff to the other over the interior loop of boom.

Once on the barge, Paul and I moved to the edge of the stern where the fishing poles were kept and a picnic table had been set up. Paul checked a tide chart to see when he should do his work, which consisted of working through the barge's inventory sheets and filling out his reports, and when he should fish. Since he had so little work to do, fishing was the first priority.

Paul owned a roofing and rain-gutter business in California. A friend from his Vietnam days had arranged for him to be taken on by the Crawford Insurance Company. At about that time, Crawford monitors had begun to turn up everywhere in the oil spill region. I would see one in Exxon's Homer office, a Bartleby-like figure surrounded by heaps of papers and ledger sheets, and several in Cordova, in Valdez. . . . They wore dark blue peaked hats with gold scroll work and the name of their Crawford division. They commanded instant respect. Paul said he shouldn't talk to me at all, but he did. He said that Crawford was there to check for graft. "There is graft," he said, "such as people turning in duplicate work sheets with overtime." By that time, this was not news to me, but it was interesting to hear it coming from one whose job was to ferret out such mischief. He told me about a young woman who had hooked up with a man in one of the offices and had arranged to work overtime in two different places at once. When I told him what Carl Pulliam had said about the $200,000 in wasted wages, Paul said, "No doubt. Exxon's been taking a beating." Nearly a year later, in the late spring of 1990, the towns would begin to buzz with rumors that information gleaned by the Crawford monitors, among others, was to lead to suits brought by Exxon against local persons and businesses. By summer, but for a couple of cases, the rumors had not been realized.

Seeing that the tide wasn't to come in for a while, Paul went into the office to do his paperwork and I moved toward the bow of the barge, where I'd arranged to meet Jim Miller, the community alcoholism counselor for Port Graham and English Bay. He was also working on the barge. Jim is a Native from southeastern Alaska, married to a woman from Port Graham. He was the board president of the "other" church in Port Graham, an unaffiliated charismatic church, the Church of the First Born, that had grown up after the Baptists had left seven years before. The Russian Orthodox Church tended to include the more traditional element in the village, Jim told me. "Our church is strict. It's language, food, and religion that makes you an Aleut in this village. If you don't do those, then you're not a real Aleut. But even Walter," Jim said, "has to admit that we're a sober bunch."

Charismatic churches, I understood, had become common in Native communities of the area, and they were especially attentive to matters of sobriety. In that respect, they were forward-looking. Drugs and alcohol , the chemicals of despair, were a serious problem in the villages, and Jim was worried about it, now. We sat at the edge of the big stack of absorbent pads, looking off the side of the barge toward the mouth of the long bay. Slowly, the light was fading. To our left, several clean fish totes stood on end. So far as I could tell, they were the same ones Martin had cleaned the night before. Jim had a short crop of dark hair and a bony face. He sat still and spoke quietly. "My feeling is that the money will finally cause more problems than it'll solve, especially with the alcoholics and addicts. We have some of those. Exxon money accentuates the spill, and this'll take effect in the winter because of the depression. We'll have more suicides than usual.

"At first, we were really scared," he said. "The people were afraid to eat anything. And they didn't know what to do, because in the annual cycle the spring and summer are the time to do all the work. So they were lost for a while. But now they're gathering again. Financially," he said, "the villages are much better off than they've ever been. For people who use the money wisely, it's good. They can find a self-respect out of being self-supporting. But the anger from the oil, and then the pride, jealousy, and greed that comes from the money, it all comes from the spill and it affects the spiritual world of the people. That's not a good thing. There's a real take 'em for what you can get attitude. Spiritually, it's not a good thing."

A young man, Jim had been educated differently than most of the Port Graham people, he told me. He'd been to college. He was independent, personally hopeful, and prepared to enter the world outside. His preference was to take the shares he'd received through the Alaskan Native Claims Settlement Act of 1971 and sell them so that he could start up his own business. This touched upon a controversial question among Native people. Besides converting Native claims into the 13 regional corporations and over 200 village corporations, ANCSA also included a provision by which individuals received share allotments that could be sold in 1991. Some people felt very strongly that ancestral claims should be held collectively for the sake of future generations.

Jim's wife didn't want to sell her shares, he said. That was fine with him because then their children would inherit her shares and they could use his money. He said, "I like being on a boat, but I don't like fishing. There's a lack of opportunity here. I'd like to relocate and start a business. Someday I'd like to write a book. I want land, but I want to buy it when and where I want. I had a chimney cleaning business for a while. I can't picture myself ever being out of work. It's become very clear to me that my people can't rely on world systems for their security."

Inside the Korean shipping container that served as the office on the barge, Paul was teaching the game of craps to Fiona Sawden and two other older women who, along with Jim Miller, made up the work crew. Paul and the three women were clumped around one end of a long bench that stretched most of the way along a wall. The office was a dense place. In the open space past the end of the bench, two rows of folding chairs faced each other from opposite walls. At the far end of the bench, George Hiller, the supervisor, was organizing papers. There was an attached storage room loaded with supplies and snacks. On the bench was a coffee pot. Above the bench, the wall was plastered with photographs of the crews, and warning and safety posters and regulations — what to do in case of a tsunami, drug testing procedures, Coast Guard regulations, alcohol regulations, emergency procedures, emergency numbers. On all the cleanup vessels safety had become the number one priority. Zero tolerance for additional spills of any sort was the second priority.

Paul had a notepad on the bench, and he was explaining the rules of craps to the women. One of them would roll the dice, and he would explain what the roll meant. They were intensely interested in the game, particularly Fiona Sawden. They played a few mock rounds. One rolled and they all looked at the dice, then over at Paul. They laughed, softly rocking in their chairs as he explained how they might have lost or won. Paul told them how the game was played in Las Vegas. Fiona had been to Reno. Paul worked the odds of the rolls on the pad of paper, making an elaborate chart for them. There was an intriguing heaping up of elements in the scene . . . the bunch of us pressed into the Korean container, its walls loaded with Exxon posters and regulations, and the container mounted on a barge from Portland that did no work, lying still here in the bay, put here to quiet the villagers, and the Crawford monitor whose job it was to dig out graft teaching the women how to play craps.

I learned that Fiona, a plump, attractive woman in her fifties, was a bilingual teacher and had been involved with translation. When I asked if I could speak with her sometime, she said, "We can meet in the banya."

Not understanding that a banya was a bath, a steam house, I said, "Where?"

"In the banya," she said, leaning back and laughing. Everyone in the office looked at me and laughed at my foolishness.

I talked to her the next day in the living room of her home. It is a comfortable place with a thick carpet, a sofa, and easy chairs. On the walls are pictures, family photographs, and Russian Orthodox icons. Her husband was out working and her two grandchildren were there, visiting from Los Angeles. Their father, she said, was up on the Kenai. Occasionally, she would get up and tend to one of the children. "The oil didn't have much impact here," she said, "except for making money. At first it scared the heck out of us. There were a lot of dead salmon fry on the booms, but we won't know about them for three, four years. How long is Exxon going to be around? If I don't smell the oil, I'll eat the food. We've been eating birdarki [chiton], and now the clams and cockles are starting to build up. A couple of weeks ago we got birdarki, built a fire, cooked them, and ate them. We didn't get sick.

"But now there's not much fishing because of the working," she said. "I'm working on the barge to make money. I'm just as greedy as the next person." She smiled. "If they want to make money, I want to make money. It's the greed Exxon is bringing out in us. The greed is bad. Families are fighting amongst themselves and nepotism is going on. A lot of families are not taking care of their kids. They're working, or if they're home, they're too tired. And we're worried about what the money will do to the people this winter with the drinking. The winter is long."

One of her grandchildren, a boy of three or four, had snuggled up next to her on the sofa. I asked her about the Church of the First Born, and she smiled again and said, "The trouble is they can't sin. The Russian Orthodox don't have such rules. The born agains can't dance, and now our kids don't know what a dance is. We have masking in our church. It's all that's left from the old days before the Russians came. It comes during Christmas. We have to wash the masks each year to purify them. The traditional masks were burned."

Fiona was a part of a movement in many Alaskan villages to rediscover and record their own history so that traditional languages and values could be preserved for the young and serve as a buffer against white culture and its extractive economies. "My great-great-grandfather was a Russian priest from San Francisco. Before the Russians, Shaman was our religion. I learned that at the bilingual conferences," she said.

After the shift change at midnight on my second and third nights on the barge, Jim Miller and the women went home and the younger crew came on. Paul Katroscik and I then fished off the end of the barge deep into the morning. We were fishing for halibut, a bottom feeder. We caught nothing, but sat there, baiting and rebaiting our hooks, reeling them out and reeling them back in. An older man from the village came and set a line and tied it off on the barge, and came back every half hour or so to check it. He caught fish.

I thought about Fiona, about how impressed I was by her bearing, her calm, her humor, her acceptance of herself. I thought about the momentous distinction Thomas Berger made in his book on the Settlement Act, *Village Journey*, between the Native regard for the earth as inalienable and the white regard for it as endlessly alienable. For the one people the earth was never a stranger. For the other, the relationship was one of estrangement. It seemed to me that the grace with which Fiona and others like her had positioned themselves in a world loaded with contrarieties came from a deeply felt sense of her own inalienability. The capacity to contain the contradictions of the world and human behavior and yet to act with grace, to not suffer the defeat of a complete change of heart, seemed to be the measure of character the oil spill had mounted.

On the third night, Martin and Anna Sue were out at the stern for a while. They had a ghetto blaster and played a Dolly Parton tape. For a while, they jiggled around voluptuously to the music. They knew what a dance was. Slowly, the light began coming back into the sky. Martin and Anna Sue went into the office to watch television with the others, and Paul's and my place at the stern fell silent. The hump of the landform across from us took shape against the pale air. The tide ran hard and the loops of boom were drawn almost to a point on the high side of the barge. White jellyfish floated slowly by in the dark like flowers. Paul told me the story of his lost love, a woman he was going to marry when he was 29. She was killed in an automobile accident a few days before they were to move into a new house. The story was perfectly told, filled with emotion and yet devoid of self-pity. The oil spill seemed to do that to some people, to carry them to the edges of themselves and to open them to the seams of the world.

A year later, Walter Meganack told me that Port Graham was still not normal. "Some people used the money they made wisely," he said. "They are doing good. The others have a problem. Some of them now have income tax problems, especially the ones that worked on the barge. The fish did not show up this year. We are waiting for them. There are good reports and bad on the shellfish, and we don't trust the reports, so we don't use the shellfish."

16

MASKS

In July, I went into the Homer Exxon office in hopes of meeting Dean Peeler. The receptionist said he was not in, but that his assistant would meet with me. I gave her the letter from my editor that I carried with me in lieu of a press card. The receptionist disappeared with the letter down the hall, then she returned. She was a friendly woman whose telephone rang constantly. Behind her on the wall was a long poster that read, "Hip, Hip, Hooray, for the Gang Away . . . From The Folks You Left Behind." Beneath the poster was a photograph from the *Anchorage Daily News* that showed a smiling woman holding an otter pup. The caption to the photograph read, "One tough pup beats the odds." The poster was laced with the signatures of those who had left; only a few of the Exxon people had been here continuously from the beginning. The poster and newspaper photograph were an expression of team spirit, at a time when the local firestorm of criticism was just beginning to wane. I waited 15 or 20 minutes. Waiting was a part of the game.

Several times, the receptionist walked down the hall, then came back, and each time she told me that someone would see me in a minute. I began to get the feeling that my letter was being checked out. Eventually, the assistant, a young woman, did come out. She led me down the hall to a back room and introduced me to Dean Peeler, who I'd just been told was not here. He led me into yet another room, deeper into the complex of offices. He offered me a Coke and a doughnut. I understood that it was admirable that graciousness could persist under these circumstances and also that it meant nothing. Peeler was a large man, tall, bearded, young, and friendly. He was from New Orleans and spoke with a soft accent that gently rounded off the edges of his words. More than once, I had heard the oil industry people switch from flat accents to the most beguiling of South Atlantic and Gulf Coast drawls. Peeler wore a white striped shirt, pale blue denims, and white Reeboks. Had I not already seen him at the Homer MAC meetings cutting a community representative to the quick,[59] and had I not seen the iron under his gracious surface, I would have found it impossible not to like him. We sat across from each other at a table and he affably informed me that he could not answer my questions, that instead he had questions for me. He wanted to know what I was interested in.

I told him — the barge in Port Graham, the state of the cleanup in his region, the continued use of dispersants on shorelines, bioremediation, the local controversies over the Exxon and Veco presence, the sinking oil question, the otter recovery center at Jackolof Bay, the disposition of archeological materials that members of the Shoreline Cleanup Advisory Teams had been finding, the structure of Exxon management, and the matter of reliable information. He said he'd been on the phone to Valdez. I discerned that while I'd been waiting in the lobby, he'd been getting his directions for dealing with me. He said that what I needed was a briefing, that if I went to Valdez they would answer all my questions. What information he then was willing to give me came in an indirect form, such as his to my question about the idleness of the barge at Port Graham — "So, now you know."

---

[59] The discussion concerned whether or not Exxon would approve and fund Billy Day's rock-washing machine. The heated exchange turned not on the merits of the rock washer but on what had happened to the memos that had traveled the loop back and forth between the Homer MAC, the Coast Guard, and the Exxon headquarters, and where the rock-washing machine was.

He did have something he wanted to show me, a portion of a videotape. It was the *U.S.A. Today* show on the oil spill. It included segments from the notorious, staged cleanup operation at Gore Point and a cutting from the equally notorious Marilyn Monroe ad. The ad was part of a campaign developed after *Alaska* magazine devoted its June 1989 issue to the oil spill. The magazine's forthright portrayal of the damage resulted in the withdrawal of all advertising by the Alaska Tourism Marketing Council, which represented a major portion of the magazine's advertising. The editor of the magazine, Ron Dalby, stood his ground. Exxon gave $4 million to the state tourism division, citing the urgent need for image enhancement. The state tourism division gave the money to the Alaska Visitors Association, which had ties with many of the same parties as the Alaska Tourism Marketing Council. The Visitors Association[60] spent some of the money to retain a public relations firm that also represented Alyeska. Under the guise of supporting worried tourism interests, Exxon was funding its own image enhancement. The result was the Marilyn Monroe ad, which appeared nationally in magazines and on television in the lower forty-eight and was shown to Exxon shareholders.

Marilyn Monroe was presented as Alaska. Her famous mole had been airbrushed from her face. The absent mole represented Prince William Sound, without which, the ad implied, Marilyn and Alaska were still equally beautiful.

Dean Peeler looked at me and smiled. We were to enjoy this man-to-man. In his expression, however, there was a hint of apology, a slight crack in the mask, as if to inform me that he understood I was not so stupid as to not know what a fraud the ad was. "It's a great idea, though," he said. "I really admire the person who thought that up."

In between my time in Homer and Valdez I had communicated several times with Exxon's Valdez headquarters. They asked for my list of questions, which I revised and sent on. I was assured that the proper persons to answer my questions would be provided. I could expect an encounter with a battery of experts. When I arrived in Valdez on September 19, Karsten Rodvik came out and asked if I could come back a few hours later. I agreed to do so. Rodvik introduced me to another spokesman, Joe Ferguson, with whom I

---

[60] The Alaska Visitors Association is the same organization that sponsored another advertisement run on network televison (notably CBS) during the early fall of 1990. This ad invited would-be tourists to come to Alaska, and in particular to Prince William Sound, where they would "see its pristine shoreline nearly recovered now from the oil spill."

had talked previously, although Ferguson insisted that we had never spoken before. The fact that he had forgotten me, considering the numbers of people who had been through those offices, was hardly surprising. It was his emphatic denial of a meaningless lapse of memory that seemed curious. Surely, it was not important, and yet the inclination of Exxon people to protect themselves against often nonexistent rebuffs or threats tended to draw attention to them. Each of the men looked tired.

When I returned later that day for my appointment, I waited for 45 minutes or so in the small lobby and watched two construction workers just outside a window. I had seen them earlier. They were setting sono tubes to make footings for what would be a covered walkway to the building. As it happened, there was a controversy in Valdez at the time over what would happen to the building when the Exxon headquarters moved to Anchorage. Questions over its disposition would continue through the winter into the next summer. It was a steel-sided modular building with a well-appointed interior that had been hauled in on trucks and thrown up to make the Valdez headquarters. Exxon had refused to commit itself to leaving the building behind when it moved but left open the possibility that it would be knocked apart and shipped back out.

Valdez wanted the building. Everything considered, it was a minor question, an isolated fulcrum point in the chaos that had overrun Valdez. The city's normal population of about 5,000 had swelled at one point to over 11,000. Carol Smith of the city's community development department told me that through most of the summer the population was in excess of 7,000. There was not anything approaching sufficient housing, or sufficient office space. There was no available storage space. Subcontractors, such as Norcon and Veco, threw up trailer and container camps just outside town, Workers lived there, or sometimes in tents in campsites. The drug trade had exploded. The bars were loaded. The city jail ran out of space. The court system and police department were overtaxed.

The shortages continued into 1990, well after Exxon and its subcontractors had pulled out of town, because of continued increased employment there for government agencies and Alyeska's upgraded system, which included the addition of 125 oil spill response positions. At the same time the established stores and businesses had difficulty finding employees because so many had made so much working on the cleanup. The counseling center had been stretched beyond its capacities. The hospital found itself left with a huge operating debt as a result of unpaid bills stalled in litigation that was connected to claims. All through 1989 and 1990 the city services, including the development department, were run ragged. Since Valdez did not have a sales tax, the city treasurer, Don Gill, was unable to estimate the total amount of money that came into the city. There was a little over $2 million, Gill said, in expenditures by the city directly connected to the spill and cleanup presence. It went for things such as extra snow removal, extra employees, office supplies, overtime, police, campsite construction, remodeling. Those expenditures were funded by Exxon. Because of litigation, I was told by Exxon representatives, the company would decline to estimate for me the money it spent in Valdez or any other community.

As I waited in the lobby of the Valdez Exxon headquarters, the guard at the podium next to the door asked me if I thought the workers were making any progress. Earlier, we had talked about the walkway. I had observed that the sono tubes had been set below the frost line. If Exxon took the building out, some pretty good footings were going to be left behind. It seemed to be Exxon's way. Driven by codes, regulations, insurance, and bad feeling, the company threw money at construction, supplies, equipment, safety regulations, testing procedures, research, and personnel while the real question of what would be done with the building or, more generally, about the oil, remained unanswered.

So far as I could tell, in the time between early morning and now, about 1:45 in the afternoon, the workers hadn't moved the work forward an inch. They were still standing around, occasionally fooling with their tape measures and string lines. The guard looked around to make sure no one but me was in hearing distance, then said, "They're paid by the hour, too."

I learned that I was not to speak with Rodvik, nor with Joe Ferguson, but with yet another man, Bleu Bethard. Since Bethard was a senior staff adviser, I had apparently come up a bit in the world. He met me in the lobby and led me back through the hallway to his office, offered me a Coke, then sank into the chair behind his desk. A middle-aged, slightly overweight man, he appeared extremely tired. His face had a gray cast and there was a heaviness in his carriage and an almost paralyzed deliberateness in his movements. He leaned on his elbows and looked up at me briefly, then back down at his desk, and said he wanted to find out what interested me. I replied that I had already sent on a list of questions and subjects. He said, yes, that he was looking at it. I straightened up in my chair and peered at his desk. He stared fixedly down at the surface. There was nothing there between his arms, no paperwork at all, and I had an eerie sensation, but then Bethard slowly revolved his head to the right and stared at the computer screen mounted there.

He began to speak in a monotone, and for a long time did not look at me at all, shifting his gaze between the computer screen and his desk. The usual slippery friendliness had fallen away to reveal something nearer to a death mask. Every once in a while, he reached out and touched a key on the computer keyboard. I presumed he was scrolling the material on the screen, that my questions and whatever other information Exxon had about me were stored there. A version of my reality was in there made out of electricity and amber light, while the other me, whose presence the reality of the file might yet find to be a mistake, merely sat in the room and breathed the air.

Bethard said he would answer what questions he could, and apologized for his failure otherwise to provide me with the information I wanted. He said that because of the withdrawal of the cleanup machinery and forces, they didn't have the time to do many interviews, and that if I could come later, perhaps even a month later, after they had moved to Anchorage and things had settled down, they could set up a series of briefings for me. When I said I had been informed that that was my reason for coming here, Bethard again expressed his apologies.

"We've given the press complete access to the scene," Bethard said. "We ran the press out in helicopters. We had two flights a day for weeks. We told the pilot to take the people anywhere they wanted to go."

I said nothing. His statement was true in a way. It was also true that at times it took the persuasion of a national network to get the press tours to move, and that such tours were compromised twice over — first by Exxon sponsorship and then by network agendas, their obsession with photo opportunities. The labors of the cleanup crews as they were depicted in the national media did not jibe at all with the stories told by workers: the stories of graft, goldbricking, senseless assignments, discouragement, and speedups when incoming flights and boats came near. For those reasons, I had taken no interest in Exxon-sponsored press tours.

Bethard told me about the numbers of workers Exxon had employed, and the number of boats it had leased. "Exxon had zero employees here four months ago," he said. "Now they have four hundred Exxon people from round the world, and contracts with another ten thousand. Our main camp has support for seven hundred people. We serve them four meals a day, including one at midnight. The speed with which we did this," he said, "is unbelievable."

Perhaps this was true, but it hadn't worked.

One of the questions I had sent in had to do with the gag orders attached to the contracts Exxon had first issued to fishermen who leased out their boats. Bethard said, "When you work for Exxon, you agree that you don't speak for Exxon. That's all."

I said that that wasn't exactly what the fishermen in Cordova had reported.

Bethard looked up at me briefly. It was a glimmering of contact, but then he looked back over at the computer, stared at it fixedly, and said, "The story that we were paying fishing skippers not to talk to the press is not true. We have tried to be open and we've given a lot of access to the press."

This was not exactly correct, either. The initial contracts the fishermen received did contain an explicit stipulation that contractees not speak to the press without permission.[61] What this would have meant in practice was that only fishermen willing to speak favorably of Exxon would be allowed to speak to the press. It was also not correct in my experience that openness was the common practice — access, maybe, according to Exxon's guidelines, and obviously in accordance with Exxon's schedule, but openness only when the questions were the ones Exxon wished to answer. It was common for Exxon to refuse to answer questions, particularly when they touched upon specific matters of finance, science, and law. I was interested in breakdowns on projected expenditures — how much for research, animal rescue, reimbursements to communities, how much paid to cleanup workers. Bethard said that they didn't have those figures. I was extremely interested in scientific findings, but because of litigation they were unavailable. I was interested in corporate structure as Exxon had implanted it here on the shores of Prince William Sound because of the obvious incompatibility between the structure of response and the reality of oil on the water.

When I raised the question of corporate structure, Bethard said, "Oh, you mean an MBA type thing."

I was interested in language, in the way Exxon (and, incidentally, government agencies, as well) used language not as a means of transporting information but as a kind of veil dance that always promises but never reveals. The Exxon press releases were filled with such vaporous stuff:

> One of Exxon's top concerns was working with fishing groups to identify critical areas for deployment of the first available containment booms.

[61] Clause #8 of the contract offered to fishermen read, "Contractor agrees to avoid unnecessary publicity and to make no statements, admissions or representations on behalf of EXXON or purporting to be on behalf of EXXON. Further, all press releases and/or contacts with the press, television, radio or other media discussing the services performed hereunder shall require the prior written approval of EXXON before being released." Bethard's point was true for the first part of the clause, but clearly not for the second part.

Wiping oil covered boulders

Injection cleaning, one of the "aggressive" methods

Rock polishing

"Hot water wash" from a ship based crane

Workers clean a beach on Green Island, an all-out attack

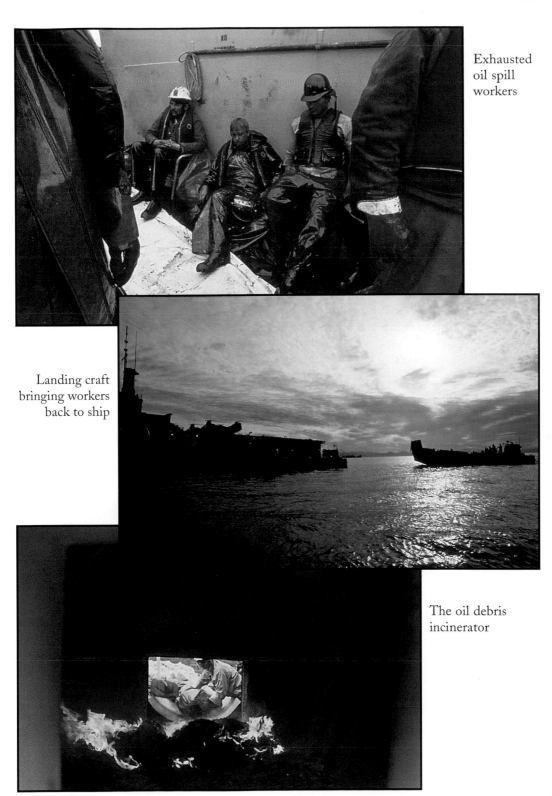

Exhausted
oil spill
workers

Landing craft
bringing workers
back to ship

The oil debris
incinerator

Mountains above Unakwik Inlet

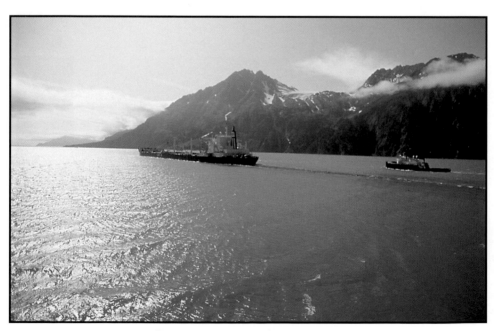

Out going tanker and escort vessel

Cordova
Harbor

Marie Smith Jones and
David Grimes (left), the
"mini-blockade"

Dune Lankard in an Eyak Corporation clear-cut on the Copper River Delta

Herring Bay, Knight Island
Inset: new shoots after oiling

From the onset, "helping people help themselves" has been Exxon's way of operating.

The mammals most impacted by the oil spill were the sea otters and Exxon's response to their plight was swift.

Within the first few days of the spill, Exxon invited the Tourism Bureau and the Alaska Seafood Marketing Institute to make suggestions on how Exxon might help alleviate their customer concerns. The dialogue led to an Exxon grant of $4 million to the Alaska Visitors Association for an immediate advertising campaign.

Exxon deeply regrets the oil spill, has acknowledged responsibility, and accepts the obligation to mitigate its impacts.

. . . current plans and schedules indicate that all significantly impacted shorelines will be treated prior to September 15, 1989.

The massive effort undertaken during 1989 was successful in significantly improving shoreline and water conditions in Prince William Sound and the Gulf of Alaska. The resulting stable conditions minimized the likelihood of harm to the area's wildlife, while the extensive activities provided a foundation for natural forces to accelerate the cleansing process during the harsh Alaskan winter.

The half-truths in the statements are evident: Exxon worked with fishermen only after the fishermen took action on their own, and in some instances Exxon submarined the people's efforts to "help themselves." The response to stricken animals was forced upon Exxon by the Department of the Interior and the public. Exxon's interest in tourism was also one of alleviating its own bad reputation; most of the 1,090 miles of oiled shoreline had been insufficiently treated. Even more troubling in my view, however, was the resort to vagueness, the flimsily cast language of corporate kitsch: *concern, dialogue, mitigate, obligation, significant, stability, minimize, likelihood, cleansing process*, and the most overused buzzword of all, *impacted*, which in a previous life I had thought referred to a tooth lodged in the jaw. Such obscure wording muddled the issues. Because there was so little in it to hang on to, it prevented examination.

Naturally, I found it impossible to establish a ground upon which Bleu Bethard and I could discuss the matter of language. The question he did want to answer had to do with bioremediation. "It's working better than we thought it would," Bethard said. "It's a great follow-up tool. We also think Corexit is a net benefit for the environment. We wanted to use that on some of the areas that have oil stuck on the rocks. Corexit is even faster than bioremediation. We've got environmental studies going. We'll probably have more information than anybody in the U.S."

I asked about the availability of that information.

He said, "It's not in our nature to put out preliminary results."

He went on: "We'll never get it completely clean. Maybe we'll get all the oil off some of the shorelines, and some off the rest of them. We've cleaned some sections five to ten times. We have scientists working for us and we're not paying them to tell us fairy tales. Some of the beaches, you wash again and again and you can't get it all out. We'll get it off to varying degrees. We will not leave a shoreline where it'll be an environmental threat to birds and otters and sea life. I hate to say Mother Nature will help, but it's true. We have both high and low energy shorelines, though. Some of the oil will be absorbed in nature, and then we'll have to decide — now what do we want? More people on the beaches?"

"We've spent eight hundred eighty million so far, and there's another four hundred million in insurance that we expect to be added to that. This doesn't include litigation, which will probably go primarily to the fishing industry.[62] I'm just a PR man," he said. "I'll be perfectly happy if I can get the public to understand what we have done and nothing more. I'd be happy if we can just tell the facts well."

I didn't interrupt him, but thought that the "well" part of that statement was the rub.

"One of our problems," he said, "is that the state of Alaska is perceived as an independent party, and it's not. It has a vested interest. If people would scrutinize their opinions as closely as ours, they'd see that."

Bethard had begun to look at me a little more often. His gaze now seemed about equally divided between computer screen, desk top, and me. We'd been in close physical proximity for well over an hour. Despite myself, I'd begun to feel a sympathy for him. He was easily the least slippery and most credible of the Exxon PR people I had spoken with. His face remained gray, his voice

---

[62] A month later, when I talked to Exxon officials in Anchorage, I found them surprised to learn that I had those figures. By late fall, the total had climbed to $1.4 billion. By the end of the second summer, it would be $2.5 billion.

soft and expressionless. The mask remained fixed, but out from under it came glimmers of character. He told me that the Exxon employees here had mental health counseling, that there was a fishing boat to take them out on the water for relief, that it was not uncommon for them to work past midnight, that some of them had had to be sent home. He paused and glanced out toward the hallways where there was a bustle of activity, then looked back at me. "We have a lot of pride in Exxon."

"Pride" seemed to me to be the most dangerous buzzword. It represented the screen behind which the Exxon people could hide their own anxieties and questions.

Bethard said, "And now suddenly we're the object of national scorn. Many of us think it's the worst thing that's ever occurred."

A woman came into the room, and left a stack of papers on Bethard's desk. His face brightened. The woman went out. She was young, blond, and attractive. Bethard told me that she was from the Valdez city offices. "She's always pleasant," he said. "She always has a smile." In a moment, the woman returned and stood just outside the doorway, talking to someone else. Bethard had to go to a meeting. He began talking to the woman near his doorway, then got up from behind his desk. There was a spring in his step, as if he were about to be freed from captivity. Suddenly, he moved through the doorway, forgetting me completely.

Later that afternoon, I had some time to kill until my ride on the float plane back to Cordova. I made my way to the docks to look around, and ended up talking for while to a man who introduced himself to me as Roger Shaw. We sat across from each other in his four-seater aluminum boat, which he said was fast, and used for deliveries and emergencies. "It's a hell of a mess, ain't it?" he said. His boat was attached to Task Force II, a group of work crews that had been located off Ingot, Eleanor, and the northwest end of Knight Island. "It's a funny deal, too," he said, and then he leaned back and laughed, displaying his bad teeth. The laugh sounded like a bray.

Several school buses had pulled in above us on the access road, and not far away a couple of tour boats leased out as delivery vessels had just docked to unload workers. Over Shaw's shoulder, I watched a long line of a hundred or so men and women walking up the metal gangway toward the buses, which were there to taxi them out to the ready-made camps outside town. The workers appeared sullen and weary, and the heavy, rhythmic thud of their boots on the gangway made a sound like distant thunder. Further away and a little to the south of us lay the open bay and at the far end of it the Alyeska

Terminal. Two tankers rested in the water. Above them, and above the huge holding tanks, the mountains rose precipitously, their blue streaked with white glaciation. Like dragonflies and gnats, airplanes and helicopters buzzed to and fro, ceaselessly going out into the sound and coming back.

Shaw had swung around to watch the workers, then he turned back to me, shaking his head and grinning. "Take the bear watch," he said. "They give you an air horn and a can of mace and a whistle and hope to hell you've got a big set of balls. No guns allowed. Guns are against the rules. So the bear watch guys damn sure don't want to be back there too far in the woods like they're supposed to be. There might be bears in there. So they find a tree up from the beach and go to sleep, and when the boat comes back for the shift, they're the first ones out. It's just a funny deal."

He told me he used to work for Veco at Prudhoe Bay, but was laid off in early March. When he heard about the spill, he bought the boat and engine, and came down here. "I had to hound them for a month to take me on," he said, "but now these boys are paying me good money. Best money I ever made in my life."

I had a glimmering of recognition that made me wonder if I'd happened upon the same guy I'd encountered in the Fish and Game offices back in the April — the shark, the one with the fast boat who'd tried to hustle a job out of Bill Allen on the KIMO show. It was possible. If so, he'd been eating well enough to put on a little weight, and he'd bought new clothes. I wasn't sure.

He reached back to pull a sheaf of papers from under his instrument console, and passed a sheet to me. "Look for yourself. I make eleven twenty-five a day. I've been working three months and I've got another two to go. Figure it out for yourself."

I saw the figure, $1,125, and did some math in my head: Say, five days a week, though he probably worked six or seven and had overtime, as well. Say, $5,600 a week, or $22,500 a month, or a total in excess of $112,500.

When I looked up he grinned again and said, "And it's more than you think. They bring me everything. They bring my food to this vessel. They pay everything while the vessel is working. They pay insurance. Whatever I need, they give it to me. I got no expenses. It's crazy. They don't know what they're doing. They're not keeping count. Sometimes they get people up at 5 A.M. and then the crew sits half a day like a herd of cattle. A lot of it is BS. Everybody's always laughing. You got to have a sense of humor. What else do you got to do? Sometimes the crews'll sit on a beach a whole day waiting.

"They keep giving me life vests. I trade them off. They give me more. They're brand new. The chemicals they're using don't work, but the bacteria

. . . it eats the shit right up. What a life. The crews are crowded in like sardines on the navy ship and in the camps. The food's terrible, though in town they eat good. Here, I get what I want. Do you want steaks? I got it. They put you on the beach, you do nothing, the bear watch sleeps under a tree, then you all go back. You just laugh all the time."

Two men walked down along the dock, stopping at Shaw's boat. They said they'd come to be taken out to the navy ship. "Okay," Shaw said. "No hurry." The men laughed. Shaw asked me if I wanted to go along, but I couldn't because of the float plane ride back to Cordova. Before I stood, Shaw leaned close toward me and laughed outrageously again, showing the gaps in his teeth like a jack-o-lantern mouth. His skin was shiny and drawn tightly over the bones of his face. He put his hand on my knee and said, "Ain't it something?"

CHAPTER
17
NO ROAD

This damn town has been smeared with money.

— A Cordova fisherman, 1989

Besides Exxon and Veco, the full complement of the national and international press came to Cordova, and came again and again. A Cousteau Society team, filming an oil spill special, had come to town several times. The heads and representatives of environmental organizations came and went. State politicians came and went. Agency heads came. Agency representatives established a semi-permanent presence. Oil observers from foreign countries came. Coast Guard admirals came. Members of Congress had been here, and so had Vice President Quayle, who was kept sealed up inside a security phalanx as he passed over the board walkway built to keep his shoes clean. For a while, it was thought that President Bush would come, but he didn't, preferring to hold the same distance as Exxon chief executive officer Lawrence Rawl.[63] The singer John McCutcheon came. John Denver gave a benefit concert. James Naughton, the actor, appeared with Chuck Hamel, the oil broker, and there was a buzz about a Paul Newman-financed feature movie. Economists came to study the contours of economic windfalls made in a small community. A group of social scientists from Alabama came to study the effects of disaster.

Mental health researchers came to watch the course taken by post-traumatic stress syndrome, which a striking number of Cordovans would eventually suffer, the consequence of a violent alarm over the threat to the very substance of their life, and the long hours spent battling that threat as it stretched into months, and then the precipitous dip in energy, the confusion over the simple details of daily life, and the depression. In August, John Crowley, who worked in the mental health outpatient division of the local hospital, said that the number of cases had increased fivefold, but he also said, "Each case has had a history of fragility that the spill itself, the destruction of nature, or the financial stress triggered." It was a reminder of the tweak to a system that Dan Reed had talked about on the *Alpha Helix*. In these cases, the tweak was to the psychic systems of humans.

Back at the end of May, the town had rolled out the red carpet for the crew of the Russian oil skimmer *Vaydaghubsky*. The largest and most effective skimmer in the world, the ship had an oil storage capacity of 670,000 gallons and a recovery rate of 200,000 gallons per hour, but it was far too large to negotiate the narrows and shallows near the shorelines. By the time it arrived at Resurrection Bay on April 19 (following yet another bureaucratic snarl, this one with the U.S. Customs Department over the question of allowing a Russian vessel to enter U.S. waters, which was finally resolved by having it fly both Russian and U.S. flags), the oil had scattered and formed mousse. Attempts to modify the ship's machinery proved only marginally successful, and ultimately very little oil was collected. If a ship like the *Vaydaghubsky* had been on the scene during the first few days of the spill, it would have made a difference.

The people of Cordova, understanding that the skimmer was anchored idly off Knight Island, invited the crew to town. The ship moved to Nelson

---

[63] Years later, Rawl would claim that he had paid a secret visit to Valdez during the early days of the spill, and had not appeared in public in order to avoid creating a distraction.

Bay just up the coast from Cordova and the townspeople ferried the crew and themselves back and forth between town and the ship, threw a five-hour party with food, music, and dancing, and so entered the realm of foreign relations.

Money poured into town. By June of 1990, Exxon money that had entered through the city government in the form of grants totaled $744,000. From this, $196,000 was devoted to various means of rectifying the housing shortage during the summer, $18,000 was devoted to child care, and some $530,000 went to reimbursements of different types, including the Cordova Oil Spill Disaster Response Office (COSDRO).[64] Unlike Valdez, Cordova had a sales tax, and revenues generated through it were the best available measure of the effect of the presence of outsiders and of income earned by Cordovans, including fishermen who worked for Exxon. Sales tax revenues increased by 22 percent. In June, Dale Daigger, city finance director, said that further reimbursements from Exxon or Veco remained "under discussion."

PWSAC, upon which the fishermen relied heavily for its hatchery system, had received by June a total of $8 million from Exxon. The bulk of this money was channeled through a containment and management company called Spill Tech, which had been hired soon after the oil spill to protect the PWSAC hatchery system. Besides management costs, money went for the actual purchase of boom and related hardware, boat charters, people, and overtime work in the PWSAC offices as well as in the field. PWSAC had also instituted a permanent storage system for boom and other protective gear at the hatchery sites. This was a part of Alyeska's new contingency plan.

According to Cordova District Fishermen United's Executive Director, Marilyn Leland, her organization's budget was normally about $50,000 per year. Although CDFU had received a payment of $250,000 from Exxon in mid-April 1989, the money was gone by the following September. Leland told me in June that CDFU had projected its oil spill-related expenses to reach the $350,000 and $400,000 range, but that she anticipated no difficulty in obtaining the additional money from Exxon.

The Cordova Science Center, a new project triggered by the alarm of the spill and modeled upon Woods Hole and the Moss Landing Institute in California, was established early in the summer. Under the acting directorship of John Harville, the founder of Moss Landing, the science center would

---

[64] COSDRO was the yet more strongly community-oriented equivalent in Cordova of the MACs in Seward and Homer.

soon appear to be well on its way to success, and for the time became the crown jewel of the city's response. It received a total of $100,000 from Cordova in the form of a loan, $250,000 from legislative action in the U.S. Congress, and by fall of 1989, $85,000 in donations from organizations and individuals. According to Nancy Bird, who began as a local volunteer, worked at COSDRO, and then became the coordinator of the Science Center, the support given by the city was made possible by the presence of Exxon funds.

From the start, the large and small doses of capital that passed through Cordova fed into all the interstices of daily life — in the restaurants, grocery stores, the liquor store, through the extra flights to Anchorage, Seattle, Hawaii, and back and forth between Cordova and Valdez, in the long-distance calls, newspaper subscriptions, and boat purchases. Marilyn Leland told me that CDFU went through twenty or thirty cases of photocopy paper in a year as opposed to the usual four or five. Close on the heels of the paper came the maintenance of copying machines, copying fluid, and wages for additional help and overtime to run and maintain the machines, to file the copies, or to find copies in the files. Such expenditures were in part a result of the work being carried out by CDFU itself and also because photocopying services were made available without charge to everyone in town. Paper was a primary tool of the intense community effort.

In mid-August 1989, I met with Brenda Guest, COSDRO deputy director. She had replaced Susan Ogle, who had worked as a volunteer. Brenda had arrived in Cordova from Anchorage, and had fallen in love with the town and its spirit. She said people walked freely from the street into the COSDRO office to read the latest letters to Exxon off the computer. As arrangements were being made for the visit of the *Vaydaghubsky*, she'd gone around securing supplies for the celebration, and local businesses had accepted purchase orders with very little idea of how they were going to be paid, or by whom. "These people fought to get what they needed. Ultimately they've done really well," Brenda said.

At the time, I was trying to sort out where right-minded outrage ended and opportunism began in Cordova. I asked her where she thought the heart of Cordova was. She paused for a moment, looking away, then beckoned me to follow her outside. We climbed into a pickup and drove along the old New England Road, passing by the house filled with Filipino cannery workers, past the canneries themselves, the Veco boat-cleaning lot, the ferry terminal, and toward the old New England cannery since taken over by the Chugach Native Corporation.

We stopped first at what was commonly known as Hippie Cove, though its proper name was Shelter Cove. It was a shallow inlet and creek drainage backed by a steep slope. We looked at a sauna that had mystic symbols on its walls and a sign inviting anyone to refresh themselves here so long as they left the sauna clean and re-stocked it with firewood. Just above the sauna, almost hidden in the foliage, was a small hand-built house, and above it another house. Brenda said there were more houses up there. She led me 100 yards or so along the edge of a pool in which a lone, spawning salmon struggled to enter the creek bed. We climbed the slope, winding our way through the dense woods to a string of campsites and dwellings built out of wood salvaged from a wrecked ship down below. No one was in sight, but left in the campsites and shelters were suitcases, bags, and cooking gear. Higher up on the hill, Brenda said, were yet better-built dwellings. She mentioned that Gene wasn't here, and I wondered if that meant we were looking for him, or if what she'd already shown me — the mix of semi-permanent and strictly temporary, ramshackle dwellings — was supposed to form her answer to my question.

From there we drove to a set of campsites COSDRO was building to help accommodate the overflow of people in town, then as we headed for the Chugach Corporation, we came upon Gene as he walked along the side of the road — Gene Rossellini, a member of a prominent Washington State family and now, according to Brenda, the unofficial spokesman for Shelter Cove. He wore a ragged pair of black shorts and ragged brown T-shirt. The pack on his back was filled with rocks, which he made a practice of carrying in order to keep what he referred to as his "primary means of transportation" in good condition. Often, he conveyed building materials up the slope at Shelter Cove. His dark brown hair was cropped short, his face weathered, and his eyes as clear as those of Dr. James Payne. Behind a strap that passed across his chest was wedged a tiny, plastic prescription bottle filled with water — just enough water to sustain him on his walk in accordance with his principle of no excess.

He spoke with difficulty, as if he weren't used to talking. He and Brenda began a negotiation. Brenda was making arrangements to move a trash bin and two Porta-Potties to Shelter Cove and to build a fire ring there. The reason for such "development" was the influx of people. Gene approved of the Porta-Potties and the fire ring but not of the trash bin. He didn't want trash removed from the sites. "Besides, there's a new theft problem," he said. He meant that on general principle he didn't want people getting the idea that things could be either taken or thrown away. "I can't leave anything valuable in my cabin, anymore. I have to carry my money with me."

As we drove back to town Brenda told me she was surprised that he had money. She said that earlier in the summer he'd gone to the police chief to inform him that he would be appearing in town a little more regularly now, that he wanted to prepare the police for that. "The children love him," Brenda said.

I was now beginning to understand her answer to my question: It was the exquisite and Spartan campsites, built with Exxon money; it was Shelter Cove which for years had been a refuge for those in transition as well as for many who came here seeking their future, such as Heather and Max McCarty, and others who had "dropped out" in the late sixties and seventies, and had now "grown up" into independent fishing people, business people, and members of the city government; and it was Gene Rosellini, offspring of wealth and influence from "outside" who I would later hear had come here years before to study firsthand the Eyak people and language, and in the mean-time became an eccentric loner. Now, by the duration of his presence in Shelter Cove, and his labor, he had found himself the trusted spokesman who nego-tiated the most extreme and flimsiest tailings of Exxon largesse. Porta-Pot-ties and fire ring, yes. Trash bin, no. It was a good answer.

A year and a half later, though, Gene would be found dead of a knife wound in Shelter Cove. At first, it was suspected that his fears about Hippie Cove's new problems had been confirmed by an act of murder, but then it was determined that he had taken his own life in the Japanese fashion. His was, no doubt, a sensitive psyche, and yet a grim afterthought to his loss was that the turmoil in the place he loved had finally carried him beyond the limits of his forbearance. Almost equally grim was the thought that Gene himself was an indicator and that the moment in which he found his own way of participating in community life had passed forever.

Clearly, one of the more unsettling aspects of the spill emanated from the uses to which the Exxon money was put. In Cordova there were in-stances of graft, nepotism, and profit-taking. In the early days, rifts and ac-cusations of favoritism developed over the assignment of skippers and their boats by CDFU or PWSAC to the cleanup or hatchery defense. Prices in some public establishments were jacked up. There were tales of a Veco super-visor who skipped town with funds. Some residents billeted out their homes at exorbitant rates. As the growing flood of big money created a new class of spillionaires, so too it evinced envy, bitterness, and isolation. The money was always incendiary and even well before Gene Rossellini's suicide it had threatened to undo the old solidarity and split the town in half.

Although instances of graft and greed seemed not to represent the town's fundamental response, the money was incendiary. By the end of 1989 and on into the '90s, it threatened to tear the town apart. Many community groups and institutions that had received funding would find themselves way out on the ends of limbs. Some, such as the Cordova Science Center and COSDRO, which had sponsored the *Vaydaghubsky* party and had paid for it with Exxon money, were created after the spill. Others, such as CDFU and PWSAC, had been in existence long before the spill. To those citizens who preferred to follow what they might call the moral high road, the use of Exxon money for any purpose not connected strictly with the cleanup and reparations was wrong. Such people came from both ends of the spectrum: those who hated Exxon and wished to have nothing to do with its money, and those who applauded Exxon's cleanup efforts and wished to prevail no further upon the company's indulgence. Among the remainder, particularly those adept at managing money, were some for whom the presence of Exxon capital in large quantities created an opportunity to extend the meaning of reparation. The Cordova city government came to lean in that direction, and COSDRO was its arm.

In the beginning, the oil spill had startled many Cordovans into thinking seriously about economic diversification as a defense against the unknown effects of the spill, possible future spills, and of their dependence on a fishing monoculture. COSDRO hired a professional business consultant, Mead Treadwell, to head its operations. A resolute young man, a member of an old Alaskan entrepreneurial family, and a graduate of Yale and Harvard Business School, Treadwell had previously been associated with Walter Hickel's venture company, Yukon Pacific Corporation, and would later leave Cordova to serve in Hickel's administration following Hickel's election as governor in 1990.[65]

As the summer of 1989 wore on into August and then into September, it had gradually become manifest that Exxon would indeed live up to its prom-

---

[65] Hickel, who had previously held the Alaskan governorship, then a cabinet position as Secretary of the Interior in the Nixon administration, had been instrumental in establishing the Alaska pipeline system. In the fall of 1990, he made an eleventh-hour entry into the Alaska gubernatorial race, financing his campaign with his personal fortune and running as an independent on a pro-development platform. He won the race by carrying the principal cities, Anchorage and Fairbanks, and Prince William Sound, but lost everywhere else in Alaska. He expressed a "soft spot" in his heart for Prince William Sound and promised to negotiate a strong oil spill settlement between Exxon and the federal and state governments, and to insist that settlement moneys be devoted to restoring and enhancing damaged habitats.

ise to extract its cleanup forces from Prince William Sound by mid-September — the 11,000 workers, 14,000 vessels, 80 aircraft, and most of the offices, bureaucrats, and public relations specialists, as well as its open vaults, which by then had poured forth close to a billion dollars. The Cordova claims offices were slated to be closed. The presence of state and federal agencies would be reduced. The population of observers and hangers-on would melt away, and Cordova's brief, high-velocity stint as a weird, disaster-fed company town would be over.

The town found itself hanging between returning to something resembling what it had been before the spill (a complete return was patently impossible) or putting the best face on the changes that had come to it. "Exxon," Mead Treadwell told me then in August, 1989, "keeps saying that they don't want to pick up garbage that's not theirs." From Exxon's perspective, such garbage consisted of a range of things running from trash left by others on the beaches to mental stress and economic dislocation stemming from causes not clearly related to the oil spill. "But my attitude," Treadwell said, "is, 'Go jump in the lake, guys. You certainly won't be able to pick up all your own garbage.' This city is trying to recover from an economic disaster, and I don't see anything wrong with trying to mount a deeper keel to stabilize the city."

The "deeper keel" included community development projects. One of these was the science center. Another was a deep water port, which through commercial logging was tied to the interests of the Chugach Regional Corporation and the Eyak Village Corporation, centered in Cordova. Yet another was the road through the Copper River Delta, over the Million Dollar Bridge, and on to Valdez and Anchorage. All three projects had been longstanding concerns in the community. Again, those who took the moral high ground asserted that such projects had nothing whatsoever to do with the oil spill and that even to study them with Exxon money was a form of gouging. Others said that the possibility of another oil spill in the future, and the likelihood that Alyeska would again be unable to deal with it necessitated such considerations.[66] With the help of Treadwell, the city government prepared economic projections. Treadwell knew that the city government remained worried about the potential long-term effects that the spill would have on fish processing in Cordova and on the number of boats for which

---

[66] The new Alyeska contingency plan released in 1990 included this statement: "Alyeska anticipates that in many circumstances spills of fewer than 1000 barrels (42,000 gallons) can be substantially controlled and recovered. There will be few circumstances in which a catastrophic spill (over 4.2 million gallons) can be substantially contained." Improved though the state of preparations may be, the meaning of this caveat for *Exxon Valdez*-sized or larger spills is clear.

Cordova was the home port. Both the boats in the harbor and the canneries (through a raw fish tax that brought about a million dollars annually into the city coffers) had a direct effect on the economic and social fabric of the town. "Twenty-nine families have left town because they made so much money on the cleanup that they had no reason to stay," Treadwell said. "It's what's called a pattern dislocation in our economy, and Cordova will be feeling it for years."

Some argued that the Cordova airport — the best in Prince William Sound — was a good reason for Exxon and Alyeska to use Cordova as a staging ground for any future oil response and that they should be courted toward this end. One such person was Connie Taylor, a member of the Oil Response Committee and president of the Cordova Chamber of Commerce. Earlier on, the Cordova business community had split between the old-line Chamber of Commerce people, led by Taylor, and a newer, more aggressive group, Main Street Business, led by Bob Van Brocklin. A bitter rift developed between the two groups stemming from the question of who should represent Cordova businesses to Exxon and the state government.

In the October municipal elections, Taylor was elected to the city council and Van Brocklin was elected mayor. The rift deepened through the following year, culminating in Taylor bringing suit against Van Brocklin and council members R.J. Kopchak and Jeff Hawley for allegedly holding secret meetings in her absence in violation of the Alaska Open Meetings Act. In turn, Taylor was accused of channeling information from council executive sessions to Exxon, including information connected to possible future suits for reparations from Exxon. The city council appropriated $75,000 to defend Van Brocklin, Kopchak, and Hawley against Taylor's suit. The consequence was that Taylor won a portion of her original suit, the city expended about a million dollars it didn't have, Taylor was recalled by vote from the city council, Kopchak and Hawley resigned, and Van Brocklin declined to run for office again. For a year following, the division and paralysis that had struck Exxon and the state and federal governments was echoed in the chambers of Cordova's city government. Later, in 1992, a despondent Van Brocklin would join Gene Rossellini by committing suicide.

A rift had developed on the CDFU board, too, over questions of legislative lobbying, Alyeska's revised Oil Spill Contingency Plan, and the appropriate level of cooperation between CDFU and the new Alyeska head, James Hermiller. The town's old debate over the road that would connect it to Anchorage and Valdez percolated through it all. Connie Taylor had been pro-road. Van Brocklin had been anti-road, or so it seemed. The lack of the road, some argued, was part of the reason the town had been passed over as a winter staging ground and that therefore less money had come into town. Proponents wanted the road built for the sake of future development. To some, the answer to all problems seemed to rest in completing the road and using it to facilitate shipping, to provide access to additional resources, including timber, possibly coal, and to open up opportunities for road-based tourism.

The coming settlement between Exxon, the U.S. government, and Alaska would play into the road question, as well. The newly elected governor, Walter Hickel, reneged on his campaign promises to Prince William Sound constituents by supporting a settlement that would have been favorable to Exxon, then once the 1991 $1.025 billion settlement was in place, he set about lobbying for the use of funds to build the road to Cordova, a gambit quite contrary to the stated purposes of settlement money.[67] Later in 1991, Hickel vetoed a bill from the Alaska legislature that would have dedicated a portion of settlement money to the purchase and set-aside of timber rights in the sound. The idea he was attempting to counter was contained in the settlement agreement ("acquisition of equivalent resources"), and was one that had emanated in 1989 and early 1990 from Steiner, Grimes, Ott, and the organization they had founded, the Coastal Coalition. Coastal Coalition people well knew that several Native corporations, including the Eyak Corporation, were gearing up to resume logging, and they aggressively argued the idea that, first, Prince William Sound was best left to heal itself, and second, that clear-cut logging would actually constitute another "hit" to marine habitats, which interlocked with adjacent woodlands. Further, because of the high cost of shipping and the relatively low value of the trees, logging had so far operated at a loss in the sound and promised nothing different for the future. The proposal to acquire timber rights came to be supported in some form by most fishing people and many Native people, as well, who did not necessarily agree with actions taken by the corporations in which they held shares. Hickel's view, which was and is common enough in Alaska, was that the state was best treated as a resource colony. He was therefore much less interested in restoring the sound or in nurturing the balance of communities such as Cordova than in furthering his own view of "enhancement," which meant cracking open access to remote regions, and in the case of Cordova of having the road to maximize that access.

---

[67] Namely, the "restoration, rehabilitation, or replacement of natural resources, natural resource services, or archeological sites and artifacts . . . or acquisition of equivalent resources." For further discussion of the *Exxon Valdez* settlement, see the "Conclusion."

More typical of the feelings of Cordovans toward the road question were those of fishing families who were stunned at first by the oil spill and who then grew increasingly outraged at the ever-deepening bureaucratic imbroglios attached to righting the wrong in which they, in order to survive, were forced to participate. First they had to get somebody to do something about the oil, then they had to do something about it themselves on Exxon's payroll. They had to try to collect their claims against Exxon for losses suffered during the 1989 fishing closures and watchdog Alyeska's new contingency plan, and in the meantime adapt to a profoundly altered financial reality. They feared for the salmon hatchery system to which they were inextricably bound. Finally, many simply wanted to see Exxon and any other corporate interloper shut up and get out. Community polls and the 1992 mayoral election of Kelly Weaverling — by his own description the highest elected member of the Green Party in the country — suggested that the majority of Cordovans at that time remained opposed to the road.[68] Mead Treadwell, even as he argued for diversification, had told me back in 1989 that he "wouldn't touch the road question with a ten-foot pole."

Cordova fishermen owned 55 percent of all limited-entry permits in Prince William Sound. Fifty percent of Cordova's labor force was employed in fishing and fishing-related industry. In addition, 90 percent of Cordova's base population engages in some form of subsistence economy — hunting, fishing, gathering. This makes Cordova what sociologists refer to as a "renewable resource community," one utterly dependent on the yields of the natural world. The three fisheries upon which Cordovans and other Prince William Sound fishermen most rely have been the Copper River Delta wild salmon runs (including the famous Copper River Reds), herring, and the hatchery salmon runs.

The Copper River fishery, located as it is well over in the eastern portion of the sound and untouched by oil from the spill, has continued to succeed since 1989. The herring fishery, on the other hand, is generally considered to have suffered a dramatic population collapse as a direct result of the oil spill contamination of roe (eggs). Herring are on a four-year spawning cycle, and

[68] Weaverling lost his bid for reelection in 1994 by exactly one vote. Although Weaverling himself remained philosophical about the outcome, others raised objections to the fact that Alyeska abruptly scheduled an oil-spill response training exercise on the day of the election, which made it impossible for a number of Weaverling supporters (fishing skippers) to vote. Weaverling was replaced by Margie Johnson who is related by marriage to Luke Borer, the principal timber-cutting proponent from within the Eyak Corporation. Johnson herself was a road and development advocate.

fishing was curtailed in 1993 (the 1989 return) and closed from 1994-96. By 1997, a limited fishery opened, but generally herring returns remain quite weak compared to pre-oil spill years. The 1998 report from the *Exxon Valdez* Oil Spill Trustee Council notes that an area of concern is "the possibility that herring genetically damaged by exposure to *Exxon Valdez* oil would perpetuate abnormalities in the gene pool."

The salmon hatchery system — by far the first in order of commercial importance of the three fisheries — comes with its own built-in hazards: die-outs, disease, effects of changes in weather and current systems, shifts in predation patterns, ambush by high seas drift-netting fleets, and the quirks of the marketplace, which for Prince William Sound fisheries has been 80 to 90 percent Japanese. These are all typical shortcomings of a monoculture, or of converting fishing into something a little like dairy farming. The sameness of the stock creates vulnerabilities both in the stock itself and its effect upon habitat, and these make yet more emphatic the vulnerability of a resource-dependent community. The Prince William Sound Aquaculture Corporation has its program, of course, for renewing wild runs in order to replenish the genetic mix of its own stock with wild-run eggs.

For both wild and hatchery runs, the fry and eggs must not be subjected to pollution, as both the hatchery fry released in 1989 and the spawning run very likely were. Although as it happened, the 1988 pink salmon brood, released as fry in 1989 following the spill, produced the largest return on record (an estimated 43 million pink salmon). This immediately resulted in a barrage of Exxon press releases and advertisements claiming that the oil spill had hardly damaged the ecosystem. In truth, however, what the 1990 return might have validated was what had been observed in the weeks following the spill — that the all-out effort of fishermen to protect that year's hatchery stock had succeeded. It said nothing of the multifarious factors that might, for better or worse, affect a run at sea, or of the possible effects of oil and the various cleanup procedures upon the spawn of 1989, or, most importantly, of the fact that 1990 was not the year biologists expected to see the results of negative effects.

In 1991, the salmon returns also set records, but for numbers only. The fish were small, behaved erratically, and arrived three weeks late, and were therefore too advanced in their spawning cycle ("overripe") to be of value. Two million fish were dumped at sea because they had been refused by the canneries, and more, otherwise unmarketable, were shipped to Russia as charity. In 1992 the returns were a third of what was expected, and the 1993 returns (the offspring of fish spawned the year of the spill) fell to 5 million.

According to Alaska Fish and Game, this marked the first time that the Prince William Sound hatchery system registered a decline for three consecutive years since its inception in the early seventies, while in the same year many other areas of Alaska had record and near-record runs. Prince William Sound hatchery returns in the five following years (1994-98) have generally been strong — within the top 10 percent of all years since 1971, but still below the growing hatchery system's projected levels. The reason for the population shifts and whether or not there has been significant genetic damage to salmon remains a topic of debate among experts, and according to Cordova-based Alaska Fish and Game biologist, Dan Sharp, the two sides of the debate continue to be taken up in a predictable fashion by Exxon and the state of Alaska. Whatever strength hatchery runs have shown in recent years, however, is offset from the fisherman's perspective by a continuing price collapse. A result of this, Sharp informed me, is that in 1998, of the 264 permits allotted for pink salmon hatchery runs, only 50 boats turned up for the opening. Sharp said, "What has happened is that the returns are too small to support the past levels of the fishing industry."

Wild salmon runs are finally of far greater importance than hatchery runs because everything — the health of both wild and hatchery runs, and indeed of species survival — depends absolutely upon a vigorous and varied gene pool. The wild runs in the western portion of the sound were already under stress because of what the state of Alaska and Cordovans in particular had created — the hatchery system itself. When millions of hatchery fish arrive more-or-less simultaneously in the Gulf of Alaska, then swim through the sound to their spawning grounds (hatchery site bays), the marine environment's capacity to sustain wild fish running in on their own diverse schedules is severely taxed. The stressed system for wild salmon may have been tweaked in 1989 by the heavy oiling of the many discretely located stream beds, very few of which were given the same level of cautious attention as hatchery outlets. For several years afterward, streams yielded high levels of egg mortality, lesions, and other abnormalities in the fish, and reduced numbers. To this is added impending damage all over the sound by clear-cut logging along waterways and shorelines, the silting over of stream beds, the dessication of organic detritus, the creation of new barrens.

Clearly, the disaster that struck Cordova and the other towns of the sound has differed from most natural disasters in three important ways. First, rather than one catastrophic event, it has been a persistent sequence of braided-together events that have remained disruptive for years because of the oil spill and cleanup's lingering effects upon fishing, and because of lingering questions about those effects. It is now generally agreed that the cleanup was as damaging to wild shoreline habitats as the oil spill itself.

Second, what Mead Treadwell called "pattern dislocation" has continued to take its toll through the years that have followed, as those who profited from the money spill either left town with their riches, squandered it, or invested it in high-priced "over-teched" fishing boats with which to prowl an increasingly less lucrative fishery. Those who had not profited had to check their enmity toward rich friends and neighbors. Some — discouraged, or filled with despair — pulled up stakes and left town. Max and Heather McCarty came to be among these.

I saw Heather in 1993 — after the second hatchery run failure in a row, and after the fishermen, furious, fearful, and frustrated by the lack of information, the snail-like movement of their class action suit against Exxon, and by the activities of the *Exxon Valdez* Oil Spill Trustee Council, came together in a last collective act of defiance, the blockade of the tanker channel that they'd been talking about for four years.[69] I asked Heather about her plans, and she told me they were leaving. "It's very grim in Cordova," she said. "It's too hard. But if you live here you're never sure why." This is the third difference, the human-connected obscurity and doubt. Many of the claims filed by fishermen against Exxon would remain unresolved for years, even up to the time of this writing (1998). Such people carry with them personal expense and heartache.

Because the spill was a technological disaster caused and compounded by a sequence of human errors, and because many Cordovans participated in the cleanup sham, a haunting sense of guilt throws even the victims into the same realm of culpability as the perpetrators. Steven Picou, a sociologist from the University of South Alabama, whose specialty is technological disasters and who with his associates conducted a four-year study of Cordova, affirmed the important distinction between natural disasters, which are accepted as "acts of God," and technological ones, which carry with them the suite of distinctly human secondary disasters. In particular, this suite includes, as he explained to me, the inclination in our culture to turn to litigation for resolution, and to expect more satisfaction from litigation than it can possibly give. He echoed Heather McCarty's sense of the obscurity as he spoke of the litigation-driven scientific secrecy, saying, "It's criminal. Communities like Cordova should be allowed to know what is happening to them."

---

[69] See "Conclusion" for discussion of the blockade.

The town's roadlessness, the nearness of the oil shipping channel, the PWSAC-administered hatchery system, and back in 1989 and early nineties the impending Eyak Corporation logging enterprise all spoke to the deep contradiction Cordovans were, and continue to be, forced to face. Cordova does have, it should be reiterated, connection by sea and air, but the physical fact of the lack of a road to the outside world in the age of the automobile makes a metaphor for the Cordovan contradiction, which in its turn is a metaphor for the growing limitation of the world. Cordova's roadlessness nurtures, on the one hand, the isolated intimacy of the town, and stimulates the town's atunement with and passion for community and nature, its genius of spirit. On the other hand, modern Cordova had been first a port for the Kennecott mine. The proposed new road would likely run as far as the mine site on the railbed of the old copper ore transport system. The opportunistic outward movement toward resource and capital has always been very much alive in the town. Indeed, there are Cordovans who can think in no other terms . . . witness the spillionaires, the proposed deep water port, the impending and historically ironic logging enterprise at the hands of the Eyak Corporation, and the hatchery system itself, opportunistic and extractive as it is, and upon which in recent times the town has been absolutely dependent. Along with the genius, energy, and love of the world here, a melancholy dissonance reverberates from out of the depths of the contradiction.

18

GHOSTS

Boone's genius was to recognize the difficulty as neither material nor political but one purely moral and aesthetic. Filled with the wild beauty of the New World to over-brimming so long as he had what he desired, to bathe in, to explore always more deeply, to see, to feel, to touch — his instincts were contented. Sensing a limitless fortune which daring could make his own, he sought only with primal lust to grow close to it, to understand it and to be part of its mysterious movements — like an Indian. . . .taciturn in his demeanor, symmetrical and instinctive in understanding, Boone stood for his race, the affirmation of that wild logic, which in times past has mastered another wilderness and now, renascent, would master this, to prove it potent.

— William Carlos Williams, *In the American Grain*, 1925

I'd first heard of David Grime's boat, the *Orca II,* in July 1989 at Mavis Mueller's cabin near Homer. Larry Smith had taken me to meet Mavis, an artist, who was at that time involved in organizing the Geo-Textile Banner project through which large banners were to be hung in Kodiak, Homer, Seldovia, Valdez, Cordova, Anchorage, Fairbanks, San Diego, and Tijuana to protest the spill. It was also her desire to commemorate the arrival of the *Exxon Valdez* in San Diego for repairs. Mavis's cabin had barely enough room for a kitchen and a bed, and yet there were six or seven of us in there — Larry, Mavis, myself, and a group of Earth First! people, whose arrival had caused a kind of panic among the police and Exxon people. The FBI had come to Homer. Most of the Earth Firsters were from California. One young woman who happened to be from Homer had been arrested and then released for chaining herself to the doors of the Exxon offices in Valdez.

Mavis, who was solid, committed, and funny, described herself as a "deep ecologist," one who believed in the kinship of all living things. The Earth Firsters struck me as being surly and a bit puffed up with themselves. They had the "they" lingo down pat, the use of the pronoun which usually meant Exxon but also served as a catchall receptacle for vaguely defined forces of evil. As it turned out, though, the Earth Firsters proved their mettle later on by going to work on the Mars Cove volunteer effort. A part of the story of the oil spill was the constant presence of activist elements, a roiling just beneath the surface. There had been demonstrations, such as the one staged by the woman from Homer, and the "liberation" of 12 otters from holding pens in Valdez on the night of July 12. Greenpeace staged events, but most of the local people felt that they were essentially media spectacles that had little to do with their needs. A regatta, or mock raid, organized by Kelly Weaverling and Riki Ott for the Port of Valdez in mid-September 1989 served to solidify feeling among the participants in the waning days of the oil spill, but fewer boats came than expected and the event made no more than a ripple in the national coverage. What was interesting was that there were moments, especially in the early days of the spill, when it would have taken very little to galvanize the activists of the left and right and the independent-minded fishermen into action, such as a blockade of the channel, or sabotage. Indeed, to the end of 1989 and through the following year, successful fishermen with families and mortgages continued to speak of a blockade of the tankers as an entirely reasonable line of action. During the spring and early summer, it had been a near happening. The ingredients were there: a disaster, followed by inept and paralyzed authorities, and most importantly a powerful, articulate, and organized body of victims — the fishing people, who might well have lent spine to the diffuse activism of the left.

One reason why it didn't happen then was that the fishermen had made some progress working inside the channel — for example, with the improved Alyeska contingency plan. Another was the insidiously divisive effect of money. A third was that although the battle was being fought at a critical link in the oil delivery system, the Port of Valdez remained a remote outpost. Even though there had been a string of spills elsewhere that seemed intended to remind the nation of the condition of the delivery system[70] support from the outside came mainly in the form of lip service as opposed, say, to a selective petroleum boycott. Ultimately, the people of south-central Alaska recognized that they could not (and cannot to this day) fight Alyeska or Exxon alone.

On that day in July, however, Mavis Mueller's tiny cabin happened to be a hot spot in insurrectionist feeling. The talk swirled around a room that smelled strongly of fish. People shifted here and there, jockeying for standing space. The air was suffused with existential anticipation, and of something momentous about to occur that might carry everyone with it. Just what that thing was remained unclear. What did become clear three or four weeks later was that for whatever reason, their moment had already passed.

Mavis and I found ourselves next to each other in front of an Edward Abbey Monkey Wrench Gang poster. Mavis invoked the *Orca II*. "It's a spirit vessel used as a sanctuary," she said. "A support vessel for wildlife. It's a vehicle for creative response."

Just past noon on September 25, ten days after the official deadline for the pullout of Exxon's cleanup forces, the *Orca II* pulled out of the Cordova harbor. It stopped at the fuel dock to tank up on gasoline, then went on northeasterly along Orca Inlet past the Chugach Corporation cannery and veered outward to the center of the channel in order to avoid the logs that had broken loose from a raft in the storm that had ripped through during the last few days. Logs lay low in the water and were visible only at close range. The three of us — David, Lynn Schooler, and myself — were in the wheelhouse, looking out intently.

---

[70] Among them were three spills within 12 hours on June 23 and 24, 1989. A Greek tanker ran aground in Narragansett Bay near Newport, Rhode Island, spilling 420,000 gallons of fuel oil; a Panamanian freighter collided with an oil-carrying barge in the Houston Ship Channel, spilling 250,000 gallons of heavy crude oil into Galveston Bay; and a Uruguayan tanker hit a rock in the Delaware River near Claymont, Delaware, spilling 310,000 gallons of fuel oil.

Stray logs occasioned a brief, grim exchange between Lynn and David. Lynn was from Juneau in southeastern Alaska, where there is strong feeling over timber cutting in the Tongass National Forest. Federal subsidies for logging and a guaranteed profit contract held by the Alaska Pulp Corporation and Louisiana Pacific had made the Tongass one of the biggest money-losing national forests in the country. Meanwhile, watersheds were being despoiled and the slopes clear-cut down to the water. The destruction to wildlife in southeastern Alaska from logging would far exceed that of the oil spill in Prince William Sound.[71]

The immediate subject of discussion between Lynn and David was the logs that were cabled together in huge rafts along the banks of Southeast waters and that sometimes broke loose and became a menace to boats. "It's a fact of life down there," Lynn said. In Prince William Sound, loose logs were much less common because of the lower level of cutting, but here, just outside Cordova, storms regularly broke up the rafts. One log could rip a boat apart, particularly a fast-moving gillnetter. It remained a sore point that raised the larger, smoldering issue of logging in the sound, and of the questionable financial practices attached to it. The issue had receded from attention during the oil spill but bracketed it in time. From the perspective of fishermen, the eroding silt loads caused by logging on the slopes adjacent to marine habitats and spawning streams also presented a serious threat to their livelihood, and indeed the logging question generally resonates with many of the same economic, political, and cultural issues as the oil spill itself.

Prince William Sound, the Kenai Peninsula, and the Kodiak archipelago constitute the northernmost occurrence of a vast temperate rain forest that has its southern reach nearly as far down the coast as San Luis Obispo where a few pockets of redwoods survive, tucked deeply into the central California hills. They make shaded places where an ancient exchange between bark and root, fungus, crawler, humus, bird, and beast is still conducted. The body of this forest once broadened up along 6,000 miles of coast into regions of Northern California, Oregon, Washington, and British Columbia, where 90 percent of "old growth" stands have now been cut. The forest reaches up to the southeast of Alaska and the Tongass National Forest. From there, it rims out westerly around the Gulf of Alaska to its northernmost extreme where due

---

[71] And despite reduced levels, the cutting continues at enormous expense to the U.S. taxpayer. A 1995 General Accounting Office report put the cost of the U.S. Forest Service timber program, which gives physical and technical support to private logging companies, at $995 million for the years 1992-94, and of that total the timber program in the Tongass cost $102 million. A Forest Service report put the total losses of its timber program in 1997 at $88.6 million. Of that, a third, or $33 million, was lost in the Tongass.

to glacial retreat during the last four thousand years it has "colonized" a holdfast at the margin between the precipitous, snow-topped mountains and the sea. This is a fjord-carved sub-polar region. The terrain is still interrupted by tidewater glaciers, and much of the surface of the coastline has been exposed for less than a thousand years. All the coastlines appear intricately carved — the jagged, twining line between land and sea, inlets, harbors, coves, and coves within coves, raw with extruded and cobbled rock. The further north the forest goes, the narrower the band it makes between the sea and shore, and because of the harsh conditions in the north, the more marginal it is in economic terms as a resource. With reduced harvests, however, in Oregon and Washington, and due to legislative machinations, tax schemes, and Forest Service underwriting, south-central Alaskan timber appeared more and more lucrative.

While we were on the *Orca II*, the new Chugach Native Corporation mill was nearing completion over in Seward, and logs barged from as far away as 300 miles were being stockpiled there. The mill was being built at a cost of over $20 million, 25 percent over original estimates.[72] Previously, the corporation had sold off coal and timber stocks (from the approximately one billion board feet of timber the regional corporation owned in Prince William Sound and elsewhere) in order to generate tax losses, then sold off the paper losses to profitable companies, such as General Mills, that were in search of tax write-offs, a ruse made possible by an exemption arranged by Alaska Senator Ted Stevens to the 1986 Tax Reform Act. The act disallowed the sale of what are called Net Operating Losses (NOLs), which had been a means by which corporations showing substantial losses could sell those losses to corporations showing large profits. The result was that corporations in the red received cash flow while corporations with profits too large for comfort could reduce their tax burdens. The exemption was granted for Alaska Native Corporations alone and dozens of them, particularly during the NOL heyday years of 1986-88 took advantage of it through elaborately devised shell games. The Sitka-based Shee Atika Corporation, for example, sold timber rights appraised at $177 million to a company it co-owned (Atikon, Inc.) for $10 million, then sold about $175 million in losses to Drexel, Burnham Lambert, Inc., and Quaker Oats. The Cordova-based Eyak Corporation engaged in a similar transaction by selling forest land appraised at between $17 and $34 million for $1 million, then selling the $33 million loss to a group of multinationals, including Del Webb, Walgreens, and Hilton. Such

---

[72] It would open, but less than three years later in 1992, the mill shut down due to lack of revenue.

strategies resulted in nonprofitable clear-cuts, the leveraging of Native corporations by outside interests, and for some, including the Chugach and Shee Atika corporations serious problems with the Internal Revenue Service. All this was often accomplished without the full knowledge or consent of Native shareholders and in a manner quite at odds with the traditional Native view of ownership and boundaries.

The Chugach Corporation is the regional corporation of Prince William Sound and Kenai Peninsula. It and various village corporations were in the process of selling off timber rights in 1989. The corporations, including the village corporations of Tatitlek, Seldovia, and the Eyak Corporation, had contracted for harvests of about 14,000 acres of timber in Prince William Sound, the Kenai, and the Kodiak archipelago during the next year. At the time, it seemed clearly that the wished-for result of the 1971 American Native Claims Settlement Act to capitalize and bring into development Native Alaskan lands had been achieved.

The *Orca II* moved on at a speed of about seven knots. The loose-log conversation fell away as we neared the bend in the inlet that would take us out into Orca Bay and thence to the sound itself. The tailings of the storm that had delayed our departure for two days were still with us — great gray billows of clouds before us and off portside swelling up from behind the hump of Hawkins Island. The water was dark. The wooden double-ender moved lightly through the water, and down in the hold the Chrysler flathead 6 rumbled steadily. Originally, the boat had been built as a troller, and was converted by extending the cabin to the stern. We passed by several otters. They lay on their backs, eating, or cradling their pups, and scarcely gave us notice. Our main destination was Knight Island. We would spend several days there, then head up to Columbia Glacier and come back across the channel to visit Jon Rush and Susie Gill.

I had discovered both David Grimes and the *Orca II* to be rather different from what the heady atmosphere of the meeting in Mavis's cabin had led me to expect. The boat did have its fanciful aspect — the banners that fluttered from its masts, and inside the mementos and photographs. Next to the radar screen in the wheelhouse was a liquor bottle with a bouquet of dried weeds, and hanging from the ceiling two penny whistles, a mobile, and two dried dragonflies suspended by threads. Just above the windscreen was the *Time* magazine photograph of Joseph Hazelwood, whom David referred to as the "patron saint of the sound." He said, "Hazelwood had the reputation of being the best skipper in the company, and it was because of his intimate understanding of the sea. He was a rebel. He didn't like Exxon's policy of operation by imagery. He kept the appointment for the company. I'd like to get a message out to him that we don't blame him."

David himself was far less a person who had bought into a New Age agenda than one who was struggling to emerge whole from the firestorm that began with the spill and his part in the ad hoc advisory committee along with the other Cordovans, and then went on through the making of his oil spill video, *Voices of the Sound,* the purchase of the *Orca II,* animal rescue, and "spiritual cleanup." Despite the fact that he'd been at the very heart of the turmoil, he said, "Even while my efforts were directed toward salvaging something here, I had the sense that it wasn't Prince William Sound that was at risk. More, it was L.A. and New York and the Great Lakes."

He was born in Springfield, Missouri, grew up in Columbia, Missouri, studied natural history in college, and had first come up to Prince William Sound in 1977. He skippered a salmon boat for a time, then turned to herring fishing. Like John Oliver, David cultivated his peripheral vision. "I am a fisherman," he said, "but I'm always on the outer edge of the curve. I have an ambivalence toward it. I'll see a pod of killer whales, or a mountain on Knight Island I'd like to climb. I've never been a competitive fisherman."

Lynn Schooler said that David was a changed man. Lynn himself was from Texas originally, had grown up in Anchorage, homesteaded on the sound, and fished for a time out of Seward. Expert with boats, and world wise, he'd been watching people for evidence of delayed stress syndrome while we were in Cordova and had seen it.

I had felt an increasing disquiet over the enlarging gap between the spill as a heavily moneyed political and legal event and the spill as fact. I wished — perhaps oddly, but as it would turn out, rightly — to return to the scene of destruction in hopes it would act as a restorative. I didn't seek yet another survey (by then I understood that another survey would be self-defeating), but an intense address to realities as they chose to present themselves, and the first thing had been the broken-up log raft.

By four o'clock, Knowles Head, the point of mainland at the outer, northern verge of Orca Bay, had become visible off our starboard side. Two tankers, small in the distance, awaited permission to enter Valdez Arm. We altered our course southerly, swinging in the direction of Johnstone Point on Hinchinbrook Island. The tanker channel lay directly ahead. Since we remained in the lee of Hinchinbrook Island, the swells were low. Before us, the sky was dotted with broken clouds, but at our backs the clouds were thick and vertical swatches of rain reached down to the water. Just before five, we passed Johnstone Point and came out into the channel north of Hinchinbrook Entrance. There were three-to four-foot swells, what David referred to as "the ghost of the storm." I was permitted to pilot the boat, and as we went into the swells at an angle slightly less than 90 degrees, the boat pitched to and fro like a canoe. The light shone on the water. Mixed with milky sediment, the green and blue water changed color as the sunlight passed in and out from behind the clouds. Behind us stood a double rainbow. Before us, a flock of sandhill cranes cut a long V-shaped pattern high in the sky. They were heading out for southern California or Mexico. "They had to wait for the storm to pass, too," David said. Over the radio, we heard the announcement: "The bodies of two crewmen from the tug *Steadfast* have been found 20 miles northwest of Cape Saint Elias. . . ."

A quiet fell over the wheelhouse. Lynn and David grew watchful. Two more crewmen, according to the report were either drowned or out at sea somewhere. Lynn theorized that if they were in a life raft, it might well drift up to where we were. Though Cape Saint Elias was 70 miles away, the prevailing currents could carry them around the rim of land to Hinchinbrook Entrance. Lynn knew the boat and thought it was based in Oregon. It had been a cleanup vessel, and the crewmen presumably had been headed home with their riches. The irony of that, the irony native to the hazard the sea always set against its riches, and the specific irony of this hazard driven against the lucre of the cleanup, carried with it a heavy freight of gloom. The two crewmen were never found.

Three Dall's porpoises appeared off our portside. They left small roostertails of spray in their wake and rapidly overtook us. They rode our bow wave, dove from one side, reappeared on the other, and then dove again. I climbed out onto the deck and leaned over the bow. They swam double-loops. Each would ride the wave on the surface at one side of the bow, then surf the surge of the wave underwater and hang there for a moment, and roll, then dart across the vacuum just beneath the bow. It came out on the other side, surfed the surge, rose to the surface, and swam out and across the front of the boat in a wide loop, glided back, and started in again. All three did this at once, moving in an intricate counterpoint. They were black and white, concisely colored. They had the white ovals on their bellies and up their sides, and white at the tips of their dorsal and tail fins. The blue and green and cream-colored water rippled around them as they passed through and rolled. It shuddered against their whiteness and blackness, making them shimmer as they played.

By eight o'clock, the clouds had begun to stitch back together in a mass. Green Island came into view off our portside. Knight Island appeared before us. Through an opening in the clouds, a short stretch of ragged mountain peaks raked the sky. The sky darkened and the clouds closed up. The lower slopes on the island were at first a chalky blue. As we approached, as night fell, the color deepened to a black obscurity. We entered Snug Harbor, a large bay not far above the southern end of the island. Shaped like a sideways S, its broad mouth tipped northeasterly so that it directly faced Bligh Reef up at the other corner of the sound. It had been among the hardest-hit places: oil in two-foot pools, and hundreds of large animals, birds, otters, deer, floating around in the tidepools and trapped between the rocks. This was one of the first places that Kelly Weaverling and members of the animal rescue crew had come to. It also became one of the most heavily intruded-upon sites, subjected to all manner of cleanup exercises.

Along its southern side lay the line of beaches that had been selected by the EPA's Office of Research and Development (ORD) as test sites for bioremediation. Through the agreement between ORD and Exxon, six separate, adjacent beaches had been isolated. The beaches fell roughly into two types — sand and gravel beaches, and cobblestone beaches. One of each type was used as a control, while the others were staked off in blocks that ran both parallel to the waterline and perpendicular to it, that is, running up the beach so as to include low, mid, and high tide exposures. They received two separate types of fertilization to "spike" the activity of oil-eating bacteria — the liquid Inipol treatment, and granular or briquette fertilizer applications. As discussed earlier (Chapter 14), the experiment was the first of its kind in the field, was continued through 1990 with uncertain results, and provided the basis for the use of similar procedures in subsequent spills, including the June 1990 *Mega Borg* spill in the Gulf of Mexico and the *Sea Empress* spill.

As we entered Snug Harbor, it was quiet and dark, the darkness of midnight made more profound by the nearness of the island. David slowly picked his way into the harbor, scrutinizing the depth finder and radar for obstructions. We set anchor, switched off the engine, and the quiet abruptly deepened. There was only the light breeze snapping the boat's banners and the water lapping against the hull. At a call from David, Lynn and I clambered out to the deck. An aurora borealis spanned the sky. Tensile like a huge rubber band, it expanded and retracted, intensifying in brightness as it stretched. It flashed against the clouds and glinted on the spruce trees near the shore, the rocks, the dark water.

At seven in the morning, the three of us took the Zodiac to shore. David was in charge, and we scarcely noted the shoreline but immediately began to hike up a steep slope to a lake. A windstorm had leveled a stretch of forest, and the going was rough. We clambered over tree after tree and tight-roped the trunks, jumped into holes between the stumps, and clambered up again, clinging to old limbs. Amongst the fallen trees and out of their capsized root systems new trees and a dense bush had sprung up. An hour or so later, we came clear of the blowdown and made our way along a bear trail to a lake and stood on the rock outcropping along its shore. Not far away, a bare, glaciated mountain peak rose into the bright blue sky.

The lake was impeccably clear, spanning 40 yards across. The reflection of the rocks and trees on the far side was perfect, but toward the center the stirring of the breeze upon the surface of the water obscured the reflection ever so slightly. The shapes and colors — gray rock, green spruce, pale trunks of the hemlocks and the leaves turning to red and yellow — remained quite recognizable, but the image was diffuse, like a Monet. It was exquisite and conceptually arresting because of the interplay of elements — shoreline, water, and wind.

We took a different way back through the blowdown, the chaos of destruction. By then the inescapable question had come to me: in the course of things, what was the difference between this and the destruction of oil on the water? The answer was simple: a blowdown was not toxic and it didn't keep walking all over itself, and the regeneration, the tangle of new growth coming up in the wealth of decay, was in its different way as wild as the destruction. The second answer — which might be cast in the perspective of the passage of geologic time, and might consider mutation as one among the forms of regeneration, and even the human role in the late twentieth century as an agent of nature's proclivity for weird catastrophe and regrowth — was far more difficult to grasp. I knew what I believed and would act on, but ultimately I could not know that answer.

We came out of the blowdown into a muskeg meadow. The ground cover was richly colored: little pools of water like dark eyes, coated with mud and organic scum, the green trailing vine, lycopodium, and delicate lichens that came in gray, green, cream, yellow, and red, and russula mushrooms, inedible but extraordinary in their phosphorescent pastels — violet, pink, pale silver, the color of fish in water.

Back down at Snug Harbor, we paused long enough where we'd left the Zodiac to see that there was evidence of oil, a darkening between stones. When dug into, the fine gravel revealed more pooling oil beneath the surface. My guess was that the beach had been cleaned with high-pressure hoses. Hunks of boom had been left in the bushes nearby, and in a streambed, transects had been set up — wires laid out in a grid and buried beneath the gravel, hooked up to something — a plate, or diodes — then run to a battery that was strapped to a tree at the edge of the stream. The battery clicked every few seconds, a signal that it was working. The research project, I suspected, had something to do with salmon, but I really didn't know. Something was being counted. I stood looking at the wires that entered the stream and found myself fighting the urge to kick them loose.

We set out in the *Orca II*, passing the test sites on the southern shore. They bled oil and the two different kinds of fertilizer into the water. Across one stretch, what looked to be large canvas sacks, and were in fact seine net bags filled with fertilizer briquettes, were strung out between metal posts, secured against the shifting tides. We entered Montague Strait and passed Hogan Bay, where even from a distance we could spot the oil. We turned around Point Helen at the southern extreme of Knight Island. To the south were Latouche, Evans, Elrington, and Bainbridge Islands. We were in the same hard-hit territory the *Alpha Helix* had come through. We passed Little Bay. A tug appeared, pulling a barge loaded with equipment — containers, small machinery, boom, and cranes. A straggler of the pullout, it caused us to realize that we hadn't seen another boat since the evening before.

There was a bench in the *Orca II's* wheelhouse, a stool, and then the skipper's chair. David was at the wheel and Lynn and I otherwise spread ourselves out. A pod of killer whales, their dorsal fins erect above the surface, appeared. We followed them for a few minutes, then let them go. In the distance off our portside, a lone humpback dove, its flukes swinging up and catching the sun, then it disappeared.

David began to talk about how, back in March, he, Riki Ott, Rick Steiner, and Jack Lamb had ended up in Valdez back in March and found themselves at the center of what he called "the power grid." There was the tension among the three principal figures, particularly between Dennis Kelso and Frank Iarossi. According to David, it was "very difficult to tell when they were speaking out of their own sense of despair and truth and when they were speaking for their constituencies." He continued, his passion rising with the memory. "At one of the meetings Kelso was trying to get Exxon off the leadership role. Iarossi said, 'If you do that, we're out of here.' Kelso said, 'And if you do that, we'll take out ads showing you promising that Exxon will clean it up.'"

What David was describing was a beginning moment of the spill when the outward signs were confusion, inaction, and rancor over what method to use, while the slick sat on the water, ominously awaiting the first, and then the second storm. At that moment in the history, a pitched battle was being waged between the state of Alaska and Exxon over who, first, was in charge, and who, second, was responsible. They were not the same thing, neither was easily resolved, and the confusion would persist for days and then for weeks and months after the spill, well into the next year. At an April 6 hearing before the U.S. Senate Committee on Commerce, Science, and Transportation, Senator Richard Bryan of Nevada, seeking the answers to the same questions, would finally show his exasperation to Samuel Skinner, secretary of the Department of Transportation, and William Reilly, the head of the EPA, by saying, "I am not trying to be critical of you or the President [Bush]. I am just trying to find out in the vernacular of the street who the hell is calling the shots."

Secretary Skinner replied that the Coast Guard was in charge, although, of course, this had never quite been the case. "One of the best sources of information on what was going to happen to this crude," he said, "was from the fishermen who have been in that area forty years watching the flow. . . . They were part of the group that we met with." This was where David, Steiner, Ott, Lamb, and the others had come in. The glibness with which Secretary Skinner alluded to their participation hardly accounted for the actual difficulties they first encountered in getting someone to listen to them about the need first of all to protect the key wild spawning streams and the hatcheries.

"We were over there in Valdez," David said. "It dawned on us that there wasn't much going on. We had to do something. What happens is you think somebody's in control and so you give up your day-to-day decision making, and we all were lulled. Somehow we had the illusion that there was this one great big not-for-profit oil company, which isn't true at all. You get this infra-structure that allows you to think that way. Our first couple days in Valdez were spent working through the cobwebs of that illusion. We were waiting for somebody to do something, and then finally it hit us that it was our home and nobody else was there to act. All the things we'd been taking for granted were gone.

"But those of us in Valdez weren't used to speaking with such authority, and so first, we had to learn what authority was about. It's doing the best you can with what you know. So far as speaking for the sound was concerned, we were the ones who showed up, that's all. When the first storm hit, Exxon had to admit the whole thing was out of control. We advised them on currents and winds, the hatchery system, fish biology. They were like kids, getting the story. We created the planning committee. It was like we'd created our own government. We had to give ourselves over to it."

Early in the afternoon, we pulled into Lucky Bay and set anchor. Because of its position in the center of the southern end of Knight Island and its shape — broad at its base, then narrow and twisting — the bay had been but lightly oiled. David set store in its name — Lucky. As we'd come into the bay, he said, "For those who know Knight Island, all you need to say is Lucky Bay." There was evidence of oil along the banks, at the bottoms of the rock faces. Above the rocks was the thick growth of bush, fern, and tree. In the water, two otters lay on their backs, feeding. A pup climbed up onto its mother's belly.

It was high tide as we headed up the slender bay in the Zodiac, and barely passed through a narrow channel bounded by rocks. We came around a bend into a pool and a dozen Canada geese fled our presence, sending out fans of water as they beat against it. They swept around the bend in the bay by which we'd just entered and disappeared. Lynn switched off the outboard. We sat still as the Zodiac twisted ever so slowly in the pool. No one spoke except to draw attention to this thing or that. Surf scoters and common mergansers had paddled away from us near to the shore but otherwise seemed unalarmed. Down in a corner of the pool, a belted kingfisher sat on a hemlock limb that overhung the water. It was gray and had the white band around its neck, the long, silvery beak protruding from the odd, hydrocephalic-looking head. It dropped like a stone into the water and caught a fish.

The Zodiac drifted. There was no evidence of oil whatsoever here, and in fact the "inner sanctum" of the bay had not been oiled. All along the banks lay the tumult of growth, fern, bush, lichen, and tree. The sun was out and everything reflected crazily in the water. A stream came softly into the pool at the top of the bay and high above it was a waterfall, a dense band of plummeting white against the dark mountain slope. Over the edge of the Zodiac, one saw, first, the reflection of one's own face, beneath that the kelp, and then what was almost indiscernible, and yet there — a line of differentiation beneath the lens of fresh water that floated on top of the salt water. Salt water came in with the tide. Fresh water flowed from the streams. White jellyfish, what David called "moon jellyfish," floated in the water, looking like big, slightly disarrayed bouquets, amorphous, the frilly white oral arms and tentacles hanging loosely from their bodies as they awaited the arrival of prey to be stung and absorbed. A bald eagle passed overhead and veered away. The Zodiac twisted slowly. The kingfisher returned to its perch. Everywhere, there was the sense of life layered upon itself.

To see this place, so near to the heart of the calamity and yet so unlike the ghetto-like shores of Snug Harbor, was a restorative. It was clear that this was what David had hoped to find here. He burned sage in honor of the place. We drifted out of the pool, and in order to maintain our sense of quiet, rowed back to the *Orca II*. We left Lucky Bay and headed for the southwestern corner of Knight Island, then turned north into a narrow, inside passage, Long Channel. Off our portside was Squire Island. On our starboard side was Deer Cove. An ebbing tide slowed the *Orca II's* pace as it labored against the power of the water. Swollen with water, the channel seemed beguilingly benign, and the rocks and nearby islands gave the sense of our being in an immense bathtub. We passed Echo Rock and stuck our heads out the windows of the wheelhouse and shouted at it. Echoes bounced back in an exact facsimile. The channel was narrow and on either side all along the shorelines were heaps of dead popweed. David slowed down further as he negotiated the rocks off the head of Mummy Island. We swung back out toward Knight Island Passage again, a more open waterway which here ran north and south. Chenega Island came into view. At six in the evening, we passed the notorious Herring Bay. Small worksheds were still visible along the shoreline and a Zodiac loaded with three persons in orange float jackets sped across it, but the human presence was nothing compared to what it had been. David said, "Back in Valdez, when the feds came in, they told us, whatever you need, we'll get it and Exxon will pay the cost.

"They gave us free rein, whatever we could think of. There was a brilliant redneck engineer who came down from the North Slope. We were trying to think up ways to clean up the oil. The skimmers they had certainly were not working. If the Soviet skimmer had been here, it probably could have got a lot of the oil. The engineer wanted to know if we could use the vacuum trucks, the supersuckers he had up on the North Slope, so we talked about that, and he said, 'Look, are you guys going to be with me on this? I'm going to be out a million dollars.' We said, yeah, we'll back you up. It was crazy. Who were we? A bunch of fishermen, but for a while, it was like we were all generals.

"The next night in the planning meeting we started to talk about alternative things, and we broke it to them then, the supersuckers. Iarossi was there and he immediately woke up and said, 'How many can we get?' We didn't know if they would work, but that was when I started to see how

Iarossi got to where he was. It was his ability to make decisions. We sent for the supersuckers, and in the meantime they were lightering the ship and all the Exxon people were kind of white in the face. You could see they were living right on the edge.

"We spent entire days on the phone and hardly got any sleep. Nobody knew who to call for anything, or what to do, where to work, where the planes were, where the oil spill tech people were. When we talked to Cordova, we said, 'Do what you have to do. Pretend you're on your own.' They ordered their own boom for Port San Juan. PWSAC and the city of Cordova all went way out on a limb with their budgets, and that was the real message of the whole thing. There was enormous parallel work going on, but if you didn't do it, it might not get done. It was a perfect mirror of the world.

"Exxon was really trying to mobilize equipment from all over the world, and they were trying to control the situation in several different ways, but you just couldn't depend on Exxon to cover the bases. They had to pay for it, so they wanted to be as sure as they could that things were needed. It was a tremendous peacetime mobilization. They were grabbing barges and planes from everywhere. The pilots were maxed out on hours. It was just what you'd have if you had a war. The volume had been turned up, but you couldn't really figure out where the knob was to get it turned back down. There were press people. You'd try to sleep, do four interviews, and talk to Australian TV, and fly out with the press, or go look at boom, or write up something, a contingency plan, a briefing on supersuckers, or why dispersants were a nonissue, or make the video. You were developing relationships with all these people, most of whom had an ego problem. You were trying to figure out who was a player, who had to get up, who would never get up to speed, and nobody knew who everybody was or what or where all the information was, and yet information was inherent in everything. If you wanted to do the work, you had to know instinctively what it took to do it. It was that simple."

A storm was approaching. We'd come up the western flank of Knight Island. Just before dark, the *Orca II* crept through a narrow slot to a bay that occupied the heart of Disk Island, a small island located between the northern end of Knight and Ingot Islands — another site of horror I'd witnessed with the *Alpha Helix* crew. The bay, so far as the three of us could make out, had no name. It was almost completely encircled by Disk Island. On a map, Disk island looked like a ragged Pac-Man head with a small, open mouth.[73] We ducked into the eastern edge of the bay, as deep into the shelter as pos-

[73] Disk Island was the second site for the EPA/Exxon cooperative research into bioremediation, conducted during the summer of 1990.

sible, and set anchor. David and I talked deep into the night, while the rain drummed against the roof of the cabin.

At sunrise, the storm continued to blow and we decided to stay put. Rain filtered down. Where we were the water was nearly calm, but through the narrow slot at the west end of the bay, looking out into Lower Passage between Ingot Island and the northern end of Knight Island, whitecapped waves raged by. During the night, two other boats, the *Monde Uni,* a seiner from Cordova, and a DEC boat had also sought refuge in the bay. From our position, the *Monde Uni* was visible to the left of the slot. The DEC boat was near to shore on our right. I spent time out in the open at the stern of the *Orca II.* The gray Zodiac swung slowly on its tether, folding back against the *Orca II,* then stretching out again while the *Orca II* traced its own arc in the current. The *Monde Uni* and the DEC boat swung, aligning themselves variously in the shifting wind. A man appeared on the deck of the *Monde Uni,* holding a cup of coffee. The bay was encircled by a line of oil, the nearly ubiquitous bathtub ring.

Back in the galley, we ate breakfast, then moved to the wheelhouse. Lynn talked about accidents, about people he had known who died at sea. He knew of a boat from Seward, the *Jon & Olaf,* which had been caught out in a winter storm. The boat was found floating and in fine shape, but covered with ice and abandoned by her three crewmen. Another boat, the scallop dragger *Saint Patrick,* was abandoned by fourteen men while still afloat. One survived, washed ashore. The crew had abandoned ship in a panic because they believed the batteries would explode when water flooded the engine room. David told us of premonitions he'd had of people who were going to die. A close friend of his had been killed some time ago. Another friend had died this year. It was the storm and this bay, which not long before had been a place of death, and perhaps the boat gently twisting on its anchor, that brought on such talk. We had a mooring in a place of refuge, almost as if we'd found the calm in the eye of the storm. David said a man had contacted Rick Steiner back in the early days of the oil spill and claimed he had a device that could turn oil to water. At first, Rick had thought it was another snake oil joke, but then he and David began to wonder what would have happened if the guy could actually do it.

After his work with the citizens' advisory group in Valdez, after he'd made the oil spill video, David accompanied Rick Steiner to the Shetland Islands. That was in May, by which time Chuck Hamel had given him some advice about Exxon. "Don't kid yourself about playing the game on their terms because they've got the heavyweights in town now," Chuck had said. Nevertheless, David had felt a compelling need to continue to do something. He said he asked himself why he was still talking to the cameras, and told himself that he needed to be able to make decisions. "The bureaucracies got left behind," he said, "and for the time being the power had returned to the people if they wanted to use it. It was hard work and you had to watch out, or everything would set up again. The oil companies were trying to reclaim the ground they'd lost. It was like something got loose and we had to try to figure out a way to keep it alive. It was a matter of dreams and hopes."

So far as the *Orca II* was concerned, I was beginning to understand that its spirituality might come from bringing sometimes unlikely people into convergence on the water. As the three of us sat in the wheelhouse and tried to discuss the metaphysical, transcendental matters, we found it difficult to speak clearly. We believed that they were the bedrock of all questions posed by the oil spill. It was best, perhaps, to come in from the sides and always look to the peripheries, to the Shetland Islands; to Juneau, where David had discovered that the *Orca II* was a boat that had "something of right livelihood moving through its history"; to the timber question (he would soon join forces with Rick Steiner in an attempt to get Exxon settlements set against the purchase of timber rights in the sound).

David was a voluptuary in the sense that William Carlos Williams described Daniel Boone as one. He recognized the difficulties as being neither strictly "material nor political" but "purely moral and aesthetic." It was expressed in his conduct — his ability to fish, to speak to people like Frank Iarossi, and to remain independent. Through his love of the wild and his inclination to affirm that "wild logic," he was able to locate the potency of a place like Lucky Bay, and to understand that potency did not mean mastery, but alignment. He was singular, but among those who answered the call of the oil spill, and struggled with it, and even made their mistakes with it, he was not alone in the possession of such qualities.

It stormed throughout the day and we decided to spend another night at Disk Island. There was an otter near the *Orca II*, who dived, then came up on the other side of the bay. Another otter appeared back where the first one had been, but then I couldn't find the first one. Perhaps it was just one otter. Bill Black and Kenny Carlson came over in their Zodiac from the *Monde Uni* to talk. They were out picking up oiled popweed. Bill Black said he didn't know what he was going to do with them — maybe take them to Valdez and let them figure it out. He would eventually do so, it would be in the newspapers, and Exxon would figure it out. Naturally, a program would be initiated for the retrieval of oiled popweed. Bill and David got out the charts and marked the places where there were rocks in the channel that should be avoided.

Bill Black said he'd heard that Billy Webber (a revered Cordova fisherman) had the idea of chaining fishing boats to the anchor lines of the tankers waiting off Knowles Head. At this, the wheelhouse of the *Orca II* swirled with a spirited, half-jocular conversation about the possible methods of blocking tanker traffic and the technical challenges presented by each. It was as if the men were seeking the story that might feasibly be acted out. The methods ran the gamut from violent to nonviolent, or nearly so — loading up the narrows with fishing vessels, casting seine nets that would jam the tankers' propellers. The beauty of Webber's idea was its simplicity, its stillness, and its accentuation of a tanker's vulnerability to its own conspicuous size. Once a fishing boat latched on to a tanker's anchor gear and observers were on the scene, the tanker would not move for fear of capsizing the fishing boat. A few fishing boats might interrupt the entire Alaskan oil trade.

After Bill Black and Kenny Carlson left, David went on talking about Billy Webber. He said that Webber could catch four times as many fish as anybody else and it never seemed to take much effort. He'd do strange things, David said, like hang back and watch while everybody else was desperately fishing, even during a short opening. Then he'd take yet more time to motor off somewhere else and find all the fish he needed where no one thought they'd be. As the stories multiplied, Webber took on a legendary quality. Rain kept falling and time grew indeterminate.

David said he'd once had a vision on the Colorado River. He'd realized there how beautiful the world was, but then he'd felt a wave of despair and inadequacy over his inability to express it. "The despair," he said, "was the sense of never being able to capture the essence of the world. I picked up the guitar and played a melody and suddenly it all broke over me. I felt Bach saying, 'Do you think it was different for me? Do you think I didn't feel helpless?'" He remembered David LaChapelle, who during his first sojourn on the *Orca II* had had a dream of all the animals killed by the oil spill hovering above the sound in a gray mist. The animal spirits said, it's true we're still here because we have a message to deliver, and it's a message of love. They were the ghosts, watching what was to follow. We three now occupied the ghost territory.

After a time, I stepped out to take a leak off the stern of the boat. I saw one otter and then the other. There were two, after all. They looked oblivious to the storm that raged outside the bay. One would dive and then the other, each head popping up with seeming whimsy in this place or that. Geese floated past me, their bodies, long necks, and heads still. A black bear appeared from behind the ridge at the edge of the bay and descended the short, steep bank nearly to the water. I studied the circular bay, the rim of oil around it, and above that the rocky bank while he investigated the shoreline. The three boats twisted on their anchors. On the other side of the slot in the bay, jagged whitecaps slid by. The black bear moved sinuously, catlike, stepping adeptly from rock to rock, passing over and under the fallen timber. He disappeared into a dense stand of bush, the occasional trembling of outer branches marking his progress. The otters dove one at a time, then reappeared. The bear emerged from the bush. He had a way of walking with the front feet turning out sideways, reaching out there. Agile and powerful and balanced, there was absolutely no waste in his motion.

THE
BUBBLE NET

When I completed the original version of this book in the fall of 1990, U.S. forces were building up in the Mideast in response to Iraq's invasion of Kuwait. The world shuddered. In order to account for their voracious appetite for petroleum, large numbers of people reawakened an ancient anti-Orientalism by assuring themselves that the president of Iraq, Saddam Hussein, was a devil. At the time, there was no telling what the situation would lead to. For months preceding what would become a war, then during the war, one had to read fairly deeply into the newspapers to find serious discussion of the fact that the U.S. response was about protecting Western oil interests, or that existing Arab boundaries had been drawn by the Western alliance with oil resources in mind, that the oil-producing state upon which we most rely, Saudi Arabia, was and is a feudal kingdom, as is Kuwait, or that much of Hussein's support came from vast numbers of disenfranchised Arabs outside Iraq. Arabia is but another, if very large and often very rich oil ghetto. The policy of the petroleum companies, American foreign relations, and the Arabian national companies, such as Saudi Aramco, seemed to have converged to make a ring of power near the site of the biblical Garden of Eden, a desert rich with the chemical detritus of past fecundity. In preparation for the invasion that would occur early in the year following, then President George Bush offered as a reason for the U.S. military build-up the need to protect the "American way of life."

One result of the Persian Gulf War was the largest oil spill on record — something in the vicinity of 200 million gallons. As it happened, only about 100 miles of coastline were struck by the oil and a superskimmer operated with great efficiency, setting a record for the quantity of oil picked up. As the Iraqis retreated from Kuwait, hundreds of oil wells were ignited and for a time 126 million gallons of oil went up in smoke every day. Birds literally dropped out of the sky. During the years that followed, the United States and other United Nations member countries have continued to skirmish with an apparently resilient Saddam Hussein over inspections for weapons of mass destruction, and now as I complete my revisitation to the text of this book late in the fall of 1998, American warships are gathering in force in the Persian Gulf in order to compel Saddam Hussein's compliance. There is talk of bombing raids. Once again, there's no telling what this will bring. It is clear that Saddam is a ruthless tyrant, but it is also clear that the United States relies absolutely on the world's oil reserves. I remember that one also had to read very deeply into the accounts of the 1991 war to learn the magnitude of American killing then — that as the column of Iraqi soldiers retreated from Kuwait, U.S. bombing raids buried upwards of 200,000 of them in the sand.

States on the Caspian Sea, recently emerged from the yoke of the Soviet Union, also control vast quantities of oil. Though the reserves have been known to have existed for more than a century (the name Azerbaijan comes from an ancient Persian word meaning "garden of fire"), the oil has become accessible more or less suddenly. American companies — Pennzoil, Chevron, Amoco, and Exxon[74] — are among the leading investors. American geopolitics are also heavily invested, and as the newly independent nations themselves arise through civil strife to new levels of opulence and corruption, the

[74] In the works at the time of this writing are mergers that would cause the reconstitution of two of these into British Petroleum-Amoco and Exxon-Mobil. Exxon-Mobil will be the largest company in the world. As the number of companies with real access to energy resources decreases, and as the size of each of the companies swells, their power individually or in concert to lobby government, affect policy, and control information will also increase.

petroleum players and interested nations maneuver and skirmish. There is a debate over where to send the oil and by what means. By pipeline, most likely. But not northward through Russia, the collapsed superpower, and certainly not southward through Iran where there are hosts of devils. Most likely eastward through either Turkey to the Mediterranean or through Georgia to the already polluted Black Sea, and thence to be shipped by tanker. Nations and petroleum companies will find ways to cooperate on the expense. The euphemistic remarks of Bill Clinton's Secretary of Energy, Bill Richardson, sound oddly familiar: "This is about America's energy security. . . . It's also about preventing strategic inroads by those who don't share our values. We're trying to move these newly independent countries toward the west."

We require stability at the wellhead so that we may bend to it and drink deeply, even in the midst of fire. Meanwhile, the real questions about our contradictory conduct run hard upon us, bearing down on what William Carlos Williams called our "agonized spirit," the "idiot" that "governs with its great muscles, babbling in a text of the dead years."

There is no question but that human mortalities associated with the *Exxon Valdez* oil spill are very low indeed when compared to war, or to the effects of other recent technological disasters, such as Bhopal or Chernobyl. In Bhopal, some 2,000 people are known to have died as an immediate result of the release of methyl isocyanate from the Union Carbide installation. With the nuclear reactor meltdown at Chernobyl, the number of deaths was first put at 37, including 32 workers, while another 240 cases of acute radiation sickness were diagnosed. Because of the radiation carried through air and river systems, a vast expanse of land was eventually left devoid of life, and a yet vaster expanse hundreds and thousands of miles away was measurably contaminated. Now, twelve years later, Ukrainian officials put the death toll in the thousands, with another hundreds of thousands presently afflicted with radiation related illnesses. Thousands more will die from the exposure. The death toll by cancer is projected to be eleven times the combined total from the 1945 bombings of Hiroshima and Nagasaki.

There is also chronic destruction at Britain's Sellafield installation, and following years of questioning and rising cancer rates in nearby farming communities on the Yakama Reservation in Washington State, where disturbing information has recently come out about radiation test plumes released during the forties and fifties at the Hanford Nuclear Reservation. Conceivably, the effect of emissions upon the ozone layer and resulting global warming have already begun to cause suffering. The results of such humanly caused disasters are not, or will not be the same in their detail, but each of them occurred in association with big money, involved the release of toxic substances, and, in the case of Bhopal, Chernobyl, and the *Exxon Valdez*, were triggered by a combination of faulty initial design and human error, followed by a woefully inadequate response capability. At Chernobyl, the initial improvisation was to dump by helicopter tons of clay upon the glowing red core. Many of the drops missed the target and to this day radiation continues to leak from what is called the "sarcophagus."

No person is known to have died as a direct consequence of the *Exxon Valdez* oil spill itself. Numerous people, however, including the crew members of the *Valdez*, government representatives, technicians and workers who were early on the scene, and residents of the villages of Ellamar and Tatitlek, were imperiled by the effect of fumes upon their respiratory systems, and there were numerous "indirect" consequences — the observed cases of delayed stress syndrome, homelessness, and in Cordova the suicides of Gene Rossellini and Bob Van Brocklin. Exxon noted that during the cleanup only two of the 11,000 persons employed died on the job — one of those a heart attack casualty, and the other crushed by a ship's dumbwaiter — and that the injury rate was 30 percent lower than the national average for heavy construction projects. In 1990, Cindy Coe, area director for the Anchorage office of the Occupational Safety and Health Administration (OSHA), confirmed the mortality rate, but added that Exxon put out the injury rate figures (in December 1989) before the company had enough data to support the claims.

If human fatalities are not among the significant issues with the *Valdez* spill, then several other matters are, including the troubling attitude toward information, and toward language and image as nothing more than a means for manipulating perception. It is true that practitioners from all camps regularly committed acts of convenient expungement. Impermeable loops were fabricated around what might, or should be known. Exxon repeatedly offered unconfirmed, incomplete, and misleading accounts to the public, and in the public relations fight over the extent of the damage, so did environmentalists and government agencies. Exxon was simply the master of the art. In July 1990, the *Valdez*, repaired at a cost of $30 million, was renamed the *Exxon Mediterranean* and reassigned to the Persian Gulf. At first, Exxon officials explained that because of the decline in Alaskan oil production,[75]

---

[75] The "decline" of oil on the North Slope is real and at the same time yet another public relations gambit employed by all involved oil companies in order to encourage acceptance of more drilling to the west and east of Prudhoe Bay.

the ship was no longer needed on the West Coast, and that giving ships names appropriate to the region they served was normal practice.[76] In 1993, the name of Exxon's subsidiary, Exxon Shipping, was itself changed to the far more mellifluous SeaRiver Maritime. Again Exxon officials disavowed any connection between the name change and the Alaskan oil spill. Familiarity with Exxon's approach to language, however, might lead one to wonder if the company hoped the new pseudonyms would wipe out the ship's former identity. *What ship?*

Consider the line of Exxon commercials that aired on network television during the summer and fall of 1992, after enough time had passed to establish a respectable distance from the settlement agreement and the end of the company's cleanup exercise. In one of these, the central totem of North American culture, a sleek, speeding car, dissolves magically into a lunging tiger. In another, a tiger runs at the edge of a deep forest. The animal is magnificent, powerful, and riveting. The photography is impeccable. For the older generation of Americans, the tiger evokes sentimental attachments to a kitsch image from the old days of the "Tiger in your tank" commercials. For the young, it suggests inexhaustible power. The vibrant natural setting, the rich colors, and the clean muscularity of the wild animal are meant to imply Exxon's ties to the natural world, and bring to an end to Exxon's bad reputation. The sorcerers who made the commercials are formidable, and for their ability to draw beguiling loops around perception, a dangerous genius in our culture.

It must be granted that the company's safety record after the oil spill itself was exemplary. Cindy Coe indicated that the final numbers would indeed show that the cleanup effort was effective so far as provisions for worker safety were concerned. It's fair to add that the work conditions were hazardous, due to oil-slickened rocks, tricky weather, rough seas, and water so cold that to fall into it meant almost certain death. In December of 1989, Exxon's health and safety manager, Fred Brown, said to me, "My goal was to not kill anyone. I was surprised by the hazards associated with the slippery conditions, but my biggest fear was of losing a boat with forty or fifty people on it." Brown's concern was no doubt genuine, as was that of Exxon employees in general for all the effects of the oil spill, but in Brown's statement one can

---

[76] The Oil Pollution act, passed by Congress in 1990, included a provision that applied a prohibition on trading in Prince William Sound to one vessel — the now-named *SeaRiver Mediterranean*. SeaRiver considers this discriminatory and is currently seeking redress through the courts. If successful, according to Exxon media representatives, the *Mediterranean* is expected to return to service in Alaska.

discern the gravitation toward depersonalization and image: Within the corporate system, the prime effect of a capsized boat full of workers would have been the splash it created in the media, not the pain of it suffered by the victims and their loved ones. In one suit brought against Exxon's insurance claims by more than a hundred of its insurers under the lead of Lloyd's of London, it was stated that "Exxon's expenditures were made solely as a prophylactic measure to protect its corporate public image and profits."

In its way, Exxon's "zero-tolerance" pollution standard applied to cleanup vessels, as I observed in Port Graham, was also exemplary. There were measures of good in the opportunities taken to research ways of responding to future spills and in the apparent willingness of Exxon to devote its considerable resources to cleanup. But at the same time, to see a hundred workers tromping up from the Valdez docks after several days of safe and often meaningless labor, or the idleness of the barge at Port Graham — a politically correct sop tossed to the Native community — or to consider the damage in much of the cleanup exercise, the wasted money, the tilt given to company-generated science for use in litigation and public relations, it all became another conquest of nature and the imagination. As discussed earlier, research devoted to dispersants and bioremediation was conducted by Exxon in cooperation with the EPA, and at times to the exclusion of other promising formulations. Because of its hold on patents, Exxon would eventually benefit from successful remedies.

The company developed a traveling science-information program, provided brochures for tourists at the Alyeska oil terminal, and produced a documentary video called *Scientists and the Alaska Oil Spill*, which it distributed nationally to public schools in 1993. While government and independent studies continued to find a high probability that oil contamination and the cleanup remained a significant factor in certain failures of recovery in the sound, Exxon asserted that there was absolutely no linkage between newly observed failures, including fishery failures, and the oil spill. Admittedly, oil spill science is arcane stuff that engenders hairsplitting disputes over sampling and testing procedures, design flaws, and statistics, and that it is made all the more impenetrable for ordinary people when the various researchers represent vested interests in contention with one another. The question, to which Prince William Sound residents most fervently wished to know the answer in the early 1990s was: Does the oil spill continue to affect the habitat and the life within it? The answer proved to be slippery, lodged as it was in a debate that ineluctably drew the players toward a legalistic and media spun black hole where finally nothing seemed to mean anything at all. In

Exxon's documentary video, which included not one image of an oiled animal but many images of cleaned-up ones, Jerry M. Neff, an Exxon consultant from the Batelle Ocean Science Laboratory, states, "The story is essentially closed. The hydrocarbons are gone."

At best that is an overstatement. While it might be argued that the story so far as what remained to be *done* about lingering oil was closed in 1993, it was far from true that the hydrocarbons were essentially gone. In the same year, researchers under the auspices of the *Exxon Valdez* Oil Spill Trustee Council (EVOSTC) observed oil residue at each of the 59 selected test sites, including 120 gallons of oily liquid collected on one beach near Sleepy Bay. To this day, oil can be found beneath the surface of heavily oiled beaches, often simply by digging a few inches down, which I myself have done. In 1997, Native residents of Chenega Bay, under the guidance of the Alaska DEC, applied a recently formulated chemical agent (PES-51, a citrus-based product that, when injected beneath the surface, binds to the oil and floats it upward, allowing both the agent and the oil to be collected with oil-absorbent pads) to beaches in the vicinity of their village. Analysis of sample sites showed quantities of residual oil — between 1 and 20 pounds of sealed-up mousse per square meter.

Independent and government scientists have charged that Exxon-sponsored research regularly works with designs and databases that lack "power," or that have insufficient range in their sampling procedures. For example, in 1993, both ADFG biologist Mark Willett and Riki Ott made the observation that juvenile wild salmon in one Exxon study didn't show increased mortality rates because they were "sheltered," or penned. Once the juveniles were released, the decreased growth rate due to oil exposure and the concomitant decrease in vitality was precisely what increased their susceptibility to predation and which the study had protected them from. When I asked Dr. Ernie Brannon, the lead author of this and another Exxon study on pink salmon, he said first that he didn't feel ADFG researchers gave their own data "the kind of rigorous interpretation that an unbiased reader would give it. I think that's symptomatic of the fact that they are vigilant resource managers. They're looking for ill effects." Fair enough. Regarding his own work, he insisted that he was given independence by Exxon, as did virtually all Exxon researchers, but granted that there was "no question about the conditions of employment always being a factor. There's always that bias if the person you work for has something at stake."

The American Society for Testing and Materials (ASTM) held a symposium in April of 1993 in Atlanta, Georgia, which Exxon employed as a showcase for unveiling portions of its research findings. Company research-ers presented study after study, including Dr. Brannon's work, that intended to show the lack of persistence of *Exxon Valdez* oil in Prince William Sound. The studies were challenged by some scientists and by a contingent of Alas-kans, including Riki Ott, who caused a minor furor by insisting that her objections be heard. Before the symposium was over, researchers from the National Ocean and Atmospheric Administration (NOAA) denounced the Exxon studies, and in a highly unusual move for members of the customarily staid agency, they distributed a public document that said Exxon scientists had skewed NOAA findings by using "selected bits from the raw database" to make their argument.

The matter of information rendered to an often unwary or ill-informed public, whether delivered in the guise of science or of straight-out advertis-ing, and particularly when the one blurs into the other, raises questions about the distinction between public and private domain so far as the American oil industry is concerned, and by implication about other resource-oriented in-dustries. Historically, the oil industry has at times pleaded its free enterprise interests, and it is winked at while it goes to the extremes of forming trusts, fixing prices, witholding information that bears upon public concerns, and at times of forming its own foreign policy. At other times, it pleads its ties to national security, through which over the years it has easily been the largest single recipient of government welfarism, including the repeated mustering of troops to protect its interests.

Is it fair to ask a company to be forthcoming and truthful about informa-tion when it holds leases on public property, is the recipient of publicly funded development and research, has received underwriting in the form of infra-structure construction with public funds, has its interests defended by na-tional troops, and has polluted public waters? It might seem so, even given such a company's inclination to compartmentalize its activities, but then the question arises: In what does a company such as Exxon find the faith to perpetuate its half-truths and outright lies? The answer, perhaps, is in the reluctance of much of the American population to penetrate the loop of power, its preference for living in a fog, and its willing acceptance of almost any-thing in return for the opportunity to keep its gas tanks topped off. We are Exxon.

The American consumer, as we have allowed ourselves to be called, is a dangerous influence — dangerous in the sense that our insatiable appetite for raw materials causes continuous and often destructive change in the world. We seem unable to attend to the effects of our habits. Our radicalism of consumption — unchecked, and even enhanced during the ten years since the Alaskan oil — has become systemic, like an organism living out its time with a case of the worms. There are statistics, the numbers, endless numbers to confirm our role — the fact that we use two and a half times as much energy per capita than the citizens of Japan and Europe, and almost forty times as much as citizens of, say, India. In the years since the OPEC embargo in the early eighties and the shortage scare, and despite corrective measures, including dramatically increased automobile efficiency, our consumption of petroleum products now exceeds the record 1978 levels. To our general profligacy, add the conspicuous consumption of a certain class of Americans, those suburbanites who purchase expensive, gas-guzzling "sport utility vehicles" equipped with four-wheel drive, racks, brush guards, winches. It's as if they've found a way to consume most brazenly and at the same time in their "road warrior" angst to have prepared themselves for the coming devastation of a post-apocalyptic world. Add also rising automobile use in "developing" nations, and the result is universal increases in oil consumption, which worldwide reached a record high of 26.16 billion barrels for the year 1997. These and yet more troubling statistics about the effects of pollution, such as the decay of the ozone layer, are available for contemplation by the American public, but we seem unable to come to grips with them. While opinion polls continue to show that Americans want environmental action to be taken, we look away when Congress fails to ratify significant international agreements, or as oil leases on public lands near and off the Alaskan North Slope are opened for auction with the product — oil — to be transported through the same decrepit pipeline system to Prince William Sound. We insist upon action only fleetingly, and only when faced with calamity. Then, as the incident in Prince William Sound would suggest, the nation flagellates itself, the press and broadcast news feed our frenzy with half-assimilated information, and we fasten on symbols in order to allay our disturbing sense of ignorance and guilt.

In the case of Prince William Sound, one symbol was Exxon, what during the press glut of 1989 many came to regard as an evil empire. Another was the sea otter, the newfound Bambi that we sought to redeem, and so to redeem ourselves. The first emanated from one of America's controlling myths, the myth of endless resource, endless consumption, and of endless time which like money always expands for our use. In this myth, we mount our elaborate armatures to pluck the fruit of the earth. The second, the otter, conjured up the myth of the lost garden. From this sprang our melancholy regard for Alaska as the last wilderness on American soil. This is what triggered the remarkable but often sentimental public response, and hence soon exhausted the outpouring of concern over the spill. Not without vitality in their substance — American pragmatism in the first, American hope in the second — the two myths and the differing ways of regarding the world that attend them came to be woven together out of the thin stuff of bad information and outright propaganda to be played on the stage of our theatrical culture. Watching, we were befogged by an illusion from which there seemed to be no escape.

During the summer of 1989, a total of 338 otters were brought into the otter rescue centers. Of these, 114 died, 28 were placed in aquariums, and 196 were released to uncertain fates. A total of 1,589 birds were received in the bird centers, of which 792 died and 797 were released. The expense for each rehabilitated otter was over $90,000 and for each rehabilitated bird, over $25,000. A small number of eagles were captured, rehabilitated, and released, at a cost of $42,000 each. The cost of wildlife rescue and rehabilitation to Exxon was $41 million. These figures only begin to suggest the total expense of additional millions for spill-connected research, observation, and rehabilitation by government and private entities for a variety of reasons, including litigation in which the assignment of dollar amounts to damage would become the subject of fierce contention.

The sea otter is a keystone predator, a species not only easily anthropomorphized[77] but actually rather like us in several ways. By its voracity for shellfish the sea otter is capable of causing precipitous change in a habitat. It eats 25 percent of its own body weight daily, far more than any other marine mammal and eight times as much as humans, although humans have found many other ways to increase the weight of their consumption. Left alone, the otter will increase its numbers beyond the capacity of a habitat to support it, and then will die off or migrate. Some of its specialized features make it particulary vulnerable to an oil spill — its proclivity for shoreline mining (large numbers of shellfish concentrate along the shore) and the loss of insulating capabilities it suffers when its fur is coated with oil. Otter rescue following the grounding of the *Exxon Valdez* became complicated, too, because of jockeying for power among the rescue centers, and disputes over whether

[77] Although I've discussed the matter of anthropomorphization with scientists and others, it remains unclear to me where the breaking point lies between excessive presumption on the part of humans that an animal will be like them, on the one hand, and on the other hand of awakening human feeling in a fashion that opens the way for an address to the shared realities of the animal world. Applied scientists in general incline toward guarding against or even fearing the loss of "objectivity" that anthropomorphization might encourage.

otters should be rescued at all (mostly, they probably shouldn't have been), and whether or not placing them in captivity actually increased their susceptibility to disease. As in so many instances with the response to this oil spill, the confused remedies mirrored the confusion of the incident.

In the rescue centers during the summer of 1989, there was a distemper scare and a herpes scare (later, according to Randall Davis, otters were found to have herpes in the wild). Some argued that the otters should not be released into waters where they might infect other otters. There was a controversy during the spring of 1990 over an otter die-off. Forty dead otters were discovered in Prince William Sound during a five-week period preceding mid-April, an unusually high number, according to Nancy Lethcoe, the Valdez coordinator of the state's winter cleanup effort. The question arose as to whether those otters had been contaminated by oil over the winter. There was another die-off among otters released with implanted radio transmitters, which raised questions as to whether captivity had weakened the animals. Since recovered otter carcasses had been carried into the secret world of litigation by the Fish and Wildlife Service, no answers were immediately forthcoming. Later, as information was released, it was concluded that stress and infections acquired during captivity had indeed weakened the otters.

As of 1998, it is estimated that 2,800 sea otters[78] died from the initial effects of the oil spill. Because of weak pre-spill baseline studies and harsh conditions, which made retrieval difficult, losses were impossible to track with precision. During the summer of 1989, nearly 1,000 otter carcasses were found, most of them in Prince William Sound. While the otter population in the eastern (largely unoiled) portion of the sound continues to increase at normal rates, the population in the heavily oiled western portion remain low. Researchers suspect that sea otters continue to suffer "subtle and difficult to detect" spill-related effects, including possible chronic liver and kidney damage.

Harbor seals were in a state of decline in Prince William Sound prior to the oil spill. Indeed, over the last 20 years their numbers have decreased by 80 percent. Like the otter, the harbor seal inclines to reside in the intertidal zone where it consumes quantities of pollock, octopus, capelin, cod, and herring. The seal itself is prey for sharks, Steller sea lions, transient killer whales, and Native subsistence hunters. The causes of the general decline of the harbor seal population are not known, but are likely due to multiple factors, including persistent oceanic pollution, increased predation by sharks, imbal-

---

[78] These and succeeding animal mortality numbers are drawn from "Updates" and "Status Reports" released under the auspices of the *Exxon Valdez* Oil Spill Trustee Council.

ances in the ecosystem created by the fishing industry, and entrapment in fishing nets. For the harbor seal, the oil spill was a sharp tweak to an already stressed system, and it is estimated that 300 seals died by inhaling fumes or by the absorption of oil through the skin as they clambered out of the water to heavily oiled "haul-out" sites. The toxic effects of oil in seals caused brain damage, lethargy, disorientation, and thus drowning — and in what we might term a "social" extension, caused affected mothers to abandon their pups. After a sharp drop in population in 1989 and 1990, the trend for harbor seals has resumed its previous steady decline of about 6 percent per year in both oiled and unoiled areas.

A total of 26,499 bird carcasses from 74 different species were recovered in Prince William Sound and the Gulf of Alaska. As of 1996, the estimates of the number of birds killed by the spill, including the far larger number of unrecovered bodies, was 250,000, of which 74 percent were murres. Some experts put the timeline for the complete recovery of the sound at 70 years or more due to lingering oil spill effects, and they project that during that period (and barring further pollution events), as many as 600,000 birds will have died. Certain species, such as the bald eagle, have proven to be resilient. Hundreds of eagles died, chiefly through the ingestion of contaminated prey, but they now appear to be rebounding. Eighty-seven yellow-billed loons were found dead, and 250 are estimated to have died, this from an endangered species whose total numbers were then between 2,000 and 5,000. The common murre, 40 percent of whose population in the sound was killed by the spill and which is now just beginning to show signs of recovery, will nevertheless take years to reach its former numbers. At the 1993 ASTM symposium in Atlanta, Exxon researchers claimed that they found no evidence that the cliff-nesting seabirds had been decimated since the spill in the sound, which provoked a response from EVOSTC chief scientist, Robert Spies, to the effect that murres were so devastated that it would take anywhere from two decades to a century for them to recover.

Of particular importance to many species of birds, as well as to sea and river otters, is the intertidal region where both the oil and cleanup activities had deleterious effects upon marine flora and fauna. In a 1993 study, biologist Charles Peterson found continued oil contamination on many beaches, and noted that "oil continu[es] to invade the food chains through uptake by mussels and subsequent consumption of those contaminated mussels by important predator species." Peterson also observed an associated and continuing effect upon predatory seabirds in the form of depressed reproductive rates (fewer eggs, thin eggshells, fewer chicks, less healthy chicks). His report states that "significant and substantial spill induced declines were identified in harlequin ducks, black oystercatchers, northwestern crows, scoters, loons, mew gulls, cormorants, and arctic terns." Further research reveals that the weakness of the intertidal zone's recovery continues through 1998, and that the breakdown of intertwined communities is sometimes exacerbated through the colonization of stressed regions by "opportunistic species." The pigeon guillemot, marbled murrelet, and harlequin duck to this day show no sign of recovery.

Ecosystem damage always extends beyond the immediately evident and quantifiable into the much more difficult-to-track community and social effects, and even into what in human culture would be called psychological effects. Such imponderables are dramatically presented by the fate of one killer whale pod in the sound. North Pacific killer whales (*Orcinus orca*, also commonly called orcas) are divided into two genetically distinct types — *resident* fish-eating whales, and *transient* mammal-eating whales. All killer whales live and travel in social groups called "pods" — family groups comprised of a female and her offspring, including adult males — although the pods of transient whales appear to be more loosely structured than those of resident whales. The hunting ranges of the two types may at times overlap (in Prince William Sound, several transient pods make seasonal entries), but generally the residents and transients avoid contact with one another. Females will be inseminated by males from outside their own pod, but always or nearly always by males of their type. These characteristics alone suggest that killer whales are sophisticated and live in a state of intricate social interaction recognizable to people by its affinity with their own social procedures. Indeed, according to researchers Craig Matkin and Eva Saulitas, "the social bonds of killer whales are considered among the strongest of any mammalian species, stronger even than those of human societies."

Killer whales also have sophisticated methods of vocal communication — what would seem to be social or conversational calls, and echolocation employed for navigation and hunting. The variations in the specific "vocalizations" and in the phrasing of them is enormous. Additionally, what are termed the "acoustic dialects" of all killer whale pods are distinct from one another, although in general the language of transient pods seems to be the less elaborate. I had the opportunity to hear communication among resident whales in the summer of 1997 while on board the research vessel *Lucky Star* with Matkin and Saulitas. On one afternoon, after we'd been in the vicinity of two resident pods for several days, Eva Saulitas dropped a submersible microphone into the water for my benefit. At that time, one of the pods had gone into a resting mode, while the other slipped in and out of sight as it prowled in a seemingly desultory fashion the shoreline of Latouche Island to the south of us. The *Lucky Star* was positioned in a large expanse of open water near the convergence of Latouche and Evans Passages. To the north lay Knight Island, and to the east a mile or more away the barrier island, Montague, with its jagged spine of snowcapped mountains.

Craig Matkin surmised that the whales had gorged themselves on chum salmon, which were schooling at the time prior to their spawning run. The resting whales, gathered in their matrilinear groups, swam around us in huge, looping rectangles — skimming the surface, briefly submerging, and skimming again like a stitching of the seam between air and water. Their black and white markings gleamed and their dorsal fins sliced the water. What emerged from the microphone and the small speaker mounted in the *Lucky Star's* cabin was at first nothing more than the sound of water lapping against the boat's hull, and then gradually first one, and then another whale call. The sound bore a certain resemblance to what I'd heard before on recordings of whales — the resonant, echolocating clicks, sometimes coming in rapid fire, and the high melodic howls. What was different and most compelling — drawn from the shifts in volume and directional orientation of the sounds, and also perhaps from the effect of our visual orientation, here near the whales, but in our own above-water expanse — was the sense that the communications below were not only measuring but also organizing a huge dimension in a way that was absolutely indecipherable to me. It was an effect far beyond stereophonic. Whales can converse with each other this way over long distances underwater — miles — and they can identify prey 600 yards away by listening as the clicks bounce off it, making an aurally perceived shape out of, say, the body of a fish. What I was hearing sounded like nothing I'd ever heard before, except maybe once when I stood in the midst of a forest during an ice storm and listened as trees spoke their sundering with sharp cracks at the rate of one or two a minute from all directions for miles around.

Of the Alaskan killer whales, there are 110 individuals in six pods that currently use Prince William Sound and the Kenai Fjords region for feeding and social activity. Most of these have maintained normal population levels since 1983, according to Craig Matkin, who has been studying and cataloguing them since that time.[79] One transient pod that was commonly sighted in

---

[79] Individual killer whales are identified by photographic records of their dorsal fins, which whale-to-whale have a unique shape, size, and scar pattern, and are as distinct as fingerprints. Craig Matkin began photographing in 1983 and has records of over 300 whales. Thus, the killer whale is one of the few species in Prince William Sound for which a comprehensive pre-1989 baseline exists.

the sound and is thought to have had direct contact with oil through encountering the spill itself or ingesting oiled prey — probably harbor seals — lost nine members. Much more telling are the losses to a resident group designated the "AB" pod. This pod has long been well known to researchers, fishermen, and other observers because of its unusual friendliness and fearlessness. Individual whales commonly approach boats closely and sometimes swim alongside them, as if in play. Indeed, while I was with Craig and Eva, we approached whales from the AB pod in a skiff to photograph them, and one of the whales swam close and looked up at us. Eva believed that the whale "knew" the skiff, as well as Craig and herself as familiars.

Prior to the oil spill, beginning in 1985, the AB pod began interfering with the commercial long-line fishery in the sound, removing as much as 25 percent of the catch from the lines. Between 1985 and 1986 six whales were lost, probably to gunshot wounds. Stricter regulations were enacted to protect the whales, and since that time no new bullet injuries have been observed. It is possible, as with the declining numbers of harbor seals, that the pressure put on the AB pod created a vulnerability in them, but there is no way of proving this. In March, 1989, the AB pod was photographed swimming in oil slicks south of Knight Island, and later three adult females and four juveniles of the thirty-six member pod turned out to be missing. Subsequently, they were confirmed as mortalities with the strong likelihood that the oil spill was the cause — probably due to the inhalation of vapors and the resulting damage to lungs, other organs, or nerve systems.

By the spring of 1990, an additional six whales (one female, one calf, four juveniles) from the pod had disappeared and were presumed dead. In the years following, three calves orphaned by the 1989 female mortalities also died. While other resident pods have increased their numbers since the oil spill, the AB pod has not. Since 1994, one matrilineal group from the AB pod split off and now travels with another pod — an unprecedented event for a resident killer whale pod, according to Craig Matkin. In their assessment for EVOSTC, he and Eva, who are a highly respectful and diligent pair, who take care to minimize their own disruption of the whales, or their opportunism,[80] note that "the drastic disruption of pod social structure with

---

[80] One of the research tools Craig Matkin has used over the years is a darting method by which tiny cones of blubber are extracted from individual whales and then tested for pollutants and used for genetic identification. The dart, which is shot from a gun, is designed to penetrate only into the layer of blubber, then to be squeezed out by pressure, and to float, and thus to be retrieved. Cognizant of the disruptive effect of such sampling, Matkin has a research protocol that allows for only one shot per whale for each encounter, whether the shot is a hit or a miss. While at sea with him, I also observed him board an approaching

the loss of females and offspring from maternal groups may further limit the potential recovery of the pod." What is being suggested here is that animals were experiencing precisely the same thing that Mead Treadwell back in Cordova in 1989 had called "pattern dislocation," the phenomenon resulting from material disruptions compounding themselves into unmeasurable community and psychic effects. Even understanding that change in the natural world, or unending revolution for that matter, is inescapable, it is sobering to consider that among the things to be lost with the AB pod, along with lives and a community, is a distinct dialect of a language, one underwater voice never to be heard again.

Coast Guard records indicate that on average an oil tanker in U.S. waters catches fire, explodes, hits a dock or another ship, breaks apart, experiences mechanical failure, runs aground, or ends up in some kind of accident — admittedly, usually minor — two of every three days.[81] The experience of the *Exxon Valdez* spill made it abundantly clear that the primary emphasis should be placed upon preventing further spills, especially catastrophic ones, and that in the event of such an occurrence, nothing approaching the confused and slipshod response to it should ever be repeated. When I wrote the conclusion to this book's first edition, I argued that a drastic reduction in the number of spills (including pipeline leaks and refinery explosions elsewhere in the United States) was well within the industry's capabilities, and that the only way industry would become accountable was for it to be too expensive, one way or another, for it not to do so. This meant that legislative loopholes

---

cruise ship and give the passengers an expert talk on killer whale behavior. This he did gratis and willingly so, in exchange for the opportunity to advise both the passengers and crew on the need not to approach the whales too closely. For her part, Eva, who did her master's thesis on killer whale vocalization, told me that she has decided not to pursue that line of inquiry any longer. Her reason, as I took it, was her reluctance to engage in a form of penetrating voyeurism upon a community that had not granted her permission to do so. Needless to say, both Eva and Craig were profoundly shaken by the oil spill and its aftermath.

[81] It should be said that only about 6 percent of the petroleum in marine waters comes from "accidental" sources. By far the majority of such pollution (84 percent) comes from land-based industry and failures in waste management. For example, 31 percent of petroleum pollution enters the oceans in the form of runoff from cities and river systems, 30 percent from the normal conduct of marine transportation (bilge bunkering, dry docking, and so on), and 10 percent from the atmosphere. Also, natural seeps are the source of another 10 percent. Since the oil carried by tankers is not weathered, however, and since it is precipitously released in quantity, it is much more toxic and more likely to cause devastation than oil from other sources.

needed to be closed, inspections vigorously conducted, regulations strictly enforced, heavy fines imposed, and shipping systems shut down when operated unsafely, and that the industry itself needed to create a much deeper cushion between standard operating procedures and operating at peak capacity. It also needed to be much less driven to supply low-cost fuel to the American public. Problems remain. Americans continue to receive unlimited quantities of cheap gas. The Alaskan system itself is coping with a rapidly decaying pipeline, as observed by Richard Fineberg, which raises the specter of a Siberian-style spill into the Copper River drainage system. At the same time, however, much has been done to correct past and potential failures within Prince William Sound and at the Alyeska terminal.

During its spring session of 1990, the Alaska legislature passed a major bill requiring the oil industry to stockpile enough equipment in Alaska to respond to a 300,000-barrel spill (12.6 million gallons) and to be prepared to import equipment to combat larger spills within 72 hours. The Alaska bill included provisions for reimbursing victims of spills and for increased state monitoring of vessel traffic and inspection of tankers and pipelines. Bills were also passed to increase criminal penalties for the reckless operation of oil carriers.

In the same year, the U.S. Congress passed and President George Bush signed the Oil Pollution Act. This legislation increased the liability by shippers for up to $1,200 per gross ton instead of the previous ceiling of $150 per gross ton. It also mandated the creation of a $1 billion oil spill response and cleanup fund with the money coming from a five-cent-a-barrel fee on both domestic and imported oil. The act requires that all new tankers have double hulls and that existing tankers be retrofitted with double hulls or taken out of service by the year 2015. It calls for the formation of regional response teams within the Coast Guard to deal with oil spills and a national response center where computers will hold lists of personnel and equipment that can be called upon. In what may be its most significant feature, politically speaking, it recognizes the primacy of state regulations.

Except for relatively minor mishaps, near misses, and spill response drills, the provisions of the new laws have yet to be tested, but there is no question that procedures for shipping in Prince William Sound have improved. A large number of provisions are now in place, beginning with the formation of the Regional Citizens' Advisory Council of Prince William Sound (RCAC), whose 18 members represent communities in the region, as well as commercial fishing, aquaculture, Native, tourism, and environmental interests. The council is under contract with Alyeska to provide information and advice in the interest of promoting safe operation of oil tankers and the Valdez Marine terminal. Of equal importance is the fact that by contract with its own companies Alyeska now has responsibility for the initial response to differing oil spill scenarios, including the 300,000-barrel spill, and then must aid in the transition of responsibility to the party causing the spill. This agreement corrects the cause of much of the initial confusion with the *Exxon Valdez* spill. A "Unified Command" system has been established to bring quickly into play Alyeska's equipment and personnel, the U.S. Coast Guard, and the company causing the spill.[82]

Oil spill response equipment, including over thirty miles of boom, is now positioned and ready for staging in the communities of Cordova, Chenega Bay, Tatitlek, Whittier, as well as Valdez. Hatchery protection equipment is staged at the five operating hatcheries in Prince William Sound. Two dispersant distribution centers are maintained at Anchorage International Airport. In addition to a 50-vessel "core fleet," approximately 325 fishing vessels are on contract with Alyeska to provide emergency oil spill response assistance. The fleet includes four escort tugs and two 5,500 horsepower Protector Class tugs, which are to be replaced by 10,000 horsepower tractor tugs presently under construction, the first of which is slated to arrive in early 1999. Each tanker entering and leaving port is accompanied by an Emergency Response Vessel (ERV) and a tug, with an additional tug assigned in severe weather. The pilot now boards and leaves oil tankers at Bligh Reef rather than nine miles nearer Valdez at Rocky Point. Other vessels include three large, self-propelled oil skimmers, as well as other smaller ones, a landing craft, and eight barges, including a lightering barge. Also, the oil industry itself has instituted a response program that includes equipment storage and deployment sites on both American coasts.

---

[82] The full scale spill response drill mounted by British Petroleum and the Coast Guard of September, 1998, had one deficiency in addition to the glitch over dispersant application mentioned in preceding pages. This was that the "Unified Command" established by protocol following an oil spill included representatives from the oil industry, the Coast Guard, and the Alaska DEC, but not from the citizens as they are to be represented by the RCAC. This means that the command system is still not truly horizontal and reopens all the possibilities for misunderstanding of and by citizens that became so evident after the *Valdez* spill. This suggests that politicians and industry remain incorrigible in their presumption of authority. John Devens, formerly mayor of Valdez and presently executive director of the RCAC, remembers how community officials "found it difficult to fit into the information and decision-making loop" back in March, 1989, how this "engendered mistrust," and how it "also deprived Exxon Corporation and government agencies of information they could have used to combat the spill."

The speed limit for tankers in all of Prince William Sound has been lowered from 12 to 10 knots. Tanker captains are tested for alcohol an hour before sailing, and crew members are tested if suspected of alcohol use. Tankers must remain in their lanes, and the radar system at the Vessel Traffic Center has been upgraded. The Alaska DEC has more money and more power to conduct effective inspections, and there is generally much stricter government oversight, including a stronger Coast Guard presence. Another, most significant provision of the Oil Pollution Act is to limit the number of hours crew members can work. They must have six hours off-duty during a twelve-hour shift. With such provisions in effect, the *Exxon Valdez* spill would likely have been a very different affair, or might not have occurred at all, although of course, no two spills are alike. No one spill will repeat the conditions of a previous one. It is utterly clear that the best of the improvements are those dedicated to preventing another spill from happening in the first place.

Much has been learned, also, about cleanup procedures in the event an oil spill breaks loose from initial response, as the *Valdez* spill certainly did. Contrary to its wishes, Exxon did return to Prince William Sound in 1990 to resume cleanup, but with a drastically reduced force of about 1,000 workers. Emphasis was placed on bioremediation and dispersant applications. Throughout the summer, Exxon and the state of Alaska disputed over chemical applications, the effects of excavation, and just what "environmentally stable" meant. Generally speaking, the state was in favor of more aggressive mechanical cleanup methods and more stringent standards, and more opposed to the use of chemical dispersants, but gradually the positions held by Exxon and federal representatives gained sway over the state's position. By midsummer, however, a group of Moss Landing Institute scientists — Michael Foster, John Tarpley, and Susan Dearn — published an article that argued that "most shoreline cleanup methods will increase immediate ecological damage and delay recovery." The three had served on Shoreline Cleanup Advisory Teams during the summer of 1989.

They pointed out that evidence concerning the ecological effect of various cleanup procedures was sketchy, but that water flushing, excavation, and the trampling of beaches certainly destroyed many oiled organisms that were still alive. This was basically the same observation that members of the *Alpha Helix* crew and James Payne had made. Foster, Tarpley, and Dearn also noted that dispersant use near shorelines introduced more toxic elements into delicate water columns. Concerning the use of dispersants generally, they repeated the doubts of other scientists concerning their effectiveness and risks and recommended site-by-site strategies and the circumspect use of manual collection by, for example, vacuum pumps and skimmers. They argued that most of the oil would degrade on beaches strongly affected by tides, currents, and waves (high-energy beaches) in a period of a few months to a few years and on protected beaches on the order of ten years. They did not address the question of sublethal effects, or of long-term benthic pollution.

Some, such as Steve Provant of the Alaska DEC, objected strenuously to Foster, Tarpley, and Dearn's observations, but Alaskan entities, in particular, had at that time a litigation-based interest in continuing to promote large capital expenditures into the cleanup. The three Moss Landing scientists were not arguing that oil remaining on the beaches would not be damaging. Rather, they were making a more discrete and telling point — simply that most available cleanup methods were more damaging than leaving the oil alone. They seem to have been basically on target. Sensitive habitats, and especially the critical intertidal zone, should be addressed with great care — booming off and skimming where possible, vacuuming here, sometimes moving rocks and cleaning them, and sometimes employing benign treatments such as the citrus-based injection method, or possibly bioremediation. Prior to that, one would hope that the deployment of superskimmers, perhaps dispersants, and even incendiary bombs during the initial stages of a large spill would reduce the amount of oil that reached the shores. To the extent that Foster, Tarpley, and Dearn's observations were correct, then to an equal extent the high-rolling cleanup exercise was unnecessary.

In December 1989, Exxon, Alyeska, and other oil industry codefendants cited in over 150 private and public lawsuits filed papers in the state of Alaska's Anchorage Superior Court requesting a sweeping order that all evidence gathered prior to trial be kept secret. Taken together, the argument went, the bits of information could create a mosaic of Exxon operations that would betray trade secrets, though in fact what was desired was to keep information out of the hands of legal adversaries. Alyeska spokesman George Jurkowich described the motion as "a broad request to protect information gained in a very wide-ranging discovery process. What that means," he said, "is if there is information out there about Alyeska, you can come and ask Alyeska about it, and we'll make a judgment about whether to release it." The motion provoked strong protests from the public, especially from those with an interest in the results of research (fishermen, for example). Many of the suits were not expected to go to trial for years. Also protesting were the state and other plaintiffs. Macon Cowles, then a lead attorney for environmental groups, said that "Exxon's basic proposal is to put all this information in a black box."

On February 27, 1990, a federal grand jury in Anchorage indicted the Exxon Corporation and its shipping subsidiary on five criminal counts (two felony charges under the 1972 Ports and Waterways Safety Act and the Dangerous Cargo Act, and on three misdemeanors under the Clean Water Act, the Refuse Act, and the Migratory Bird Act). Guilty verdicts on all counts could have resulted in fines of upwards of a billion dollars. Again, resolution of the charges, if the cases were tried, might not have come for years, and in the meantime the information would spin within the judicial system while the dead animals collected as evidence might remain forever frozen in refrigerator truck limbo up in Anchorage.

Prior to the February 27 indictment, the U.S. Justice Department had attempted to hammer out a plea bargain agreement that would have assessed about $200 million in criminal fines and required Exxon to contribute up to $550 million to a fund for environmental restoration. The plea bargain arrangement was abandoned due to a last-minute protest from the state of Alaska because a part of the agreement stipulated that the federal government would delay filing a civil suit for at least four years. Alaska said this would have cast it and all other plaintiffs adrift without any federal support as they pursued their damages.

Cordova's Marine Advisory Agent, Rick Steiner, had been involved in the collapse of the plea bargain agreement. As discussed above, Steiner learned early in 1990 from Frank Iarossi, then the head of Exxon Shipping, that Exxon and the U.S. Justice Department were finalizing in secret a settlement that would minimize both restoration penalties to Exxon and legal culpability for the U.S. Coast Guard.[83] When Steiner reported this to Alaska's At-

---

[83] In 1993, following publication of an essay under my authorship that dealt with these matters, a member of the U.S. Justice Department team involved with settlement negotiations contacted me and informed me of the U.S. government's strong interest in protecting the Coast Guard from liability in the oil spill. He also told me that what I reported in the essay and in the original edition of this book about VTS personnel on duty at the time of the spill testing positive for drug and alcohol use was intended to have been kept secret. He wanted to know how I had learned of it. The answer was in the off-the-record exchanges between attorneys and the judge in Joseph Hazelwood's trial in state court, which were included in the copy of the trial transcripts I received with the aid of an Exxon attorney. A consistently underplayed element in this story from its earliest stages, and no doubt an element that runs through all of Exxon's resistance to accepting further financial responsibility or penalty, is the Coast Guard's failure to rigorously monitor the shipping trade prior to the oil spill, and the failure of its personnel and radar system to track the *Exxon Valdez* on March 24, 1989.

torney General, "The shit," in Steiner's words, "hit the fan." The agreement
fell apart, and by July, 1990, the loosely-knit organization that Steiner, Riki
Ott, and David Grimes were involved with, the Coastal Coalition, submit-
ted its own proposal for a comprehensive settlement.

Steiner was respected by other activists for his ability to engage the upper echelons of the industry and political power structure, and to bear up
under the intense scrutiny of the press and the outright hostility of those
who counted themselves his enemies. He would eventually have to leave
Cordova because of his sense of discomfort and vulnerability there, and David
Grimes, too, would begin a protracted state of wandering. I admired in Steiner
what I had learned to admire in many others — the capacity to absorb the
powerfully conflicting forces of the oil spill and big money and yet to respond with tough action, even when the action might have seemed outrageous, such as proposing a comprehensive legal settlement, initiating legal
action, or helping to organize the 1993 fishermen's blockade of the tanker
channel. He never lost his sense of purpose, his sense of humor, nor the
ability to look beyond the edges for a kind of wild, cosmic solace. One of the
times I visited him in Cordova, we took a drive out of town along Eyak Lake,
stopped at a canyon through which ran Power Creek, and hiked upwards.
Fair-complexioned to the extreme, tall, thin, and angular, he had a scraggly
beard and a rangy way of moving. We passed a pool in the creek, loaded with
spawning salmon, and exchanged a few sardonic remarks about the origin of
the name — Power Creek — which had been given in honor of a proposed
hydroelectric plant. "But we mean a different kind of power when we call it
that," Rick said. As we hiked on, he told me that he had whiled away a few
hours calculating how many pounds of carbon had fallen to the earth's surface during the petroleum age. He wondered if our time might be merely the
capstone to the age of humankind. "It could be," he said, half in fun and yet
half-deadly serious, "that our true purpose on the planet is to prepare a car-
bon-rich environment for the next great age of plants."

It was the serious side of his nature that led him and his Coastal Coalition associates to argue that state, environmental, and Native plaintiffs be
enjoined and all resource damages from the oil spill be resolved in one stroke
by having Exxon pay $2 billion to establish a nonprofit corporation, the Alaska
Restoration Fund. The money would be used to support research, education,
sustainable economic development, and continuing restoration of resources
damaged by the spill (re-establishing herring runs and rehabilitating wild
salmon streams, for example) as provided for by the Comprehensive Environmental Response, Compensation, and Liability Act (CERCLA, other-

wise known as the "Superfund"). Also, in what would eventually prove to be one of the most striking recommendations, the fund would be used to *acquire* resources equivalent to those that were lost — in particular, forest lands adjacent to marine habitats. The system of "contingent valuation" served as one of the means for arriving at the $2 billion figure.[84]

Thus, rearing its curious visage again, was the same statistically driven system that has its roots in philosophic positivism and the economic theory of A.C. Pigou, and which is commonly employed in environmental law. By it, value is attached to the dead and to hazily perceived potentials of the world, such as how much the view through one's picture window would be worth if a neighbor hadn't put a two-story house in front of it, or of what the value of an uncut forest will be 50 years from now. This system of thought seems odd because it affixes dollar amounts to what is often clearly unmeasurable, such as what contingent valuation practitioners term "existence value" — the benefit gained by the citizenry from simply knowing that, say, a forest, a healthy yellow-billed loon population, or an intact killer whale pod exists, or that biological diversity with all its unforeseen potentials will be preserved. At the same time, the approach might be defensible precisely because it does seek to give material weight to the unquantifiable in a materialist culture that seems to have forgotten how to honor mere existence or how to grant the force of spiritual values in any form other than a demagogic one, such as the tawdry political trade in the flag and school prayer.

Anticipating that "organized science" would soon become its outright adversary, the Coastal Coalition's proposal argued that "research should be driven by fundamental scientific interest in the behavior and response of this ecosystem . . . not by the need to collect evidence for litigation." In order to justify its solution, the proposal covered several areas, notably the economic need to maintain the viability of the fisheries, especially the wild fisheries, and the related need to protect natural diversity. Among its recommendations for the use of the fund was the purchase of timber rights in the sound. Implicit in it was the argument for human alignment with the natural world. The proposal made note of the connection between land and water, and of what David Grimes is fond of saying — that "salmon are forest animals, returning from the ocean every year to spawn in their natal forest streams." The proposal also observed the necessary role of what are known as terpenes, the biogenic hydrocarbons — oil — that drip from spruce trees. Terpenes are one type of the aromatic hydrocarbons that occur naturally and are ubiqui-

---

[84] By the same system, some scientists estimate the actual oil spill damage to Prince William Sound to have been $15–20 billion.

tous. They are what we smell in a coniferous forest. They are the cause of the explosive nature of forest fires. They are washed from the ground into streams and then into coastal waters. They float. They are driven by currents and collect in varying densities in various places. They may play a role in the so-far-mysterious olfactory memory of anadromous fish — salmon. They are also the natural sustenance for the very hydrocarbon-metabolizing bacteria that were the essential element in what was thought to be the most promising oil spill restoration technology — bioremediation. Terpenes are, therefore, a case in point for a previously unforeseen consequence of a previously unanticipated diversity interface between woods and water. To cut the forests would increase the susceptibility of marine habitats to the damaging effects of crude oil. The terpene is an indicator species, in a way, of the world's mechanisms for healing itself, and it is but one very discrete, though telling example taken from a forest filled with such interconnections between alive and decaying things — trees, bush, lichen, insect, crustacean, mollusk, mammal, and fish, and especially anadromous fish for whom a clear-cut might be as lethal as an oil spill as they pass between the salt and freshwater worlds.

A settlement between Alaska, the federal government, and Exxon was reached in October of 1991, its terms being that Exxon would enter guilty pleas for violating provisions of the Federal Water Pollution Control Act, the Migratory Bird Treaty Act, and the Rivers and Harbors Act, and pay a fine of $150 million (the largest such fine ever levied), and also settle damage claims with the state and federal government in the amount of $900 million (the largest sum ever recovered in the U.S. in an enforcement of an environmentally related civil action). Of the $150 million fine, $125 million was remitted (forgiven) to Exxon for the company's previous expenses and cooperation, thus bringing the total to $1.025 billion. A previous settlement agreement had been reached in March of the same year with similar provisions, except that the amount of the fine was $100 million rather than $150 million, which U.S. District Court Judge H. Russel Holland rejected as insufficient. In addition, the earlier settlement had no provision for the release of scientific findings while the later one stipulated that government-connected research would be opened for the benefit of the public and the thousands of "third party plaintiffs" (individuals, fishermen, Native villages, etc.), though Exxon, as a private entity, was not bound by the same requirement.

The earlier version of the settlement had caused Exxon Chairman, Lawrence Rawl, to state that "the agreement in my view and that of the board is that it's in the interest of shareholders. . . . [It] will not have a noticeable effect on our financial results. . . . The customer always pays everything." Such remarks, and the public knowledge of Exxon's enormous revenues (a $5 billion net profit in 1990) precipitated another outcry. Still, the twists continued, as the terms of the later and final settlement actually came out more favorably to Exxon because of the remittance of all but $25 million of the $150 million fine, and because Exxon's payments against the $900 million were to be stretched out over ten years, while it collected interest on the balance. By law, Exxon was permitted to deduct the $900 million as a business expense. The actual cost to the company, therefore, would turn out to be approximately $500 million.

No step in the process had been taken without acrimony and there was no abatement of it as the terms of the settlement began to be applied, beginning with the news that reimbursements would not only be made to Exxon, but that the governments would also reimburse themselves for past spill-related expenses to the tune of about $215 million. The $25 million remaining from the fine was divided between deposits made into the North American Wetlands Conservation Fund and the Victims of Crime Act Account — worthy causes, perhaps, but at best very loosely connected to the oil spill in Alaska. The administration of the trust fund was given into the hands of six trustees, three each from the federal and state governments (representatives from the U.S. Department of the Interior, National Marine Fisheries Service, U.S. Department of Agriculture, and the State of Alaska's Attorney General's Office, Department of Environmental Conservation, and Department of Fish and Game).

Nevertheless, with the new settlement, Rick Steiner, David Grimes, the Coastal Coalition and like-thinking parties from other areas had achieved two very important victories: First, the stress in the "Memorandum of Agreement" upon "*ecosystem* restoration" and the directive that the Trustees ". . . shall jointly use all natural resource damage recoveries for the purpose of restoring, replacing, enhancing, rehabilitating or *acquiring the equivalent of natural resources* injured as a result of the oil spill and the reduced or lost services provided by such resources . . ." (italics mine). Secondly, the agreement stipulated that the decision-making process be fully public, and to facilitate this a number of representatives from interest groups (environmentalism, municipal and borough government, commercial fishing, the tourist industry, etc.) were appointed to advisory positions.

The stage was set. Events and efforts to leverage the trust fund would move forward, sometimes in a wildly erratic fashion, sometimes in a crunching grind, and always fraught with potential legal and political jeopardy. Disputes ran the gamut from mundane jurisdictional disputes to the most heavily freighted jurisdictional dispute of all in American government — states' rights. The newly installed Alaska governor, Wally Hickel, perceived what remained of the trust fund as a cash cow for the economic development of Prince William Sound. His administration promoted tourism, a science center in Seward linked to tourism, and road building, including the notorious Copper River Highway to connect Cordova with the outside world (which was finally not built), and incredibly in the minds of some, a road to support a logging operation on the Kenai Peninsula. In 1992, when Bill Clinton assumed the U.S. Presidency, the federal positions on the Trustee Council switched over from Republican to Democrat, creating both a somewhat more environmentally friendly tilt and frequent stalemates, since the trustees were compelled to act by consensus. In the meantime, imaginations worked way out at the nether reaches of what enhancement, rehabilitation, replacement, or restoration might mean. Hearings held through early 1993 — what would turn out to be the most important post-oil spill year — inspired scores of claims upon the funds, including those from established entities, and quixotic ones — such as a proposal to exterminate the rats deposited on the Aleutian Islands by nineteenth-century shipwrecks. Scientists wanted to continue their myriad of studies and lobbied heavily for them. By late summer 1993, the General Accounting Office (GAO) would release a report sharply critical of Trustee Council procedures and outlays. Through 1992, the $240 million received in payments from Exxon had been used primarily to reimburse state and federal agencies and Exxon itself for legal costs and previous oil spill related costs. No natural habitat protection or land acquisition had been accomplished. Weak organization, exorbitant travel and administrative costs, lack of competitive bidding, spending on questionable agency-sponsored studies (including conflict-of-interest scenarios by which agencies and individuals recommended, approved, and carried out projects) were among the problems cited by the GAO. The report also criticized the Trustee Council for the glacial pace of all its deliberations.

Simultaneously, another drama was being played out in Prince William Sound and on the Kenai Peninsula — what was sometimes referred to as the "second hit," Native corporation logging. As discussed previously, the effect of the Alaska Native Claims Settlement Act (ANCSA) was to capitalize Native holdings and to cast individual Natives in the role of shareholders. This set in motion the course toward an inescapable result, since the holdings consisted of land and its resources, and in Prince William Sound, after fish, the most available resource was trees. This is the point at which the financially strapped Native corporations of the region complicated their position by engaging in sales of net operating losses (NOLs) to large outside companies seeking to improve their tax position. Among these were the Chugach Alaska Corporation, which owns forest land throughout the sound, and several Prince William Sound and Kenai Peninsula village corporations, including the Tatitlek Corporation and the Cordova-based Eyak Corporation, which has holdings in the eastern Prince William Sound and Copper River Delta areas.

Immediately prior to the oil spill and for several years following, timber in Prince William Sound was being cut at an increasing rate, while for fishing people and many Native people, logging always inspires deep apprehension. They fear the wastelands that clear-cutting creates, the silt that washes into spawning streams and estuaries (which in the case of the Copper River Delta is one of the richest remaining "wild run" salmon fisheries in the world). After 1989 they feared the echo on land of what had just happened to the shorelines — the devastation and fragmentation of habitats — and by virtue of the interface of water and land further damage to the marine environment. In the five years from 1988 to 1993, logging in the region had increased fivefold from 40 million board feet to 200 million. As described in the previous chapter, what was being cut was the northernmost extreme of the Pacific coastal temperate rain forest, where, due to the cold and hardscrabble ground, clear-cutting creates subarctic deserts. High shipping costs of the product, usually sold as whole logs to Asian markets, result in extremely low or nonexistent profits.

Not surprisingly, Cordova was to become the site of the most intense wrangle over the logging question. The logging would be done by the Eyak Corporation, which is named after the last tribe to be officially recognized in North America, the Eyaks, who are thought to have crossed the glaciers from the interior to the coast perhaps 3,500 years ago. They see this area as their ancestral home, and yet they number 37[85] out of the 320 shareholders in the corporation bearing their name, the remainder being some Tlingit people, with whom the Eyaks share Athabaskan linguistic roots, but mainly Aleut people with whom the Eyaks have a relationship that is at times amicable enough and at other times so intense in its antipathy as to approach the

[85] The total number of people with blood ties to the Eyak tribe thought to remain is estimated to be about 100. Most of these live to the south of Cordova, beyond the range of the Eyak Corporation, and were included as members in other tribal corporations at the time ANCSA was enacted.

levels of race-hatred. The Eyaks, having suffered Russian incursions, then American incursion and domination in the copper mining days, and again incursion by the American fishing industry, have become a tribe on the verge of disappearing. Among their numbers remains one living speaker of the Eyak language, Marie Smith Jones, with whose death the language may well pass into extinction.[86] The deep ironies here in human culture as they relate to the preoccupations of environmentalists and scientists with ecosystem health, animal extinction, and diversity, as well as to the efforts of one part of the white culture to compel Alaskan Natives into assimilation, and of another part to keep them as they are — poor and *preserved* — become, I trust, manifest.

The Eyak Corporation did its first cutting in the Copper River Delta in 1992 in what is referred to by some as a "sport kill" — a trial balloon. Later that year and then on into 1993, the cutting continued and the log trucks began rolling through the town of Cordova to the great alarm of fishing people. These cuts, made by three different logging subcontractors, yielded, according to a former Eyak Corporation board member, Glen E. "Dune" Lankard (an Eyak Native), a net loss to Eyak's "wholly owned" logging subsidiary, Sherstone, Inc. Sherstone was created through a Byzantine set of maneuvers that began with the capitalization of Native Land by ANCSA, and then during the eighties by the Net Operating Loss tax scheme, which heightened the temptation for financially strapped Native corporations to convert their resources into dollars. In the case of the Eyak Corporation, the NOL tax scheme went approximately this way: In 1987, Eyak had 86,000 acres of timber appraised at $34 million. It purposely sold that timber at a loss for one million payable over 20 years, 10 percent down, to its own subsidiary, then sold the resulting $33 million paper "loss" for $11 million to a group of corporations (Del Webb, Hilton, Walgreens), who then wrote the $33 million loss off their own taxes. Through 1993, Eyak engaged in an even more labyrinthine set of buyouts, sellouts, and bank exchanges collateralized by NOL money that backed what would become an initial 15,000 acre cost-plus clear-cut, what is called the "Sheridan Cut," after the nearby Sheridan Glacier. After that, what remained was a $4 million debt, zero revenues for Eyak shareholders, and then going into 1993 a new contract for more extensive cutting with a major timber player, ITT Rayonier. Lankard's view was that the NOL scheme actually subsidized Eyak clear-cutting, while ANCSA,

[86] Michael Krauss, a linguist at the University of Alaska in Fairbanks, has dedicated much of his professional life to the Eyak language. He has compiled tapes, a dictionary, and texts in Eyak, and also speaks Eyak on occasion with Marie Smith Jones.

which he called "legalized cultural genocide," had created the necessity of extracting resources by capitalizing them in the first place.

Marie Smith Jones, a woman in her mid-seventies at the time, had been watching Dune Lankard for about a year as he challenged the corporation for not being responsive to shareholders. She told him that she would like to help him, that she'd "been waiting for someone like you to come along for sixty years." She would say, "He's got the know-how. I don't have the big doctor words. I'm the chief. I'm supposed to have a warrior, which Dune is. God sent him to me." A union soon evolved between the young firebrand and the elder chief, who herself was emerging from a lifetime of trouble that included, as she has publicly stated, alcoholism and abusive relationships, and who saw a last opportunity to assert her tribe's identity.

During the summer of 1993, Marie Smith Jones, Lankard, and a group of other Eyaks filed for a temporary restraining order against Eyak Corporation logging, claiming that trees were being cut on sacred Eyak ground.[87] They and a slowly increasing number of fellow advocates, engaged in what is called the "mini-blockade" by water (actually a "show" of protest by about 15 fishing boats), a temporary road blockade of a logging site in the delta, and the ceremonial internment of the skeletal remains of an Eyak man returned after resting in the Smithsonian Institution for 60 years. Marie was convinced that the bones belonged to an Eyak healer, and she saw the entire ceremony, to which townspeople and loggers had been invited, as a healing ritual. A year later, at the first potlatch the Eyak tribe would have had in decades, Rick Steiner and David Grimes were admitted as honorary tribal members as a mark of respect for their support.

Enter into this already complicated scenario a potential solution and yet another potent irony, *a deus ex machina* poised and ready to arrest the action by lowering vats of money into it — the *Exxon Valdez* settlement. Negotiations between the Trustee Council and the Eyak Corporation to bring an end to the logging by purchasing either Eyak trees by conservation easement or the land outright (fee simple) began soon after the settlement was resolved in 1991 and ran through a string of offers, rejections, and counter offers for several years. The process was complicated by political swings on

---

[87] The filing did delay logging for a time, but the temporary restraining order was eventually denied in court and the trees were cut. A resulting lawsuit appealed to the Alaska Supreme Court led to a precedent-setting 1996 opinion in favor of the Eyak tribe, granting them "public interest litigant status," thus freeing them from liability for the opposing Eyak Corporation's substantial legal fees. The court found that the Eyaks, and indeed any culture legitimately seeking to protect its sacred institutions and way of life, served the public interest and therefore should not be prevented from entering the court for fear of financial ruin.

the EVOS Trustee Council, shifting attitudes about the appropriateness of "habitat acquisition," and by Eyak Corporation efforts to continue to develop capital projects. A tricky and pivotal point in the negotiations upon which many, including Eyak Corporation people, the "dissident" Eyaks, and the Coastal Coalition people who were advocating forest protection, agreed was that Native people should expect continued access to the land in order to pursue traditional subsistence activities as well as to have its use for future revenue producing activity — possibly tourism. While certain environmental interests are enamored with the notion of completely off-limits "wilderness preserves," Lankard, Smith Jones, Steiner, Ott, Grimes, and many others believed that ecosystems were in fact more likely to be protected if there were also human habitation by those whose way of life required engagement with a healthy habitat.

Finally, one more set of ingredients came to be added to the long summer of 1993: the collapse of the pink salmon fishery, the fishermen's frustration with the EVOS Trustee Council's painstaking slow pace with releasing scientific assessments of the fishery and of the general condition of the sound, the pain and anxiety the logging caused them, and their ever-mounting fury at legal maneuvering and delays with the civil suit against Exxon for oil-spill-related damages into which several thousand complainants had joined. From this suit, fishermen hoped to recoup losses from fishery closures and failures during the years since 1989. By August 1993, the seine fleet, further piqued by Exxon's geared-up public relations campaign and its claim that health had been restored to Prince William Sound, was galvanized by Cordova fisherman Jim Gray's proposal to "call bullshit on Exxon's media blitz."

On August 19, the fleet abruptly abandoned the failed salmon run and set out that night in gale-force winds for the Port of Valdez. By the next morning, 65 seiners had gathered in Jack Bay, an inlet just off Valdez Narrows. More fishing boats were on their way. The fishermen awaited Exxon's *SeaRiver Baton Rouge*, which they planned to "symbolically blockade" and then escort to the terminal in hopes of raising awareness of their cause. They talked by radio and held impromptu conferences on one another's boats. Hours passed, and as the *Baton Rouge* missed its scheduled arrival time, the group which the fisherman Bill Webber described to me as "very determined and very edgy" then found itself actively contemplating the high-stakes intrigue of an actual blockade. The *Baton Rouge* further postponed its arrival to 5:00 P.M., then to 9:00, and then to the next day. In the meantime, other tankers scheduled after the Baton Rouge and not wishing to take the heat intended for Exxon, remained outside the sound, as well. When the last of the tankers taking on crude oil at the terminal left late on the night of August 20, the fishermen believed that for the first time since the opening of the Trans-Alaska Pipeline System in 1977, there was not a single tanker anywhere within the sound's 2,500 square miles.

I sailed from Cordova that night after the storm had abated. This was a passage I had by then made many times, and as we passed Knowles Head, where tankers normally await permission to enter Valdez Narrows, the anchorage seemed eerily quiet and peaceful, devoid of the humming ships lit up like factories. It was as if the place were stunned to rediscover its own skin of water and headland by which it had addressed the rest of the world for aeons. We turned northward, entered the tanker channel past the red warning light for Bligh Reef, easing against the ebb tide. Off to starboard, pale lights emerged through the mist from Jack Bay, where lay now a floating village of nearly 80 boats that extended deep into the tongue and hard upon the hump of land, silhouetted against the dawn. The next morning, informed that a British Petroleum chartered vessel had entered the sound, the flotilla deployed across Valdez Narrows. Tired of waiting for Exxon, British Petroleum decided to take matters into its own hands. Soon, the BP ship, *Atigun Pass*, appeared in the distance. A Coast Guard helicopter thumped in the air, and cutters prowled the water. Then more tankers, the *Arco Alaska* and at last the *Baton Rouge,* entered the sound. The flotilla didn't move. When asked by the Coast Guard what his intentions were, Jim Gray, who had emerged as the spokesman for the demonstrators, replied evenly, "Commander, I've lost control of my fleet."

Men, women, and children on the fishing boats put on survival suits and prepared for what fisherman Max McCarty referred to as "the last resort" of laying out their seines and creating a "quarter-mile-long, 65-foot-deep nylon barrier capable of choking even the giant prop of a supertanker." The *Atigun Pass* slowed to three knots but kept coming, growing ever larger against the horizon, until a BP executive in a helicopter high overhead ordered its captain to turn around. The fishermen had accomplished their primary objective, which according to Gray was to make a statement.

Governor Hickel's response was to say that "If I were a fisherman, I'd probably be out there, too." The local Coast Guard personnel seemed in the main sympathetic to the fishermen over Exxon, having gone through the trauma of the oil spill themselves, but a Coast Guard gunship from California was rapidly steaming its way toward Alaska with orders to break the blockade and see to the arrest of the demonstrators. President Clinton's Secretary of the Interior, Bruce Babbit, who as the fishermen had well known, happened to be in Alaska at the time, flew to Valdez. Three days after the blockade began, he met with representatives of the fishermen, and convinced them that they had reached the top of their curve and made their point. Now was the time to withdraw their boats. In exchange, he assured them that he would use his influence to encourage the Trustee Council to address the fishermen's demands, which they'd outlined in a "white paper" to use settlement funds for meaningful research, restoration of the ecosystem, and acquisition of forest land. The fishermen also requested a resolution to the stalled civil litigation against Exxon, and Babbit promised to look into the matter.

Trustee Council operations did become markedly more effective, perhaps because of Babbitt's influence, the soon-released and embarrassing GAO report, new administrative officers, and dogged public pressure. Rick Steiner, for one, would persistently track Trustee Council affairs through the several succeeding years, maintaining a steady correspondence, requesting pertinent material (employing the Freedom of Information Act when necessary), and sometimes filing for legal action. Later that year, the Trustee Council would begin to finalize agreements with some Native Corporations for forest protection or acquisition.

The civil trial would not open until May 9, 1994, and it would last through August 16.[88] Two striking consequences would emerge from it: first, the amount of the punitive damages award to plaintiffs from Exxon — $5 billion — and second, the revelation in the closing stages of the trial about a deal that Exxon had cut earlier with a group of seafood processors (the so-called "Seattle Seven") to whom Exxon had paid out a $70 million settlement for fishing losses. What was not known about the deal was that the Seattle Seven had agreed secretly that if there were a later award for punitive damages they would apply for their share of it, and then, also secretly, hand that money back to Exxon. This arrangement, and the fact that it had been kept from the notice of the court and its jurors, provoked a rebuke from 5th District Court Judge Russel Holland so sharp that it raised questions about possible censure by the Bar for Exxon attorneys. "What is really pernicious about the Seattle Seven issue," Judge Holland states in his Opinion, "is that Exxon sought to reduce its exposure to punitive damages twice: once by informing the jury of its voluntary payments to the seafood processors, and a second time through its secret agreement with the Seattle Seven. The court will not countenance Exxon's astonishing ruse and allow it to manipulate the jury and negate its verdict. Since the outset of *Exxon Valdez* litigation, the court has been singularly impressed with the apparently fair, professional, and responsible man-

---

[88] For a complete treatment of the civil trial, see the book, *Cleaning Up*, by David Lebedoff.

ner in which Exxon has managed its legal proceedings. Yet in this instance, Exxon has acted as a Jekyll and Hyde, behaving laudably in public, and deplorably in private. The court is shocked and disappointed that Exxon entered into such a repugnant agreement with the Seattle Seven. Although the court does not so find, it is probable that more than one of the many attorneys who represent Exxon and the Seattle Seven violated Rule 3.3 of the Alaska Rules of Professional Conduct requiring candor toward the tribunal."

An Exxon request for a new trial on the grounds that one of the jurors was harassed into agreement with the amount of the punitive damages was denied late in 1998. Exxon's appeal of the decision is expected to be heard in January, 1999.

I had met with Dune Lankard on several occasions, including in March of 1995 when we flew over Eyak forest lands, which at that time were still the subject of intense dispute. As we ascended from the Cordova airport, the expanse of the Copper River Delta opened itself before us in the curious way landscape has of seeming to rise to the eye even as the eye rises from it. We passed over the Scott River, one of several that wound their way into the flatland and fed into the big one — the Copper River itself. Behind us to the north lay the Chugach Mountains. To the east lay more of the flats and the broad mouth of the big river opening into the sea. The Egg Islands became visible along the horizon to the south, marking the outer limit between the Copper River Flats and the Gulf of Alaska, and the southeastern edge of the sound. Rounded and low, from this distance they did indeed look like eggs. They were the color of pale brown eggs, unlike the other dark, basaltic islands. Above them floated a heavy bank of luminous gray storm clouds, headed for the sound. We passed over the Sheridan Cut and Eyak Lake, where more cutting was threatened, over Cordova and out into the edge of the sound.

We were communicating through headsets in the small Cessna, and as we went Dune talked to me, showing me where the "sport kill" had been, the Sheridan Cut, and where in the woods Eyak burial sites and two old village sites were. At that time, he was actively considering filing another request for a temporary restraining order. "There'll be no profit if they cut more," he said. "The roads cost one-fifty to two hundred thousand per mile and the corporation will have to cover that cost." We flew through the slot between mountains and turned up Orca Narrows toward Shepherd Point, passing along the inside of Channel Island and over the "old cannery," what Dune told me was the last subsistence site of the Eyak people and where now the

Chugach Corporation proposed to build a deep water port for shipping and tourism. Soon, we passed over Nelson Bay and came upon Sheep Bay and flew over it into the Rude River Valley. Dense stands of hemlock and spruce lay before us, bounded by forbidding walls of rock. Out of the head of the canyon tumbled the tumultuous river, a line of froth glimmering in and out of our sight. "It's so beautiful here," Dune said softly. "It's an old hunting ground. Just looking at it, you can see why it's so important to protect it. So, we'll be happy enough if the Trustees purchase timber rights to it all." The small plane jittered and bumped in the air currents as we banked hard near to the precipitous slope at the back of the valley, and turned a loop to take us out again over the water. The black and the green and then the aquamarine rushed by us as we flew toward the approaching clouds.

The day before, I'd talked with another former Eyak Corporation board member, the main mover of the logging enterprise and the president of Sherstone, Luke Borer. He would tell me that Dune was interested mainly in money, but when I asked for details and an explanation, he declined to respond, stating only that "Lankard has cost the corporation hundreds of thousands of dollars" through his legal actions. Borer had a merchant's view of the forest and the corporation: Their essence lay in the capital they represented.

Luke Borer took me on a drive ten miles east of Cordova on the Copper River Highway into the delta — a small piece of the terrain Dune and I would fly over. As we rode along, he said, "It's some of the most beautiful land in the world, and yes, timber harvesting is ugly. All the board members don't like logging. But five to seven years from now it'll all be green again." His remarks put me in mind of a comment the corporation president, Kathyrn Anderson, had made about the stripped-away hills: "It's gorgeous. Now you can see all our lands."

Borer was a fit man of Aleut extraction, and the stepson of Margie Johnson, the new pro-development mayor of Cordova who'd defeated Kelly Weaverling in the election by one vote. He lifted a hand off the steering wheel and gestured toward what he claimed were clear-cuts of forty and fifty years ago — one just outside town on the far side of Eyak Lake, another near the Cordova airport. He pointed out stumps in the woods and large spruce and hemlock trees, saying that forests had been clear-cut out at the new site on Orca Bay, too. "Some of the shareholders' ancestors did clear-cutting," he said, without explaining how they did it or what ancestors he was referring to. "The regeneration cycle is 80 to 120 years to harvest."[89]

He turned down a gravel road and we came out at the Sheridan Cut. Borer's stated objective was to show me how the seedlings were regenerating already, but there was absolutely no such evidence. A solitary scraggly two-foot spruce stood off the edge of the roadway. Hundreds of acres of gray slash and disgorged stumps were piled chest-high all the way to the distant, glaciated slopes. I took Borer himself to be a little daunted by the prospect before us, or even lost for a moment in its desolation. As if to grant this, he said, "We want to start up another enterprise with some of the money. We want to use the land in some fashion that's non-consumptive."

Dune Lankard had scoffed at the enormous irony in Borer's comment when I mentioned it to him on our overflight the next day. "Then what's he doing?" Dune asked.

The day after that, Dune took me to meet his sister, Pamela Smith, at her house just outside Cordova. Smith's primary energies had come to be directed toward rediscovering her people's nearly lost traditions, to seek out identity in that fashion. We sat at her kitchen table, eating from a dish of salmon that she'd smoked and put up. At her elbow rested a small skin drum she had made for the spring potlatch. Outside lay two feet of snow dropped by the storm that had blown in the day before, and a bleaching light flooded through the windows. A daughter was home sick from school, and now and again Smith would get up and go to a nearby room to check on the young girl. Smith told me that she'd had a moment of discovery, a life change, when she had questioned corporation policies concerning the logging in a meeting and was "accused by an elder of asking 'white man' questions. That's when the picture came clear to me," she said. "What were we trying to hide here? When one of us [Eyaks] starts speaking, we're called dissidents and rabble-rousers."

While Pamela was poised and calm, her brother, seated near to her, bristled with energy. Smart, passionate, and handsome, formerly a high-school basketball star, he had by then surely become a political force. He said, "We're not dissidents. We're descendants. What Luke won't say is that to them the

---

[89] Steve Bodnar, an independent Cordova researcher working under a U.S. Forest Service contract with Paul Alaback of the University of Montana on forest regeneration cycles in Prince William Sound, asserted that the cycle to maturity in this region is more likely to be 200 years, and that Borer's figures might have been drawn from a more southerly location, possibly Southeast Alaska. Bodnar also said that none of the forests Borer pointed out to me had ever been clear-cut, but rather logged selectively in the 1910s and 20s, decades before the advent of the chain saw.

corporation's a holding. To us it's a way of life. What they're trying to do is intimidate the shareholders so they don't ask questions. But once they start asking questions, they see they've been taken advantage of. Shareholders come up to me and say, 'You keep going at them. We're wondering when you're going to get shot.'"

I had taken an interest in the drum on the table, and on our way out, Pamela led me through the knee-deep snow to the woodshed where she kept another drum she'd made, a big one a good three feet across with a pale skin drawn taut over one side of the ribwork. It was a fine piece of work, meticulously made, and deep and resonant in its sound. When I expressed my admiration, Pamela smiled with pleasure. I couldn't help but ask her what songs her people played, and she looked away for a moment, then back, saying, "We don't know our songs anymore. We sing some of the Tlingit songs that we know."

In 1998 a deal would be finally struck between the Trustee Council and the Eyak Corporation. In a combination of fee simple purchases and conservation or timber conservation easements, the Trustee Council would protect nearly 70,000 acres of Eyak lands, including those near Port Gravina, Sheep Bay, Simpson Bay, Nelson Bay, across the Narrows at Windy Bay, and around Eyak Lake. These are added to acquisitions and conservation easements previously arranged with Native corporations by the Trustee Council on or near Chenega Bay, English Bay, Port Graham, Kenai Fjords, Kachemak Bay, Seal Bay, and on Afognak and Kodiak Islands. The Council has now spent about $350 million[90] on acquisitions and protective arrangements for over 650,00 acres.

Not everyone is satisfied, of course, and the ironies of history and present intent persist. A troubling issue continues to be the fee simple sale of some of the parcels versus the sale of conservation easements for habitat conservation. Many Natives in the region, such as Dune Lankard, have wished to be part of restoration but not on the condition of selling away ancestral lands by whole cloth to the same government from which they were so hard won in the first place. The Trustee Council, not always content to just buy timber

[90] As of 1998, Trustee Council estimates of total expenditures through the end of the settlement revenues are: reimbursements to governments and Exxon, $213 million; research, monitoring and restoration, $180 million; habitat acquisition and protection, $392 million; science management, public information, and administration, $31 million; and funds set aside in a restoration reserve, $108 million. A second GAO report issued in 1998, found that most of the shortcomings noted in the 1993 report had been addressed and corrected. An exception was "redundant" science.

rights in perpetuity from Native landowners, has often insisted that no habitat deals would be done without outright sale. Traditional peoples with ancestral ties to the land continue to be encircled by three beasts: the colonialist mindset of government and industry that encourages the rape of the land, their own "Native" corporations that have come to ape the rapists, and finally, a mirror image, those environmentatlists who would re-make natural habitat into untouchable, virginal gardens. Lankard responds with his own triumvirate, saying that the future of the Eyaks resides in what he calls the three S's — "spirituality, sovereignty, and subsistence."

Dune Lankard, Rick Steiner, David Grimes, Marie Smith Jones, and Riki Ott (now deeply involved with a new organization — the Copper River Watershed Project) all hold to the belief that the most meaningful way to restore the oil spill region is to protect both the wild habitat and those life-supporting human economies attendant upon it. This is hardly a novel idea, but rather one quite in sympathy with the principles of bioregionalism and reinhabitiation as articulated by a number of environmental theorists, including Peter Berg, Raymond Dasmann, Gerry Mander, and Stephanie Mills. Here, however, and at the very moment of this writing, ways of reestablishing a sustainable mode of conduct that will be watchful of the world, respectful even when harvest is required, and that will finally grant the fullness of all of life include modest, selective, value-added logging, and properly managed fishing, along with subsistence activities, requires a very different kind of consciousness from that with which the mainstream in our culture has so far made its approach.

Grimes, who likes to quote Vice President Al Gore's statement in his book, *Earth in the Balance* — "research in lieu of action is unconscionable" — lays out a basic case in which he conjoins the response to the depredations of both the oil spill and timber clear-cutting by saying that "only time and mother nature will heal the ecosystem's wounds. Thus, as human healers, our triage work should follow the Hippocratic oath and 'First, do no more harm.'" Although a scientist himself, Rick Steiner has long been particularly provoked by Trustee Council expenditures on research. A couple of years ago in a moment of vitriole, he said to me, "This is already the most studied oil spill in history. I am absolutely furious at the self-centeredness of science. If they could spend all the money on science, they would. A lot of what they've done is so-what science. We know oil is bad for seals. Why do we need to know every excruciating detail about how oil affects seals' brains?" There were echoes in his statement of John Oliver's parable of the can full of oil with all the scientists holding their cups out to it, hoping to catch some of the lucre but not to dirty themselves in the process. By implication, what Rick was addressing was the seemingly unassailable class advantage of the whole of the American scientific establishment, well-heeled and smart as it is, often wedded to powerful goverment and corporate forces, and often assuming the mindset that it is nothing more than the prestidigitating, incisive edge of American opportunism.

But when I last talked to Rick not long ago, he surprised me by acknowledging that everything considered, he and the Coastal Coalition had accomplished "ninety percent of what they could have hoped for." In my judgment, his estimate seemed a little high. I'd have said — maybe 75 percent — but I understood the proviso in his phrase — "what we could have hoped for" — and also that he and the others had certainly succeeded with one very important thing, which was to convince the Trustee Council that habitat protection in some form constituted a viable and necessary use of settlement funds. His words, and the unmistakable fatigue, or even sadness that I sensed in his voice took me back to when I'd first talked with him at length in 1990 down in Sitka Sound. We were on a boat that was following two humpback whales. The whales swam in the shadows near the shoreline, scouting a herring school. Their long dark backs were visible to us. Periodically, they dove, one after another, lifting their flukes to the air. Their method of capture was to swim upwards in circles from the deep, beginning beneath the fish. As the whales circled, they released air, creating a curtain of bubbles called a "bubble net." It was an original form of seining, actually, although in this case the net was an illusion. The herring apparently considered themselves trapped, and their impulse was to swim higher and higher to try to get over the top, but of course the bubbles that made the net also rose to the surface.

From the boat, what we saw was the dark whales cruising the surface, then turning downwards. Their flukes hung for an instant as the animals gathered themselves for the dive. Then there was a quietude, nothing at all on the surface, and then a white circle of bubbles appeared on the water, often a good distance away from where the whales had dived. In another moment, the herring suddenly appeared, scores of them desperately churning the surface inside the ring. They seemed frantic. They looked like knives cutting repeatedly through the water as they tried to fly straight up into the air. One of the whales (they took turns at this) breached the water with its huge jaws agape, the inside of its mouth white against its dark body, the dark water, and dark shore as it gulped the fish. Finally, the whale settled back into the water, cruising and blowing a cloud of vapor.

Rick and I had been talking admiringly of the whales, and of pollution and whales, since we were not far from the Alaska Pulp Corporation that disgorged a brown discharge into the bay. Since that time, the mill has closed down. Our conversation turned to what he was most concerned with even way back then — clear-cutting, habitat fragmentation, the breaking up of habitats that is caused by logging, development, by the noise of machines, the trampling of humans coming *en masse*. We talked about genetic diversity and the exquisitely balanced chaos of the world. He was filled with vinegar and combative enthusiasm. It occurred to me that the trick was to enter the chaos, not to control it, not to wipe it out with one form of monomania or another, not to turn away from it in defeat or deceit, and yet at the same time to hold fast to a sense of right conduct, to keep looking outward, to try not to get trapped inside the illusory nets our culture has ready-made for us. At the time, I also remembered the description Bruce Martin gave me of the dimensions of the world as we two stood at the *Alpha Helix's* rail looking out on the *Exxon Valdez* — the several of those dimensions always simultaneously present, and among them the so-called real and spiritual always indivisible from each other. That, and Rick Steiner's vibrant energy, his readiness to step out into battle, remain resonant in my memory as the ringing core of the best that would come to pass in the late-century event of the Alaskan oil spill.

I have learned to be angry with the scale of American consumption and aggression, with the ruthless and estranging mindlessness of it all, the tons upon tons of our waste, our arrogant posture of superiority, our newfound propensity in the millisecond of history to become the world's supercorporate state and to accept all the encirclements that go with that — funding oppression and environmental destruction abroad, launching missile strikes willy-nilly to make our point clear, and the enormous anti-critical whitewashing of commercially driven information. But I can also see that Martin's old alert way of thinking and Rick Steiner's purposeful action exemplify the best and only possible remedy. I long to be in the company of the remarkable people I met at Prince William Sound — Rick Steiner, David Grimes, Pamela Smith, Dune Lankard, Marie Smith Jones, Bruce Martin, John Oliver, Larry Smith, Riki Ott, Craig Matken, Eva Saulitas, and the many of them.

In my protracted witnessing of the story here recounted, I perceived that the hope lies in what these people have done to embrace the weight of contradiction, the tumult of the world's chaos, even its fearsome extinctions, to resist the powerful forces that make tempting a comfortable state of powerlessness, and to take heart and go forward nevertheless. However much these people might have wished for it, they did not truly expect their dreams or their vision of what was right to be perfectly realized. There is no perfect accomplishment, nor any perfectly satisfying redress for wrongs, just as there never was any such thing as pristine, but even so, burdened and compromised as they might have felt, or weary though they now may be, they have managed to part the net and to brighten the way into a more metaphysic and less alien dark.

NOTES

The principal sources for this book have been, first, the experience as told to me by the residents of south-central Alaska, and second, the accounts of those in official capacities with federal, state, and local governments, and with the Exxon Corporation. In addition, beginning on the day of the oil spill, government agencies and private and public institutions have generated vast quantities of written material in the form of press or public information releases and memoranda. When such documents contained significant information, my approach was to check them one against another and whenever possible to speak directly to people in the institutions. These sources have been cited in the text.

Certain documents, articles, and books proved central to the original edition. Among the documents are the National Transportation Safety Board

(NTSB) hearings, *The Grounding of the U.S. Tankship Exxon Valdez;* the Alaska Superior Court transcripts of the trial of Joseph Hazelwood; the Alaska Oil Spill Commission's four-volume publication, *Spill: The Wreck of the Exxon Valdez;* Engineering Computer Optecnomics' *An Assessment of Tanker Transportation Systems in Cook Inlet and Prince William Sound*; the National Oceanic and Atmospheric Administration's daily overflight charts of the course of the oil spill; and the *State and Federal Natural Resource Damage Assessment Plan for the Exxon Valdez Oil Spill.* For the new edition, the annual *Status Report* and *State/Federal Natural Resource Damage Assessment and Restoration Plan* issued by the *Exxon Valdez* Oil Spill Trustee Council (EVOSTC) have been regularly examined, as have numerous in-house white papers and documents from the Eyak Native Corporation, the Coastal Coalition and media relations reports from Exxon, Alyeska, and the *Exxon Valdez* Oil Spill Trustee Council. The last group of sources are for the most part not listed in the bibliography.

The books and articles I consulted fell into two general categories. Some provided scientific and technical information. Among the most useful of these were the National Academy of Science's *Oil in the Sea: Inputs, Fates, and Effects* and *Using Oil Dispersants on the Sea*; Lou and Nancy Barr's *Under Alaskan Seas*; Pete Mickelson's *Natural History of Alaska's Prince William Sound*; D. K. Button's work on terpenes; and James Payne and Daniel McNabb, Jr.'s work on oil in the marine environment. Other works provided a sense of historical and intellectual context. Among these, I was especially attentive to Thomas Berger's *Village Journey: The Report of the Alaska Native Review Commission*; Robert Engler's *The Brotherhood of Oil* and *The Politics of Oil*; Morgan Sherwood's *Exploration of Alaska*: 1865–1900; Susan Sontag's *On Photography*; Walter Mead's *Mortal Splendor: The American Empire in Transition*; and William Carlos Williams's *In the American Grain.*

For the first two or three years following the oil spill, there was intense and often overlapping newspaper coverage in and out of Alaska, and after that time, bursts of coverage as important developments ensued, such as the 1991 settlement agreement between Exxon and the state and federal governments. I have regularly read the newspapers listed in the bibliography, but have cited them as sources only when the material is explicit and critical.

Between the first and second editions of this book, there has been extensive magazine journalism and scholarly and scientific writing produced in connection with the oil spill, some but not all of which will be cited in my bibliography. After Art Davidson's *In The Wake of the Exxon Valdez: The Devastating Impact of the Alaska Oil Spill* (1990), and my own book, a third book

that undertakes comprehensive discussion has appeared: Jeff Wheelwright's
Degrees of Disaster. Although Wheelwright's work and mine disagree on several basic issues, including the relationship of adjacent forest and marine habitats, his treatment of spill-connected scientific inquiry would make a good counterpart to my account. Two other books of importance are David Lebedoff's account of the civil action suit against Exxon, *Cleaning Up*, and Conrad Smith's *Media and Apocalypse*. It should be noted that the Oil Spill Public Information Center Library in Anchorage maintains an excellent collection of books and documents.

The references that immediately follow, named by author, or sometimes by title and date in the case of periodicals and documents, are to works listed in the bibliography.

Chapter 1. INTRUDERS

The naming of Bligh Island, whether by Cook or Vancouver, is variously reported. See Pethick, p. 178. Cook first gave the name Sandwich to the sound, then King William Sound. Subsequently the name was changed to Prince William Sound. See Cook (ed. Price), p. 228.

Chapter 2. THE SCREENS ON THE STAGE

For the account of Fidalgo's exploration and the naming of the port after him, see Lethcoe, p. 34. Early history of settlement and development is derived from Naske and Slotnick, passim. For an account of ANCSA and its effects see Berger, passim, and for subsistence see Berger, Stratton and Chisum, and Stanek, passim. For the death of Cook, see Cook (ed. Price), p. 255 ff., and for the personal history of Joseph Hazelwood, see *Time*, July 24, 1989. Background material on the oil industry was derived largely from Engler (both books), passim. For somewhat different perspectives, see also Adelman, Turner, and Sampson. Oil earnings figures are derived from industry accounts and Horton, p. 57. Production figures are taken from R. Smith, pp. 4-5. For accounts of Alyeska's troubles with pollution regulations and mechanical breakdowns, see the hearings of the National Transportation Safety Board, passim; LaResche, "Appendix C"; *Anchorage Daily News* (Epler), October 22, 1989 and October 29, 1989; Horton, p. 58 ff.; *Wall Street Journal* (McCoy), July 6, 1989; and Davidson, p. 79, passim. For quoted material from Eward, Woodle, Blake, Lawn, and Tom McCarty, see *Wall Street Journal* (McCoy), July 6, 1989; for quoted material from LaResche and Lawn, see Davidson, p. 94, and p. 83 ff.; for quoted material from Purtell, see Luoma. The material on the *Thompson Pass* spill is reported in Davidson, pp. 5-7 and corroborated in conversation with Charles Hamel. For information on the Alaskan tankerage fleet, see Luoma, *passim*, and Bell, *passim*. Material regarding Ott's experience is derived from interviews with her and from her "O.C., Inc.," *passim*.

Chapter 3. THE CHANNEL

My own observation of Prince William Sound was augmented by Dold and Soucie, and Mickelson, *passim*.

Chapter 4. THE IMAGINARY JOURNEY OF CAPTAIN JOSEPH HAZELWOOD

For events pursuant to the grounding of the *Exxon Valdez*, see the Superior Court transcripts of the Joseph Hazelwood trial, the NTSB hearings, LaResche, transcripts of the civil action suit, and Lebedoff, all *passim*. When the accounts vary the court transcripts are given precedence. For the misidentified blood samples and 1990 Coast Guard hearings, see *Anchorage Daily News* (Deutsch and Campbell), July 26, 1990, and Lebedoff. For Hazelwood's personal history see *Time*, July 24, 1989. For the results of the Coast Guard study, see Bell, *passim*. Information on Hazelwood's current status derived from conversation with Tom Russo of the law firm, Chalos and Brown. For a complete account of the 1996 civil trial, see Lebedoff. Additional information regarding the grounding was obtained from the transcripts of the 1996 civil trial, and from transcripts of FBI interviews conducted in early April, 1989, the latter acquired through the Freedom of Information Act. Neither Captain Hazelwood's nor Third Mate Cousin's interviews were included among the released FBI transcripts.

Chapter 5. CITY LIFE

Here and elsewhere, the chronology of the spill and response is derived from Lethcoe and Nurnberger, pp. 1-4, and from *Spill: The Wreck of the Exxon Valdez*, vol. 4, *passim*. For material on the Alyeska response, see the 1987 *Alyeska Oil Spill Contingency Plan*. Many of the pertinent facts within the *Plan* are also widely reported in books and articles. For specific Alyeska failures according to the *Plan*, see Davidson, *passim*; Horton, p. 57 ff.; *Wall Street Journal* (McCoy), July 6, 1989; *New York Times*, April 3, 1989; and *Anchorage Daily News* (Epler), October 22, 1989 and October 29, 1989. For quoted material from Ott, see Davidson, p. 26; for the account of Steiner's observation flight (subsequently confirmed in conversation with Steiner), see Sims, p. 42; and for quoted material from Brennan, see Horton, p. 58. The attempts to use dispersants are recounted in testimony before the National Transportation Safety Board (especially Iarossi, Kelso, and McCall). See also Davidson, p. 29 ff. For the Exxon suit against the state of Alaska, see *Anchorage Daily News* (Toomey), October 24, 1989. For information on the regulations applying to the use of dispersants in Prince William Sound and on the nature of dispersants, see 1987 *Oil Spill Contingency Plan*, pp. 3–51ff.; Lethcoe and Nurnberger, pp. 38–53; and Butler, passim. For material quoted from Butler, see p. 249. Updated and footnoted material in this chapter concerning lightering operations and the quantity of oil spilled is drawn from accounts, expert analyses, and ullage reports contained in documents from the Oil Spill Public Information Center Library, *Volume of Oil Spilled Documents*, recorded under the number "COL-00025."

Chapter 6. CORDOVA

Material from Kumins is as cited in the text. My conversations with Cordovans are augmented by the account in Sims, and in Ott, "O.C., Inc.," passim. The quotation from Steiner concerning logistical support is drawn from Davidson, p. 110. Regarding Copeland's efforts, see Davidson, p. 109. Weaverling's account, as told to me, is augmented by information in Davidson, p. 134 ff. For salmon spawning, see Netboy, p. 32 ff. For toxic effects on herring, see Kocan, passim.

Chapter 7. SHOWTIME

Don Moore's statement is recorded in the video, *Voices of the Sound*. Bill Allen's personal history and information regarding Veco International are drawn from various newspaper accounts, including *Anchorage Daily News*, November 21, 1989 (Mauer), an internal memo from Veco's marketing division by Todd Bureau, and from *Alaska Business Monthly*, October 1990 (Tyson). For a complete account of Veco and Allen's role in the gray whale rescue operation, see Rose. For the quoted material from Yost, see Davidson, p. 124.

Chapter 8. THE TEARS OF SCIENCE

For atmospheric and marine conditions, see *Spill: The Wreck of the Exxon Valdez*, vol. 2, pp. ii–1 ff. For the chemistry and behavior of oil, see Payne and McNabb, passim, Butler, passim, and Lethcoe and Nurnberger (Ott), pp. 30-37.

Chapter 9. THE RAPTURE OF MACHINES

For supplementary data on marine life, see Barr, passim. The test beach controversy was presented in the *Anchorage Daily News* on February 20, 1990 (Wohlforth) and March 2, 1990 (Maki). The quotations by Yost and Robbins are from Davidson, pp. 124,190.

Chapter 10. THE RAPTURE OF SCIENCE

Abstracts of research administered by the EVOSTC contained in the annually released *Natural Resource Damage Assessment and Restoration Plan*.

Chapter 11. GUESTS

For comparative data on the Sullom Voe and Alyeska Contingency Plans, see Lethcoe and Nurnberger (Ott), pp. 102–3.

Chapter 12. THE VALUE OF THE DEAD

Supplementary information on the response of Kenai Peninsula people, including the "bird burning" and Gore Point material, has been derived from the *Homer News*, March–July 1989. For quoted material from Flagg, see Davidson, p. 257. As noted in the text, for "contingency valuation" see Krutilla, and Freeman and Kopp, passim.

Chapter 13. SELDOVIA

Supplementary information is derived from accounts in the *Homer News*. For the response from Kenai Fjords National Park, also see Davidson, p. 240 ff.

Chapter 14. THE TRUTH ABOUT OIL

For background information on crude oil, see Payne and McNabb, Gourlay, Steele, Butler, Neff, and Baker, all passim. See also Lethcoe and Nurnberger (Ott), pp. 30–35. For results of bioremediation field tests, see Levin and Gealt, "Chapter 12" (Pritchard).

Chapter 15. CRAPS

Passages from the text of Meganack's address are drawn from Frost, pp. 6–8. McMullen's remarks are reported in the *Anchorage Daily News*, June 19, 1989. For Engler's description, see Engler, "Portrait of an Oil Spill."

Chapter 16. MASKS

For Alaska magazine background material, see Davidson, p. 207.

Chapter 17. NO ROAD

Some of the late 1989 and early 1990 information is drawn from the *Cordova Times*. Information concerning the herring fishery from Korcan, passim. Information concerning the pink salmon fishery from Mundy, passim. Additional information on fisheries from the Alaska Department of Fish and Game and the EVOSTC "Status Reports." The Shee Atika NOL scheme was reported in the *Anchorage Daily News* (Hal Benton), March 18, 1990.

Chapter 18. GHOSTS

Information on bioremediation field tests drawn from Levin and Gealt, "Chapter 12" (Pritchard).

Conclusion. THE BUBBLE NET

Wildlife mortality figures have been widely reported, beginning with the *Anchorage Daily News*, October 8, 1989. Oil pollution statistics are drawn from Hyland, p. 493. Information on Alyeska and tanker traffic preparedness derived from Stan Jones, passim, and from information provided by Alyeska Media Relations. Information on Caspian Sea oil from "On Piping Out Caspian Oil," *New York Times*, Stephen Kinzer, November 8, 1998. Rehabilitation costs are derived from Exxon press material, substantiated at a slightly lower figure by EVOSTC assessments. For cleanup assessment, see Foster, passim. For the quotation by Cowles, see *Anchorage Daily News*, December 28, 1989. For information on animal health and mortality, see, Andres, Kuletz, Frost, Brown and Carls, Matkin and Saulitas, and EVOSTC *Resource Damage Assessments*. For the NOAA response to Exxon science, see NOAA. For an account of the 1998 BP/Coast Guard oil spill drill and Devens' remarks, see *RCAC Observer*, v.8, no. 3. Information on the oil spill settlement and *EVOSTC* drawn from numerous contemporaneous newspaper accounts, including the *Anchorage Daily News, New York Times, Business Insurance,* and *Alaska's Marine Resources*, v. VII, no. 3, and also from settlement documents and EVOSTC Status Reports. Information on Prince William Sound logging drawn in part from contemporaneous accounts in the *Anchorage Daily News* and the *Cordova Times*. For terpenes, see Button and Button and Juttner, passim. For The Coastal Coalition's proposal, see Steiner, passim. For information on the Eyak people and language, see Krauss, Enge, and De Laguna. For information on coastal rainforests, see Alaback, passim. Other general information on events since 1991 drawn from conversations with David Grimes, Riki Ott, Rick Steiner, Dune Lankard, Luke Borer, and Marie Smith Jones.

SELECTED
BIBLIOGRAPHY

BOOKS

Adelman, M. A. *The World Petroleum Market.* Baltimore: Johns Hopkins University Press, 1972.

The Alaska Almanac. 1989 ed. Edmonds and Anchorage: Alaska Northwest Books, 1989.

Alvarez, A. *Offshore: A North Sea Journey.* Boston: Houghton Mifflin Co., 1986.

Armstrong, Robert H. *Guide to the Birds of Alaska.* Anchorage: Alaska Northwest Publishing Co., 1983.

Arvidson, Rose C. *Cordova, The First 75 Years, a Photographic History.* Cordova: Fathom Publishing Co., 1984.

Barr, Lou, and Nancy Barr. *Under Alaska Seas*. Anchorage: Alaska Northwest Publishing Co., 1983.

Berg, Peter, ed. *Reinhabiting a Separate Country: A Bioregional Anthology of Northern California*. San Francisco: Planet Drum Books, 1978.

Berger, Thomas R. *Village Journey: The Report of the Alaska Native Review Commission*. New York: Hill and Wang, 1985.

Brody, Hugh. *Maps and Dreams*. New York: Pantheon Books, 1982.

Brundtland, Gro Harlem, et al. *Our Common Future: World Commission on Environment and Development*. Oxford and New York: Oxford University Press, 1987.

Butler, James N., et al. National Research Council. *Using Oil Spill Dispersants on the Sea*. Washington, D.C.: National Academy Press, 1989.

Cook, James. *The Journals of Captain James Cook on His Voyages of Discovery*. Edited by J. C. Beaglehole. Vols. 1–4. Cambridge: Hakluyt Society, 1955-67.

Cook, James. *The Explorations of Captain James Cook in the Pacific as Told by Selections of his Own Journals 1768-1779*. Edited by A. Grenfell Price. New York: Dover, 1971.

Darwin, Charles. *The Origin of Species*. New York: NAL Penguin, 1958.

Davidson, Art. *In the Wake of the Exxon Valdez: The Devastating Impact of the Alaska Oil Spill*. San Francisco: Sierra Club Books, 1990.

Dumond, Don E. *The Eskimos and Aleuts*, rev. ed. New York: Thames and Hudson, 1987.

Engler, Robert. *The Brotherhood of Oil*. Chicago: University of Chicago Press, 1977.

————, *The Politics of Oil*. New York: Macmillan, 1961.

Gourlay, K. A. *Poisoners of the Seas*. London and Atlantic Highlands, New Jersey: Zed Books, Ltd., 1988.

Greene, William N. *Strategies of the Major Oil Companies*. Ann Arbor: UMI Research Press, 1982.

Heise, Kathy, Graeme Ellis, and Craig Matkin. *A Catalogue of Prince William Sound Killer Whales*. Homer: North Gulf Ocean Society, 1992.

Johnson, Jon F.C., ed. *Eyak Legends of the Copper River Delta, Alaska*. Anchorage: Chugach Heritage Foundation,1983.

Klein, Janet. *A History of Kachemak Bay: The Country, The Communities*. Homer: Homer Society of Natural History, 1987.

Kundera, Milan. T*he Art of the Novel*. Transl. by Linda Asher, New York: Grove Press, 1986.

Langdon, Steve J. *The Native People of Alaska*. Anchorage: Greatland Graphics, 1987.

Lebedoff, David. *Cleaning Up: The Story Behind the Biggest Legal Bonanza of Our Time*. New York and London: The Free Press, 1997.

Lethcoe, Jim, and Nancy R. Lethcoe. *Cruising Guide to Prince William Sound*. Valdez: Prince William Sound Books, 1985.

Lethcoe, Nancy R., and Lisa Nurnberger. *Prince William Sound Environmental Reader 1989—TV Exxon Valdez Oil Spill*. Valdez: Prince William Sound Conservation Alliance, 1989.

Levin, Morris A., and Michael A. Gealt, eds. *Biotreatment of Industrial and Hazardous Waste*. New York: McGraw-Hill, Inc., 1993.

Mangusso, Mary Childers, and Stephen W. Haycox, eds. *Interpreting Alaska's History: An Anthology*. Anchorage: Alaska Pacific University Press, 1989.

Matkin, Craig. *An Observer's Guide to the Killer Whales of Prince William Sound*. Valdez: Prince William Sound Books, 1994.

Mills, Stephanie. *In The Service of the Wild: Restoring and Reinhabiting Damaged Land*. Boston: Beacon Press, 1995.

Mickelson, Pete. *Natural History of Alaska's Prince William Sound*. Cordova: Alaska Wild Wings, 1989.

Muir, John. *Travels in Alaska*. San Francisco: Sierra Club Books, 1988.

Naske, Claus-M., and Herman E. Slotnick. *Alaska, A History of the 49th State*, 2nd ed. Norman and London: University of Oklahoma Press, 1987.

Nelson, Richard K. *Hunters of the Northern Forest*. Chicago: University of Chicago Press, 1986.

Netboy, Anthony. *Salmon: The World's Most Harassed Fish*. Tulsa: Winchester Press, 1980.

O'Donoghue, Brian. *Black Tides: The Alaska Oil Spill*. Anchorage: Alaska Natural History Association, 1989.

Pethick, Derek. *First Approaches to the Northwest Coast*. Seattle: University of Washington Press, 1979.

Picou, J. Steven, Duane A. Gill and Maurie J. Cohen, eds. *The Exxon Valdez Disaster: Readings on a Modern Social Problem*. Dubuque: Kendall Hunt Publishing Co., 1997.

Repetto, Robert, ed. *The Global Possible: Resources, Development, and the New Century*. New Haven and London: Yale University Press, 1985.

Robinson, Marilynne. *Mother Country: Britain, the Welfare State and Nuclear Pollution*. New York: Farrar, Straus, and Giroux, 1989.

Rose, Tom. *Freeing the Whales: How the Media Created the World's Greatest Non-Event*. New York: Carol Publishing, 1989.

Sampson, Anthony. *The Seven Sisters: The Great Oil Companies and the World They Shaped*. New York: Viking Press, 1975.

Sherwood, Morgan B. *Exploration of Alaska: 1865–1900*. New Haven and London: Yale University Press, 1965.

Smith, Conrad. *Media and Apocalypse: News Coverage of the Yellowstone Forest Fires, Exxon Valdez Oil Spill, and Loma Prieta Earthquake*. Westport: Greenwood Press, 1992.

Sontag, Susan. *On Photography*. New York: Farrar, Straus, and Giroux, 1977.

Steele, John H., et al. *Oil in the Sea, Inputs, Fates, and Effects*. Washington, D.C.: National Academy Press, 1985.

Turner, Louis. *Oil Companies in the International System*. London: The Royal Institute of International Affairs/George Allen and Unwin, 1978.

Wheelwright, Jeff. *Degrees of Disaster*. New York: Simon and Schuster, 1994.

Whitaker, John O., Jr. *The Audubon Society Field Guide to North American Mammals*. New York: Alfred A. Knopf, 1980.

Williams, William Carlos. *In the American Grain*. New York: New Directions Books, 1925, 1956.

ARTICLES, OFFPRINTS, PAMPHLETS

Alaback, Paul. "Ecological Characteristics of Temperate Rainforests: A Broadscale Perspective on the Forests of Prince William Sound." Unpublished, 1994.

Alaback, Paul, and Glenn P. Juday. "Structure and Composition of Low Elevation Old-Growth Forests in Research Natural Areas of Southeast Alaska." *Natural Areas Journal*, 9 no. 1, 1989.

Alaback, Paul, and James Welgand. "The Status of Temperate Rainforest in British Columbia." *Conservation International and Earth Life Canada Foundation*, Dec. 1990.

Andres, Brad A. "Black Oystercatcher." Unpublished, *EVOSTC Notebook Series*, 1997.

Baker, J. M., R. B. Clark, P. F. Kingston, and R. H. Jenkins. "Natural Recovery of Cold Water Marine Environments After an Oil Spill." Paper presented at the Thirteenth Annual Arctic and Marine Oil Spill Program Technical Seminar, June 1990.

Bodkin, J.L. and B.E. Ballachey. "Sea Otter." *EVOSTC Restoration Notebook*, 1997.

Brown, Evelyn D. and Mark G. Carls. "Pacific Herring." *EVOSTC Restoration Notebook*, 1998.

Button, D. K. "Evidence for a Terpene-Based Food Chain in the Gulf of Alaska." *Applied and Environmental Microbiology* (1984) pp. 1003–10.

Button, D. K., and F. Juttner. "Terpenes in Alaskan Waters: Concentrations, Sources, and the Microbial Kinetics Used in Their Prediction." *Marine Chemistry* 26, (1989): 57-66.

Cernetig, Vladimiro, Jr. "Black Waters." *Equinox* 46 (July/August 1989): 40–48.

De Laguna, Frederica. "Eyak." *Handbook of North American Indians* 7 (1990).

De Laguna, Frederica. "Chugach Prehistory: The Archaeology of Prince William Sound, Alaska." *University of Washington Publications in Anthropology* 13 (1956).

Dold, Catherine A., and Gary Soucie. "Just the Facts: Prince William Sound." *Audubon Magazine* 91, no. 5, (September 1989): 80.

Enge, Marilee. "The Fighting Eyak." *Anchorage Daily News* (August 22, 1993).

Foster, M. S., J. A. Tarpley, and S. Dearn. "To Clean or Not to Clean: The Rationale, Methods, and Consequences of Removing Oil from Temperate Shores." *Northwest Environmental Journal* 6 (1990): 105–20.

Freeman, A. Myrick III, and Raymond J. Kopp. "Assessing Damages from the Valdez Oil Spill." *Economist* (summer 1989): 5–7.

Frost, Kathryn J. "Harbor Seal" *EVOSTC Restoration Notebook*, 1997.

Gilliland, Jennifer R. "Moving Alaskan Crude: Who's in Charge?" *Audubon Magazine* 91, no. 5 (September 1989): 87.

Hodgson, Bryan. "Alaska's Big Spill." *National Geographic* (January 1990:) 5–42.

Horton, Tom. "Paradise Lost." *Rolling Stone*, (December 14–28, 1989).

Hyland, Jeffrey L., and Eric D. Schneider. "Petroleum Hydrocarbons and Their Effects on Marine Organisms, Populations, Communities, and Ecosystems." Paper prepared for symposium. "Sources, Effects and Sinks of Hydrocarbons in the Aquatic Environment." American University, 1976.

Krauss, Michael E. "Alaska Native Languages: Past, Present, and Future." *Alaska Native Language Center Research Papers*, no. 4. Alaska Native Language Center, University of Alaska, Fairbanks, 1980.

Krutilla, John V. "Conservation Reconsidered." *American Economic Review* 57, (summer 1967): 777-86.

Kuletz, Katherine J. "Marbled Murrelet" *EVOSTC Restoration Notebook*, 1997.

———,"Pigeon Guillemot" (unpublished), *EVOSTC Notebook Series*, 1997.

Laycock, George. "The Baptism of Prince William Sound." *Audubon Magazine* 91, no. 5 (September 1989).

Luoma, Jon R. "Alaska's Aging Tanker Fleet." *Audubon Magazine* 91, no. 5, (September 1989): 77–91.

Manville, Albert M. II. "Oiled Aftermath." *Defenders* 64, no. 4 (July/August 1989): 13-17.

Matkin, Craig, and Eva Saulitis. "Killer Whale." *EVOSTC Restoration Notebook*, 1997.

Neff, J. M. "Water Quality in Prince William Sound." Batelle Duxbury Operations, Duxbury, Mass., April 1990.

Nickerson, Sheila, ed. "*Exxon Valdez* Oil Spill." Special oil spill issue, *Alaska Fish and Game* 21, no. 4 (1989).

Ott, Riki (Fredericka). "O.C., Inc." Unpublished.

———,"Oil in the Marine Environment: An Update." Anchorage: Oil Reform Alliance, 1990.

Payne, James R., and G. Daniel McNabb, Jr. "Weathering of Petroleum in the Marine Environment." *Marine Technology Society Journal* 18, no. 3 (1984): 24–42.

Schoen, John W., Matthew D. Kirchhoff, and Jeffrey H. Hughes. "Wildlife and Old-Growth Forests in Southeastern Alaska." *Natural Areas Journal* 8, no. 3 (1988).

Sims, Grant. "A Clot in the Heart of the Earth." *Outside* (June 1989).

Thedinga, John F., et. al. "Effects of Logging on Size and Age Composition of Juvenile Coho Salmon (*Oncorhynchus kisutch*) and Density of Presmolts in Southeast Alaska Streams" *Canada Journal of Fisheries and Aquatic Science* 46, (1989).

DOCUMENTS

"Alaskan Oil Spill Bioremediation Project." Publication of the United States Environmental Protection Agency. Document number EPA/600/8-89/073. August 1989.

Alaska's Marine Resources, Vol. VII, No. 3, Marine Advisory Program, Alaska Sea Grant College Program, University of Alaska, Fairbanks, October 1992.

Albert, Tom. "Trip Report: (1) Joint U.S./Canadian Meeting in Seattle, Wa., to Review Hydrocarbon Developments in the Beaufort Sea; (2) Meeting in Anchorage of National Research Council Panel to Review Environmental Studies Program of the Minerals Management Service; and (3) Meeting in Anchorage with Soviet Scientists Regarding Cooperative Marine Mammal Study this Summer in Soviet Far East." Memorandum to Ben Nageak, Director, North Slope Borough, Department of Wildlife Management, Barrow, Alaska, May 1989.

Alyeska Oil Spill Contingency Plan, 1987.

An Assessment of Tanker Transportation Systems in Cook Inlet and Prince William Sound, Engineering Computer Optecnomics, Inc., Annapolis, Maryland, Nov. 4, 1989.

Bell, H. H. (rear admiral and chairman, Coast Guard Safety Study Group) et al. "Report of the Tanker Safety Study Group." October 1989.

Collingsworth, D. W., W. Stieglitz, M. A. Barton, and S. Pennoyer (members of the federal and state Trustee Council following the *Exxon Valdez* spill). *State/Federal Natural Resource Damage Assessment Plan for the Exxon Valdez Oil Spill, August 1989, Public Review Draft*. Juneau, 1989.

————, *The 1990 State/Federal Natural Resource Damage Assessment and Restoration Plan for the Exxon Valdez Oil Spill*. Vols. 1 and 2. Juneau, 1990.

Deakin, Edward B. "Oil Industry Profitability in Alaska: 1969 through 1987." Report prepared for the State of Alaska Department of Revenue. March 1989.

Exxon Valdez Oil Spill Trustee Council: *Status Reports, Natural Resource Damage Assessment and Restoration Plans, Invitations to Submit Restoration Proposals, Draft Work Plans, and Comprehensive Habitat Protection Process: Large Parcel Evaluation and Ranking, Restoration Workshops, Abstracts of Restoration Projects*, most issued annually, Juneau & Anchorage, 1992–1999.

Exxon Corporation 1989 Annual Report. Exxon Corporation. New York, 1990.

Fineberg, Richard A, Pipeline In Peril: *A Status Report on the Trans-Alaska Pipeline*, Alaska Forum For Environmental Responsibility. Valdez, 1996.

Hearing Before the Committee on Commerce, Science, and Transportation, United States Senate, One Hundred First Congress, First Session on Exxon Valdez Oil Spill and Its Environmental and Maritime Implications. Washington, D.C.: U.S. Government Printing Office. April 6, 1989.

Holland, J. S. FRED *1988 Annual Report to the Alaska State Legislature* 89. Division of Fisheries Rehabilitation, Enhancement and Development. Juneau, 1989.

Jones, Stan, "Changes in Prevention and Response Since the 1989 *Exxon Valdez* Oil Spill." Unpublished, Regional Citizens' Advisory Council, 1998.

Kodiak Island Area Local Fish and Game Resource Guide. Kodiak Area Native Association with Assistance from the Alaska Department of Fish and Game, Division of Subsistence, December 1983.

Kocan, Richard M., *"Toxic Effects of Exxon Valdez Oil on Prince William Sound Herring,"* supplemental report to attorneys for civil action suit, 1993.

Kumins, Lawrence C. "CRS Report for Congress: The Alaskan Oil Spill and Gasoline Prices." Congressional Research Service, Library of Congress. April 17, 1989.

LaResche, Robert E. (oil spill coordinator, State of Alaska). *Before the National Transportation Safety Board, Washington, D.C.: Proposed Probable Cause, Findings and Recommendations of the State of Alaska.* July 1989.

Lee, Martin R. "The *Exxon Valdez* Spill." Environment and Natural Resources Policy Division, Congressional Research Service, Library of Congress. September 5, 1989.

"Oil Pollution Liability and Compensation Legislation After the *Exxon Valdez* Spill." Environment and Natural Resources Policy Division, Congressional Research Service, Library of Congress. September 5, 1989.

Logan, Sid, et al. *Cook Inlet Regional Salmon Enhancement Plan*, 1981–2000. Cook Inlet Regional Planning Team, 1982.

Matkin, Craig, David Scheel, Graeme Ellis, Lance B. Lennard, and Eva Saulitis. "Comprehensive Killer Whale Investigation." Restoration Project 95012, for EVOSTC, Anchorage, 1996.

Mundy, Phillip R. "Long-Term Salmon Damages in Upper Cook Inlet, Kodiak, and Prince William Sound as a Result of the *Exxon Valdez* Oil Spill," supplemental report to attorneys for civil action, 1993.

"Natural Resources Restoration: Use of *Exxon Valdez* Oil Spill Settlement Funds." U.S. General Accounting Office, Washington, D.C. August 1993.

"Natural Resources Restoration: Status of Payments and Use of *Exxon Valdez* Oil Spill Settlement Funds." U.S. General Accounting Office, Washington, D.C. August 1998.

"NOAA Response to Exxon Challenge to *Exxon Valdez* Natural Resource Damage Assessment Database." National Oceanic and Atmospheric Administration, U.S. Department of Commerce, Washington, D.C. April 27, 1993.

Parker, Walter B. et al. *Spill: The Wreck of the Exxon Valdez, Implications for Safe Marine Transportation.* Report of the Alaska Oil Spill Commission, Executive Summary and Appendices. Vols. 1-4. Anchorage, 1990.

Peterson, Charles H., "Supplementary Report on Coastal Ecosystem Damages from the *Exxon Valdez* Oil Spill." Supplemental report to attorneys for civil action, 1993.

Preliminary 1988/89 *Herring Season Catch Summary.* Alaska Department of Fish and Game, 1989.

Preliminary Review of the 1989 Alaska Commercial Salmon Fisheries. Alaska Department of Fish and Game, 1989.

Restoration Following the Exxon Valdez Oil Spill. Proceedings of the Public Symposium Held in Anchorage, Alaska, March 26-27, 1990. Restoration Planning Work Group, July 1990.

Savikko, Herman. *1988 Preliminary Alaska Commercial Fisheries Harvests and Values.* Regional Information Report No. 5J89-03. Alaska Department of Fish and Game. Juneau, 1989.

Smith, Rodney. "1989 Review of Hydrocarbon Development in the Beaufort Sea: Highlights of U.S. Oil and Gas Activities." Marine Management Service (included as an attachment to Tom Albert's North Slope Borough Memo).

Spill: The Wreck of the Exxon Valdez. Appendix. Vols. 1-4. Alaska Oil Spill Commission. Juneau, 1990.

Stanek, Ronald T. *Patterns of Wild Resource Use in English Bay and Port Graham, Alaska.* Technical Paper No. 104. Alaska Department of Fish and Game, Division of Subsistence, 1985.

State of Alaska (Plaintiff) v. Joseph Hazelwood (Defendant). State of Alaska, Third Judicial District. Transcript of Proceedings Before the Honorable Judge Karl S. Johnstone. Vols. 1-30. Anchorage, 1990.

Steiner, Rick. "Draft Proposal for a Comprehensive Settlement of Natural Resource Damages from the 'Exxon Valdez' Oil Spill." Coastal Coalition, July 1990.

Stratton, Lee, and Evelyn B. Chisum. *Resource Use Patterns in Chenega, Western Prince William Sound: Chenega in the 1960s and Chenega Bay 1984-1986.* Technical Paper No. 139, Alaska Department of Fish and Game, Division of Subsistence, December 1986.

United States of America (Plaintiff) v. Exxon Corp., et al (Defendant). Civil Action No. A91-082, U.S. District Court, District of Alaska, April 1991.

United States of American, (Plaintiff, consolidated) vs. Exxon and Joseph Hazelwood (Defendants). U.S. District Court, District of Alaska, Civil Action No. A89-0095-CV, Judge's Opinions, Order Numbers 264, 265, 267, 317, District Court for the District of Alaska, Opinions of June 11, 1996 (decided and filed), January 27, 1995 (decided and filed).

U.S. Department of Justice, Federal Bureau of Investigation, Interviews of *Exxon Valdez* crew members, April 5-12, 1989, File No. 197-AN-8251

VIDEOS

Voices of the Sound. Film Center for the Environment, 1989.

Scientists and the Alaska Oil Spill, Exxon Corporation, Houston, 1993.

NEWSPAPERS AND MAGAZINES

Alaska Business Monthly, Alaska Fish and Game, Alaska's Marine Resources (Marine Advisory Program, Alaska Sea Grant College Program, University of Alaska Fairbanks), *Anchorage Daily News, Anchorage Times, Cordova Times, Homer News, Los Angeles Times, The Nation, National Fisherman, Newsweek, New York Times, The Observer* (Prince William Sound Regional Citizens' Advisory Council), *Seattle Times,* Spokane *Spokesman-Review, Time, Valdez Vanguard, Wall Street Journal.*

ACRONYMS

ADFG	Alaska Department of Fish and Game
ANCSA	Alaska Native Claims Settlement Act
ANWR	Arctic National Wilderness Refuge
ARCP	Alaska Regional Contingency Plan
CDFU	Cordova District Fishermen United
CERCLA	Comprehensive Environmental Response, Compensation, and Liability Act
COSDRO	Cordova Oil Spill Disaster Response Office
DAP	Damage Assessment Project
DEC	Department of Environmental Conservation (Alaska)
DFG	Department of Fish and Game (Alaska)
DNR	Department of Natural Resources (Alaska)
ERV	Emergency Response Vessel (Alyeska)
EVOSTC	*Exxon Valdez* Oil Spill Trustee Council
EPA	Environmental Protection Agency (U.S.)

GAO   General Accounting Office (U.S.)
HARC   Homer Area Recovery Coalition
IBRRC   International Bird Rescue and Research Center
ICS   Incident Command System
MAC   Multi-Agency Coordinating Group
MMS   Minerals Management Service (U.S.)
NOAA   National Oceanic and Atmospheric Administration (U.S.)
NOL   Net Operating Loss
NTSB   National Transportation Safety Board (U.S.)
ORD   Office of Research and Development (U.S. Environmental
               Protection Agency)
OSC   On Scene Coordinator (U.S. Coast Guard)
OSCO   Oil Spill Coordinating Office (Homer)
OSHA   Occupational Safety and Health Administration (U.S.)
PWSAC   Prince William Sound Aquaculture Corporation
RCAC   Regional Citizens' Advisory Council (Prince William Sound)
RRT   Regional Response Team
SAIC   Science Applications International Corporation
SCAT   Shoreline Cleanup Assessment Team
SERVS   Ship Escort Response Vessel System (Alyeska)
SPARC   South Peninsula Area Recovery Coalition
TAPS   Trans-Alaska Pipeline System
USFWS   United States Fish and Wildlife Service
VTC   Vessel Traffic Center (U.S. Coast Guard)
VTS   Vessel Traffic Service (U.S. Coast Guard)

INDEX

Numbers in brackets denote photographs. Numbers followed by "n" denote a footnote.

Veco Environmental and Professional
    Services, 103
Veco International, 103, 106, 178–179,
    191–192, 193–195, 203, 205–206,
    208, 258–259
  cleaning barges, 228, 231–232, 234–
    235, 236–239
  cleanup operations contracts, 234
Velikanje, George, 85, 99–100
Vessel Traffic Service, U.S. Coast
    Guard (VTS), 42, 43, 44, 48, 53
Voices of the Sound (video), 175, 281
VTS. *See* Vessel Traffic Service, U.S.
    Coast Guard (VTS)

W
Warren, Bob, 207
Watt, James, 215–216
Weaverling, Kelly, 80, 93–94, 96–97,
    270, 276, 283
Webber, Billy, 292, 323
Whales, 108, 125, 306–309
Willard, Jerry, 206
Willet, Mark, 300
Williams, Terrie, 71
Wohlforth, Charles, 146
Woodle, James, 21, 22

Y
Yost, Paul, 52n, 68, 104, 152
Young, Don, 211